Windows XP Taskbar and Window Components

W9-AHU-522

Desktop · Title Bar · Minimize Button · Maximize Button · Close Button

Internet Explorer · NetMeeting · Show Desktop · Tasks

Windows XP Desktop Components

Desktop Shortcuts · Desktop · Window

Windows® XP
Home and
Professional Editions
Instant Reference

Denise Tyler

San Francisco • Paris • Düsseldorf • Soest • London

SYBEX®

Associate Publisher: Richard J. Staron
Acquisitions Editor: Ellen Dendy
Developmental Editor: Raquel Baker
Editor: Pete Gaughan
Production Editor: Molly Glover
Technical Editor: James Kelly
Book Designer: Franz Baumhackl
Electronic Publishing Specialist: Franz Baumhackl
Proofreaders: Emily Hsuan, Laurie O'Connell, Nancy Riddiough
Indexer: Nancy Guenther
Cover Designer: Design Site

Library of Congress Card Number: 2001093080
ISBN: 0-7821-2986-2

For Ed,
always a source
of inspiration.

Acknowledgments

It takes a team of people to put any published work together, and I would like to take this opportunity to thank many talented individuals for the making of this guide. It has truly been a pleasure working on this project with all the people at Sybex; they have been fabulous to work with.

First, to Chris Denny, who paved the way for this opportunity: thanks as always for your ongoing friendship, support, and technical savvy. Next, to Ellen Dendy, who gave me the opportunity to work on this guide: I very much appreciate your keen advice and expert suggestions on the best way to approach and coordinate all the material. Later in the project I was introduced to Raquel Baker, who saw the development of the book to its completion. Thanks, Raquel, for all your positive feedback, cheery attitude, and your patience as the many, many pages took shape.

As the book went into production, I had the pleasure of working with Molly Glover, Production Editor, who kept things running smoothly as the chapters flowed to the right places. I'd also like to thank Pete Gaughan, Senior Editor, for his impeccable suggestions and edits as he molded the material into its final form. Special thanks go to Jim Kelly, the technical editor on this project, for his helpful comments and suggestions as he verified all the material in this guide.

Finally, I would like to thank my mom, dad, and brothers for teaching me that good things happen when you follow your heart. Your constant love and support is always an inspiration to me.

Introduction

Windows XP Home and Professional Editions Instant Reference is the complete "quick guide" to Microsoft's latest operating system. Windows XP Home Edition and Windows XP Professional are built on Windows 2000 technology. They provide you with many familiar features and functionality found in earlier versions of Windows, but also include a wealth of new and enhanced features and functionality. With a new, sleek, user-friendly interface, you get increased stability along with improvements in networking, connectivity, security, and multimedia; and this *Instant Reference* makes it easier for you to take advantage of all these benefits. Some of the functions available in earlier versions of Windows are moved to different locations or have changed names; this book tells you how to access any covered function.

How This Book Is Organized

This book is a detailed, alphabetical guide to the major features and commands found in Windows XP Home and Professional. Each entry in this guide provides you with a description of the feature or command, tells you how to access it, explains the interface (such as screens, menus, and toolbars), and, in many cases, provides step-by-step instructions to perform tasks related to the command or function. Most entries also contain one or more cross-references to other entries so that you can easily find related information. Throughout this guide, you'll also find graphic images that illustrate topics or tasks that are being discussed.

Who Should Read This Book and Why?

Windows XP Home and Professional Editions Instant Reference was written for beginning, intermediate, and advanced users as well as technical personnel (such as administrators and technical support personnel) who will be using Windows XP. In this book, you'll find information on anything from using the Start button and menu, to configuring your Desktop environment, to creating and configuring objects in the console. No matter where you are on the learning curve, you'll find this book useful. Each entry in this guide covers the subject at hand thoroughly but doesn't get bogged down in details. And, because the book is organized alphabetically, you'll be able to quickly find entries regarding the subject you're interested in. Using this book, you'll be able to gain an understanding of a given topic and learn how to perform related tasks, thus making you more proficient.

Setup Considerations

The setup used in the writing of this book was a Windows XP computer, using a dual-boot configuration with default options installed for both Home and Professional versions. Both operating systems were installed on drives formatted with the NTFS file system as recommended for Windows XP. If your setup is different, available commands and functions may vary. This guide indicates when a function or command is available only in Windows XP Home Edition or only in Windows XP Professional.

Conventions Used in This Book

Throughout the book, you'll find consistently used conventions that make it easier to find information. You'll see graphic images of menu options and/or icons just below each entry title (where applicable) so that you can easily tell what topic is being discussed. You'll also often find graphic images or icons that are being discussed within a topic included as a visual reference.

At the end of an entry, you may find **See also** references. These references point you to other entries in the book and may provide either information necessary to use the currently discussed feature, or information that is simply related and will provide you with greater understanding. For example, under the entry for My Computer, you will see the following reference:

See also   Control Panel, Explorer, My Documents, My Network Places, Shared Documents

You'll find additional information provided in the form of Notes, Tips, and Warnings, as described below:

NOTE   Notes provide additional information about the current topic.

TIP   Tips give you information on how to better use a function, alternative ways to perform a task/function, or shortcuts to a task/function.

WARNING   Warnings alert you to potential problems when using a feature or performing a task.

Terms Used in This Book

The following terms are used throughout the book to indicate specific actions:

Click   Move the mouse pointer over an item and press and release the left mouse button. This action often selects an item.

Double-click   Move the mouse pointer over an item and press and release the left mouse button twice in fast succession. This starts an action (such as running a program or opening a folder).

Drag   Move the mouse pointer over an item, press and hold down the left mouse button to select it, then move the pointer to a different location. Release the left mouse button at the desired destination.

Right-click   Move the mouse pointer over an item, then press the right mouse button. This activates a pop-up menu, or "shortcut menu," that contains options appropriate to the item you right-clicked.

Windows XP

Home and
Professional Editions

A–Z

Accessibility

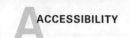 Program group that helps adjust the computer to users' needs. Choose Start ➤ All Programs (or Start ➤ Programs from the Classic Start menu) ➤ Accessories ➤ Accessibility to access the Accessibility Wizard, Magnifier, Narrator, On-Screen Keyboard, and Utility Manager. For more information on these tools, see their respective main topics and the following subsections.

Accessibility Options

 Configures settings that make using the computer easier for users who have physical disabilities, such as hearing and vision impairments, as well as users who have difficulty using the keyboard and mouse.

Choose Start ➤ Control Panel (or Start ➤ Settings ➤ Control Panel from the Classic Start menu) and click Accessibility Options to open the Accessibility Options window.

Accessibility Options Window

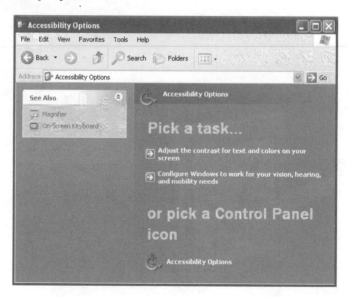

The Accessibility Options window consists of three main areas, which provide the following options:

See Also   Contains links to two accessibility features that you can customize to suit your needs. Use Magnifier to enlarge areas of your screen while you move your mouse. On-Screen Keyboard lets you use a mouse or other pointing device to enter text into dialogs or other software programs.

Pick a Task   Click "Adjust the contrast for text and colors on your screen" to open the Accessibility Options dialog to the Display tab. Select "Configure Windows to work for your vision, hearing, and mobility needs" to open the Accessibility Wizard. Further information on this dialog and wizard appear in the following sections.

Pick a Control Panel Icon   Click the Accessibility Options icon to open the Accessibility Options dialog, described next.

Accessibility Options Dialog

The Accessibility Options dialog contains five tabs: Keyboard, Sound, Display, Mouse, and General. Select the appropriate check box to turn on a feature, and click the Settings button to adjust the default settings.

 TIP   You can use keyboard shortcuts to turn many of the Accessibility Options on and off. The shortcuts are turned on by default; to turn them off, click the appropriate Settings button and deselect the Use Shortcut check box.

Keyboard tab Contains the StickyKeys, FilterKeys, and ToggleKeys options, which are useful for those who have trouble using the keyboard. You can also specify that programs display additional keyboard-related help. The StickyKeys feature keeps the Shift, Ctrl, Alt, or Windows logo key activated until you press another key in a keyboard shortcut (such as Ctrl+A or Alt+F). A tone also sounds when you press a key. FilterKeys either repeats or ignores short keystrokes and slows down the repeat rate. ToggleKeys sounds a tone when you press the Caps Lock, Num Lock, or Scroll Lock key.

TIP If you have shortcuts enabled, press the Shift key five times to toggle Sticky-Keys on. Hold down the Right Shift key for eight seconds to toggle FilterKeys on. Hold down the Num Lock key for five seconds to toggle ToggleKeys on.

Sound tab Contains the SoundSentry and ShowSounds options, which are useful for those with hearing impairments. SoundSentry flashes an on-screen alert when the system generates a sound. ShowSounds displays text or icons to represent speech or sounds that programs use.

Display tab Contains the High Contrast option, which is useful for those with vision impairments. High Contrast displays fonts and colors that make reading the screen easier. The Cursor Options section also allows you to adjust the blink rate and width of the cursor.

TIP To toggle on High Contrast, press Left Alt+Left Shift+Print Screen.

Mouse tab Contains the MouseKeys option, which allows you to control the mouse with the numeric keypad.

TIP To toggle on MouseKeys, press Left Alt+Left Shift+Num Lock. For a complete explanation of the MouseKeys feature, search the Help and Support Center index for the keyword *MouseKeys*.

General tab Contains options for Automatic Reset, Notification, Serial-Key Devices, and Administrative Options. Automatic Reset turns off accessibility options after the computer is idle for a specified period. Notification displays warning messages or sounds when you turn features on and off using shortcut keys. SerialKey Devices enables support for a serial input device other than keyboard or mouse. Administrative Options applies default settings for new users and for the logon Desktop.

Accessibility Wizard

Accessibility Wizard   Helps you configure accessibility options to make Windows XP and your computer easier to use if you have difficulties with your vision, hearing, or mobility. To start the Accessibility Wizard, choose Start ➤ All Programs (or Start ➤ Programs from the Classic Start menu) ➤ Accessories ➤ Accessibility ➤ Accessibility Wizard.

Once you have launched the wizard, make the choices and settings indicated in each screen and click Next to continue. You'll be able to:

- Select the smallest text size that you are able to read.

- Enable or disable options that allow you to read text more easily (such as changing the interface font size), switch screen resolution, or use personalized menus.

- Indicate types of features that are difficult for you to use.

- Adjust the size of scroll bars and window borders if needed.

- Change the size of icons (normal, large, or extra large).

- Choose from several color schemes that alter the contrast of text and colors on the screen.

- Change the size and color of the mouse pointer.

- Change the cursor blink rate and width.

- Display visual warnings when system events occur.

- Display captions for speech and sounds.

- Use StickyKeys, which makes it easier to use multiple keystroke combinations.

- Use BounceKeys, which ignores repeated keystrokes.

- Use ToggleKeys, which plays a sound when you press the Caps Lock, Num Lock, or Scroll Lock.

- Show extra keyboard help when applicable and available.

- Use MouseKeys to control the mouse pointer through the numeric keypad.

- Select a right- or left-handed mouse and adjust the mouse pointer speed.

- Turn off StickyKeys, FilterKeys, ToggleKeys, and High Contrast features when the idle time exceeds a specified period.

- Configure all these settings as the default for new user accounts or for the current user only.

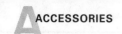

On the Completing the Accessibility Wizard screen, review your choices. If you want to make changes, use the Back button to return to a choice and change it. Finally, click Finish. Windows XP applies the changes when you exit the wizard.

See also   Magnifier, Narrator, On-Screen Keyboard, Utility Manager

Accessories

Accessories ▸ Predefined program group that includes many programs to help configure and maintain your Windows XP computer and network or Internet communications. It also provides access to Windows XP multimedia features, games, and other helpful programs that allow you to create documents, work with images, and explore and synchronize Internet content. To access the Accessories group, choose Start ➤ All Programs (or Start ➤ Programs from the Classic Start menu) ➤ Accessories.

The programs and program groups available in Accessories depend on the choices you made during the Windows XP installation and may include additional items if you installed other programs. If you install Windows XP with the default configuration, the Accessories group includes the following:

Programs	**Program Groups**
Address Book	Accessibility
Calculator	Communications
Command Prompt	Entertainment
Notepad	System Tools
Paint	
Program Compatibility Wizard	
Scanner and Camera Wizard	
Synchronize	
Tour Windows XP	
Windows Explorer	
Windows Movie Maker	
WordPad	

 TIP   For more information on these items, see their respective main topics.

Active Directory

Scalable directory service that is a feature of Windows XP Server. Active Directory allows you to identify resources in the network and makes those resources accessible to users via a single logon. Examples of resources are users, users' data, groups, computers, servers, and printers. Active Directory has a component called the Directory, whose function is to store information about these resources, as well as store services that make that information available. Because all network resources are represented as objects in the Directory, Active Directory provides single-point administration.

NOTE Active Directory is not a feature of Windows XP Home Edition or Windows XP Professional. It's installed on Windows XP Server computers only. But if your computer is on a network, it could be a member computer of Active Directory, and you might see references to some of the elements described here.

In Active Directory, a computer administrator creates a directory *structure* that organizes the network resources logically according to your company's internal structure, rather than based on the physical location of resources. (Active Directory does keep track of the physical network as well, through the assignment of *sites*.)

The Active Directory structure consists of *objects* (which represent resources in the network such as user accounts, computers, printers, files) as well as hierarchical collections of objects (such as organizational units, domains, trees, and forests). An *organizational unit (OU)* is a container object that holds other objects, such as users, groups, printers, other OUs, and computers. An OU might represent a small department or a building, for example. *Domains* are larger container objects that logically group objects in the network; an organization might decide to have all its Marketing computers in one domain and all of Distribution in another, or it might group domains by geography instead. One or more domains that use the same contiguous name space form an Active Directory *tree*, and trees are grouped into *forests*. Forests enable communication across the entire organization even though domains and trees in a forest operate independently of one another.

Trust relationships can exist between domains to enable user access from one domain to objects in another domain. Two types of trust relationships exist:

Two-way transitive trust Automatically established between parent and child domains in a *particular* tree or forest. Enables access from all domains to all objects in all other domains in that tree or forest. Also used between top-level domains in a forest.

Explicit one-way trust   Used to establish trusts between domains in *separate* trees. Enables backward compatibility with Windows 2000 and Windows NT 4.*x*.

Active Directory employs the *multimaster replication* model, whereby all domain controllers are peers to one another—or, put a different way, no one domain controller is the master domain controller, and each domain controller stores a copy of the Directory. Changes to the Directory can be made to any of the copies on any of the domain controllers in the domain, and are replicated to all other copies. This ensures fault tolerance. Should a domain controller become unavailable, another domain controller is still present to provide services and information to users.

Add New Hardware

 Starts the Add Hardware Wizard, which helps you add, remove, and troubleshoot hardware on your system, such as network cards, modems, disk drives, and CD-ROM drives.

NOTE   You can search the Windows XP Help and Support Center index for the Add Hardware topic and open the Add Hardware Wizard through a link in the Details pane.

The wizard guides you through the steps to add new device drivers to a Windows XP computer after you physically install the associated hardware. You can also prepare Windows XP before you physically remove or unplug hardware from the computer, or troubleshoot a device that is experiencing problems. The Add Hardware Wizard automatically makes the necessary changes, including changing the Registry and configuration files and installing, loading, removing, and unloading drivers.

 NOTE   You must have administrative privileges to add, remove, or troubleshoot hardware with the Add Hardware Wizard.

 TIP   The Add Hardware Wizard installs device drivers for Plug and Play, non–Plug and Play, SCSI, and USB devices.

Before you start the Add Hardware Wizard, power off your computer, and install the hardware device or plug it into the appropriate port. Turn your computer back on. If Windows XP detects a Plug and Play device for which it has drivers, it automatically installs the drivers and no further action is required.

If Windows XP does not detect your hardware, follow these steps:

1. To open the Add Hardware Wizard, choose Start ➤ Control Panel (or Start ➤ Settings ➤ Control Panel from the Classic Start menu) ➤ Printers and Other Hardware. From the See Also tasks in the left pane of the window, click the Add Hardware link. Click Next to continue.

2. The Add Hardware Wizard asks whether you have connected the hardware. If you choose No and click Next, the wizard provides an option to turn off the computer when you click Finish, so that you can install the hardware. Click Yes if you have connected the hardware, then click Next to continue.

3. Windows XP searches the hardware that is installed on your computer and displays a list of items that it detected. Select Add a New Hardware Device, and click Next.

4. The wizard asks whether you want to search for and install the new hardware, or select it manually from a list. Even though the wizard did not detect the hardware the first time, it may find it if you search for it now. If you know the manufacturer and model of the hardware you want to install, choose to select it manually from a list. Click Next.

NOTE If you allow Windows XP to detect the new hardware, be patient. Searching for the different categories of hardware devices may take some time.

5. The remainder of the process varies greatly, depending on the method you selected and the type of hardware you install. Follow the on-screen instructions or the instructions that were furnished with your hardware.

6. After Windows XP configures the settings for your hardware, a screen informs you that the installation is complete. Click Finish to close the wizard.

See also Help and Support Center, System, System Information

Removing/Unplugging Hardware

See Device Manager (Action Menu)

Troubleshooting a Device

See Hardware Troubleshooter

Add or Remove Programs

 Installs or removes programs and Windows XP components from your computer. Examples of programs are Microsoft Word or Microsoft FrontPage; examples of Windows XP components are Administrative Tools or networking options. You can also use Add or Remove Programs to install other operating systems on different partitions.

To open Add or Remove Programs, choose Start ➤ Control Panel (or Start ➤ Settings ➤ Control Panel from the Classic Start menu) and click the Add or Remove Programs icon. The left pane of the following window contains three buttons that allow you to change or remove programs, add new programs, or add or remove Windows XP components (described in the following sections). The information in the right pane changes based on the option you choose.

Change or Remove Programs

Changes or removes programs installed on your Windows XP computer. The Currently Installed Programs box displays a list of programs that are currently installed on your computer.

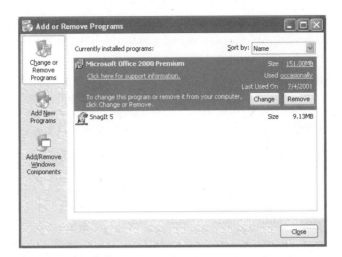

When you select a program in the list, you may see some or all of the following additional information and options:

Size   The amount of space the program takes up on your hard drive.

Used   How often you have used the program in the last 30 days (possible values are Rarely, Occasionally, or Frequently).

Last Used On   The date that you last used the program.

Change, Remove   To change or remove a program, select a program from the list and click the appropriate button. The steps that follow vary, depending on the program you selected. A wizard may guide you through the steps to change, reinstall, or remove the program. Windows XP may prompt you to confirm the removal of program files, program groups, and registration and configuration file entries, or to verify that you want to remove the program before changes are made.

WARNING   After you click the Change or Remove button, Windows XP may remove some programs immediately without showing any warning messages.

Add New Programs

Adds new programs or program updates to your Windows XP computer. Click the Add New Programs icon in the left pane to display two options that allow you to install a new program from CD or floppy disk, or to add new features, drivers, or updates from the Microsoft Web site.

CD or Floppy   To add a new program from CD or floppy disk, click the CD or Floppy button. A wizard guides you through the individual steps that are required to install the program.

From Microsoft   You can use the Windows Update feature to add Windows XP system updates, new features, and device drivers. After you establish an Internet connection, click the Windows Update button to display the Microsoft Windows Update home page, which allows you to download product updates or to view support information.

TIP   In the Classic Start menu, you can also choose Start ➤ Windows Update to access Windows Update.

From Your Network   If you're connected to a network, any programs that have been published in the Active Directory and to which you've been given access will appear in the Add Programs from Your Network list box at the bottom of the screen. A network administrator may have placed programs into different categories; select different categories (if available) in the Category drop-down list to find the application you're looking for.

Add/Remove Windows Components

Add/Remove
Windows
Components

Allows you to add or remove options from your Windows XP installation. When you click the Add/Remove Windows Components icon, the Windows Components Wizard appears.

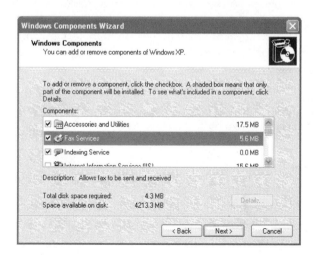

This wizard helps you install, configure, and remove Windows XP components. Follow these steps:

1. In the Components list, select a component to display its description. Clear the check mark to remove a program, or check a component to add it to your Windows XP installation. When you check a component, the bottom of the dialog also displays the total disk space required to add the program and the amount of free space on your hard drive.

2. Some Windows components have subcomponents that you can add or remove. To see the list of subcomponents, click the Details button after you select a component from the list. All subcomponents are selected by default. Check or uncheck subcomponents you want to include or remove.

3. Each subcomponent includes a description and disk space information, and may include additional subcomponent levels. After you make your subcomponent selections, click OK until you return to the Windows Components screen. Then click Next to continue.

4. The wizard makes component configuration changes and installs or removes the components you selected. The wizard may prompt you to insert your Windows XP CD, or prompt you to provide an alternate path to Windows XP files. Follow the prompts to complete the changes.

5. When the installation is complete, click Finish to exit the wizard.

TIP You must configure some Windows XP components before you can use them. In these cases, the wizard displays two choices: choose Configure to configure components, or Components to add or remove components.

See also Windows Update

Address Book

 Address Book   Allows you to manage your contact information, such as postal and e-mail addresses, telephone numbers, business and personal information, and home page addresses. You can also use Address Book together with other programs, such as Internet Explorer, Outlook, and Outlook Express.

TIP To open Address Book from Outlook Express, click Addresses on the toolbar.

Address Book Window

To open Address Book, choose Start ➤ All Programs (or Start ➤ Programs from the Classic Start menu) ➤ Accessories ➤ Address Book. The Address Book window contains a list of contacts, a toolbar, and a menu bar. To display folders in the left portion of the window, choose View ➤ Folders and Groups.

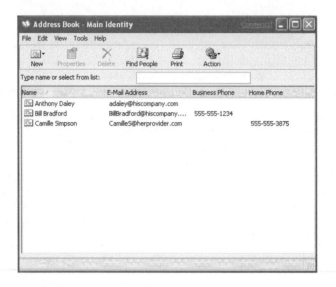

The entries in Address Book can include contacts (individual persons) or groups (two or more contacts to whom you can send e-mail at the same time). A business card icon appears beside contacts; two people appear over the business card for a group.

The contact list displays information about each entry in Address Book, including name, e-mail address, and business and home phone numbers. Click a column heading to sort the list in ascending or descending order by the category that you choose. Click the column heading again to sort the list in the opposite order.

To view or specify additional information about a contact, double-click an entry in the contact list, or select an entry and click the Properties button on the toolbar. You can go directly to an entry in the list by entering the name of a person in your contact list into the Type Name text box.

Address Book has some familiar as well as some unique menu options. Some of these menu commands can be quickly accessed on the Address Book toolbar.

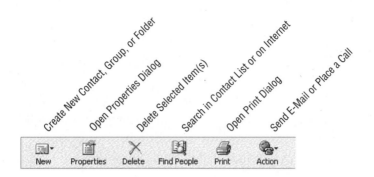

NOTE Some menu commands and options are not available when you log on with the default Administrator account.

File Menu

New Contact   Creates a new contact.

New Group   Creates a new group.

New Folder   Creates a new folder.

Properties   Opens the Properties dialog for the currently selected contact or group.

Delete   Deletes the currently selected contact, group, or folder. Windows XP also removes a contact from any groups in which the contact appears.

Import   Imports other Windows Address Books (WAB files), virtual business cards (VCF files), or other types of address books, such as those from Eudora or Netscape.

Export   Exports your contact list to a WAB file, a VCF file, or other address book file formats.

Print   Opens a dialog where you can print the current contact, multiple contacts, or the entire address book in one of three formats: for each contact, Memo format prints all information, Business Card format prints business information, and Phone List format prints only phone numbers.

Switch Identity   Allows you to switch to a different identity when multiple identities are created.

Show All Contents   Displays the contents of the contact list in a separate Address Book window.

ADDRESS BOOK

Edit Menu

Copy   Copies an Address Book contact or group.

Paste   Creates another Address Book contact or group using the information that you copied.

Profile   Allows you to create a contact list entry that you can use as your Internet profile. Some Web sites allow you to submit profile identities instead of manually entering your information.

Find People   Opens the Find People dialog, where you can search for addresses in the contact list or on the Internet.

View Menu

Folders and Groups   Shows or hides the Folders and Groups view.

Sort By   Sorts the contact list by name, e-mail address, business phone, home phone, first name, last name, ascending, and descending.

Tools Menu

Accounts   Allows you to view, add, remove, import, and export directory services, such as Active Directory and Internet Directory Services. You can also configure the properties of each directory service, designate a directory service as the default, and change the order of directory services.

Options   Allows you to share, or to not share, your contact information with other users on the computer.

Action   Allows you to send mail to the selected contact or group, dial the contact's phone number, or place an Internet call to the contact.

TIP   You can also right-click a contact or group in the contact list and choose Action to access these options.

Creating a New Contact

To create a new contact, choose File ➤ New Contact. The Properties dialog appears.

TIP   Alternatively, you can right-click a contact, group, or folder and choose New ➤ New Contact; or click New on the toolbar, then choose New Contact to open the Properties dialog.

The Properties dialog has seven tabs: Name, Home, Business, Personal, Other, NetMeeting, and Digital IDs.

Name Tab

Enter the first, middle, and last names of the contact, as well as a title and nickname. Based on the name you enter, the Display drop-down list allows you to select how you want the name to appear in the contact list (for example, last name first, or with/without commas). You can also type a display name into the Display text box.

TIP Each contact must have a display name. You cannot enter blank text in the Display text box.

To add an e-mail address for a contact, enter the address in the E-Mail Addresses text box and click Add. Repeat this for each e-mail address for the contact. If a contact has more than one e-mail address, highlight one in the list and click Set as Default to assign it as the default for this contact.

To edit or remove an e-mail address, select it from the list and click the appropriate button. Check the Send E-Mail Using Plain Text Only check box if the contact cannot receive e-mail messages that contain formatting (such as with stationery or a Web page background).

Home Tab

Enter personal postal information (street address, city, state/province, zip code, and country/region), and phone, fax, and mobile phone numbers for the contact. Check the Default check box to designate this address as the default. If your contact has a Web page, enter the URL in the Web Page field. Click the Go button to open the Web page in your browser.

Click View Map to display a map for the address that you enter. Your browser obtains the map information from the Microsoft Expedia Web site.

 TIP You must connect to the Internet to display map information.

Business Tab

This tab is very similar to the Home tab; it allows you to add business address information for the contact (company name, street address, city, state/province, zip code, and country/region). You can also add other information (job title, department, office, and phone, fax, pager, and IP phone numbers). Check the Default option to designate this address as the default. Click View Map to view a Microsoft Expedia map for the information you entered. If the contact has a business Web page, enter the URL in the Web Page text box; you can click Go to access the page.

Personal Tab

Here you can enter other personal information about the contact, such as gender and the names of spouse and children. To add a child's name, click the Add button, replace the words New Child with the child's name, and press Enter. Click the Edit or Remove button to change or delete the name of a selected child. To enter birthday and anniversary dates for the contact, click the arrow next to the appropriate drop-down list to select a date from the calendar.

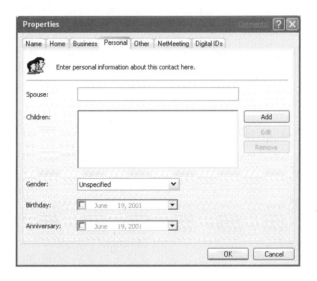

Other Tab

This tab allows you to add notes that provide additional information about the contact. Type the information in the Notes text box. The Group Membership box lists the names of the Address Book groups in which the contact appears. The Folder Location field displays the path to the Address Book folder.

TIP You must create a contact before you add the contact to a group.

NetMeeting Tab

Specify the conferencing server and address that you use to establish NetMeeting conferences with the contact. Enter the name of one or more servers in the Conferencing Server text box. Use the Conferencing Address box to enter the conference e-mail address for the contact; click the Add button to add the information to the list. The first directory server you add is automatically set as the default server. Click the Set as Default button to specify the selected server as the default directory server.

To change an entry, select it in the list and click the Edit button. Click the Remove button to remove a selected entry. To select another server to use as a backup when the default server is unavailable or busy, select another server and click the Set as Backup button. Click Call Now to open NetMeeting and immediately call the selected directory server.

Digital IDs Tab

Here you can add, remove, and view *digital IDs* for the contact—certificates that confirm the identity of the contact. To add a digital ID, click Import. Browse to the digital ID file, select it, and click Open to add it to the list on the Digital IDs tab. To view the properties for a digital ID, select it and click Properties. To remove the selected ID, click the Remove button. To set the selected ID as the default, click the Set as Default button.

Creating a Contact Template

If many of your contacts use the same contact information (such as the same business address, phone number, fax number, and so on), you can create a new contact that serves as a template. Later, you can copy the information from the contact template to each individual contact to which the information applies.

First, create a new contact. Enter all of the common information that applies to each contact for which you will use the template.

To use the template information, highlight the template contact in the contact list. Choose Edit ➤ Copy to copy the information to the Clipboard. Then choose Edit ➤ Paste to open the contact's Properties dialog. Change or add any information that is unique to the new contact you are creating, then click OK to add the new contact to the contact list.

TIP You can also create a new group and use it as a template in the same manner.

Creating a New Group

An Address Book group allows you to send e-mail to all members of that group. To create a group, click New on the toolbar, then select New Group to open the Properties dialog. It has two tabs: Group and Group Details.

TIP Alternatively, you can choose File ➤ New Group, or you can right-click a contact, group, or folder and choose New ➤ New Group.

Group Tab

This properties page allows you to enter a name for the group, and to assign
Address Book contacts as members. First, enter a name for the group in the
Group Name text box.

To add a new contact to the group *and* to your contact list, click the New Contact button to open the contact's Properties dialog. Enter the information for the
contact, and click OK to return to the Group tab.

To add a new contact to the group but *not* as a separate entry in your contact
list, enter a name and an e-mail address in the text fields at the bottom of the
tab. Then, click Add.

To remove a contact from the group (but retain its entry in your contact list),
select the contact in the Group Members list box and click Remove. To view and
edit a contact's property sheet, click Properties.

To quickly add members who are already in your contact list, click Select
Members to open the Select Group Members dialog. By default, the list of contacts in your Contacts folder appears in the left side of this dialog. Expand the
drop-down list to select another contact list if available. Choose a contact from
the left pane, and then click Select to move the contact to the right (Members)
pane. Alternatively, enter a name in the text box and click the Find button to
search for contacts in Address Book or on the Internet. Click the New Contact
button to create a new contact for the group. Click the Properties button to view

the properties for the selected contact. After you add all members, click OK to return to the Group tab.

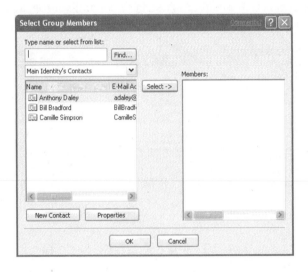

Group Details Tab

This tab is much like the Home tab of an individual contact's properties pages. Here you specify other information for the *group*, such as postal information (street address, city, state/province, and so forth), phone and fax numbers, and notes about the group. Click the View Map button to display a map for the group address in your browser. Enter a Web page URL for the group in the Web Page text box, and click the Go button to access the Web page.

Folders

Folders allow you to organize your contacts. Windows XP creates two folders by default: the Shared Contacts folder and the Main Identity's Contacts folder. To see folders, choose View ➣ Folders and Groups.

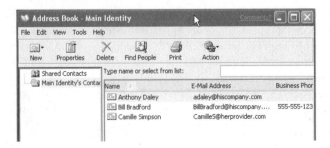

Creating a New Folder

New folders appear as a subfolder of the current identity's Contacts folder. To create a new folder, click New on the toolbar, and then choose New Folder to open the Properties dialog. Enter a name for the folder in the Folder Name text box and click OK to create the folder. The newly created folder then appears in the Folders and Groups view.

TIP Alternatively, you can choose File ➤ New Folder, or you can right-click a contact, group, or folder and choose New ➤ New Folder.

Address Book always saves contacts and groups into the currently selected folder. After you create your folders, choose the folder into which you want to place new contacts and groups. Then, create the new contacts and groups for the selected folder. Here you see a new folder, named Family and Friends, with one contact already added.

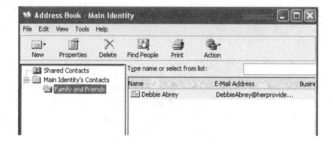

TIP To change the name of a folder, right-click the folder, then choose Properties to display the Properties dialog. Enter a new name in the Folder Name text box and click OK.

Contact and Group Properties

Every contact and group has a Properties dialog, which displays the same tabs that you see when you create a new contact or group. To view the Properties dialog, select a contact or group from the Contacts list, then click the Properties button on the toolbar or choose File ➤ Properties. The property sheet for contacts features an additional tab: The Summary tab displays a summary of information that appears in other tabs, such as name, e-mail address, home and business phone, and personal and business Web-page addresses.

TIP You can also access this tab by right-clicking a contact or group in the contact list and choosing Properties.

Creating Additional Identities

By default, Windows XP creates one *identity* (the main identity) for Outlook Express and Address Book. You can create additional identities for other users in either program. Each user can read their own mail in Outlook Express and see their own contacts and groups in Address Book. Additionally, you can share contacts and groups among different identities.

To create an additional identity in Address Book, follow these steps:

1. Choose File ➤ Switch Identity.

2. Click Manage Identities, then click New. Enter a name in the Type Your Name text box.

3. To password-protect the identity, select Require a Password. The Enter Password dialog appears. Enter the password in both the New Password and Confirm New Password text boxes and click OK.

4. Click OK to create the new identity.

5. Click Yes if you want to switch to the new identity right away; click No to return to the Manage Identities dialog box. The new identity appears in the list of identities. Click Close, and then click Cancel to return to Address Book, or click New to create another identity.

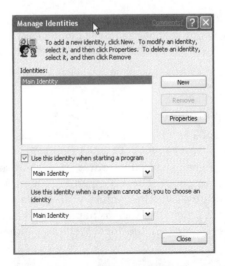

Switching Identities

To switch identities, choose File ➤ Switch Identity, then select the identity you want to switch to from the list. Enter the identity password if required, and click OK. Address Book displays the contacts, groups, and folders for the selected identity.

Sharing Contacts and Contact Folders between Identities

You can share individual contacts with other users (for whom an identity has been created). With the Folders and Groups view displayed, drag a contact from the contact list to the Shared Contacts folder. All other identities can click the Shared Contacts folder to see the contacts that you add.

When you drag a contact to the Shared Contacts folder, you remove the contact from the original user's list and place it into the shared contact list. You cannot *copy* a contact into the Shared Contacts folder (the Paste option is disabled). Instead, to put the contact in both places, drag the contact to the Shared Contacts folder, then paste a copy back into the original identity's folder. Note, however, that these entries are separate; information about the contact will get out of synch if you do not make equivalent changes to both copies.

See also   Outlook Express, Internet Explorer, Search

Administrative Tools

Administrative Tools ▶ | Collection of MMC tools you can use to administer every aspect of your Windows XP computer configuration. The list of available tools depends on whether your computer is a Windows XP Home or Professional computer and which services are installed on the computer.

To access Administrative Tools, choose Start ➤ Control Panel (or Start ➤ Settings ➤ Control Panel from the Classic Start menu) ➤ Performance and Maintenance, then click the Administrative Tools icon.

Common Administrative Tools for both Home and Professional include Component Services, Computer Management, Data Sources (ODBC), Event Viewer, Performance, Services, and Server Extensions Administrator. Windows XP Professional computers can also include Internet Services Manager and Local Security Policy.

Each of the Administrative Tools available in Windows XP Home and Windows XP Professional are covered in separate sections of this book.

See also Active Directory, COM+, Computer Management, Data Sources, Event Viewer, Local Security Policy, Microsoft Management Console, Performance, Services

Advanced System Information

See System Information

Appearance and Themes

 Control Panel category that provides access to several utilities that help you configure your display properties and the appearance of Windows XP. To display the Appearance and Themes category, choose Start ➤ Control Panel (or Start ➤ Settings ➤ Control Panel in the Classic Start menu) and then click the Appearance and Themes control panel icon. The individual utilities that are associated with the Appearance and Themes category are discussed under their own main topics in this book.

See also Accessibility, Display, Folder Options, Fonts, Mouse, Taskbar and Start Menu

Autodial

See Network and Internet Connections

Automatic Updates

See Windows Update (Receiving Update Notification)

AutoPlay

Windows XP feature that automatically starts programs or displays media files when you insert removable storage media into the appropriate drive. To configure options for AutoPlay, choose Start ➤ My Computer, right-click a removable storage device (such as a CD-ROM drive or digital camera), and choose Properties. Select the AutoPlay tab. For each media type, click the radio button that describes how you want Windows XP to work when that device is activated: take an action (that you choose in the list box), prompt you for an action, or do nothing.

Backup

WINDOWS XP PROFESSIONAL   Backup is a feature of Windows XP Professional only.

 Backup Allows you to safeguard the data stored on your computer, or on network drives to which you have access, by copying the data to a data storage device, such as a tape drive or additional hard disk. Should there be a problem with your live data (such as disk failure, accidental deletion of files, or file corruption), you can restore data from a backup.

NOTE   Supported file systems include FAT and NTFS.

You must have administrative privileges to perform backup- and restore-related functions.

Choose Start ➤ All Programs (or Start ➤ Programs in the Classic Start menu) ➤ Accessories ➤ System Tools ➤ Backup to open the backup utility.

By default, the Backup or Restore Wizard appears when you choose the backup command. To switch to the advanced backup utility, click the Advanced Mode link on the first screen of the wizard. To return back to the wizard, click the Wizard Mode link in the Welcome tab of the advanced Backup Utility.

Backup or Restore Wizard

The Backup or Restore Wizard guides you through the process of configuring the parameters for backup jobs. You can then run these backup jobs to back up files.

Backing Up Files

To create a backup with the Backup or Restore Wizard, follow these steps:

1. On the Welcome screen, click Next.

2. On the Backup or Restore screen, choose Back Up Files and Settings. Click Next.

3. On the What to Back Up screen, choose one of the backup options. If you select the Let Me Choose option, click Next; the wizard will let you check or uncheck files and folders from various folders and drives. You can expand or collapse the hierarchy tree to select files, or double-click a folder in the tree to display its contents on the right. After you select your backup option and any files and folders, click Next.

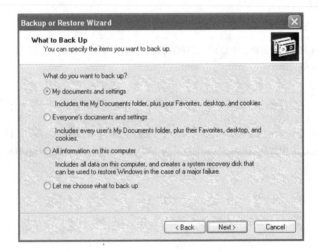

4. Select the drive to which you want to perform the backup. Floppy drives and removable drives appear in the list by default. Choose Browse to back up the files to a location that you specify. Enter a name for the backup and click Next.

5. The Backup or Restore Wizard applies several default settings about the type of backup, verification, compression, and job scheduling. If you want to tailor these settings yourself, click Advanced and make your choices in the appropriate screens. When you're finished, click Next to continue.

6. Verify that the information on the Summary screen is correct and click Finish. Your backup job either starts immediately or at the scheduled time.

The Backup Progress dialog will inform you when the backup is complete. It also displays additional information, such as the media name, status of the backup job, time elapsed during the backup, and the number of files and bytes processed. Click Close to close the dialog, or click Report to see more detailed information about this backup job.

Restoring Files

To restore files that have previously been backed up with the Backup or Restore Wizard, follow these steps:

1. On the Welcome screen, click Next.

2. On the Backup or Restore screen, choose Restore Files and Settings. Click Next.

3. The What to Restore screen displays backups that you previously created with the wizard. Navigate the available backup sets by using the plus and minus signs or double-click the available media and folder names. The left pane shows you the entire folder structure; the right pane shows only the contents of the currently selected drive or folder. Select files or folders from either pane. Click Next.

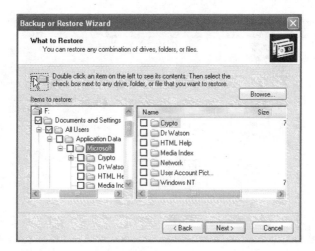

4. By default, files are restored to their original locations, but the utility does not replace files that already exist. If you want to change these and other settings, click Advanced. When you're finished, click Next to continue.

5. Read the summary screen and click Finish to start the restore operation.

Follow any additional prompts, which may vary depending on your backup media. When the restore begins, you'll see the Restore Progress dialog with the same information as the Backup Progress dialog. When the restore is complete, click Report if you wish to see more detailed information about the process, or click Close to dismiss the dialog.

Advanced Backup Mode

When you first open the Backup or Restore Wizard, the opening screen displays a link to switch to Advanced Mode. Click it to switch to advanced mode; the Backup utility then consists of five menus and four tabs that allow you to perform backups, restores, and automated system recovery operations. These commands allow you bypass the wizard if you are familiar with settings required to back up or recover your data. The utility has some familiar menus and menu options and some unique ones. The options available on each menu change depending on which tab you have selected.

Job menu   Commands to create a new backup job, start a backup or restore job after you select files, load a previously saved backup job script (Load Selections), save a backup job as a BKS script (Save Selections), save a backup script under a different name (Save Selections As), select a recent file, and exit the Backup utility.

Edit menu   Commands to select a drive, folder, or file on the Backup and Restore tabs, deselect a folder or file, or move up to the next-higher level from the currently selected item.

View menu   Commands to display or hide the Backup toolbar, display or hide the status bar at the bottom of the backup window, display the Backup tab and the Restore and Manage Media tab as lists or as details, and refresh the views in the backup and restore trees.

Tools menu   Commands to switch to the Backup or Restore Wizard (Switch to Wizard Mode), run the advanced Backup Wizard, run the advanced Restore Wizard, run the Automated System Recovery Wizard (ASR Wizard), create a catalog of any backup file that you have created, delete a previously created catalog (Media Tools ➤ Delete Catalog), open a backup job report, and configure backup and restore options.

Welcome tab   General information about Backup's features and buttons to access the Backup Wizard (Advanced), Restore Wizard (Advanced), and Automated System Recovery Wizard.

NOTE   The Backup Wizard (Advanced) and Restore Wizard (Advanced) display options that are similar to those you see in the Backup or Restore Wizard and its advanced options. The Automated System Recovery Wizard is described later in this section.

TIP   You can also access these wizards through options on the Tools menu.

Backup tab   Allows you to select the files you want to back up and to specify a backup destination and backup media or filename. The left pane displays the entire file system structure (local and network file systems to which you have access). The right pane displays the contents of the currently selected drive or folder, including files. In either pane, select drives, folders, and files to back up by checking their boxes.

Select a backup destination from the drop-down list. Assign a name for the backup in the Backup Media or File Name box, or click Browse to choose a location. Click Start Backup to start the backup; the Backup Job Information dialog opens. Enter a backup description and specify whether you want to append or replace data on the media. If you choose to replace the data, check or uncheck the option to allow only the owner and the Administrator to access the data.

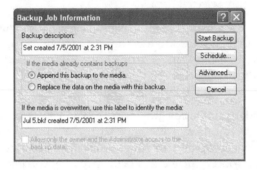

Click Schedule to schedule the backup job to run at a later time. The utility prompts you to save your backup selections. Click Yes to save your selections as a selection script, or No to change your selections. Click Advanced to configure additional backup options. Select a backup type (normal, copy, incremental, differential, or daily). You can back up data that is in remote storage, verify data after backup, compress backup data to save space (if available), back up system protected files with the system state (if available), and disable the volume snapshot. Click OK to return to the Backup Job Information dialog.

After making all selections, click Start Backup in the Backup Job Information dialog box.

Restore and Manage Media tab   Allows you to select, from any available backup set, the files you want to restore from the backup media to disk and then to start the restore operation. The left pane displays the backup sets and folders available in backup sets under each created media. The right pane shows the contents of the currently selected created media, backup set, or folder, including files. Choose backup sets, folders, and files to restore by checking their boxes in either pane.

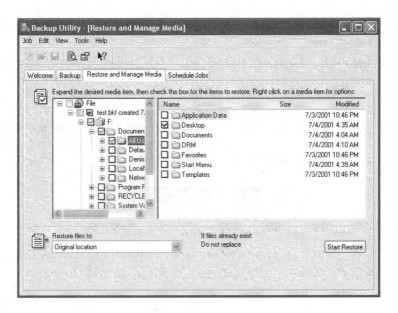

Backup sets that have not yet been cataloged display a question mark; you cannot access files and folders in these sets. To catalog a backup set or media, right-click it and choose Catalog.

TIP Question marks for backup sets that are not cataloged may not appear right away. You may have to close and restart Backup or even restart the computer.

You can also choose a location for the restored files by selecting Original Location, Alternate Location, or Single Folder from the Restore Files To drop-down list. Click Start Restore to begin the restoration. You'll have a chance to set advanced restore options by clicking Advanced in the Confirm Restore dialog.

Schedule Jobs tab   Allows you to choose the start date for a backup job and runs the Backup Wizard to create the backup job. Use the left and right arrows to navigate to the previous and next month. Click Today to return to the current date. Double-click a date, or select a date in the calendar, then click Add Job to start the Backup or Restore Wizard, described in a previous section.

Options

In advanced backup mode, you can access Backup options in two ways: choose Tools ➤ Options, or click the Options button on the toolbar. The Options dialog box contains five tabs: General, Restore, Backup Type, Backup Log, and Exclude Files.

General tab   Allows you to make general choices regarding backups. You can instruct Backup to calculate the number of files and bytes to be backed up or restored, use catalogs on the media to create catalogs on disk, verify the backup data after the backup completes, and back up the contents of mounted drives. You can also display alert messages for several different backup-related scenarios and allow use of recognizable backup media without prompts. Select the appropriate check box to make your choice.

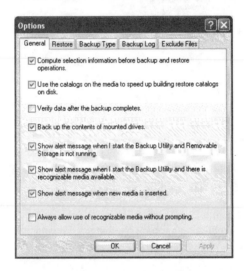

Restore tab   Allows you to specify the action you want Backup to perform when you're restoring a file that is already on your computer. You can choose to not replace the file (the default and recommended option), replace the file if it is older than the backup version, or always replace the file.

Backup Type tab   Allows you to select a default backup type. From the drop-down list, choose Normal (the default), Copy, Differential, Incremental, or Daily. A description of the selected option appears below the drop-down list.

Backup Log tab   Allows you to specify the level of detail of backup log file you want to create: Detailed, Summary (the default), or None.

Exclude Files tab   Allows you exclude specific files or file types from the backup. You can tell Backup to exclude files for all users or for the administrator by clicking the Add New button under the appropriate list box. To edit or remove an excluded file or file type, select it in the list box and click the corresponding button.

When you click an Add New button, the Add Excluded Files dialog appears. To exclude files by extension, select one or more registered file types from the list, or enter a specific filename or file type in the Custom File Mask text box. Verify or change the path to which the selection applies. Finally, select or deselect the Applies to All Subfolders check box, and then click OK to save the change.

Automated System Recovery Wizard

 Allows you to back up your data and create an Automated System Recovery (ASR) disk. Use the recovery disk along with the data backup to repair your Windows XP system when your system does not work properly anymore.

To create a data backup and ASR disk, click the Automated System Recovery button on the Welcome tab of the advanced Backup utility. Enter information and insert media as prompted.

 NOTE Make sure that you choose a media type that is suitable for storing large backups (such as tape media or another hard disk). The wizard prompts you to insert additional media into your drive if necessary to complete the backup.

After the backup is finished, the Backup utility prompts you to insert a blank 1.44 MB formatted floppy disk into your floppy drive to store recovery information. Click OK after you insert the disk. When the utility is done with this, remove the recovery disk and label it as shown in the dialog. Click OK to close the dialog and return to the utility. Store the ASR floppy disk and your data backup media in a safe place.

See also   Scheduled Tasks, System Information

Browse

Browse...   Used to find files and directories on the computer or in the network. This button appears in many dialog boxes where you need to provide the name and path of a file or folder or specify an Internet or intranet address.

Click Browse to open the Browse dialog. The left side of the dialog displays shortcuts to various locations on the computer or network where you can look for the files you want. Click one of these shortcuts or enter a folder in the Look In field. The contents of the selected folder appear in the window below. Double-click folders in the window to move further down the directory structure.

Use the Files of Type drop-down list to specify the type of files you want display in the Browse window, or choose to see all files of all types.

Select a file to display it in the File Name field, then click Open. You return to the dialog box from where you were browsing, and the name and path to the file appear in the appropriate field.

Calculator

 Calculator Allows you to perform mathematical calculations. To open Calcula-
tor, choose Start ➤ All Programs (or Start ➤ Programs in the Classic
Start menu) ➤ Accessories ➤ Calculator. You can display Calculator in either Standard view or Scientific view; it opens to the view you last used.

To enter numbers and operators, use the mouse to click the buttons or press
the matching keys on the keyboard. Different options appear depending on
whether you're in Standard or Scientific view. The following buttons are available in either view:

Button	Function
Backspace	Deletes a single digit to the left of the cursor.
CE	Erases the last entry (pressing the Delete key does the same).
C	Erases the entire calculation.
MC	Clears the calculator's memory.
MR	Recalls a number from memory.
MS	Stores a number in the calculator's memory (in place of any pre-viously stored number).
M+	Adds the displayed number to the number in memory.

Switch to Scientific view to perform scientific calculations. Select the appropriate radio button for the desired number system (hexadecimal, decimal, octal,
and binary). Enter a number, choose an operator, enter any other numbers and
operators necessary for the calculation, and click = to display the result. Use Calculator's memory functions as necessary.

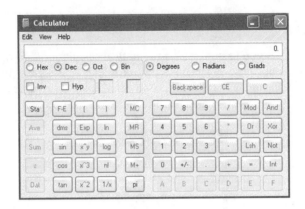

To perform a statistical calculation, switch to Scientific view and enter the first number. Then click Sta to open the Statistics box. Next, click Dat to enter the number. Enter additional numbers and click Dat after each number. Click Sta to display the statistical data you're entering and Ret to return to Calculator. In the Statistics box, you can also click Load (to display in Calculator the number selected in the Statistics box), CD (to clear the selected number), or CAD (to clear all numbers). After you enter all the data, click the statistical function you want to apply: Ave (average), Sum (sum), or S (standard deviation). Calculator will then display the result.

Capturing Images

Windows XP allows you to capture screen images to the Clipboard, which you can then paste into a document. To capture and paste an image, follow these steps:

1. To capture the entire screen, press the Shift+Print Screen key (often abbreviated as PrtSc). To capture an active window, press Alt+Print Screen.

NOTE Note that you won't see anything happen on the screen when you capture a screen or window with Print Screen.

2. Place the cursor where you want to insert the image in your document.

3. Press Ctrl+V or choose Edit ➤ Paste. Windows pastes the image into your document.

CD Writing Wizard

Windows XP allows you to write files and folders to your CD-R recorder or CD-RW rewriteable drive. After you copy files, you can "burn" them to a CD.

1. In Windows Explorer, copy the desired files and folders to your CD drive. (See the main topic "Copying Files and Folders" for further instructions.)

2. Insert a blank, writeable CD (or even a partly written CD-RW disk) into your CD-R or CD-RW drive.

3. After you copy files, the notification area displays a message that there are files waiting to be written to the CD. Click the message to display the files and folders, or select the drive in Explorer. They appear in a temporary staging area named Files Ready to Be Written to the CD. Verify the list of items to copy.

NOTE When you insert a CD into a CD-R or CD-RW drive, Windows XP prompts you to open the writeable CD folder or take no action. You can make either of these choices the default option.

4. From the Tasks area, select Write These Files to CD. The CD Writing Wizard appears. If the CD does not have enough space to hold all the files, the wizard prompts you to reduce the amount of files before you continue.

5. Assign a name to the CD, or accept the default (the date). Check or uncheck the option to close the wizard after you write the CD. Then click Next to continue. The wizard copies the files to your CD writer. A progress bar displays the amount of time remaining while the files are written to the CD.

6. After Windows XP writes the files to the CD, it ejects the CD from your CD recorder. If you elected to keep the wizard open, the wizard displays a message that the CD is complete. The option Write These Files to Another CD lets you burn another copy; if you're done, click Finish. Review the contents of the CD that you burned to confirm that all of the files were copied.

NOTE If you chose to close the wizard after burning the CD, Windows XP automatically deletes the files that were copied from the staging area and closes the CD Writing Wizard.

Character Map

 Character Map Allows you to display and copy characters for any installed font or characters you created with the Private Character Editor. Character Map displays Unicode (default), DOS, and Windows character sets. To access Character Map, choose Start ➤ All Programs (or Start ➤ Programs in the Classic Start menu) ➤ Accessories ➤ System Tools ➤ Character Map.

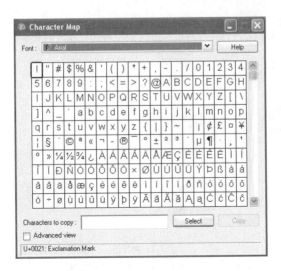

To display character sets for a font, select a font from the Font drop-down list. Click a character to enlarge it. The status bar at the bottom of the Character Map dialog displays the name and Unicode value (hexadecimal equivalent) for the character. You may also see a keyboard shortcut for the character if one is available.

TIP The phrase *(Private Characters)* appears after the font name in the drop-down list for fonts that are linked to characters created with the Private Character Editor.

Character Map allows you to copy characters to the Windows XP Clipboard and then paste them into other programs. Click a character and then click Select, or double-click a character, to place it in the Characters to Copy text box. Then click Copy to copy all selected characters to the Windows XP Clipboard.

TIP You can also select a character in the character set and then drag and drop it into an application that supports drag-and-drop.

Select Advanced View to display additional Character Map–related options. You can select the character set you want to display, group the Unicode character set by Unicode subrange, search for a specific character, or go directly to a character in the Unicode set.

TIP You cannot resize the Character Map window. If the window does not fit on your screen, you may have to move the window to see certain portions of it.

Instead of displaying all characters in a Unicode character set, you can display only the characters that are part of a selected subrange. This makes it easier for you to find a specific character. To group characters by Unicode subrange, select Unicode Subrange from the Group By drop-down list, then select a subrange in the following dialog.

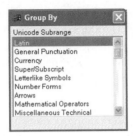

To search for a character, enter all or part of its name in the Search For text box and click Search. Or, select Unicode from the Character Set drop-down list and enter a Unicode value in the Go to Unicode text box. In either case, Character Map takes you directly to the desired character.

See also   Fonts, Private Character Editor

Checking Drives for Errors

To check a floppy or hard disk for any file system and physical errors on the disk, follow these steps:

1. In Explorer, right-click a drive and select Properties. The Properties dialog appears.

2. In the Error-Checking section of the Tools tab, click Check Now. The Check Disk dialog appears.

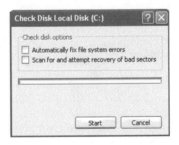

3. Check or uncheck options to automatically fix file system errors or to scan for and attempt recovery of bad sectors, then click Start.

4. After Windows XP scans your disk, the Checking Disk dialog notifies you that the check is complete. Click OK to close the dialog, and click OK again to close the Properties dialog.

See also   Explorer

Clipboard

Temporary holding place for data. When you use the Cut or Copy command in programs running on a Windows XP computer, the selected data is placed into the Clipboard. Use the Paste command to retrieve the contents of the Clipboard. To view the contents of the Clipboard, use the ClipBook Viewer.

WARNING The Clipboard stores only one item at any time. When you cut or copy a new item, it replaces the contents currently on the Clipboard. You can use ClipBook Viewer to save Clipboard contents into your local ClipBook.

ClipBook Viewer

ClipBook Viewer allows you to view and save the contents of the Windows XP Clipboard. To open ClipBook Viewer, choose Start ➤ Run, then type **clipbrd** and click OK. ClipBook Viewer has two windows: the Local ClipBook and the Clipboard. Maximize or resize the Clipboard to view its contents.

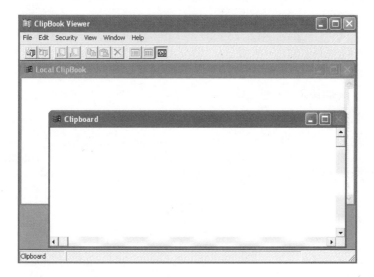

You can save the contents of the Clipboard either to a file or to the local ClipBook.

Saving the Clipboard Contents to a File

To save the contents of the Clipboard to a file (with a .CLP extension), open ClipBook Viewer and click somewhere in the Clipboard window to activate it.

Choose File ➤ Save As, browse to the folder where you want to save the file, enter a name for the file, and click Save.

Saving the Clipboard Contents in the Local ClipBook

When you save the Clipboard contents to your local ClipBook, you can share ClipBook pages with other users. You can also set up permissions and auditing for each ClipBook page (for remote user access after you share a page) and take ownership of a page, via the options on the Security menu.

After you place pages in your local ClipBook, you can display them using the Table of Contents view (the default), Thumbnail view, or Full Page view (which displays the contents of the selected page). Access the views either from the View menu or by clicking a toolbar button.

To save the contents of the Clipboard to a page in the local ClipBook, perform the following steps:

1. Click inside the ClipBook window to activate it.

2. Choose Edit ➤ Paste. The Paste dialog appears.

3. Enter a name for the ClipBook page you're creating. Select Share Item Now if you want to share the page.

4. Click OK. The page is added to the ClipBook. If you selected the Share Item Now option, provide the necessary information in the Share Clip-Book Page dialog (see following section).

Sharing a ClipBook Page

To share ClipBook pages with other users, follow these steps:

1. In the local ClipBook, select the page you want to share.

2. Choose File ➤ Share or click the Share button on the toolbar. The Share ClipBook Page dialog appears.

3. Select Start Application on Connect to automatically open the application that was used to create the contents of the page when another user accesses the page. Choose Run Minimized to run the application in a minimized window.

4. Click Permissions to configure the users and groups that are allowed to access the page, and the type of access they should have. Click OK to return to the Share ClipBook Page dialog.

5. Click OK to share the page. A hand appears at the bottom of the page's icon to indicate that the page is shared.

To stop sharing a page, select the page in the local ClipBook and choose File ➤ Stop Sharing, or click the Stop Sharing button on the toolbar.

Accessing Pages in Another User's ClipBook

To access pages in another user's shared ClipBook, choose File ➤ Connect or click the Connect button on the toolbar. In the Select Computer dialog, browse to and select the computer to which you want to connect, then click OK. A list of all shared ClipBook pages appears; double-click the ClipBook page you want to open.

To disconnect from the remote computer, choose File ➤ Disconnect, or click the Disconnect button on the toolbar.

Close

Closes the currently open window or application. You'll find this button in the top-right corner of any open window, next to either the Restore Down or Maximize button.

See also Maximize and Minimize, Restore Down

COM+ (Component Services)

Component Services
Shortcut
2 KB

MMC snap-in that includes a collection of services based on the Component Object Model (COM) and Microsoft Transaction Server extensions. COM+ provides application administration and packaging, component load balancing, improved threading and security, object pooling, transaction management, queued components, and in-memory database. To open Component Services, choose Start ➤ Control Panel (or Start ➤ Settings ➤ Control Panel in the Classic Start menu), click Performance and Maintenance, click Administrative Tools, then double-click Component Services. For further information about Component Services, choose Help ➤ Help Topics from the Component Services window.

Command Prompt

 Command Prompt Used to execute command-line functions and utilities, such as MS-DOS commands and programs. Examples of MS-DOS commands are del, dir, path, more, and print. Type **help** at the command prompt to display a list of available commands.

To open the Command Prompt window, choose Start ➤ All Programs (or Start ➤ Programs in the Classic Start menu) ➤ Accessories ➤ Command Prompt. You can now enter commands at the command prompt (by default, C:\).

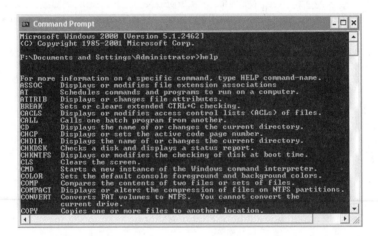

TIP To switch the Command Prompt window to a full-screen view, press Alt+Enter. This may be necessary for some programs that can't run in a Command Prompt window. Press Alt+Enter again to switch back.

Net Commands

Enable you to perform networking-related functions from the command prompt. Examples of net commands include net print (which displays print jobs and shared queues) or net group (which displays all groups in the security database).

To See This	Enter This at the Command Prompt
A complete list of net commands	**net help** or **net /?**
Explanation of net help syntax	**net help syntax**
A list of services that you can start with the net command	**net help services**
More detailed help information about a specific net command	**net help** *command name*— for example, **net help group**

Some net commands prompt you to enter either yes or no at certain times. Use the **/yes** and **/no** switches at the end of the command to automatically answer yes or no to those prompts.

```
Command Prompt                                    _ □ ×
NET HELP
command
      -or-
NET command /HELP

  Commands available are:

    NET ACCOUNTS          NET HELP          NET SHARE
    NET COMPUTER          NET HELPMSG       NET START
    NET CONFIG            NET LOCALGROUP    NET STATISTICS
    NET CONFIG SERVER     NET NAME          NET STOP
    NET CONFIG WORKSTATION NET PAUSE        NET TIME
    NET CONTINUE          NET PRINT         NET USE
    NET FILE              NET SEND          NET USER
    NET GROUP             NET SESSION       NET VIEW

    NET HELP SERVICES lists some of the services you can start.
    NET HELP SYNTAX explains how to read NET HELP syntax lines.
    NET HELP command | MORE displays Help one screen at a time.
```

Communications

 Communications Predefined program group from which you access the following communication-related program groups: Network Setup Wizard, HyperTerminal, New Connection Wizard, NetMeeting, Network Connections, Phone Dialer, Remote Desktop Connection, and Fax. These items are described in detail throughout this book, each under its own main topic. Choose Start ➤ All Programs (or Start ➤ Programs in the Classic Start menu) ➤ Accessories ➤ Communications to access the Communications program group.

Compressing Drives, Folders, and Files

You can compress NTFS-formatted drives, and individual folders and files on NTFS drives, to save on disk space. If you copy or add a file into a compressed drive or folder, it is automatically compressed. If you move a file off of an NTFS drive, the file remains in its original compressed or decompressed state.

WARNING Before you compress a drive, run Scandisk to make sure the drive is free of errors. You should also back up your data before you compress files, in case corruption occurs. Performance may suffer if you compress files that you frequently access.

To compress an NTFS drive, open the Explorer window, right-click the drive, and select Properties. On the General tab of the Properties dialog, check Compress

Drive to Save Disk Space, and click OK. In the confirmation dialog, specify whether you want only files and folders at the root of the drive to compress or you want subfolders and files compressed as well. Click OK.

To compress an individual file or folder on an NTFS drive, right-click the item in Explorer and select Properties. On the General tab, click Advanced, then check Compress Contents to Save Disk Space, and click OK. Click OK again to close the Properties dialog. If a folder contains subfolders, Windows XP prompts you to confirm the change and to specify whether you want the changes to apply to any subfolders and files as well. Click OK.

TIP To display compressed files and folders in a different color, select the View tab in the Folder Options dialog. Check "Display compressed files and folders with alternate color."

See also Folder Options, Explorer

Computer Management

Computer Management
Shortcut
2 KB

MMC snap-in that allows you to manage various aspects of your computer. To access Computer Management, choose Start ➤ Control Panel (or Start ➤ Settings ➤ Control Panel in the Classic Start menu) ➤ Performance and Maintenance, click Administrative Tools, and then double-click Computer Management.

Three categories appear in this console tree under Computer Management (Local): System Tools, Storage, and Services and Applications. Each of these contains other items you use to manage your local computer by default that depend on the options you select during Windows XP installation. (These items are discussed under separate main topics throughout this book.) To manage remote computers, select Computer Management (Local) in the console tree and choose Action ➤ Connect to Another Computer. Select a computer from the list and click OK.

Control Panel

Control Panel

Allows you to configure and personalize settings for many Windows XP functions and features. Control Panel items are described in individual main topics throughout this book.

To access Control Panel, choose Start ➤ Control Panel (or Start ➤ Settings ➤ Control Panel in the Classic Start menu). You can also access Control Panel through My Computer and Windows Explorer.

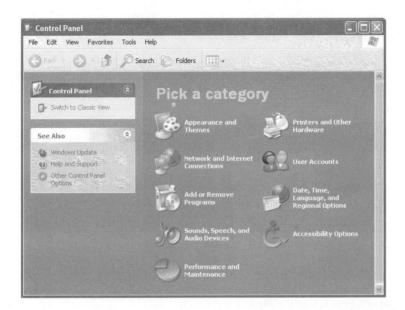

See also   Accessibility, Add or Remove Programs, Appearance and Themes, Date/ Time, Regional and Language Options, Network and Internet Connections, Performance and Maintenance, Printers and Other Hardware, Sounds and Audio Devices, User Accounts

Copy Disk

Copy Disk...   Copies the contents of a floppy disk to another. The two disks must be of the same type; for example, you can copy one 3½-inch high-density disk to another 3½-inch high-density disk. To copy a floppy disk, insert the source disk into your floppy disk drive. From Windows Explorer, right-click the source drive and choose Copy Disk. Select the source and destination (these are the same if you only have one floppy drive) and click Start.

WARNING   Make sure that you do not have data you want to keep on the target disk. The Copy Disk command overwrites its contents with the contents from the source disk.

See also   Explorer

Copying Files and Folders

Copy   You can copy files and folders to another location, leaving the original
        items intact in their original locations, using Windows Explorer. To do
so, first select one or more files or folders from the right pane of the Explorer
window. Hold down the Shift key to select contiguous items, or the Ctrl key to
select separated items. Then perform *one* of the following:

- Choose Edit ➤ Copy (or Ctrl+C). Select the destination folder, then choose
  Edit ➤ Paste (or Ctrl+V).

- Right-click the selected item or items and choose Copy from the shortcut
  menu that appears. Then right-click the destination folder and choose Paste.

- If both the source and destination folders are visible, you can use drag-and-
  drop. Hold down the Ctrl key, then left-click and drag the selected item(s)
  to the destination folder. (If you don't hold down the Ctrl key, Explorer *moves*
  the selection to the destination instead of copying it.)

See also   Explorer, Moving Files and Folders

Creating New Folders

Windows Explorer allows you to create new folders so that you can organize the
files on your computer. To do so, select the drive or folder in which you want to
create the new folder. Choose File ➤ New ➤ Folder, or right-click the drive or folder
and choose New ➤ Folder from the shortcut menu that appears. A new folder
appears beneath the drive or folder you selected. Replace the name New Folder
with a descriptive name of your choice. Then press Enter to assign the name.

See also   Explorer

Creating Shortcuts

▣ Shortcut   Shortcuts let you access programs, files, folders, printers, comput-
              ers, or Internet addresses without having to go to their permanent
locations. Windows XP allows you to create shortcuts in many ways.

To create a shortcut in Windows Explorer, select an item and then use *one* of
the following methods:

- Choose File ➤ New ➤ Shortcut, or right-click the item and choose New ➤
  Shortcut from the menu that appears. Explorer places the new shortcut

in the same folder. Drag the shortcut to a new location (such as another folder, the Desktop, or the taskbar).

- Press the Ctrl+Shift keys while you left-click and drag the shortcut to a new location.

You can instead right-click the Desktop and choose New ≻ Shortcut. The Create Shortcut Wizard then guides you through the process of creating a new shortcut.

TIP For information on how to add a shortcut to the Start menu, see the main topic "Taskbar and Start Menu."

You can also access items through My Computer, My Network Places, and My Documents. They all open Windows Explorer to a different, specific place in the Windows XP file system structure.

After you create a shortcut, you can right-click it and choose Properties to get details about the shortcut (such as file type, size, creation and modification dates) and configure characteristics such as its name, attributes (Read-Only, Hidden, Archive, etc.), target, window type, and (on NTFS drives) permissions.

Data Sources (ODBC)

Data Sources (ODBC) Allows you to configure and store information that deter-
Shortcut   mines how users connect to data sources such as dBase,
2 KB   Excel, and Access files. Use the ODBC Data Source Administrator dialog to configure your ODBC connections. To open this dialog, choose Start ≻ Control Panel (or Start ≻ Settings ≻ Control Panel in the Classic Start menu) ≻ Performance and Maintenance ≻ Administrative Tools, then double-click Data Sources (ODBC).

The ODBC Data Source Administrator dialog consists of seven tabs: User DSN, System DSN, File DSN, Drivers, Tracing, Connection Pooling, and About. Each of these tabs includes several buttons in common:

- Click the OK button to accept changes in the current tab and to close the ODBC Data Source Administrator dialog.

- Click the Cancel button to close the ODBC Data Source Administrator dialog without applying the changes you made in the current tab (changes you made in other tabs will apply).

- Click the Apply button to accept changes in the current tab and to keep the dialog open.

- Click the Help button to obtain help on the features included in the current tab. **51**

User DSN Tab

The User DSN tab allows you to add, delete, or configure data sources with user data source names (DSNs). The data sources that you configure in this dialog are accessible only by the current user of the local computer.

The User Data Sources list contains user DSNs that the current user can access on the local computer. Double-click an item in the list, or highlight an entry and click Configure, to configure the data source name, description, database version, and directory and index information.

Click Add to add a new data source; select a driver in the following dialog and click Finish to configure the data source information. To remove a DSN from the list, highlight an entry and click Remove.

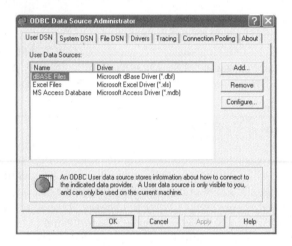

System DSN Tab

The System DSN tab allows you to add, delete, or configure data sources with system data source names (DSNs). The data sources that you configure in this dialog are accessible by any user who has user privileges on the local computer.

The System Data Sources list displays a list of System DSNs that users can access on the local computer. Double-click an item in the list, or highlight an entry and click Configure, to configure the data source name, description, database version, and directory and index information.

Click Add to add a new data source; select a driver in the following dialog and click Finish to configure the data source information. To remove a DSN from the list, highlight its entry and click Remove.

File DSN Tab

The File DSN tab allows you to add, delete, or configure data sources that are accessible by any user who has the same drivers installed. The data sources do not have to be user-dedicated or local to the computer.

The Look In box initially displays the default directory that stores database drivers. Click the down arrow to select any directory from the entire directory structure. Click the Up One Level button to replace the directory shown in the Look In box with the directory that is one level above. Click the Set Directory button to use the directory that appears in the Look In box as the new default directory.

When you select a folder in the Look In box, the tab displays a list of DSNs and subdirectories in that folder. Double-click an item in the list, or highlight an entry and click Configure, to configure the data source name, description, database version, and directory and index information.

Click Add to add a new data source. The following dialog prompts you to select a driver for the current data source. After you select the driver, click Finish to configure the data source information. To remove a DSN from the list, highlight its entry and click Remove.

Drivers Tab

The Drivers tab displays information about ODBC drivers that appear on the local computer. To install ODBC drivers, use the driver setup program that is specific to the data source to which you want to connect. After you install your drivers, the tab displays the driver name, version, company, filename, and creation date of each ODBC driver on the computer.

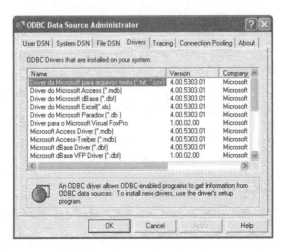

Tracing Tab

The Tracing tab specifies how the ODBC driver manager traces any calls to ODBC functions. The driver manager can trace calls continuously, or for one connection only. It can also perform dynamic tracing, or you can assign a custom DLL file.

By default, Windows XP stores the trace log in a file named SQL.LOG. Enter a new filename and path in the Log File Path field, or use the Browse button to select another location or file.

Windows XP uses the odbctrac.dll file (shipped with the MDAC SDK) by default to perform tracing. To specify a different trace DLL file, enter the path and filename in the Custom Trace DLL field, or click the Select DLL button to select a folder and file.

To start continuous dynamic tracing, click the Start Tracing Now button. Windows XP establishes a connection to the data source and traces the connections until you click Stop Tracing Now.

You can also enable or disable the Visual Studio Analyzer to debug and analyze your distributed application. Click Start Visual Studio Analyzer to use this feature, or click Stop Visual Studio Analyzer to turn the feature off.

NOTE Additional information about the Visual Studio Analyzer appears in the MSDN Library, which is available on CD-ROM or at `http://msdn.microsoft` `.com/library`.

Connection Pooling Tab

Use the Connection Pooling tab to configure connection retry wait times and time-out periods when you use connection pooling. You can also enable and disable performance monitoring to record a number of statistics.

The ODBC Drivers list displays the name of each driver and the associated connection pooling time-out option. To configure a time-out option, double-click a driver in the list, or highlight a driver in the list and click Connection Pooling Timeout, to open the Set Connection Pooling Attributes dialog. This dialog allows you to enable or disable pooling and to specify the number of seconds that unused connections remain in the pool. After you configure the pooling options, click OK to return to the Connection Pooling tab.

Click the Enable radio button to enable performance-monitoring counters for connection pooling, or the Disable radio button to disable them. Use the Retry

Wait Time field to enter the number of seconds (six or fewer numerals) that the OBDC driver will wait before it tries again to make a connection to the database server.

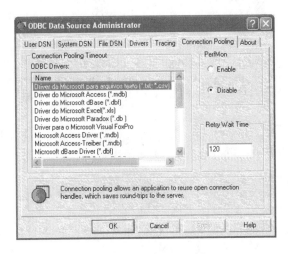

About Tab

The About tab displays information about the ODBC core components. These components include the Driver Manager, cursor library, installer DLL, and other core component files. The files appear in the Core Components list and include information such as the file description, version, filename, and location.

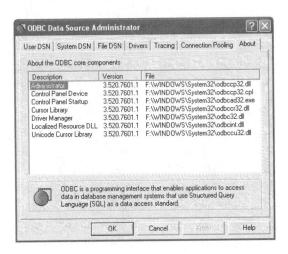

Date/Time

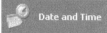 Settings used by Windows XP to assign dates to files when you create or modify them. It is important to set the correct date, time, and time zone on your system clock. To do so, choose Start ➤ Control Panel (or Start ➤ Settings ➤ Control Panel in the Classic Start menu). Click Date, Time, Language, and Regional Options, and then click the Date and Time icon to open the Date and Time Properties dialog. This dialog includes three tabs: Date & Time, Time Zone, and Internet Time.

 TIP Double-click the system clock in the notification area of your taskbar to quickly open the Date and Time Properties dialog.

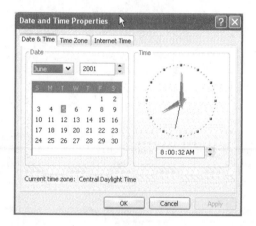

Date & Time tab Select the month from the drop-down list, and use the up and down arrows to select the year. Use the calendar display to click the day of the month. To set the time, click to select the hour, minutes, seconds, or AM/PM. Enter the correct value, or use the up and down arrows to change the value. Your current time zone appears at the bottom of the dialog.

Time Zone tab Select the correct time zone from the drop-down list. If daylight savings changes apply to your time zone, check the Automatically Adjust Clock for Daylight Saving Changes option; Windows XP will automatically reset your clock for daylight savings time when appropriate.

Internet Time tab Use this tab to synchronize the clock on your computer with a time server on the Internet. Synchronization only occurs when your computer is connected to the Internet. You may not be able to use this feature if you connect to the Internet through a proxy server or firewall.

To enable this feature, check the Automatically Synchronize with an Internet Time Server option. Use the drop-down list to select an Internet time server.

Click Apply to apply any changes you make without closing the dialog, or click OK to save changes and close the dialog.

 TIP Use Regional and Language Options in Control Panel to change the format in which short and long dates and times display in the taskbar, as well as in the Date and Time Properties dialog.

See also   Regional and Language Options, Taskbar

Desktop

The Windows XP workspace that allows you to organize your folders, files, and shortcuts to frequently used programs. When Windows XP first opens, you see the Desktop, which by default displays a shortcut to the Recycle Bin. The Start button and the taskbar appear at the bottom of the screen.

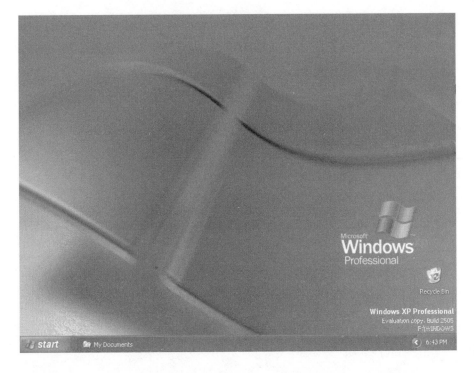

As you install new programs or make changes to your environment, Windows XP adds new icons to the Desktop and taskbar and may remove others. When you open a program, its user interface appears in front of the Desktop so that you can use the program.

The Display Properties dialog allows you to specify the appearance of your Desktop, as well as other settings. To open the Display Properties dialog, right-click an empty space on your Desktop and choose Properties. For further information on this dialog, see the main topic "Display."

See also Control Panel, Display

Device Manager

 MMC snap-in that displays a list of all hardware installed in the computer and provides information about this hardware. Use Device Manager to verify that your hardware is working properly after you install new hardware. You can also use Device Manager to enable, disable, configure, and check the status of devices and to view and update device drivers.

TIP You must log on as a computer administrator to make certain changes to devices in Device Manager.

To access Device Manager, choose Start ➢ Control Panel (or Start ➢ Settings ➢ Control Panel in the Classic Start menu) ➢ Performance and Maintenance. Next, click the System control panel icon to open the System Properties dialog. Select the Hardware tab, and click the Device Manager button.

Device Manager lists the hardware on your computer in several different classes (for example, Display Adapters or System Devices). To view the devices in each class, click the plus sign at the left of the class name. Each device appears in the list with an icon, followed by the name of the class or device.

 NOTE If the device icon contains a yellow question mark, the device is unknown. Unknown devices are typically non–Plug and Play devices for which you must install drivers that came with your hardware.

 NOTE If the device icon contains a yellow exclamation point, a hardware or software problem exists for the device. Double-click the problem device to open the Properties dialog. Click the Troubleshoot button in the General tab to open the Hardware Troubleshooter.

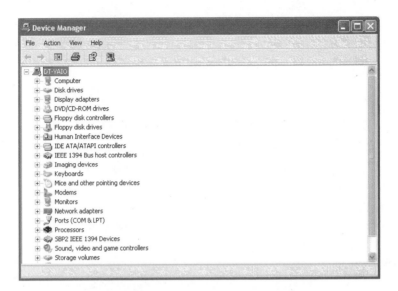

As with all MMC consoles and snap-ins, Device Manager has Action and View menus that contain options specific to the currently active MMC snap-in.

Action Menu

Action Select a device in Device Manager, and then use commands in the Action menu to perform device-related actions. Commands unique to this menu include Update Driver, Disable (which toggles to Enable), Uninstall, and Scan for Hardware Changes.

TIP An alternative method for accessing the options available under Action is to select a device and right-click. If you select a device class, only the Scan for Hardware Changes and Properties options are available. If you select the workstation itself, the Disable option won't be available.

Disable and Enable

Disable Temporarily disables a Plug and Play device. When you disable a device, you do not have to physically remove it from the computer to avoid having Windows XP load drivers for the device.

Use this feature to set up different hardware profiles—for example, one profile to attach your laptop to a docking station and another to use when your laptop is not docked. To explain further, when your laptop is docked, you might use a network adapter to connect to the Internet and to your company network. When the laptop is not docked, you might use a modem instead.

NOTE The Disable and Enable options appear only if you have administrative privileges.

After you choose Disable, Windows XP informs you that your device will not function after you disable it, and prompts you to confirm your selection. A red X appears over the device icon when it is disabled.

To enable the device later, right-click the device and choose Enable, or use the Action ➤ Enable command. The red X disappears, indicating that the device is enabled again.

Uninstall

Uninstall Allows you to remove a device driver from your Windows XP computer. After you uninstall a device driver, you need to physically remove the hardware device from your computer; otherwise, Windows XP will reinstall the drivers the next time you start up.

When you uninstall a device driver, Windows XP asks you to confirm your action. Click OK to uninstall the device from Device Manager. Then, turn your computer off and physically remove the device.

If you later need to reinstall the device and the device driver, install the hardware in your computer according to the manufacturer's recommendations. Windows XP automatically installs device drivers for Plug and Play devices when you restart your computer. Use the Add New Hardware Wizard to install non–Plug and Play devices.

NOTE The Uninstall option is available only when you log on as a computer administrator.

TIP Another way to uninstall a Plug and Play device is to shut down the computer (necessary for most devices), physically remove the device, and then start Windows again. Windows XP automatically removes the device.

Scan for Hardware Changes

Scan for hardware changes Allows you to manually scan your computer to see whether hardware changes have occurred, such as a device being removed from or added to the computer.

If Windows XP detects changes in your hardware, it takes appropriate action. Windows XP may remove or add devices to the list, and may display messages about the changes it makes. For example, when you remove or unplug a device before you disable the service, Windows XP displays the Unsafe Removal of Device dialog.

WARNING You should always disable a device before you remove it from the computer; otherwise, serious problems may result. Many devices also require that you power off the computer before you remove the device. Consult your hardware documentation for more information.

Print

Print Allows you to print a hard copy of your system summary, information on a selected class or device, or all devices and a system summary. Select the items you want to print (choose Computer from the Device Driver list to print all items), and select report options from the Report Type section of the Print dialog. Then click Print to print the report to your printer.

Properties

Properties Allows you to view and change properties of the selected device. To display the Properties dialog, highlight a device in Device Manager and choose Action ➤ Properties, or right-click the device and choose Properties from the menu that appears. The tabs and settings that appear in the Properties dialog vary depending on the device you select. The most common tabs are General, Driver, and Resources.

TIP You can also click the Properties button in the Device Manager toolbar to display properties for a device.

General tab Displays general information about the device, such as device type, manufacturer, location of the device, and the device status. If the device status indicates that the device is not working properly, click the Troubleshoot button to open the appropriate Windows XP Troubleshooter. Use options in the Device Usage drop-down list to enable or disable the device.

Driver tab Displays information about the device driver used for the selected device. Information may include driver provider, date, and version, and digital signer. Four buttons appear in the Driver tab:

Driver Details Opens a dialog that displays the paths to the driver files that are installed for the device. The information that you see in the Driver tab is repeated in the lower portion of the Driver File Details dialog.

Update Driver Opens the Hardware Update Wizard, which allows you to install software for your device. You can install software automatically or select devices from a list or specific location.

Roll Back Driver Allows you to revert to a previous version of a device driver when you experience trouble with your computer after you change a device driver. If no previous driver files are backed up for the device, Windows XP asks whether you want to launch the Troubleshooter. If one or more previous versions of the driver exist on your system, follow the prompts to select the version of the driver that you want to revert to.

Uninstall Allows you to uninstall the device driver. Windows XP asks you to confirm the removal.

Resources tab Displays information about the system resources the device is using. Device information includes the I/O (input/output) port address range, IRQ (interrupt request), DMA (Direct Memory Access) channel, and memory address range. Windows XP automatically assigns resources for Plug and Play devices. For non–Plug and Play devices, you may have to manually configure resource settings.

If a conflict exists, the Conflicting Device List displays the device with which your current device conflicts. You will need to select different settings to resolve the conflict. To select different settings, deselect the Use Automatic Settings check box. Then, select a different hardware configuration from the Setting Based On drop-down list, until you locate a setting that does not conflict with other devices or drivers. Alternatively, deselect the Use Automatic Settings check box and select a resource from the Resource Settings list. Then, click the Change Setting button to manually change a resource setting. You cannot change some resource settings.

 WARNING Change resource settings only if you are very comfortable with device hardware settings. Otherwise, the device or other devices may no longer function properly after you make a change.

View Menu

View   The View menu in Device Manager allows you to display devices and resources by using various sorting methods. It also allows you to display hidden devices and customize the view.

Devices by Type   Displays hardware devices in alphabetical order by device type (the default setting).

Devices by Connection   Displays hardware devices in alphabetical order by device connection. The devices are listed in relation to the interface or bus to which they connect.

Resources by Type   Displays the devices by the type of resources they use. Devices are arranged by DMA, I/O, IRQ, and memory resources that they use.

Resources by Connection   Displays the devices in a combination of the types of resources they use (DMA, I/O, IRQ, or memory) and the interface or bus to which they connect.

Show Hidden Devices   Displays devices that are not visible by default. They can include items such as non–Plug and Play drivers, printers, and other (unknown) devices.

Customize   Opens the Customize View dialog, which allows you to show or hide items in Device Manager. Check or uncheck options to show or hide the console tree, standard menus (Action and View), standard toolbar, status bar, description bar, and taskpad navigation tabs. You can also show or hide Device Manager menus and toolbars.

Additional Toolbar Buttons

In addition to the Action and View menus, the Device Manager MMC snap-in toolbar contains some of the buttons commonly found on MMC consoles, such as Back, Forward, Up One Level, Show/Hide Console Tree/Favorites, and Help. It can also contain various buttons depending on whether you selected the workstation, a device class, or a device, and whether a device is disabled or enabled; these are self-explanatory, except that the Update Driver button opens the Hardware Update Wizard, which allows you to update the driver for the selected device.

See also   Add New Hardware, Administrative Tools, Computer Management, Microsoft Management Console, System (Hardware tab)

DHCP

Dynamic Host Configuration Protocol, managed on Windows XP Server computers by an MMC snap-in. DHCP eases the administrative burden of Internet Protocol (IP) address management and overall IP client configuration. Every computer in an IP network must be assigned a unique IP address to be able to communicate with other computers in the network. You can assign this address either manually or automatically (via DHCP). DHCP also enables automatic configuration of associated configuration options on DHCP-enabled client computers.

Any client computer that runs a Microsoft Windows operating system can function as a DHCP client.

Enabling DHCP on a Windows XP Client

In order for the DHCP server to dynamically assign an IP address to a Windows XP client computer, you must enable DHCP at the client. To do so, follow these steps:

1. Choose Start ➤ Control Panel (or Start ➤ Settings ➤ Control Panel from the Classic Start menu) ➤ Network and Internet Connections ➤ Network Connections.

2. Right-click the Local Area Connection icon that connects to the DHCP server, and then click Properties to open the Local Area Connection Properties dialog. The dialog displays the General tab by default.

3. Select Internet Protocol (TCP/IP) in the list of components used by this connection and click Properties.

4. In the upper portion of the Internet Protocol (TCP/IP) Properties dialog, check Obtain an IP Address Automatically.

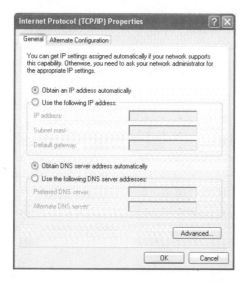

5. Click OK to exit the dialog, then click OK to exit the Local Area Connection Properties dialog.

See also Microsoft Management Console, Network and Internet Connections

DirectX

A system of components that enhance the display and performance of multimedia on your computer. DirectX features are typically found in games, 2-D and 3-D graphics programs, and multimedia-related software. Windows XP supports DirectX 8.

DirectX includes the following components that are built into your Windows XP operating system:

Microsoft DirectDraw   Supports extremely fast access to the video adapter on your computer, and is typically used in games, 2-D graphics programs, and digital video codecs. Uses standard methods to display graphics on all video adapters, but also provides support for accelerated drivers.

Microsoft Direct3D   Provides an interface to 3-D rendering functions that are built into most new video adapters.

Microsoft DirectSound   Provides a link between software programs and an audio adapter, to utilize the sound-mixing, -playback, and -capture capabilities of the adapter.

Microsoft DirectMusic   Adds interactive audio to DirectX and allows software developers to create dynamic soundtracks that respond to changes in the software. Captures and plays digital sound samples, and allows you to work directly with digital audio samples that work with your sound card or software synthesizer.

Microsoft DirectInput   Provides advanced input for joysticks, mice, keyboards, and other similar input devices used in games.

Microsoft DirectPlay   Supports game connections over a modem, the Internet, or a LAN, allowing game players to communicate with each other in a multiplayer game. Also supports voice communications over a network.

Microsoft DirectShow   Provides high-quality capture and playback of multimedia files on your computer and on the Internet. Supports several audio and video formats.

DirectX Diagnostic Tool

Allows you to obtain information about Microsoft DirectX application programming interface drivers and components installed on your computer. You can also use it to check components and to disable some hardware acceleration features. You can provide the information you obtain to support personnel who are helping you troubleshoot a problem.

NOTE You can also use the Games and Multimedia Troubleshooter to diagnose problems with DirectX. See the topic "Games and Multimedia Troubleshooter" in the Windows XP Help and Support Center.

To start the DirectX Diagnostic Tool, choose Start ➤ Run, and enter **dxdiag** in the Run dialog.

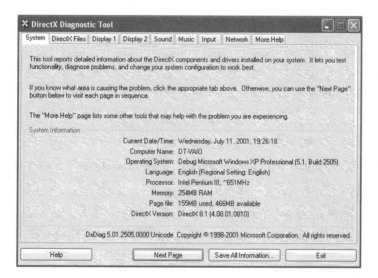

Problem Types

If you have problems with a DirectX application, they might be caused by one or more of the following, as well as other causes not listed here:

- Incorrect or beta versions of DirectX components

- Uncertified drivers

- No hardware acceleration, or hardware that does not fully support DirectX features

- Devices that are not connected

You can find helpful information about these types of situations on the various DirectX Diagnostic Tool pages.

DirectX Diagnostic Tool Pages

The DirectX Diagnostic Tool consists of eight different tabs: System, DirectX Files, Display, Sound, Music, Input, Network, and More Help. These tabs provide information about DirectX components. They also report problems or help you test and diagnose hardware features.

> **NOTE** If you have more than one display adapter installed (such as for a multiple monitor configuration), a Display tab appears for each adapter. Tabs are labeled Display 1, Display 2, and so on.

To move from page to page, click the Next Page button, or select a tab to move to a specific page. Each page lists information specific to its page topic. Notes, comments, and problems appear in the Notes section at the bottom of each page. Click the Save All Information button to save the information contained on all of the pages as a text file, using a filename and location that you specify.

System   Displays information about your system, such as date, time, computer name, operating system, language, processor, amount of memory, page file size, and the DirectX version.

DirectX Files   Displays a list of DirectX files installed on your computer. Information includes name, version, attributes (such as Final Retail or Beta Retail), language, date, and size.

Display   Displays information about your display device, including its name, manufacturer, chip type, DAC type, total memory, display mode, and monitor. Driver information includes driver name, version, and certification status, as well as drivers used for MiniVDD and VDD.

The DirectX Features section allows you to enable or disable DirectDraw Acceleration, Direct 3D Acceleration, or AGP Texture Acceleration. Click the Test DirectDraw or Test Direct3D buttons to test either of these components on your current monitor. Follow the prompts to complete the test. When you complete the tests, results appear in the Notes section.

Sound   Displays information about your sound device, including its name, various IDs, and type. Driver information includes name, version, certification status, other associated files, and the providers of those files.

Use the Hardware Sound Acceleration Level slider in the DirectX Features section to adjust your acceleration between none and full. Click the Test DirectSound button to test DirectSound features on your sound device. When you complete the test, results appear in the Notes section.

Music   Displays information about each of your installed music ports, including their description, type, kernel mode, input/output, whether the port supports DLS, whether the port is an external device, and whether the port is the default port. The DirectX Features section allows you to enable or disable default port acceleration (if available). To test DirectMusic, select a port from the Test Using This Port drop-down list, then click Test DirectMusic. Follow the prompts; results appear in the Notes section.

Input   Displays information about each of your installed input devices (such as joysticks or steering controls) and their associated drivers. Input device information includes name, provider, ID, and status for both device and port. Device driver information includes Registry key, whether the driver is active, device ID, matching device ID, 16-bit driver, and 32-bit driver.

Network   Displays information about your installed DirectPlay service providers (such as Internet TCP/IP Connection for DirectPlay) and registered "lobbyable" DirectPlay applications. Service provider information includes name, registry, file, and version. Registered application information includes application name, registry status, filename, version number, and a globally unique identifier (GUID).

To test DirectPlay features, click the Test DirectPlay button. Enter a username, choose the service provider, and specify that you want to create a new session. Click OK to start the session. Now have another user join this session from a computer on the network by following the above procedure but selecting the option for joining an existing session. Once both users have joined the session, enter messages and press Send to test the chat session. Both computers should display all messages. Click Close to finish; results appear in the Notes section.

More Help   Contains additional help options. Click the Troubleshoot button to open the Help and Support Center's Games and Multimedia Troubleshooter. Click the Sound button to open the Sound Troubleshooter. Click the MSInfo button to start the Microsoft System Information Tool. Click the Override button to override the refresh rate of your monitor (recommended for advanced users only).

See also   System Information

Disk Cleanup

Disk Cleanup   Finds files on your hard disk that can be deleted to free up hard disk space, including temporary files, unnecessary program files, Windows XP components no longer used, cache files, and files in the Recycle

Bin. You then have the option to delete some or all of the files, components, or programs.

Using Disk Cleanup

The Disk Cleanup utility runs automatically every 60 days, but you can also free up space on your hard disk at any time. Follow these steps:

1. Choose Start ➤ All Programs (or Start ➤ Programs in the Classic Start menu) ➤ Accessories ➤ System Tools ➤ Disk Cleanup. The Select Drive dialog appears.

TIP Alternatively, you can right-click a disk in the Explorer window, select Properties, and click Disk Cleanup from the General tab.

2. Select the drive you want to clean from the Drives drop-down list. Click OK. Windows XP scans the drive, and then displays the Disk Cleanup for (*drive letter*) dialog.

3. Select the Disk Cleanup tab. Place a check mark next to the type of files you want to delete. Options include:

   - Downloaded program files (removes ActiveX controls and Java applets that you downloaded automatically while you were viewing Web pages)

   - Temporary Internet files (removes Web pages that are stored on your hard disk in your Internet cache)

   - Offline Web pages (removes Web pages that you stored on your hard disk for offline viewing)

   - Recycle Bin (empties your Recycle Bin)

   - Temporary files (removes temporary files and folders used during program installation or created when programs are improperly terminated)

   - Catalog files for the content indexer (removes Indexing Service files that are left over from previous indexing operations)

TIP To view a list of files that Windows XP will delete for an option, select one of the categories and click the View Files button.

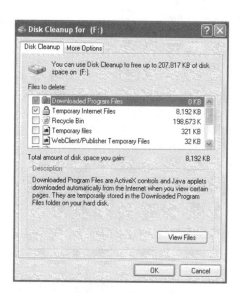

4. Choose the More Options tab to remove additional Windows components (through the Windows Components Wizard), installed programs (through the Add or Remove Programs dialog), or all but the most recent System Restore point. Click the associated Clean Up button to remove the items that you select.

5. After you complete your selections, click OK.

6. A dialog asks you to confirm that you want to delete files. Click Yes. After Windows XP deletes the files, you return to your Desktop.

See also Add or Remove Programs, Recycle Bin, Windows Components

Disk Defragmenter

Disk Defragmenter MMC snap-in for Windows XP Home and Professional that organizes fragmented files and arranges the files on your hard disk so that they load more efficiently.

When you install software, create documents, and download files from the Internet, Windows XP stores the files in any free space that is available on your hard disk. Sometimes, Windows XP uses several small chunks of available space in various places on your hard disk to store a large file. When this occurs, the file is *fragmented*. It takes longer to read a fragmented file, because the read/write head on your drive has to move to several places to read the file.

When you defragment your drive with the Disk Defragmenter, Windows XP puts the fragmented sections of your files back together and places them into contiguous space on your hard disk. This allows you to access your programs and files more quickly. In addition, it rearranges the files so that the free space on your hard disk appears contiguously. As a result, less fragmentation occurs when you add additional content.

TIP To keep your programs and files running at peak proficiency, you should periodically defragment your hard disks. If you do this on a regular basis, subsequent defragmentation sessions do not take as long as the first one. If you are a light user, once a month may be sufficient; if you are a heavy user, once a week might be better. You can use Scheduled Tasks to defragment your hard disks on a regular basis.

Disk Defragmenter MMC Console

Choose Start ➤ All Programs (or Start ➤ Programs in the Classic Start menu) ➤ Accessories ➤ System Tools ➤ Disk Defragmenter to start Disk Defragmenter.

TIP You can also choose Start ➤ Control Panel (or Start ➤ Settings ➤ Control Panel in the Classic Start menu) ➤ Performance and Maintenance ➤ Administrative Tools, and then double-click Computer Management. Expand the Storage category to select Disk Defragmenter.

The top pane of the Disk Defragmenter MMC console displays the volumes (or drives) that are available for defragmentation. Take note of the other information available regarding the volume, such as Session Status (for example, analyzing or defragmenting), File System, Capacity, Free Space, and % Free Space.

The lower portion of the console contains two graphical displays, each of which represents the state of your hard disk before and after you defragment it:

- The Analysis Display shows the state of the hard disk before you defragment it. Fragmented files are indicated in red, contiguous files in blue, unmovable files (typically system files) are green, and free space in white.

- The Defragmentation Display updates the graphical representation of your hard disk during the defragmentation process. Initially, the defragmentation display looks identical to the Analysis display, but as defragmentation pro-gresses, the fragmented files (red) and contiguous files (blue) are moved toward the beginning of the hard disk and all turn blue. Unmovable files (green) are not touched. Free space (white) takes up the remaining space.

Analyzing a Volume

To analyze a volume on your computer, perform these steps:

1. Select a volume in the list of available volumes in the upper pane of the Disk Defragmenter MMC console.

2. Click the Analyze button to start analyzing the volume. This can take some time on larger hard disks. Click Pause or Stop at any time to pause or stop the drive analysis; click Resume to continue after pausing.

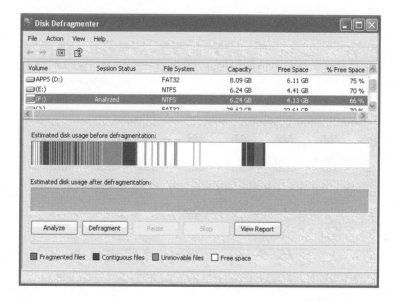

 TIP Alternatively, you can choose Action ➤ Analyze to start the analysis.

3. Disk Defragmenter displays a message when the analysis is complete and advises whether defragmentation is necessary. Click View Report to see a report about the analysis, click Defragment to defragment the volume now, or click Close to close the message and return to Disk Defragmenter.

Defragmenting a Volume

To defragment a volume on your computer, perform these steps:

1. Select a volume in the list of available volumes in the upper pane of the Disk Defragmenter MMC console.

2. Click the Defragment button to start the defragmentation. Disk Defragmenter analyzes the volume first, even if you have already analyzed it. Defragmentation starts immediately after the analysis is complete. This process may take quite some time to finish, depending on the size and state of the volume. Click Pause or Stop at any time to pause or stop the defragmentation process.

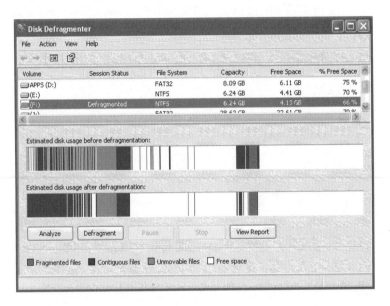

3. Disk Defragmenter displays a message when the defragmentation is complete. Click View Report to see a detailed report regarding the defragmentation, or click Close to return to Disk Defragmenter.

Viewing Reports

After you analyze or defragment a volume, Disk Defragmenter creates a report that provides you with detailed information about the action. The report contains information about the volume and about the fragmentation of the volume, file, pagefile, directory, and Master File Table (MFT). It also includes information about files that did not defragment during the defragmentation process. You can print the report or save it to a file. To view the report at the end of the operation, click the View Report button that appears when the operation is complete. If you want to refer to a report later, click the Save As button to save the report to your hard disk.

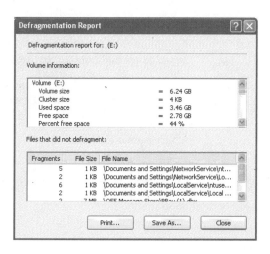

At any time, you can choose Action ➤ View Report or click the View Report button at the bottom of the console to view the report that corresponds to the most recent action you performed.

See also   Computer Management, Microsoft Management Console

Disk Management

Disk Management   MMC snap-in for Windows XP Home and Professional that allows you to manage disks and volumes in a graphical environment. To access Disk Management, choose Start ➤ Control Panel (or Start ➤ Settings ➤ Control Panel in the Classic Start menu) ➤ Performance and Maintenance ➤ Administrative Tools, and double-click Computer Management. Expand the Storage category to display the Disk Management snap-in.

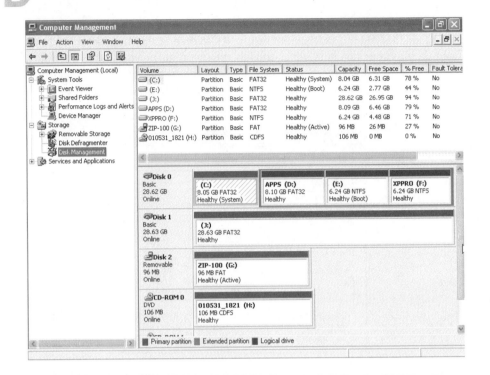

TIP You must log on as a computer administrator or be a member of the Administrators group to use Disk Management.

Use Disk Management to change drive letters and paths, format disks, create or delete partitions, upgrade basic disks to dynamic disks, and eject removable media (such as Zip disks, Jaz disks, CDs, and DVDs). You can also create and work with simple, spanned, striped, mirrored, and RAID-5 volumes for both basic and dynamic disks.

WARNING If you upgrade a basic disk to a dynamic disk, you cannot access the disk with any operating system other than Windows XP.

By default, the Disk Management Details pane displays a top and bottom window. The top window displays the volume list, and the bottom window displays a graphical view of your disks. Use commands in the View menu to customize the display to your liking.

Basic Disks

Basic disks are hard disks that contain primary and extended partitions, and logical drives, as well as mirrored volumes, striped volumes, spanned volumes, and RAID-5 volumes. Basic disks can contain a maximum of four primary partitions per disk, or three primary partitions and one extended partition (which can contain multiple volumes or logical drives). Windows XP and earlier versions (including Windows 3.1, 95, 98, Me, NT 4, and DOS) can access basic disks.

Action Menu

The Action menu for a basic disk includes many unique items, on the menu or its All Tasks submenu. The options available depend on which item you've selected in the Details pane and whether you have selected the Disk List or the Volume List.

Refresh   Updates the disk and volume views.

Rescan Disks   Rescans all available disks.

Eject   Ejects removable media from the drive.

All Tasks ➤ Open   Opens the drive in Windows Explorer without an Explorer Bar view selected.

All Tasks ➤ Explore   Opens the drive in Windows Explorer with the Explorer Bar Folders view selected.

All Tasks ➤ Mark Partition as Active   Marks the currently selected partition as active.

All Tasks ➤ Change Drive Letter and Paths   Allows you to change the drive letter and path of a volume.

All Tasks ➤ Format   Allows you to format the drive. You can choose a volume label, file system (NTFS or FAT32), and allocation unit size.

All Tasks ➤ Delete Partition   Deletes the selected partition.

All Tasks ➤ Properties   Opens the drive's properties.

All Tasks ➤ Delete Logical Drive   Deletes the selected logical drive.

Creating Partitions

To create a partition or logical drive using unallocated space, right-click unallocated space in the Graphical view and choose Create Partition, then follow the wizard's instructions.

View Menu

The View menu contains the following unique options when working with basic disks:

Top, Bottom   Each contains a submenu that allows you to select what to display in the top or bottom window of the Details pane. Choices include Disk List, Volume List, and Graphical View.

Settings   Allows you to configure the color and pattern for each of the disk regions in the Graphical view, such as primary partition, free space, and simple volume. Also allows you to configure the proportion for how disks and disk regions display in the Graphical view.

All Drive Paths   Displays all drive paths.

Dynamic Disks

Disk Management allows you to create dynamic disks (hard disks that contain dynamic volumes). There are five types of dynamic volumes: simple, spanned, mirrored, striped, and RAID-5.

NOTE   Only Windows XP and Windows 2000 can access dynamic disks. You can create an unlimited number of volumes on a dynamic disk. However, you cannot create partitions or logical drives on a dynamic disk.

Simple   A volume that is made up of disk space from a single physical disk. You can extend the amount of space at any time unless the disk is mirrored.

Spanned   A volume that consists of disk space on more than one physical disk. You can extend the amount of space at any time unless the disk is mirrored.

Mirrored   A volume that is an exact duplicate of a simple or spanned volume. The same drive letter is used for both copies of the volume. Mirrored volumes are available only on computers running Windows XP Server. You can use Windows XP Professional to create a mirrored volume on a remote computer that is running Windows XP Server.

Striped   You need at least two dynamic disks, with a maximum of 32 disks, to create a striped volume. Striped volumes are not fault tolerant, and you cannot extend or mirror them.

RAID-5   RAID-5 volumes provide fault tolerance. If you use three 10 GB disks to create a RAID-5 volume, the RAID-5 volume has a 20 GB capacity, and the remaining 10 GB is used for parity. You need at least three dynamic disks, with a maximum of 32 disks, to create a RAID-5 volume. RAID-5 volumes are available only on computers running Windows XP Server. You can use Windows XP Professional to create a RAID-5 volume on a remote computer that is running Windows XP Server. You cannot extend or mirror RAID-5 volumes.

NOTE You cannot create dynamic disks on portable computers, removable disks, or detachable disks that connect to your computer through USB, FireWire, or shared SCSI interfaces.

Creating a Dynamic Disk

In order to create a dynamic disk, you must format one or more existing drives to create unallocated space on each drive that you want to convert to a dynamic disk. After you format the disk, you can use the New Volume Wizard to step you through the process of creating dynamic disks.

WARNING You must be logged on as a computer administrator or member of an administrator group to format and create dynamic disks. If your computer is on a network, verify that your network policy settings allow you to complete this procedure.

WARNING Perform these steps only if you are certain that Windows XP is the only operating system that will access any file stored on or copied from the dynamic drive. DOS and Windows versions earlier than Windows 2000 cannot access dynamic drives. For example, if you copy a file from the dynamic drive to a floppy disk, a Windows 98 or Me computer will not be able to read the file on the floppy disk because it was originally stored on a Windows XP dynamic drive.

To create a dynamic disk, follow these steps:

1. From the Computer Management window, right-click the volume that you want to format and choose Format from the shortcut menu. The Format dialog appears.

WARNING Do not select the system or boot volume.

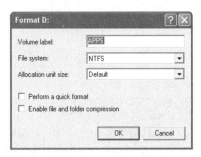

2. Enter a volume label, select a file system (FAT32 or NTFS), and choose an allocation unit size (default, or values between 512 and 64K). Check the Quick Format option only if the disk has been previously formatted and you are certain that the disk is not damaged. Check the Enable File and Folder Compression option if you want to create a compressed NTFS volume.

3. Click OK to format the volume.

4. After you format the volumes necessary to create your dynamic disk (as discussed in Dynamic Disks above), return to the Computer Management window. Right-click the unallocated space on the volume you want to use for your dynamic disk, and choose New Volume from the shortcut menu to open the New Volume Wizard.

5. Click Next to continue. The wizard asks what type of dynamic volume you want to create.

6. Select the dynamic volume type (simple, spanned, mirrored, striped, or RAID-5), and follow the remaining prompts in the Wizard to complete the process.

See also   Microsoft Management Console

Disk Space

Windows Explorer allows you to see how much disk space a file uses. From any Explorer window, select a folder in the Folders pane, then select one or more files from the right pane. The status bar displays the amount of space that the file or files use (choose View ➢ Status Bar to display the status bar if it is not visible).

To determine the amount of disk space a folder uses, select a folder in the Folders pane. Choose File ➢ Properties, or right-click and choose Properties from the short-cut menu, to open the Properties dialog. The General tab displays the total size of the folder (including all subfolders and files contained within it), the size it consumes on the disk, and the number of files and folders that are included in the folder.

See also   Explorer

Display

Used to configure the look of your Desktop. Allows you to choose multimedia themes, configure the appearance of your Desktop, choose or disable screen savers, customize the look of dialog boxes and text, and select the resolution and number of colors that your video adapter and monitor display.

Choose Start ➤ Control Panel (or Start ➤ Settings ➤ Control Panel in the Classic Start menu) ➤ Appearance and Themes, then click the Display control panel icon to open the Display Properties dialog. This dialog has five tabs: Themes, Desktop, Screen Saver, Appearance, and Settings. Click Apply any time you want to apply changes to your Desktop without closing the Display Properties dialog.

 TIP An alternative method for accessing the Display Properties dialog is to right-click anywhere on the Desktop and choose Properties.

Themes Tab

Allows you to choose from a number of pre-configured multimedia themes that consist of sounds, icons, and other multimedia elements. After you select a theme, you can use other options in the Display Properties dialog to customize your Desktop, and then return to the Themes tab to save your custom theme.

The Themes tab contains the following options:

Theme   Use the Theme drop-down list to select the theme you want to use. As you select a preconfigured theme, a preview of the theme appears in the Sample window. You can also choose one of the following special options:

- Select My Current Theme to retain your current theme.

- Choose More Themes Online to download theme files from the Microsoft Web site.

- Choose Browse to select a custom theme that you previously saved to your hard disk using the Save As button.

Save As   As you customize your Desktop using the remaining tabs in the Display Properties dialog, the Theme drop-down list displays an option called My Current Theme (Modified). To save this theme to your hard disk, click the Save As button in the Themes tab. You can select this theme at any time by choosing Browse from the Theme drop-down list.

Delete   Deletes the theme that currently appears in the Theme drop-down list.

Desktop Tab

The Desktop tab allows you to select a picture or an HTML document as the wallpaper for your Desktop. In the list box, select the background you want to use. The following options appear in this tab:

Background   Displays a selection of background images and Web pages from which you can choose as a background for your Desktop. The monitor at the top of the Desktop tab displays a preview of the item you select.

Browse   Allows you navigate to a different folder to select an image or Web page. You can select any image with a BMP, GIF, JPG, JPEG, DIB, or PNG extension, or any Web page with an HTM or HTML extension. Initially, the Browse dialog opens to your My Pictures folder, but use the Look In drop-down list to select any other folder on your computer. After you select an image or Web page, click Open to return to the Desktop tab.

Position   If the image that you choose is too small to fill the screen completely, use options in the Positions dialog to adjust the image. Choose Center to center the image on your Desktop. Choose Tile to repeat copies of the image so that it completely fills your screen. Choose Stretch to stretch the image horizontally and vertically so that it fills your screen.

Color   Allows you to select a solid color to display on your Desktop. This solid color also surrounds your background image when it does not completely fill the screen. Click the Color button to select from 20 default colors, or choose the Other option in the Color drop-down to select a custom color.

Customize Desktop   Click the Customize Desktop button to open the Desktop Items dialog, which allows you to customize the items that appear on your Desktop. This dialog consists of two tabs: General and Web.

General tab   Use this to show or hide various shortcut icons on your Desktop. You can select appropriate icons from the icon display in the center of the dialog, or click the Change Icon button to select any other icon file that appears on your computer. Click the Restore Default button to use the settings that were originally configured when you installed Windows XP.

The General tab also allows you to remove unused icons from your Desktop and store them in an Unused Desktop Shortcuts folder on your computer. The Desktop Cleanup Wizard runs automatically every 60 days unless you uncheck the appropriate option here. To run the Desktop Cleanup Wizard at any time, click the Clean Desktop Now button.

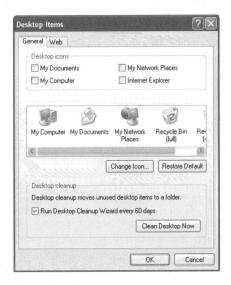

Web tab   Use this to display and customize the Web page that appears on your Desktop. The right section of the Web page displays a list of pages from which you can choose. Select an item in the Web Pages list to display it on your Desktop. Click the Properties button at the right side of the list to view the properties of the selected item, or click the Delete button to remove the item from the list.

Click the New button to open the New Active Desktop Item Wizard, which allows you to select a Web page from the Internet or from your local computer. To choose a Web page, use one of the following methods:

- Click the Visit Gallery button to select from the Desktop gallery on Microsoft's Web site. Your browser navigates to http://www.microsoft.com/windows/ie/gallery/. After you choose a Desktop item, your Desktop

83

displays the selection, and the URL appears in the Web Pages list on the Web tab.

- Enter the URL of a specific Web page on the Internet (such as your own Web site, or a favorite Web site), and click the Customize button to enter a name and password for the site if it is required. The wizard copies a version of this Web page to your hard disk and stores it for offline viewing. To update the content at any time, select the URL from the Web Pages list on the Web tab, and click the Synchronize button.

- Click the Browse button to select a Web page from any folder on your computer.

NOTE When you display a Web page on your Desktop, Maximize or Minimize buttons in the upper-right corner of the page allow you to display the Web page so that it either completely fills your Desktop or fits within a small window that appears over any other Desktop selections you make.

Screen Saver Tab

Used to select a screen saver. Screen savers display images that continuously change. Windows XP activates a screen saver after the computer has been idle for a certain amount of time.

The following options appear in the Screen Saver dialog:

Screen Saver   Select from many different screen savers that are stored on your computer. When you select a screen saver, a preview appears in the monitor at the top of the dialog.

Settings   Allows you to configure additional options for the screen saver when available. The options you see in the Properties dialog for the selected screen saver vary depending on the screen saver. You may be allowed to customize text, graphics, motion, display times, fonts, and more.

Preview   Provides a full-screen preview of the screen saver you select.

TIP   If the preview continues to run and does not return you to the Display Properties dialog, press any key to stop it.

On Resume, Password Protect   Check this option to protect your computer when you walk away from it for an extended period. When the screen saver appears on your Desktop, you must enter a password in order to return your computer to the Desktop and continue your work.

Wait   Allows you to set the amount of idle time that elapses before your screen saver appears. The default is 6 minutes, and Wait is adjustable from 1 to 999 minutes.

Power   Opens the Power Options Properties dialog, which allows you to configure energy-saving power features for your computer. For additional information, see the Power Options topic elsewhere in this guide.

Appearance Tab

Controls the appearance of dialog boxes that appear when you use your Windows applications. You can configure the appearance of windows, buttons, color schemes, and font sizes. The preview window displays a graphic representation of your choices while you make them.

Use the Windows and Buttons drop-down list to select a style for your dialog boxes and buttons. You can choose the new Windows XP style or the Windows Classic style.

Use the Color Scheme option to select a color scheme for your dialogs. Choices include default (blue), olive green, or silver.

The Font Size drop-down list sets the size of text that appears in the title bar of your dialog boxes. Choices include normal, large fonts, or extra large fonts.

Clicking the Advanced button opens a dialog that allows you to configure font size, colors, and styles for individual Windows XP items. Select an item (such as active title bar, menu, or ScreenTip) from the Item drop-down list, and use the font and color option drop-down lists to choose colors, fonts, and font styles.

Effects

Click the Effects button on the Appearance tab to open the Effects dialog. This dialog allows you to use animated menus and dialogs, and the appearance of icons.

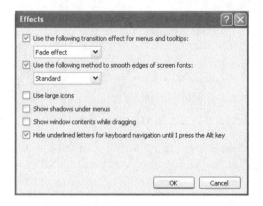

To use transition effects when you open menus and ScreenTips, check the first option (checked by default) and select an effect, such as Fade Effect or Scroll Effect, from the drop-down menu.

By default, the edges of fonts are smoothed so that your fonts do not appear "blocky." You can specify the way Windows XP smooths the fonts by checking the second option and then selecting a method (Standard or Clear Type) from the drop-down list. Uncheck this option to display text that is not smoothed.

Four additional options appear in the Effects dialog. Select the Use Large Icons option to display larger icons in menus. Select the Show Shadows Under Menus option to display shadows beneath the icons. Select the Show Window Contents While Dragging option to continually display the contents of a dialog or window while you drag it to a new location. Select the Hide Underlined Letters for Keyboard Navigation Until I Press the Alt Key option to turn off the display of underlined letters that are used for shortcuts. When you press the Alt key, Windows XP indicates the shortcut key by underlining it.

Settings Tab

Used to specify the color palette and display resolution you want to use for your display adapter, whose name appears under Display.

NOTE If you have more than one video adapter and monitor installed (such as for a dual monitor setup), the preview window displays more than one monitor, and numbers your primary monitor as 1. Drag the monitor icons to match the physical arrangement of your monitors. To configure the adapter that is associated with a specific monitor, select the associated adapter from the Display drop-down list. For further information on multiple monitor configurations, refer to the "Multiple Monitors Overview" topic in Windows XP Help and Support Center.

Screen Resolution   Adjusts the resolution of your video adapter. Higher resolution displays more information but decreases the size of each item that appears on your screen. The minimum resolution that you can choose is 800 by 600 pixels, and the maximum resolution depends on the features and capability of your graphics card. Move the slider left to decrease the resolution, or right to increase the resolution.

Color Quality   Select the maximum number of colors that your video adapter displays. Choices include Medium (16-bit), which displays a maximum of 65,536 colors, High (24-bit), which displays a maximum of 16 million colors, and Highest (32 bit) which displays 16 million colors and transparency (or alpha channels). The higher your color palette setting, the truer colors appear on the Desktop.

Use This Device as the Primary Monitor   Appears only if you have a multiple monitor configuration and select a monitor that is not the primary monitor.

Extend My Windows Desktop onto This Monitor   Appears only if you have a multiple monitor configuration and select a monitor that is not the primary monitor.

Troubleshoot   Opens the Video Display Troubleshooter in the Help and Support Center window. This troubleshooter steps you through the process of resolving problems that might occur with your graphics adapter. Follow the prompts in the troubleshooter to obtain help in resolving the problem.

Advanced   Opens the Properties dialog for your monitor and graphics adapter. This dialog consists of five tabs that allow you to configure general, adapter, monitor, troubleshooting, and color management options. Options in this dialog are discussed in the following subsection.

Advanced Display Settings

When you click the Advanced button in the Settings tab (mentioned above), a Properties dialog appears for your monitor and adapter. The Monitor and Graphics Adapter properties dialog consists of five tabs: General, Adapter, Monitor, Troubleshoot, and Color Management.

General tab   Use the Font Size drop-down list to increase or decrease the size of text beneath icons or in dialog boxes. Choose Normal Size (96 DPI) or Large Size (120 DPI) to size fonts automatically, or choose Custom Setting to scale fonts to an absolute size.

The Compatibility section allows you to choose Windows XP's response when you change your screen resolution. Some changes may adversely affect the way that items appear on your Desktop, requiring you to reboot your computer. By default, Windows XP prompts you to apply the new settings without restarting your computer. Other options allow you to restart your computer automatically, or prompt you to restart before the new settings take effect.

Click the link at the bottom of the General tab to open the Help and Support Center window for information on how to switch your display to 256 colors.

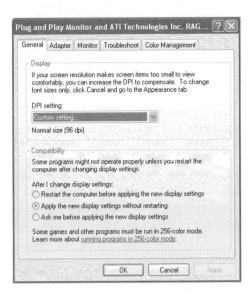

Adapter tab   Displays information about your graphics adapter, including chip type, DAC type, memory size, adapter string, and BIOS information (if available). Click the Properties button to view additional driver and resource information in the Graphics Controller Properties dialog. Click the List All Modes button to select from a list of valid graphic display modes.

TIP   After you select a new graphics mode, click the Apply button at the bottom of the Adapter tab. This gives you the opportunity to test the new setting before you exit the dialog, and you can immediately select another setting if the results are unsatisfactory.

Monitor tab   Used to view and specify settings for your monitor. Click the Properties button to display general and driver information in the Monitor Properties dialog. Use the Screen Refresh Rate drop-down list to select a new refresh rate for your monitor.

WARNING   Improper refresh rate settings can adversely affect the performance of your monitor, or even cause permanent damage. Do not deselect the Hide Modes That This Monitor Cannot Display option (which is on by default) without consulting the user manual that came with your monitor or contacting its manufacturer for recommended settings.

Troubleshoot tab   Used to select hardware acceleration options for your video display. Move the Hardware Acceleration slider toward None (left) to decrease hardware acceleration, or toward Full (right) to increase acceleration. Select the Enable Write Combining option to increase the rate at which your screen displays information. This option can improve video performance in some cases, but turn it off if your screen display becomes corrupted.

Color Management tab   Use the Color Management tab to add, remove, or configure color management options for your monitor. Color management profiles allow you to display colors on your monitor exactly as they appear when you print or scan them. Click the Add button to add a color profile to the list. Click Remove to remove the selected color profile from the list. If you have multiple color profiles, select one and click the Set as Default button to use it as the default color profile.

See also   Power Options

Drag-and-Drop

Functionality you can use to copy, move, and delete files and folders in many application programs and on the Desktop. To drag and drop a selection, place the mouse pointer over any item (or items). Press and hold the left mouse button while you move the mouse to drag the selection to another folder or drive, to your Desktop, or other destination. Place the pointer over the destination to highlight it, and then release the left mouse button.

The result of the drag-and-drop items can differ, as outlined below:

- If you drag a file or folder to a folder on the same disk, Windows moves the item. To copy the item instead, press the Ctrl key while you drag and drop the selection.

- If you drag a file or folder to a folder on a different disk, Windows copies the item. To move the item instead, press the Shift key while you drag and drop the selection.

- If you drag a file or folder to the Recycle Bin, Windows deletes the item (this is not permanent until you empty the Recycle Bin).

- If you drag a file to a printer shortcut on the Desktop, Windows prints the file.

See also   Explorer

Dr. Watson

Error-debugging program that automatically diagnoses and logs Windows XP program errors. Support personnel can then use this information to troubleshoot the problem. Dr. Watson starts automatically when a Windows XP program error occurs.

To access and configure Dr. Watson, and to view application errors, choose Start ➤ Run, and enter **drwtsn32** in the Run dialog. The Dr. Watson for Windows dialog opens.

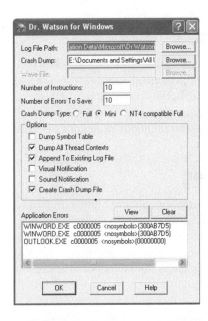

In the Dr. Watson window, you can configure the following items:

- Log file path

- Crash dump file path (if Create Crash Dump File is selected)

- Wave file path (if you select Sound Notification)

- Number of instructions

- Number of errors to save

Several options appear in the options section. For example, you can choose to dump the symbol table (which might make your log file very large) and to dump all thread contexts (not just the one causing the error, which is the default). You can also append information to an existing log file, receive visual and/or sound notification when a Windows XP program error occurs, and create a crash dump file.

When an application error occurs, it appears in the Application Errors list box at the bottom of the Dr. Watson window. Two buttons are available: The View button allows you to view detailed information in the Log File Viewer after you select an error, and the Clear button clears the selected error from the log file.

Entertainment

Entertainment   Program group that provides access to the Sound Recorder, Volume Control, and Windows Media Player. These items are discussed in detail under their own respective main topics in this book. Access the Entertainment program group by choosing Start ➤ All Programs (or Start ➤ Programs in the Classic Start menu) ➤ Accessories ➤ Entertainment.

Error Reporting

Automatically reports software errors to Microsoft. You can enable or disable this feature in the Error Reporting dialog. To display this dialog, choose Start ➤ Control Panel (or Start ➤ Settings ➤ Control Panel in the Classic Start menu) ➤ Performance and Maintenance. Select the System control panel icon to open the System Properties dialog. Click the Advanced tab, and click Error Reporting near the bottom of the dialog.

The following options appear in the dialog:

- Enable Error Reporting is checked by default and sends program and Windows operating system errors to Microsoft.

- To prevent any errors from being reported to Microsoft, select the Disable Error Reporting radio button. If you still want notification when critical errors occur on your system, select the But Notify Me When Critical Errors Occur check box.

- To include or exclude specific programs from error reporting, click Choose Programs to open another dialog. You can report errors for all programs, enable reporting for Microsoft programs or Windows components, and add, remove, or exclude specific programs from reporting.

Event Viewer

 MMC snap-in that maintains logs relating to the programs, security, and system events on your computer. These logs allow you to troubleshoot Windows XP when problems occur, or if you want to monitor Windows security events.

To access Event Viewer, choose Start ➤ Control Panel (or Start ➤ Settings ➤ Control Panel in the Classic Start menu), and select the Performance and Maintenance category. Next, click the Administrative Tools icon. From here, you can access the Event Viewer in one of two ways:

- Double-click the Event Viewer icon to open the Event Viewer dialog.

- Double-click the Computer Management icon and expand the System Tools category to display Event Viewer. When you choose the Application, Security, or System categories, the logs appear in the right pane of the Computer Management screen. You will not have access to *all* Event Viewer features (such as event filtering) when you view the event logs in this mode.

Event Viewer Logs

By default, Event Viewer contains three logs: Application, Security, and System. Each log displays different types of events. Additional logs may appear, depending on your configuration and on whether the computer is running Windows XP Home or Windows XP Professional.

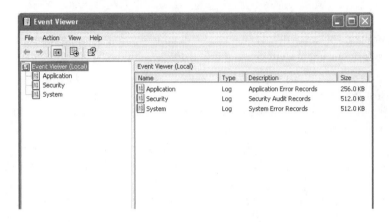

Application log   Displays events generated by such applications as installation programs and database programs. The application developer programs the events to be logged in the application.

Security log   Only available if you are logged in as a computer administrator. This log records valid and invalid logon attempts, and events that relate to resource usage (such as creating, opening, and deleting files and folders). A computer administrator can specify which events are recorded in this log.

System log   Displays events that relate to Windows XP components, such as failed attempts to load drivers, renaming hard disks, or rebuilding user disk quotas.

Event Types

The Event Viewer Details pane displays the following event types:

Error   A serious problem, such as a service that fails to load.

Warning   An event that may present a problem in the future, such as the browser not being able to obtain a list of servers from the browser master on a domain controller.

Information   A successful event, such as loading a service successfully.

Success Audit   A successful, audited event, such as a successful system logon.

Failure Audit   An unsuccessful, audited event, such as an unsuccessful system logon.

Event Log Properties

Use the Event Viewer dialog to customize event log properties. Select the Application, Security, or System log from the console tree and choose Action ➤ Properties. The Properties dialog has two tabs: General and Filter. In either tab, click Restore Defaults to return to the default configuration.

General tab Lets you change the display name and maximum size of the log. You can also select to overwrite event logs as needed, to overwrite events that are older than a specified number of days, or to overwrite events only when you manually clear the log with the Clear Log button.

Filter tab Lets you select event types to include or exclude Information, Warning, Error, Success Audit, or Failure Audit events. Use the Event Source and Category drop-down lists to narrow down the list to the type you select. Or limit the event list to a specific user or computer by entering the name in the appropriate field. You can also list events that occur within a specific time frame.

TIP You can choose View ➤ Filter to access the Filter tab.

Event Information

When you select the Application, Security, or System event log from the console tree, all events currently in the log appear in the Details pane at the right side of Event Viewer. You can see some preliminary information about each event under the column headings. The column headings give you information about the event, such as its type; the date and time the event occurred; the source and category of the event; an event ID, if applicable (this helps you classify and resolve the causes for the error); and the name of the user and computer on which the event occurred.

Viewing Detailed Information

To view detailed information about an event, double-click it, or right-click and choose Properties. The Event Properties dialog displays the date, time, type, user, and computer information that appeared in the Details pane. You also see a detailed description of the event, along with the byte or word data associated with it (if available). Click the up or down arrows in the Event Properties dialog to see the next or previous event in the log. Click the Copy button (symbolized by two sheets of paper) to copy the event details to the Windows Clipboard.

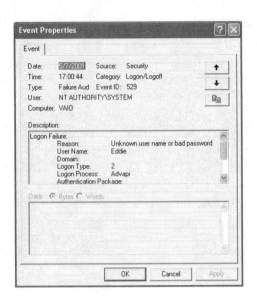

Ordering Events

By default, events in the Details pane display chronologically with the newest event first. You can reverse this order by choosing View ➤ Oldest First.

 TIP You can also display events in the details by column header. Click a column header to sort log events in ascending or descending order by type, date, time, source, category, event, or user.

Finding Events

To search for a specific event, choose View ➤ Find to open the Find dialog. Select one or more event types. Narrow the search further by choosing a specific event source or category. You can also enter an event ID, user name, computer ID, or description. Specify the search direction (Up or Down), then click Find Next.

Viewing Logs on a Remote Computer

By default, Event Viewer displays the event log files for the local computer. To access log files that appear on another computer on your network, highlight Event Viewer (Local) in the left pane. Then choose Action ➤ Connect to Another Computer. You must have administrative privileges to perform this procedure.

See also Clipboard, Computer Management, Microsoft Management Console

Explorer

Windows Explorer   Windows XP program used to work with files and folders on a local or network computer. Use Windows Explorer (the full name of this program) to display and navigate the hierarchical structure of drives, folders, and files on your computer, as well as on any mapped network drives. Explorer also allows you to create, copy, move, rename, and delete files and folders. You can also run programs, search for files, view the properties of files, and perform many other file- and folder-related functions.

To open Explorer, choose Start ➤ All Programs (or Start ➤ Programs in the Classic Start menu) ➤ Accessories ➤ Windows Explorer. This opens Explorer to the My Documents folder (a Desktop folder).

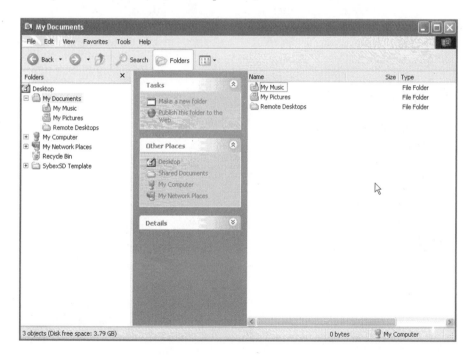

Alternatively, you can right-click Start and choose Explore. This opens Explorer to the Start Menu folder.

The Windows Explorer window displays a menu bar and toolbars at the top of the window. The left pane displays the Explorer bar, and the right pane displays the main Explorer pane. The status bar appears at the bottom of the window.

Explorer Menus

Windows Explorer menus allow you to perform all necessary file- and folder-related functions. The options that appear in each menu depend on what type of object you select in the main Explorer pane. Some Explorer menu commands are also available from the toolbars.

> **NOTE** Many of the same menu options are also available when you open My Computer, My Network Places, and the Recycle Bin.

File Menu

File Presents you with file management choices you can use to perform the following function. Some functions are available on the file menu only when an item is selected in the right pane, not in the Explorer bar, or when you right-click an item in the Explorer bar to open a shortcut menu. Besides the common commands (such as Delete, Rename, and Print), the File menu also includes these:

New   Allows you to create a new folder or shortcut, or new documents of various types.

Properties   Allows you to view and customize the properties.

Close   Closes the selected file or folder.

Open With   Opens the selected file with a program that you specify.

Send To   Allows you to create a compressed folder, or to send the selected item to your Desktop (creating a shortcut), to a mail recipient, to a floppy disk, to the My Documents folder, or to the Web Publishing Wizard.

Map Network Drive   Allows you to assign a drive letter to the selected network drive. This option is available when you select a network folder.

When you select a folder, disk, or computer, the name of the selected item appears in the File menu, directly under the Properties command. An additional submenu there displays commands that allow you to explore, open, search, or share the item. You can also format a drive that you have selected. Choose Properties to display or customize the properties of the selected item.

Edit Menu

Edit Lets you perform all the usual editing functions (undo, cut, copy, paste, and select) on files and folders. Use Cut or Copy to place the contents of an entire folder into your Clipboard, then use Paste to paste the contents elsewhere on your computer. Some functions are not available if you select an item in the Explorer bar.

View Menu

View Lets you configure what is displayed in the Explorer window and how it appears. The following options appear in the View menu:

Toolbars   Allows you to display or hide the Standard Buttons, Address Bar, and Links toolbars. You can also lock or customize the toolbars.

Status Bar   Displays or hides the status bar.

Explorer Bar   Allows you to choose a view for the Explorer bar in the left pane. Choose among Search, Favorites, History, Media, Contacts, Folders (default view), or Tip of the Day.

Filmstrip   Displays items in the lower portion of the main window as a filmstrip of thumbnails. Click a thumbnail to display a larger version of an image in the upper section of the main window.

Thumbnails   Displays items in the main Explorer pane as thumbnails.

TIP   If the selected folder contains images, Thumbnails or Filmstrip are good choices for viewing its contents. You can see a preview of the image before you open it.

Tiles   Displays items in the main Explorer pane with large icons and item names.

Icons   Displays items in the main Explorer pane with medium-sized icons and item names.

List   Displays items in the main Explorer pane with small icons and item names.

Details   Displays details of the items in the main Explorer pane. By default, details include item name, size, type, and modified date. Click a column header to sort folder contents by any category in ascending or descending order. Choose View ➢ Choose Details to select additional columns to view in this mode.

Arrange Icons By   Allows you to sort folder contents by name, size, type, or modification date. You can also show similar documents in groups, have Explorer auto-arrange icons, or align icons to a grid.

Choose Details   Allows you to select the column headers that appear in the main Explorer pane, and to specify the column width and order in which they appear.

Customize This Folder   Allows you to change the appearance of a folder. Options may vary, depending on the folder you select. In most cases, you can select a template that defines folder appearance, choose pictures, and change how icons display. Templates can be used in more than one folder, if desired.

Go To   Allows you to go to the previous view, the next view, up a level, to your home page, and to folders you've previously opened.

Refresh   Updates the current view.

Favorites Menu

Favorites Allows you to add and organize your favorite Web sites or local drives and folders in the Favorites folder. When you add a favorite, it appears in an appropriate folder at the bottom of the Favorites menu. For more information about adding and organizing favorites, see the main topic "Internet Explorer."

Tools Menu

Tools Allows you to map and disconnect network drives, synchronize offline files and folders, and configure folder options.

Help Menu

Help Lets you access the Windows XP Help and Support Center, obtain information on how to determine if you have a legal version of Windows XP, and find out information about Windows XP, such as available memory and version and licensing information.

Explorer Toolbars

Windows Explorer includes four toolbars: Standard Buttons, Address Bar, Links, and Radio. Explorer displays the Standard Buttons and Address Bar toolbars by default.

Standard Buttons Toolbar

Back   Goes back to the last item you displayed. To go back to an item before the preceding one, click the down arrow at the right of this button and choose an item from the list.

Forward   Returns to an item you were viewing before you clicked the Back button. To advance to an item after the next one, click the down arrow at the right of this button and choose an item from the list.

Up   Navigates up one hierarchy level in the directory structure that appears in the Explorer bar. The display in the main pane updates accordingly.

Search   Opens the Search Companion in the Explorer bar. Use the Search Companion to find pictures, music, video, documents, other files and folders, computers, people, printers, help topics, and sites on the Internet.

Folders   Displays the Folders view (the default view) in the Explorer bar. Here, you can view and navigate the folder structure of your computer and any network to which you're attached.

Views   Allows you to select the view in which items appear in the right pane: Filmstrip, Thumbnails, Tiles, Icons, List, and Details. These options are described in the earlier subsection "View Menu."

Customizing the Standard Buttons Toolbar   To customize the toolbar for your needs, follow these steps:

1. Choose View ➤ Toolbars ➤ Customize. The Customize Toolbar dialog appears.

2. To add a button to the toolbar, select one from the left list and click Add. To remove a button from the toolbar, select one from the right list and click Remove.

3. To change the order of buttons, select one button from the right list. Click Move Up or Move Down to change its position in the toolbar.

4. To change the text display for your toolbars, use the Text Options dropdown list. Options include Show Text Labels, Selective Text on Right, or No Text Labels.

5. To change the icon display for your toolbars, use the Icon Options dropdown list. Options include Small Icons or Large Icons.

6. Click Close to exit the dialog.

TIP   To reset the toolbar to the default settings, click Reset in the Customize Toolbar dialog.

Address Bar Toolbar

The Address Bar toolbar consists of an Address field and a Go button. The Address field displays the name of the current drive, folder, or address. You can enter a new location in the field and click the Go button to go to it, or click the down arrow at the end of the Address Bar to select a previous location from the list.

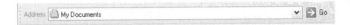

Explorer Bars

The Explorer bar displays six different views that allow you to navigate through your computer and locate files more quickly: Search, Favorites, History, Media, Contacts, and Folders.

If you don't choose an Explorer bar view, the contents of the currently selected folder or drive appear in the right pane and information about the selected folder or drive appears in the left pane. This information can include the name, size, modification date, or attributes of the folder or drive. Use the Address field on the toolbar to navigate the hierarchical structure without an Explorer bar view or while in any view except the Folders view.

Search View

To display the Search Companion, choose View ➤ Explorer Bar ➤ Search. Select a file category from the list that appears in the left pane of the Search Companion. Additional options appear that let you search for specific types of media. For example, to search for video files, you can choose the Pictures, Music, or Video option and narrow your search to video files only in the next screen.

After you select a search category, each file category screen displays a link that allows you to use advanced search options. Here, you can add additional criteria to the search, including modification date, file size, or other options. Once you define your search criteria, click Search. Use the Back button to return to previous Search Companion screens.

To search for files on the Internet, click Search the Internet. The Search Companion asks what you are looking for. Enter a word or phrase, and click Search to connect to MSN on the Internet. Search results appear in the main Explorer pane.

To change search preferences, click the Change Preferences link. This option allows you to search with an avatar (or on-screen character) that provides hints and tips. You can also enable an indexing service that provides faster results on local computers. You can change search behaviors for files and folders, or for Internet searches. Finally, you can turn off balloon tips or the AutoComplete feature.

Favorites View

To display the Favorites view, choose View ➤ Explorer Bar ➤ Favorites. This Explorer view allows you to navigate to the items you've added to your Favorites folder (and subfolders). You can also use this view to add and organize your favorites. To navigate, click an item or subitem. To add a page, click the Add button. To organize pages, click the Organize button.

 TIP Be selective with the items you add to your Favorites folder, as it can quickly become cluttered and unmanageable. Add only items you truly access often, and periodically remove items you no longer access frequently.

History View

To display the History view, choose View ➤ Explorer Bar ➤ History. This view allows you to see and access items that you've recently opened. By default, History view arranges the links by items that you visited two weeks ago, last week, and today. Click the down arrow that appears to the right of the View button to view items by date, by site, by most visited, or by order visited today. To navigate, click an item or subitem.

Media View

To display the Media view, choose View ➤ Explorer Bar ➤ Media. This view displays a media player in the left pane, and connects to the Internet so that you can search for music, radio stations, movies, and entertainment pages on the Web.

Folders View

To display Folders view, choose View ➤ Explorer Bar ➤ Folders. This view allows you to view and navigate the folders available on your Desktop, including My Documents, My Computer, My Network Places, the Recycle Bin, and Internet Explorer.

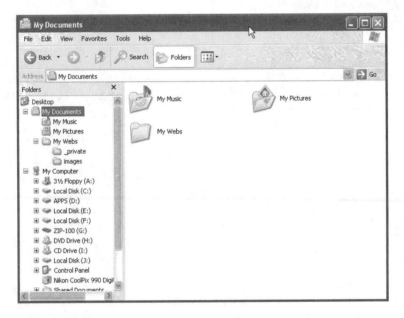

Folders view displays all items on your computer, as well as those that are shared by other computers on your network. Each item displays a name and an icon. To expand an item, double-click a folder, or click the plus sign (+) to display subfolders or drives. To collapse the expanded folder, click the minus sign (–). Select an item in Folders view to see its contents in the right pane. When you select a folder, the folder icon changes to an open folder.

Use the scroll bars at the right and bottom sides of the Folders and main panes to display contents that do not fit horizontally or vertically.

Customize a Folder

To customize the appearance of a folder, select a folder from the Folders pane. Then, choose View ➤ Customize This Folder. The Customize tab in the folder Properties dialog allows you to select from the following options:

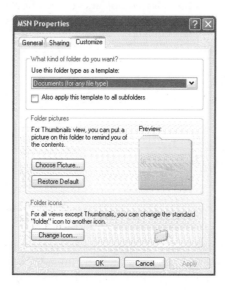

Use This Folder Type as a Template   Allows you to use settings that are common for Documents, Pictures, Photo Albums, Music, Music Artist, or Music Album. The Documents template is the default selection, and it is suitable for any file type. You can select the template that best suits the majority of items in the selected folder.

Also Apply This Template to All Subfolders   Applies the selected template to all folders that appear beneath the folder level you selected.

Choose Picture   Allows you to select an icon to represent the folder. Use the Browse dialog to navigate to any folder that contains images. Select the image and click Open. A preview of the image appears at the right of the Folder Pictures area.

Restore Default   Resets the folder picture to the default configuration.

Change Icon   Allows you to change the standard folder icon to another icon for all views except Thumbnails. Click the Change Icon button to open the Change Icon dialog, which displays several standard icons. Click Browse to locate icons in a different folder. After you select a new icon, choose OK to return to the Properties dialog. Click Restore Default to reset the icon to its default configuration.

Status Bar

To display or hide the status bar, which appears across the bottom of the Explorer window, choose View ➤ Status Bar. The status bar displays information that relates to the drive, folder, or file that you select in the Explorer pane. Details can include how many files or folders the selected object contains, how much free space is available on a drive or disk, or the total amount of disk space the files consume.

See also Folder Options, Help and Support Center, Internet Explorer, Map Network Drive, My Computer, My Documents, My Network Places, Recycle Bin, Search, Synchronize

Fast User Switching

☑ Use Fast User Switching Keeps programs running when a user logs off the computer to allow another user to log on. When the original user logs back on to the computer, the Desktop appears exactly as he or she left it.

To enable or disable Fast User Switching, choose Start ➤ Control Panel (or Start ➤ Settings ➤ Control Panel in the Classic Start menu) ➤ User Accounts, then choose Change the Way Users Log On or Off. Check or uncheck the Use Fast User Switching option.

NOTE You cannot disable Fast User Switching when multiple users are logged on to the computer. Also, only a computer administrator can enable or disable this feature.

See also User Accounts

Fax Services

☐ Fax ▶ Fax is a Start menu program group that allows you to send and receive faxes from your computer. Fax tools include the Fax Configuration Wizard, Send Fax Wizard, Fax Console, Fax Status Monitor, and the Fax Cover Page Editor. Each of these utilities is covered shortly in its own section.

To install fax services:

1. Insert the Windows XP CD into your CD-ROM drive.

2. When the menu screen appears, choose Install Optional Windows Components. The Windows Components dialog appears.

3. From the Components list, choose Fax Services, and click Next. The wizard installs the fax component files onto your hard disk.

4. After the files are installed, click Finish to exit the wizard and return to the Windows XP CD menu.

5. Click Exit to return to your Windows XP Desktop.

To configure all your fax settings, or just a single outgoing fax, you can use one of the wizards described in the next section. To manage faxes more directly—sending, receiving, and storing them—see the later sections on Fax Status Monitor and Fax Console.

 NOTE You can completely start and stop the fax service through the Services MMC plug-in.

Fax Wizards

Windows XP provides two fax wizards, one to enter information and settings that are used for all faxes and another to walk you through sending a single fax.

Fax Configuration Wizard

Allows you to configure user information that appears on fax transmissions, and to select the device or devices that you use to send and receive faxes on your computer. The Fax Configuration Wizard runs automatically the first time you choose Start ➤ All Programs (or Start ➤ Programs in the Classic Start menu) ➤ Accessories ➤ Communications ➤ Fax ➤ Send a Fax, or when you use the File ➤ Print command from any Windows application to print a document to your fax printer.

 NOTE You can run the Fax Configuration Wizard at any time by choosing the Tools ➤ Configure Fax command from the Fax Console.

To complete the wizard, you'll need to have certain information at hand:

• Personal or business information such as name, fax and phone numbers, and e-mail and postal addresses

- Transmitting Station Identifier (TSID) and Called Station Identifier (CSID): the business name or fax number that typically appears at the top of each fax page that you send or is sent to machines that you receive faxes from

- Type and model of fax device that you want to use

- Specific data such as a billing code

At each screen, make your choices or enter the requested information, then click Next to continue, Back to change information, or Finish to exit the wizard and apply your settings. When you click Finish, the Send Fax Wizard appears.

Send Fax Wizard

Send a Fax... Walks you through the steps of sending a fax via a fax printer installed on the computer. To send a cover page fax only (without a document attached), choose Start ➤ All Programs (or Start ➤ Programs in the Classic Start menu) ➤ Accessories ➤ Communications ➤ Fax ➤ Send a Fax. To fax a document with your cover page, create the document in any Windows application, then choose File ➤ Print. Select the fax printer you want to use and click Print. Either method starts the Send Fax Wizard.

The wizard will ask you to enter or choose:

- Recipient information (you can select an entry from Address Book or manually enter the data)

- Cover page template

- Your personal information (the Send Fax Wizard will default to using the information entered in the Fax Configuration Wizard)

- Delivery notification method

- Time to schedule the fax (now, when discount rates apply, or at a specified time) and fax priority

TIP Times during which discount rates apply are set up through Fax Service Manager.

At each screen, make your choices or enter the requested information, then click Next to continue, Back to change information, or Finish to exit the wizard and apply your settings. If you choose to send the fax now, then when you finish the wizard, your fax dials the number and transmits. If you choose to send the fax later, it remains in the fax queue until the specified time.

Fax Console

Fax Console   Allows you to send, receive, view, and print faxes from your computer. To open the Fax Console, choose Start ➤ All Programs (or Start ➤ Programs in the Classic Start menu) ➤ Accessories ➤ Communications ➤ Fax ➤ Fax Console.

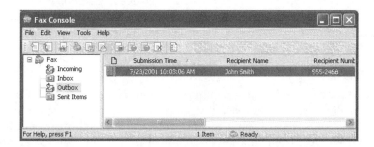

The buttons on the Fax Console toolbar perform the same functions as some of the menu commands. Menu commands that are unique to the Fax Console are covered in the following sections.

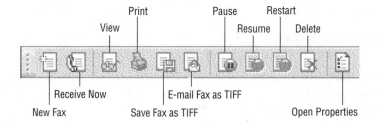

File Menu

The File menu contains the following options that allow you to send, receive, and view faxes and fax properties:

Send a New Fax   Opens the Send Fax Wizard (see preceding section) to send a fax that includes only a cover page.

Receive a Fax Now   Opens the Fax Monitor and allows you to accept an incoming fax transmission.

View   Displays a preview of your fax document in an image preview window.

Save As   Allows you to save the selected fax as a TIFF image.

Mail To   Allows you to e-mail the selected fax as a TIFF image.

Pause, Resume, Restart   Control transmission of the current fax. Restart transmits the current fax from the beginning.

Delete   Deletes the selected fax from the queue.

Properties   Opens a Properties dialog for the selected fax, with data such as the document name, subject, number of pages, size, recipient and sender information, status, current page, scheduled time, user priority, number of retries, various IDs, device, billing code, and submission time.

View Menu

The View menu contains only one unique option: The Add/Remove Columns command allows you to choose and arrange the columns that appear in the selected Fax Console view. Select the Incoming, Inbox, Outbox, or Sent Items node from the tree. Then choose View ➤ Add/Remove Columns to open the Add/Remove Columns dialog.

Tools Menu

The Tools menu contains commands to open wizards and utilities and to configure contact information for your faxes and fax utilities. These commands include the following:

Sender Information   Opens a dialog that allows you to enter personal and business contact information for the faxes you send.

Personal Cover Pages   Displays a list of personal cover pages that you created with the Fax Cover Page Editor (see later section). Allows you to create, open, add, rename, and delete fax cover pages.

Fax Printer Status   Displays the name and status of the fax printer.

Fax Printer Configuration   Opens the Fax Properties dialog, where you can view and configure properties for your fax device.

Fax Status Monitor

Monitors fax-related events, such as sending and receiving. Fax Status Monitor provides information, such as the elapsed time, about faxes currently being transmitted. It also enables you to quickly interrupt incoming and outgoing faxes and allows you to specify that you don't want to manually answer a second incoming call.

Fax Status Monitor appears in the notification area of the taskbar only during fax activity (after you send a job to the fax printer or while the job is being sent, for example).

Fax Cover Page Editor

Fax Cover Page Editor — Allows you to create custom cover pages for the faxes you send. To open the Fax Cover Page Editor, choose Start ➢ All Programs (or Start ➢ Programs in the Classic Start menu) ➢ Accessories ➢ Communications ➢ Fax ➢ Fax Cover Page Editor.

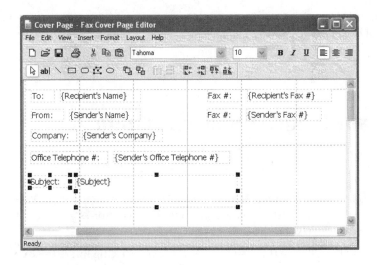

The buttons on the first toolbar—the Style toolbar—are standard Windows commands for document management, clipboard options, font formatting, and alignment. The second, or Drawing, toolbar is also similar to that found in other Windows applications, with buttons for selecting and drawing lines and shapes, adding text, and arranging selected items.

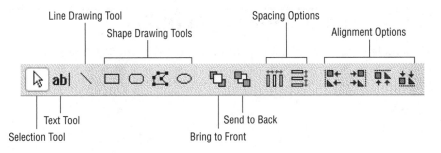

The Fax Cover Page Editor's menu bar consists of seven menus: File, Edit, View, Insert, Format, Layout, and Help. Some of these menus contain commands that are unique to the Editor:

View menu   Has commands to display or hide the Style toolbar, Drawing toolbar, status bar, and grid lines.

Insert menu   Allows you to insert various fields into your fax cover pages, to be filled in when you send a fax. Available fields include recipient name and fax number, sender information, and messages such as note, subject, date/time sent, or number of pages.

Format menu   Lets you control the appearance of the text, lines, fills, and colors on your fax cover pages.

Layout menu   Includes commands to adjust the layering, alignment, and spacing of the items on your fax cover pages.

File and Settings Transfer Wizard

Files and Settings Transfer Wizard   Allows you to transfer files and settings from your old computer to your new one. In order to transfer the files, you need to run the File and Settings Transfer Wizard on the old computer *and* the new computer. To begin the wizard, choose Start ➢ All Programs (or Start ➢ Programs in the Classic Start menu) ➢ Accessories ➢ System Tools ➢ File and Settings Transfer Wizard.

The wizard guides you through the process of transferring Internet Explorer and Outlook Express information, Desktop and display settings, dial-up connections, and other files from your old computer to your new one. After you select the items that you want to transfer, you can save the files to floppy disk or to another folder on your hard disk. Run the wizard on your new computer to retrieve the files. You may also be prompted to insert your Windows XP CD during the process.

File Signature Verification Utility

To maintain system integrity and detect changes to system files, system files are digitally signed by the software manufacturer to ensure authenticity. The File Signature Verification utility allows you to check for critical system files that should be digitally signed but aren't. To start the utility, choose Start ➤ Run, then type **sigverif** in the Run dialog. The File Signature Verification dialog appears.

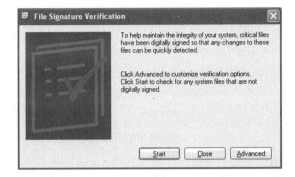

Click the Advanced button to configure verification options such as receiving notification when system files are not signed, narrowing your search to certain file types or locations, or saving results to a log file. When you are done setting these options, click OK to return to the File Signature Verification dialog.

Click Start to begin the file signature verification process. A progress bar appears in the dialog while the utility scans your files. Wait for the process to finish, then do one of the following:

- If you receive a message that tells you all files are digitally signed, click OK to return to the File Signature Verification dialog, then click Close to exit the dialog.

- If some files are not digitally signed, the Signature Verification Results dialog displays the names of those files. The status bar displays the numbers of files found, signed files, unsigned files, and files not scanned. Make note of the files that are not signed, and click Close.

NOTE After you create a log, you can return to the Logging tab in the Advanced File Signature Verification Settings dialog at any time, and click View Log to view a complete log of the files that were reported as signed, unsigned, and not scanned.

Folders

Folders are part of the Windows XP file system structure. You use folders to organize files on your computer. Folders can contain files and subfolders.

To view a folder, open Windows Explorer. Use the Folders tree in the left pane to find the folder. Select a folder name to display its contents in the main pane. You can also double-click a folder in the main pane or on your Desktop to view its contents.

Right-click a folder name and select Properties to open the Properties dialog, which can have any or all of the following tabs:

General   Displays the folder's name, type, location, size, content count, and creation or modification date. You can choose to apply the Read-Only and Hidden attributes (and the Archive attribute if formatted with FAT). If the drive is formatted with NTFS, click Advanced to configure additional attributes such as archiving, indexing, compression, and encryption attributes.

Web Sharing   Allows you to share a folder on a Web site. Available on Windows XP Professional computers with IIS installed.

Sharing   Allows you to share a folder with other users on the network. For more information, see the main topic "Sharing."

Customize   Allows you to use the display options of the current folder as a template for other folders. You can configure the folder to store documents, pictures, photo albums, or music files. You can also choose a picture that reminds you of the contents that are stored in the folder, and select a custom folder icon to use for all folders.

See also   Explorer, Shared Folders, Sharing

Folder Options

   Controls the appearance and use of files and folders and configures file associations. Any settings you make determine how folders are displayed and used in Windows Explorer, My Documents, My Network Places, My Computer, and Control Panel.

To open the Folder Options dialog, choose Start ➤ Control Panel (or Start ➤ Settings ➤ Control Panel in the Classic Start menu) ➤ Appearance and Themes ➤ Folder Options. The Folder Options dialog contains four tabs—General, View, File Types, and Offline Files.

 TIP You can also access Folder Options from the Tools menu of any Windows Explorer window.

General Tab

Controls how folders appear and work. The tab is divided into three sections:

Tasks Allows you to display common tasks in folders (default), or to use Windows classic folders.

Browse Folders Allows you to open a new folder in the same window (default) or in its own window.

Click Items as Follows Allows you to open items with a single click or a double click (default). You can also choose to underline icon titles as configured in your Web browser, or only when you point at them.

 TIP If single-clicking is specified, move the mouse pointer over an item to select it.

You can return to default values by clicking Restore Defaults.

View Tab

Controls the appearance and advanced settings for folders. Click the Apply to All Folders button to apply the View tab settings from the current folder to all other folders. This button is available only when you access the Folder Options dialog from the Tools menu of Windows Explorer. You can reset the view of all folders to the default setting (Large Icons) by clicking Reset All Folders.

In the Advanced Settings list box, select check boxes for the settings you want to apply, such as displaying the full path in the title bar, hiding file extensions for known file types, and showing hidden files and folders.

File Types Tab

Controls which file types are associated with which file extension (.XXX), and the default application used to open a file type. The Registered File Types list displays all registered file types and their extensions. The following buttons are available on the File Types tab:

New   Allows you to create a new file extension. Click the Advanced button to associate a new or existing file type with the new extension. You can also enter an existing file extension and then change the file type associated with the extension.

Delete   Allows you to delete an existing file extension and associated file type.

Change   Allows you to change the default application that Windows uses to open files of the selected extension and file type.

Advanced   Allows you to change the selected file type's associated icon and actions. Any configured actions appear in the File menu and shortcut menu for the item. You can configure a new action by clicking New and then specifying the action as well as the application that is supposed to perform that action. You can also edit or remove existing actions, and you can specify whether you want files to open immediately after they have finished downloading. Finally, you can choose to always show file extensions and to enable browsing in the same window.

Offline Files Tab

Used to configure whether files on the network are available when you are not connected to the network. On this tab, you can choose to: enable or disable offline files, synchronize files when you log on or before you log off, display reminders at regular intervals when you are working offline, encrypt these files to secure data, and adjust the amount of space to store offline files.

The following three buttons appear on the Offline Files tab:

Delete Files   Allows you to delete temporary offline files or all offline files.

View Files   Displays files that are in the Offline Files folder.

Advanced   Allows you to choose events that occur when you lose connection to the network. You can request notification and continue to work offline, or you can choose to never allow the computer to go offline. You can also configure exceptions for specific computers.

See also   Explorer, Internet Explorer, Synchronize, Make Available Offline

Fonts

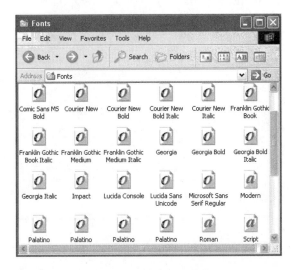

Folder used to view and manage the fonts (type styles) that are used by Windows XP and Windows applications. To open the Fonts folder in an Explorer window, choose Start ➤ Control Panel (or Start ➤ Settings ➤ Control Panel in the Classic Start menu) ➤ Appearance and Themes.

From the See also list in the left pane, click Fonts to open the Fonts window. All fonts that are currently installed appear in this window.

Windows XP supports TrueType fonts, Open Type fonts (an extension of True-Type), Type 1 fonts (by Adobe Systems), vector fonts, and raster fonts. The icon in the Fonts folder displays an indicator for each font type. For example, Open Type fonts show an *O* in the font icon; TrueType fonts show two *T*s, and Type 1 fonts display an *A* (for Adobe).

Viewing Font Examples

Double-click a font icon to open a window that contains examples of the font in different sizes. You'll also see information such as font type, typeface name, file size, version, and copyright information. Click Print to print the font example.

If you have many fonts installed on your system, it can get difficult to keep track of what fonts you have available and what they look like. The View menu of the Fonts folder includes two options that make it easier to keep track of your fonts:

List Fonts by Similarity Produces a drop-down list where you choose a font that you are familiar with. Fonts are then listed by name, arranged by similarity to the font you selected. You can also click the Similarity button on the toolbar to display this view.

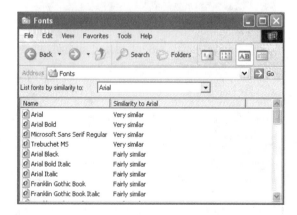

Hide Variations (Bold, Italic, Etc.) Lists only main fonts and does not show the variations of the font (such as bold or italic). This reduces the number of items in the list and makes it easier to find or choose a font you're looking for.

Adding New Fonts

You can add new fonts to your computer at any time by following these steps:

1. Choose File ➤ Install New Font.

2. Browse for the location of the new fonts.

3. Select one or more fonts from the List of Fonts list box, and check or uncheck the option to copy the fonts to your Fonts folder.

4. Click OK. Windows installs the fonts and returns you to the Fonts folder.

See also Explorer

Forgotten Password Wizard

Allows you to create a *password reset disk*. You can use this disk to log in to your account if you forget your password.

NOTE The proper time to create a password reset disk is *while you remember what your password is*. Consider creating this disk the first time you log on to your new account. The Forgotten Password Wizard prompts you to enter the *current* password while you create the password reset disk for the account.

To open the Forgotten Password Wizard, use one of the following methods:

- If you are logged on as a Computer Administrator, choose Start ➤ Control Panel ➤ User Accounts. From the Pick a Task section, click Change an Account, then select an account to change. In the Related Tasks list in the left pane, choose Prevent a Forgotten Password.

- If you are logged on as a Limited user, choose Start ➤ Control Panel ➤ User Accounts. From the Pick a Task section, click Create a Password Reset Disk, then click the Create Disk button.

If you do not remember your password when you log on, you can use the password reset disk to log on to your computer:

- In a domain environment, you can press Ctrl+Alt+Del at the Welcome screen and attempt to enter a password. The Logon Failed dialog appears. Click Reset, and insert your password reset disk into your floppy drive. Follow the instructions to create a new password.

- In a workgroup environment, click your user name on the Welcome screen, then attempt to enter a password. The Did You Forget Your Password dialog displays an option to use your password reset disk. Click the option and insert your password reset disk into your floppy drive. Follow the instructions to create a new password.

NOTE After you use the password reset disk to create a new password, you will need to create a new password reset disk with your new password.

See also   User Accounts

Format

Format...   Allows you to format a disk for first-time use, or completely erase the disk's contents. Formatting is required in order for Windows to be able to save information to and read information from any disk device, including hard disks and floppy disks.

NOTE To format a floppy disk, first insert the disk into the floppy disk drive.

WARNING Make sure the disk you are formatting is either blank or a disk whose contents you don't need anymore. Formatting a used disk erases all of the contents of the disk.

To format a disk, perform the following steps:

1. Open My Computer or Windows Explorer and select the disk that you want to format.

2. Choose File ➤ Format, or right-click the disk and choose Format. The Format dialog appears. Choose settings from the drop-down lists as needed.

 TIP You cannot format a floppy disk with the NTFS file system.

3. Choose whether you want to perform a quick format. Do this only if you know that the disk does not have any bad sectors. A quick format takes less time because Windows XP does not scan the disk for bad sectors.

 TIP You cannot quick-format a blank, non-formatted disk.

4. If you're formatting a hard disk with NTFS, specify whether you want to enable compression.

5. To make the disk bootable, check Create an MS-DOS Startup Disk.

6. Click Start to begin formatting. A dialog asks you to confirm your action. Click OK to continue.

7. When the format is complete, click OK, then click Close.

See also   My Computer, Explorer, NTFS

FTP

Acronym for File Transfer Protocol, a common method for transferring files to or from a remote host (a computer on an IP network). It supports many file types, including ASCII, binary, and EBCDIC. You can also use FTP to display directory lists and file lists.

In Windows XP, FTP is a text-based program that you run from the Windows XP command prompt. To run it, choose Start ➤ Run, enter **ftp** and click OK. A Command Prompt window opens to an FTP prompt (ftp>).

You can type **?** or **help** at the ftp> prompt to display all available FTP commands. You can also type **help** followed by the name of a command to see an explanation of what the command does.

Many of the commands are used for troubleshooting purposes and to navigate the local or remote directory structure. The following commands are most commonly used for file transfer purposes:

open　Opens a connection to the remote computer. You can then enter the IP address of the computer to which you want to connect to establish the connection. You can often use **anonymous** as the username and your e-mail address as the password.

TIP　When anonymous FTP access is allowed, you don't have to use a valid e-mail address; as long as you're following e-mail address format, you'll be allowed access to the remote computer. However, it's considered good Internet etiquette to provide your actual address.

ascii　Establishes the file transfer type as ASCII.

binary　Establishes the file transfer type as binary.

put　Transfers a file you specify from your computer to the remote host.

get　Transfers a file you specify from the remote host to your computer.

quit　Closes the connection to the remote host and ends the FTP session (the **bye** command does the same). You return to the Windows XP Desktop.

Game Controllers

Installs, removes, and configures game controllers, such as game pads, joysticks, flight yokes, and steering wheel/accelerator pedal controllers. To open the Game Controllers dialog, choose Start ➤ Control Panel (or Start ➤ Settings ➤ Control Panel in the Classic Start menu). Click Printers and Other Hardware, and then click the Game Controlers control panel icon. The dialog contains the following options:

- Click Add to open the Add Game Controller dialog, which allows you to install standard or custom game controllers.

- To remove a game controller, highlight it in the list of installed game controllers, then click Remove.

- To test and calibrate an installed game controller, select it from the list and click Properties. Use options in the Text tab to verify that your controller is installed properly. If the test is unsuccessful, click the Settings tab, then click Calibrate to perform a calibration with the Game Device Calibration Wizard.

- To configure support for older programs, click the Advanced button. Select your preferred device from the list and choose OK to return to the Game Controllers dialog.

- Click Troubleshoot to open the Games and Multimedia Troubleshooter. Follow the instructions in the troubleshooter to remedy the problem.

Games

Program group that contains ten games. You can play FreeCell, Hearts, Minesweeper, Pinball, Solitaire, and Spider Solitaire on your local computer. Five additional games—Internet Backgammon, Internet Checkers, Internet Hearts, Internet Reversi, and Internet Spades—require an active Internet connection and allow you to play with other users over the Internet. To access the Games program group, choose Start ➤ All Programs (or Start ➤ Programs in the Classic Start menu) ➤ Games. Choose Help from the game menu to learn how to play the game.

Group Policy

 WINDOWS XP PROFESSIONAL Group Policy is a feature of Windows XP Professional only.

MMC snap-in and Windows XP component that allows you to control the computing environment of users in your network. This includes the programs users can access, the programs that appear on users' Desktops, the options that appear on users' Start menus, and the script files that run at certain times. Group policies consist of settings that can be applied to all users in a site, domain, or organizational unit (OU).

Group policy administrators configure group policies to enforce company policies, such as limiting the use of applications to certain users. A group policy administrator should belong to the default Group Policy Creator Owners security group, which provides the necessary rights to modify group policies in a domain; Administrator is a member of this group by default.

Group Policy Snap-in

Windows XP Professional allows a computer administrator to use the Group Policy snap-in to configure group policies and customize settings on a local or network computer.

You can add the Group Policy MMC snap-in for a specific group policy to an MMC (see "Microsoft Management Console (MMC)" for more information on how to do this), and then add the new MMC to the Administrative Tools program group. This allows you to access it easily and more directly using the Start menu.

The Group Policy Editor has two nodes: Computer Configuration and User Configuration. Policies defined under Computer Configuration apply to *computers* in the network and take effect when the client operating system is initialized. Policies defined under User Configuration apply to *users* in the network and take effect when the user logs on to a computer in the network.

Each node has three extensions (folders)—Software Settings, Windows Settings, and Administrative Templates—which in turn can contain additional extensions and policies.

Navigate the extension structure and then use the Action menu to perform actions related to policy setting, such as changing the properties of and configuring a policy. The items available on the Action menu will vary depending on which item you have selected in the console tree or Details pane.

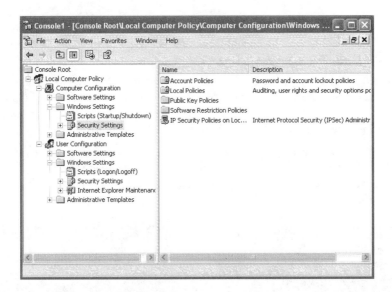

Windows Settings Extension

If you expand the Windows Settings extension, you'll find a node called Security Settings. This is where the default Domain Controller Security Policy and default Domain Security Policy are defined and configured. The Security Settings node, in turn, has subnodes that contain individual policies, such as password, user rights, and event log–related policies. Here you can also configure settings for Registry security, system service security, file security, and restricted groups.

See also   Control Panel, Local Security Policy, Microsoft Management Console, Start Menu

Hardware

See   Add New Hardware, Device Manager

Hardware Troubleshooter

Special help topic that assists you with diagnosing problems with hard disks, CD and DVD drives, network adapters, input devices, games controllers, USB devices, display adapters, modems, sound cards, and hardware conflicts.

> **TIP** The Add Hardware Wizard also helps you troubleshoot problems that you may be having with your hardware.

When you are configuring or inspecting hardware devices and associated drivers, various dialog boxes associated with the hardware or device driver display a Troubleshoot button. When you click this button, Windows XP opens the Hardware Troubleshooter in the Help and Support Center window.

To open the Hardware Troubleshooter at any time, choose Start ➤ Control Panel (or Start ➤ Settings ➤ Control Panel from the Classic Start menu), and then click Printers and Other Hardware. From the list of troubleshooters in the left pane, click Hardware.

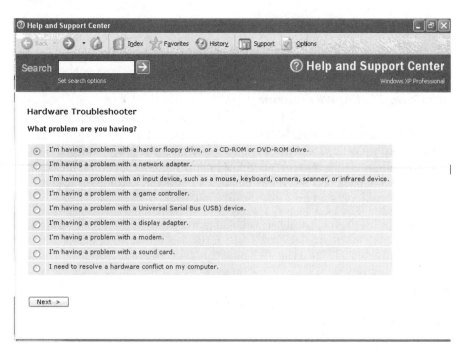

The first screen of the Hardware Troubleshooter asks what type of problem you are having. Select the option that is most appropriate and click Next to step through additional questions that pertain to the hardware item you are troubleshooting.

On each subsequent screen, choose the response that most closely matches the problem you are having and then click:

Next to continue with the diagnosis

Skip to pass by a step and try something else

Back to review a previous step

Start Over to begin an entirely new troubleshooting session

If you can't find the solution in the Hardware Troubleshooter, you can use the options in the Support screen for additional help.

See also Add New Hardware

Help and Support Center

 The Windows XP help system includes extensive explanations and step-by-step instructions for Windows XP. You can access the information contained in the system by browsing its contents, querying the index, searching by keyword, or bookmarking and checking favorite areas of Help. The help system pages are written in HTML, and as a result, if you're connected to the Internet, you can also follow links that point to pages on the Internet.

TIP For a broad introduction to Windows XP, select the "What's New in Windows XP" help topic that appears in the left portion of the Help and Support Center home page. This link allows you to read What's New topics, take tours, tutorials, or walk-throughs of Windows XP, obtain help on activation, licensing, and registration, and learn more about Windows components.

Help and Support Center Window

Choose Start ➤ Help and Support, or press F1 from the Desktop to open the Help and Support Center window. This window is divided into several different areas, described in the following subsections.

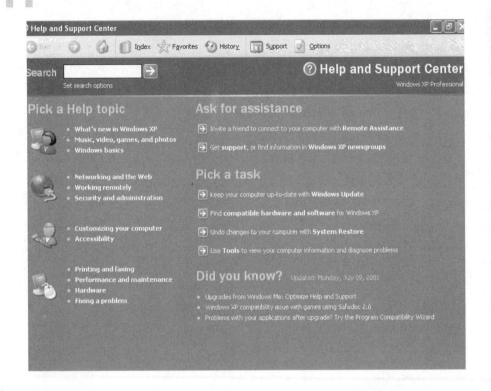

WINDOWS XP PROFESSIONAL Some options in Help and Support Center (for example, the Security and Administration topic shown here) are features of Windows XP Professional only.

Toolbar

The help system toolbar appears at the top of the Help and Support Center window. Click the buttons on this toolbar to move through the various Windows XP Help and Support Center topics and views.

Back and Forward Navigate through help pages you've opened.

Home Returns directly to the Help and Support Center home page.

Index   Opens Index view, which allows you to search through help topics by keyword or select from a list of topics.

Favorites   Opens Favorites view, which allows you to access help topics that you have added to your Favorites list.

History   Opens History view, which allows you to revisit and organize help topics that you have viewed in the recent past.

Support   Opens Support view, which allows you to get online help through various Internet and e-mail channels.

Options   Opens Options view, which allows you to configure shared help for users on a network.

 WINDOWS XP PROFESSIONAL The Options view is a feature of Windows XP Professional only.

Search Area

Use the Search area to search for particular Windows XP Help and Support topics. To perform a basic search, enter a keyword or phrase in the search box. Then click the arrow or press Enter to perform the search; a list of related topics appears in the Search Results list. Simply click a topic title to view more information in the right portion of the Help and Support Center window.

If the search takes a long time to complete, you can click Stop; a list of topics found up to that point appears in the Search Results list. If the Search Results window displays an excessive number of topics, you can narrow the search. Enter another term that applies to the topic for which you need help. Then, check the Search Within Previous Results option to search only through the topics in the Search Results list.

Click Set Search Options (the link under the search box) to enter additional search settings or to perform advanced searches. The Set Search Options window opens.

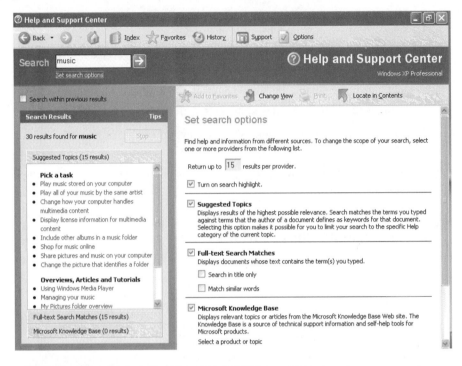

This window allows you to set several different parameters for your search:

- By default, the Search Results window displays results from three help providers: Suggested Topics, Full-Text Search Matches, and Microsoft Knowledge Base. In the Set Search Options window, uncheck providers you don't want to use in the search, and specify the maximum number of results to return from each provider.

- By default, Windows XP highlights each occurrence of the search term when you display help topics in the main pane. Uncheck the Turn On Search Highlight option to disable this feature.

- When you include Full-text Search Matches in your search, you can specify additional options. Select the Search in Title Only option to search only for titles that contain the search term you specify. Select the Match Similar Words option to return topics that contain words similar to your search term.

- When you include Microsoft Knowledge Base topics in your search, you can select a specific product or topic from a drop-down list. Use the Search For drop-down list to search for any or all of the words you enter or to search for the exact phrase or a Boolean phrase. Check the Search in Title Only box to search only Knowledge Base titles.

TIP The Windows XP help topic "Using Help and Support Center keyboard short-cuts" provides a list of shortcuts that you can use to navigate through the help viewer and its menus.

Pick a Help Topic Area

Pick a Help topic In this section of Windows XP Help, topics are organized by categories that are fairly self-explanatory. Simply choose one of these headings to display a list of related topics that you can choose from:

Category	Contains Topics That...
What's New in Windows XP	Give you a broad introduction to Windows XP.
Music, Video, Games, and Photos	Are multimedia- and game-related.
Windows Basics	Relate to core Windows tasks and essential maintenance procedures.
Networking and the Web	Relate to networking, e-mail, sharing resources, passwords, and security.
Working Remotely	Relate to offline content, Remote Desktops, and laptop computing.
Customizing Your Computer	Help you customize appearance, region, and language settings, configure for multiple users, and use handwriting and speech recognition.
Accessibility	Relate to configuring Windows XP for those who have vision, hearing, or mobility impairments.
Printing and Faxing	Relate to local and network printers and fax machines.
Performance and Maintenance	Help you keep Windows and applications running smoothly, as well as show you how to restore your system.
Hardware	Help you install and configure hardware and peripherals.
Fixing a Problem	Help you troubleshoot problems with hardware, networking, performance, startup and shutdown, and applications.

WINDOWS XP PROFESSIONAL The following help subjects are features of Windows XP Professional Edition only.

In addition to the help topics covered in both the Home and Professional editions of Windows XP, Windows XP Professional offers additional topics in the following categories:

Category	Contains Topics That...
Working Remotely	Relate to Power Options and Remote Desktop.
Performance and Maintenance	Help you back up your data and specify settings for your computer.
Security and Administration	Include security and administration tools, password and user accounts, computer management, getting system information, backing up files and folders, disk management, file encryption, removable storage, remote assistance, digital signatures, and access control.

Ask for Assistance Area

Ask for assistance The options in this section of the Help and Support Center window allow you to invite a friend to connect to your computer with Remote Assistance, to obtain Microsoft support, or to read or submit articles posted in Windows XP newsgroups on the Microsoft Web site.

Pick a Task Area

Pick a task These options allow you to connect to the Microsoft Web site for the latest Windows XP updates or for information about compatible hardware and software. You can use System Restore to restore settings to an earlier configuration to undo harmful changes, or to create restore points. The Pick a Task area also provides links to several tools that allow you to manage and support your Windows XP computer.

Did You Know? Area

Did you know? This section of the window displays links to up-to-date help and support content when you are connected to the Internet. To select one of the topics, simply click a link to view the most up-to-date information on that topic.

List and Contents Panes

Once you have chosen a help topic or task, the following four buttons appear in most Help and Support Center views:

Add to Favorites   Change View   Print...   Locate in Contents

Add to Favorites   Adds the current help topic to your Favorites list—especially handy if you need to return to a help topic several times.

Change View   Switches the window to display only the content that appears in the Contents pane. Click Change View again to return back to the full window of the current view.

Print   Allows you to print the help topic that currently appears in the Contents pane. Complete the options shown in the Print dialog box and choose Print to print your help topic.

Locate in Contents   Finds a topic in the Table of Contents while you are in the Search or Index view.

The main section of the Help and Support Center window is often divided into two panes: a List pane on the left and a Contents pane on the right. What you see in these areas is determined by the view you choose: Index, Favorites, History, Support, or Options.

Index view   Click the Index button on the toolbar. Topics included in Help and Support Center appear in alphabetical order on the left. To jump to a specific heading, enter text in the text box. As you enter your term, the list automatically scrolls to any word that closely or exactly matches. You can also use a vertical scrollbar to navigate through the topic list. To display help for a topic, simply double-click one of the items in the topic list; the help content appears on the right.

Favorites view   Click the Favorites button in the toolbar. The topics that you have entered in your Favorites list appear on the left. Double-click a topic to display its content on the right.

History view   Click the History button in the toolbar. Help topics that you have recently visited appear in the Recent Links list on the left. Double-click a topic to display its content on the right.

Support view   Click the Support button in the toolbar when you are having problems that you cannot resolve on your own. Three options appear in the left pane:

Ask a Friend to Help   Allows you to use Remote Assistance to connect over the Internet with anyone you trust to remotely view and control your computer with your permission. Both parties must be running Windows XP (or later) to use this feature.

Get Help from Microsoft   Allows you to get help over the Internet from an online Microsoft Support Professional. You will be prompted to select the product that you need help with, and then to fill out an online form that will be submitted directly to a Microsoft Support Professional. You must be connected to the Internet to submit a request and to receive a reply. The availability of this option is dependent upon warranty.

Go to a Windows Web Site Forum   Allows you to connect with online newsgroups that allow you to post messages to other Windows XP users and read their replies.

Three additional options appear in the See Also section of the Support view: My Computer Information, Advanced System Information, and the System Configuration Utility. These are described under their own main topics.

Options view   To configure Help and Support Center for your local computer and to share help options with other computers on your network, in Windows XP Professional only, click the Options button in the toolbar to reveal a list of options:

- Change Help and Support Center Options

- Set Search Options

- Share Windows Help

WINDOWS XP PROFESSIONAL   The features of the Options view are available only in Windows XP Professional.

Application and Dialog Help Features

In addition to using the Help and Support Center features, most applications have a Help menu that offers additional information about that particular program. Some dialogs may feature a Help button that you can click for additional information that relates to the options contained in the dialog.

In addition, some dialogs contain context-sensitive help. If so, you see a blue button with a question mark next to the Close button in the upper-right corner of the dialog.

Context-Sensitive Help Button

Click the blue Help button to attach a question mark to the mouse pointer. Move the pointer over any item in the dialog and click to display a ScreenTip that describes the function of that item. Click again to close the ScreenTip. Repeat this procedure for each item you want to learn more about.

Alternatively, right-click an item in the dialog to display a What's This? pop-up message (if it's available). Click What's This? to display the ScreenTip for the item and click again to close the ScreenTip.

Sometimes, the Help menu includes a What's This? choice. Select it to attach the question mark to your mouse pointer.

See also My Computer, Network Diagnostics, Offer Remote Assistance, Remote Assistance, System Configuration Utility, System Information, System Restore, Windows Update

Image Preview

Allows you to view, rotate, and add category information to images on your computer. To open the Image Preview application, double-click any image in any folder.

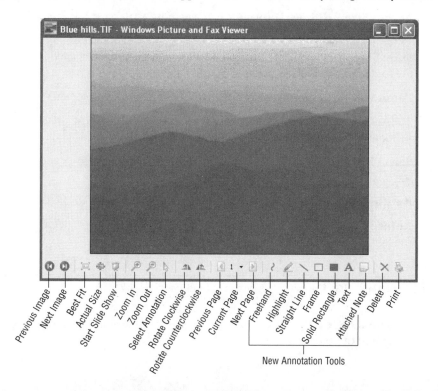

New Annotation Tools

Right-click the Image Preview icon that appears in the upper-left corner of the title bar; a menu appears. In addition to the commands that are available with the toolbar buttons described next, you can set the ima

ge as wallpaper or open the image in another application. Use the Send To command to send your image to a compressed folder, to create a shortcut on your Desktop, to send your image by e-mail, to copy the image to your floppy drive or to your My Documents folder, or to publish your image on the Internet.

The Image Preview window displays a toolbar at the bottom of the page. The available toolbar buttons vary, depending on the type of image you select. When you select a TIFF image, you see a toolbar with the following buttons (some listed with the corresponding keyboard shortcuts in parentheses):

Previous Image   (Left Arrow) Displays the previous image in the folder, based on the sort order.

Next Image   (Right Arrow) Displays the next image in the folder, based on the sort order.

Best Fit   (Ctrl+B) Sizes the image so that you view the entire image in the preview window.

Actual Size   (Ctrl+A) Displays the image in its actual size, which may be larger or smaller than the preview window.

Start Slide Show   (F11) Displays a full-screen slide show of each image in the folder, based on the sort order.

Zoom In   (+) Zooms in closer to the image to display more detail.

Zoom Out   (-) Zooms out to display more of the image in the preview window.

Select Annotation   Selects an annotation that you previously added to the image.

Rotate Clockwise   (Ctrl+K) Rotates the image 90 degrees to the right.

Rotate Counter-Clockwise   (Ctrl+L) Rotates the image 90 degrees to the left.

WARNING Rotating an image might reduce its quality.

Previous Page   (Page Up) Displays the previous page in a multipage TIFF document or fax.

Current Page Displays the current page number, and allows you to choose a specific page in a multipage TIFF document or fax.

Next Page (Page Down) Displays the next page in a multipage TIFF document or fax.

New Annotation Tools Allow you to draw or type on your image.

Freehand Draws a red freehand shape.

Highlight Highlights a yellow rectangular area.

Straight Line Draws a straight red line.

Frame Draws a red rectangular outline around an area.

Solid Rectangle Draws a solid (opaque) yellow box.

Text Adds text with a transparent background. First, draw a rectangle, then click the rectangle to add text.

Attached Note Adds text with a yellow background. First, draw a rectangle, then click the rectangle to add text.

NOTE The annotation buttons appear when you open a TIFF image. After you add annotations to your image, you can move, resize, or delete them at any time.

Delete (Delete) Deletes the image from the current folder.

Print (Ctrl+P) Allows you to print your image.

NOTE When you install third-party Windows image-editing software on your computer, images might open in your third-party application instead of the Image Preview window, due to file associations installed during your program setup.

See also Paint

Indexing Service

Indexing Service MMC snap-in that allows you to index documents (that is, extract information from them and organize it in a catalog) for faster access. This works only with NTFS-formatted drives.

Indexing Service can index various types of documents, such as HTML, text, Microsoft Office 95 and higher, Internet mail and news, and other documents for which a filter is available. The indexed information is stored in catalogs. Indexing documents speeds up searches, such as those with Search or a Web browser. You can also use the Indexing Services Query Form to perform queries on any catalog in the Indexing Service.

To access Indexing Service, choose Start ➢ Control Panel (or Start ➢ Settings ➢ Control Panel from the Classic Start menu) ➢ Performance and Maintenance. Next, click Administrative Tools, then double-click Computer Management. Expand the Services and Applications group in the console tree to display Indexing Service.

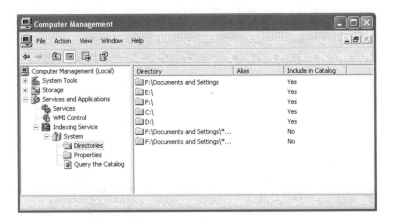

Action Menu

The Action menu in Indexing Service contains many familiar options, and some options that are unique to Indexing Service. The options that appear depend on which items you select from the console tree or Details pane and on whether Indexing Service is running:

Start, Stop, Pause   Begins, ends, or pauses the indexing service.

Merge   Merges indexes in the selected catalog; available when the Indexing Service is stopped.

New   Allows you to add a new catalog when you select Indexing Service, or a new directory when you select a catalog.

Rescan (Full)   Manually starts a complete rescan of the selected directory.

Rescan (Incremental)   Manually starts a scan of all documents in the selected directory that were modified while Indexing Service was inactive, or since the last scan.

Export List   Allows you to export a list of items that appear in the Details pane.

All Tasks ➤ Tune Performance   Enhances the Indexing Service indexing performance.

All Tasks ➤ Refresh List   Updates the Properties list.

All Tasks ➤ Empty Catalog   Removes indexing information from the selected catalog; available when the Indexing Service is stopped.

All Tasks ➤ Delete   Deletes the selected item.

Starting and Stopping the Indexing Service

To start Indexing Service, select it from the console tree and click the Start button in the toolbar (or choose Action ➤ Start). If automatic indexing is not available, the Enable Indexing dialog asks if you want Indexing Service to start automatically when you start your computer. Choose Yes or No to continue.

When Indexing Service is running, the Details pane displays information about the items that are indexed. Indexing continues until you stop the service. To stop indexing, select Indexing Service from the console tree, and click the Stop button in the toolbar (or choose Action ➤ Stop).

Catalog	Location	Size (Mb)	Total Docs	Docs to Index	Deferred for Indexing	Word Lists	Saved In
System	F:\Syste...	1	898	123	48	15	2
Web	f:\inetpub	1	294	229	0	8	0

TIP   You can also choose Pause to pause indexing. To resume, select Start again. When you restart Indexing Service, an incremental scan is performed automatically.

You can also start and stop indexing of a particular catalog by right-clicking the catalog and choosing All Tasks ➤ Start or All Tasks ➤ Stop, respectively.

Catalogs

Select Indexing Service from the console tree to see the catalogs that are available. When you install Indexing Service, Windows XP creates a default catalog called System. This catalog displays an index of the information contained on all disks attached to the computer.

WINDOWS XP PROFESSIONAL   The following IIS Web catalog is a feature of Windows XP Professional only.

When you install Internet Information Services (IIS) on a computer running Windows XP Professional, Indexing Services creates a Web catalog that contains an index for IIS.

Configuring a Catalog

Right-click a catalog and choose Properties from the shortcut menu to view and configure its properties. By default, some of the available settings are inherited from the Indexing Service Properties and you must uncheck an option to make local changes.

General tab   View the catalog name, location, and size of the index and property cache in megabytes.

Tracking tab   Specify whether you want to automatically add network share aliases. On a Windows XP Professional computer with IIS installed, you can also specify whether you want to associate a virtual World Wide Web server with the catalog.

Generation tab   Specify whether you want to index files that have unknown extensions, and whether you want to generate abstracts of files found in a search. If you choose to generate abstracts, you can specify the maximum number of characters to use for the abstract. Abstracts are returned with the results of a query.

Specifying Directories to Index

Expand a catalog in the console tree to see the Directories folder. When you select this folder, the Details pane displays information about each directory, such as the directory name, the alias name (if applicable), and whether the directory will be included in the catalog.

To include or exclude specific directories in the index, use the Add Directory dialog. Follow these steps:

1. Select either a catalog or the Directories folder from the console tree. Choose Action ➤ New ➤ Directory. The Add Directory dialog appears.

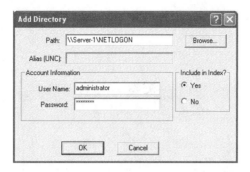

2. Enter the path to the directory and the network share alias (if applicable). If the directory is on a remote computer, enter a username and password for a user who can access the computer.

3. Specify whether you want to include the directory in the index by selecting either Yes or No. Click OK to add the directory to the list.

WARNING If you exclude a directory, all subdirectories are automatically excluded, even if you add such a subdirectory as a separate directory entry and specify to include it in the index.

To change a directory's path or network share alias, and to choose whether the directory should be included in the index, double-click it in the Details pane. Modify information as necessary.

Indexing Drives, Folders, and Files

The Indexing Service allows you to index the contents of an NTFS-formatted drive, as well as individual folders and files. When you index drives, you can access files more quickly when you perform searches.

Before you can index any drive, folder, or file, Indexing Service must be running on the computer (see the previous subsection "Starting and Stopping the Indexing Service"). Once it's started, you can include disks, folders, and files for indexing.

To index a disk, perform the following steps:

1. Open Windows Explorer.

2. Right-click any drive that is NTFS-formatted, and choose Properties to open the Properties dialog. Choose the General tab.

3. Check the "Allow Indexing Service to index this disk for fast file searching" option.

4. Click OK to apply the settings

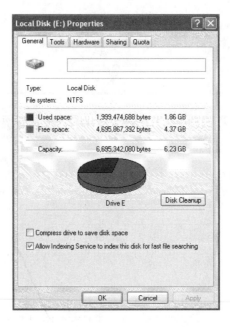

To index a file or folder, follow these steps:

1. Open Windows Explorer.

2. Right-click any file or folder on a drive that is NTFS-formatted. The Properties dialog appears. Choose the General tab.

3. Click Advanced to open the Advanced Attributes dialog.

TIP   If the Advanced button is not available, the drive is not formatted with NTFS.

4. Check the "For fast searching, allow Indexing Service to index this folder (file)" option.

5. Click OK to exit the Advanced Attributes dialog.

6. Click OK again to close the Properties dialog.

Specifying Properties to Cache

The Properties folder contains the properties and values that can be stored in the property cache; cached properties will appear in the results page of a query and will display a value in the Cached Size column. Some properties are added to the cache by default, such as document title, size, and path. To add a property to the property cache, select it in the Details pane, right-click, choose Properties, and select the Cached check box.

WARNING Adding properties to the property cache can negatively affect Indexing Service performance.

Searching (Querying) a Catalog

You can search Indexing Service catalogs using the Query form. Select Query the Catalog in the console tree, and the form is displayed in the Details pane. You might want to hide the console tree to be able to see the form better.

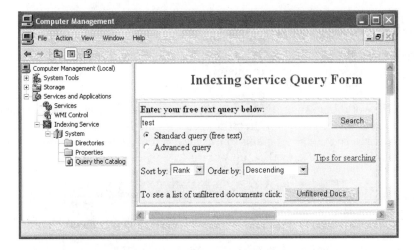

To perform a query, choose whether you want to perform a standard or advanced query, enter your query text in the text box, and then make your choices from the Sort By and Order By drop-down lists. Click Search to start the search. For detailed information on standard and advanced queries and syntax, see the "Queries, overview" entry in the Windows XP help system.

The results of your query will appear at the bottom of the query form. Scroll down and click the link to any document you would like to open. If your results contain several pages, click Next or Previous to navigate the results pages.

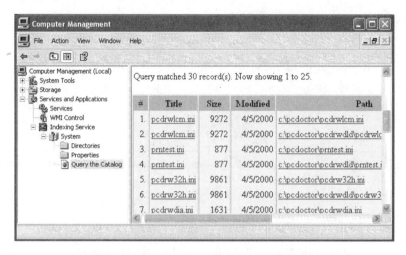

See also Computer Management, Microsoft Management Console

Internet Connection Firewall

New feature of Windows XP that provides Internet firewall protection while you are connected to the Internet through your online service provider or home network connection.

The Network Setup Wizard automatically configures and enables Internet Connection Firewall for you if you choose to use it. To run the wizard, choose Start ➤ All Programs (or Start ➤ Programs in the Classic Start menu) ➤ Accessories ➤ Communications ➤ Network Setup Wizard.

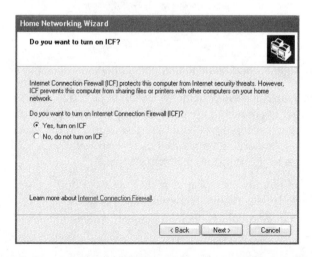

You can also enable or disable Internet Connection Firewall through Network Connections. To enable or disable the firewall for a dial-up, LAN, or network connection, choose Start ➤ Control Panel (or Start ➤ Settings ➤ Control Panel in the Classic Start menu) ➤ Network and Internet Connections ➤ Network Connections. Right-click the icon for the connection that you want to protect. Choose Properties to open the Properties dialog, and click the Advanced tab. Check or uncheck the option "Protect my computer and network by limiting or preventing access to this computer from the Internet."

Optionally, click the Settings button in the Advanced tab of the Properties dialog to configure additional settings for your home network. Use the Services tab to select or deselect Internet services that other computers on your network can access.

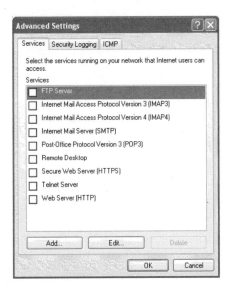

The Security Logging and ICMP tabs appear in the Advanced Settings dialog when you enable Internet Connection Firewall. Use the Security Logging tab to specify whether you want to log dropped packets and successful connections, and to configure a log file name, path, and size. Use the ICMP tab to share error and status information with other computers on the network.

NOTE If you are using Internet Connection Sharing to provide Internet access to multiple computers on your home network, you should enable the Internet Firewall Connection on the shared Internet connection. You can enable Internet Connection Firewall on any Windows XP computer that has an Internet connection.

WARNING If you are using virtual private networking, you should disable Internet Connection Firewall.

See also Internet Connection Sharing, Network Setup Wizard

Internet Connection Sharing

Allows you to share a single Internet connection with several computers that are connected on a home network. To share a connection, you must enable Internet Connection Sharing (ICS) on your host computer, which requires two connections. The first connection, typically a network adapter, connects to the other computers on your network (each of which have their own network adapters). The second connection in your host computer is a modem (56K, ISDN, DSL, or cable) that connects the host computer to the Internet. The other computers on the home network use the connection on the host computer for the Internet and e-mail.

The Network Setup Wizard detects your networking hardware and automatically provides all of the network settings you need to share your Internet connection with other computers. You must run the wizard on each one, beginning with the host—the computer that provides the physical connection to your Internet service provider, through your modem. To run the wizard, log on to Windows XP as a computer administrator. Choose Start ➢ All Programs (or Start ➢ Programs in the Classic Start menu) ➢ Accessories ➢ Communications ➢ Network Setup Wizard.

First, run the Network Setup Wizard on your host computer. When the wizard asks how the computer connects to the Internet, choose "This computer connects directly to the Internet. The other computers in my home network connect to the Internet through this computer." By choosing this option, the Network Setup Wizard automatically enables Internet Connection Sharing on that computer.

To configure ICS on your client computers, run the Network Setup Wizard on each of them. When the wizard asks how the computer connects to the Internet, choose "This computer connects to the Internet through another computer in my home network."

After you install and enable ICS, verify that all of your computers can communicate with each other on the network, and verify that they each have Internet access. Then, you can browse the Internet and send and retrieve e-mail as though you were directly connected to an Internet service provider.

See also Network Setup Wizard

Internet Explorer

 Internet Explorer Program that allows you to view and download information and Web pages on the Internet or a corporate intranet. To access information on the Internet, you must have an Internet connection established—for example, via a modem connection and an Internet account at an ISP, or via your corporate LAN.

TIP See the main topic "New Connection Wizard" for more information on how to connect to the Internet.

To access Internet Explorer (IE), use one of the following methods:

- Choose Start ➤ Internet from the Windows XP Start menu.

- Choose Start ➤ All Programs (or Start ➤ Programs in the Classic Start menu) ➤ Internet Explorer.

- Open any Web file from within Windows Explorer.

- Choose Start ➤ Run, and enter a Web URL in the Run dialog.

- Enter a Web URL in the Address bar in any Windows Explorer window and click Go.

- Open an Internet network place from within My Network Places.

- Select Internet Explorer in the Folders view (the Explorer bar of any Windows Explorer window).

- Click a link to an Internet address that appears in an Outlook Express e-mail message.

- Choose View ➤ Go To ➤ Home Page in any Explorer window.

The Internet Explorer window is very similar to a standard Windows Explorer window. It contains menus, toolbars, a main viewing area, and a status bar. Many of these items are the same as those that appear in the Windows Explorer window; however, some of the default toolbar buttons and several menu items are different.

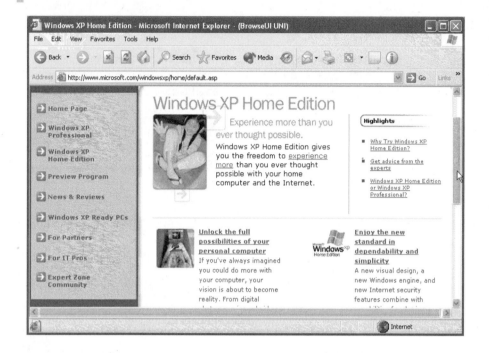

Viewing Documents

To view Internet or intranet documents in Internet Explorer, enter the address for the page (such as http://www.sybex.com/) in the Address bar. Press Enter, or click the Go button at the right of the Address bar. IE displays the page in the viewing area.

Internet Explorer Toolbars

Internet Explorer provides three toolbars: the Standard Buttons toolbar, the Address Bar toolbar, and the Links toolbar. You can lock these toolbars to prevent changes, or customize them to suit your needs.

TIP   Use View ➤ Toolbars ➤ Customize to customize the Standard Buttons toolbar.

Standard Buttons Toolbar

The IE Standard Buttons toolbar, by default, contains the following buttons:

   Back   Returns you to the page that you were viewing immediately preceding the current page.

Forward   Moves you ahead to the page you were viewing before you clicked the Back button.

Stop   Stops IE from loading a page or file from the Internet or intranet. This button is useful when the page or file contains a large amount of content or when noisy connections or server problems cause an excessively long download time.

Refresh   Updates the page that currently appears in your browser window.

Home   Displays your IE home page.

Search   Displays the Search Companion in the left pane of the IE window.

Favorites   Displays your favorites in the left pane of the IE window.

Media   Displays media links and a media player in the left pane of the IE window.

History   Displays a list of links that you viewed three weeks ago, two weeks ago, last week, and today.

Mail   Click the arrow at the right of the mail icon to choose from options that allow you to read mail, create a new message, send the current page's address as a link in an e-mail message, send the contents of the current page in an e-mail message, and open your Internet newsreader application.

Print   Prints the current document to your default printer.

Address Bar Toolbar

The Address Bar toolbar consists of an Address field and a Go button. The Address field displays the current Internet address (URL). You can enter a new URL in the field and click the Go button to go to it, or click the down arrow at the end of the Address Bar to select a previous URL from the list.

Links Toolbar

The Links toolbar holds buttons that automatically connect you to various Web pages. Use Favorites ➤ Customize to add, delete, or edit these buttons.

Internet Explorer Menus

The Internet Explorer menus contain some familiar Windows options, as well as many unique options.

File Menu

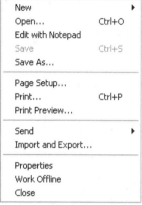

Choose File ➤ New to select from a submenu of items that allow you to perform basic tasks, such as opening a new IE window; creating a new message, post, or contact; or making a new Internet call using NetMeeting. Choose Open to open a Web document or folder. Choose Edit to edit the contents of the current page in Notepad or your default Web page editor. Choose Save or Save As to save entire Web pages to your local drive so that you can view them offline. Use the Page Setup command to configure your printing settings. Use options in the Send submenu to send the entire contents or a link to the current Web page by e-mail, or to place a shortcut to the Web page on your Desktop. Additionally, the File menu allows you to import and export favorites and bookmarks, view properties for the current Web document, work offline, and exit Internet Explorer.

Edit Menu

The Edit menu allows you to perform simple editing functions, such as cut, copy, and paste. You can also choose the Select All option, which selects the entire document, and use the Find (on This Page) option to find specific text on the current page.

View Menu

Use the View menu to choose the toolbars and Explorer Bar view you want to display, and whether you want to display the status bar. Use the Go To command to return to the previous page, move forward to the next page, go directly to your home page, or go to other pages you've accessed. Use the Stop command to stop loading the current page, and use the Refresh command to update the current page. The Text Size submenu allows you to choose the size in which you want text to display. The Encoding submenu allows you to choose from several character sets for displaying the current page. Choose the Source command to view the HTML source code of the current page. Choose Full Screen to view the current page full screen (and press F11 to return to normal view).

 TIP You can change the size used for the text that displays on Web pages. For example, you might want to use a bigger size to make text easier to read. To do so, choose View ➤ Text Size, then select a size from the submenu.

Favorites Menu

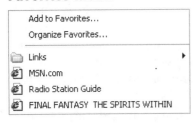

Use the Favorites menu to organize and add Web pages to your Favorites list. A list of your favorites appears at the bottom of the menu, allowing you to quickly access your favorite Web pages. Alternatively, you can click Favorites on the toolbar to access your favorites.

 TIP By default, the Favorites menu displays all of your favorites. To switch to Personalized menus, which displays only the Favorites that you most recently accessed, choose Tools ➤ Internet Options, select the Advanced tab, and check Enable Personalized Favorites Menu. Click OK to save the change.

Adding Favorites When you add pages to your Favorites list, you can navigate to the page without entering an address in the Address bar. You can also download the page so that you can view it offline, and set synchronization options that help keep your downloaded page current with the online version.

To add a page to your Favorites list, perform these steps:

1. After you navigate to a Web page that you want to add to your Favorites list, choose Favorites ➤ Add to Favorites. Alternatively, click the Favorites button on the toolbar to display the Favorites pane in the left portion of the IE window, and click Add. The Add Favorite dialog appears.

2. To download the page so that you can view it offline, check Make Available Offline. Click the Customize button to open the Offline Favorite Wizard,

which allows you to optionally download additional pages that link from the current page and to specify synchronization options.

3. Click OK to add the page directly to your Favorites folder, or click the Create In button to select another folder in your Favorites list. To create a new folder for your page, click the New Folder button and enter a new folder name. Click OK to automatically place your favorite into the selected folder.

TIP You can also access your favorites from within any Windows Explorer window.

Organizing Favorites After you add pages to your Favorites list, you can organize them. The Organize Favorites dialog allows you to delete pages that you no longer want to access, move pages to different folders, change whether they're available offline, create new folders, and rename items.

The dialog displays additional information about each Favorites page, including its URL, the number of times you have visited the page, and the date that you last visited the page. You can also check or uncheck an option to make the page available offline.

To organize your favorites, choose Favorites ➢ Organize Favorites. Alternatively, click the Favorites button on the toolbar to display the Favorites pane in the left portion of the IE window, and click Organize. The Organize Favorites dialog appears.

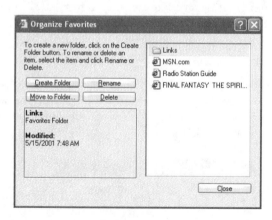

The Organize Favorites dialog displays the following buttons:

Create Folder Creates a new folder in your favorites list. If you do not select a folder from the list in the right portion of the dialog, the new folder

Checkout:

Name: ADAMS, HUGH J.
Windows XP : home and professional edit
36916000943600 Due: 10/01/07

Geeks on call Windows XP : 5-minute fix
33041013758888 Due: 09/29/07

Windows XP /
33041013166009 Due: 09/29/07

****

appears at the top level. To create a subfolder beneath any existing folder, select a folder from the list first, then click Create Folder.

Rename Allows you to assign a different name to a folder or page.

Move to Folder Allows you to move a folder or page to another folder.

TIP You can also click and drag an item or folder to a new location. Click and hold the page or folder that you want to move. As you drag the selection, a black bar indicates the new destination for the selection, or a blue box highlights the folder into which you can drop the selection. Release the mouse to drop the file or folder to its new location.

Delete Removes the selected page or folder from your Favorites list.

Tools Menu

The Tools menu allows you to read your mail, create a new message, send the contents of or a link to the current page via e-mail, and access your newsreader. It also allows you to synchronize offline Web pages, access the Microsoft Windows Update page, view links related to the current page, and configure Internet options. For more information about configuring Internet options, see the main topic "Internet Properties."

Help Menu

Use the Help menu to access Internet Explorer–related information help topics. You can also access daily tips, obtain help when you switch from Netscape, access the Microsoft Product Support page, and send feedback to Microsoft about IE.

Editing the Current Page

Internet Explorer allows you to open the source code of the current page in Notepad, where you can edit it. Afterward, you can save the edited code to your Desktop or to another location on your hard disk. To do so, follow these steps:

1. With the document you want to edit open in your active IE window, choose File ➤ Edit with Notepad. The source code opens in a Notepad window.

2. Make changes as necessary.

3. Choose File ➤ Save to save the document to your Desktop, or File ➤ Save As to save the page to another folder on your hard disk or under another name.

NOTE If you have another Web page editor (such as FrontPage) specified as your default editor, the File ➤ Edit command displays that editor instead.

Retrieving Images from Web Pages

When you hover your mouse over an image in a Web page, an Image toolbar appears, containing the following buttons:

Save Picture As   Saves the image to a folder on your local or network hard disk (by default, to the My Pictures folder).

E-mail Picture   Allows you to send the image by e-mail. You can optimize the image (compress it so that it downloads more quickly), select one or more recipients, and enter additional text for your message.

Print Picture   Allows you to configure printing options and print the image.

Go to My Pictures   Allows you to view the contents of your My Pictures folder before you choose the Save Picture As command.

Set as Background   Allows you to use the image for a full-screen desktop background.

Set as Desktop Item   Adds the image to your desktop as an Active Desktop item.

See also   Explorer, Internet Properties, Network and Internet Connections, New Connection Wizard

Internet Properties

Allows you to configure Internet settings and display options for your Windows XP computer. Among other things, Internet Properties allows you to:

- Configure your home page
- Manage temporary files
- Configure Web content colors, fonts, and languages
- Set up security
- Specify which applications to use for e-mail and Internet newsgroups

Choose Start ➤ Control Panel (or Start ➤ Settings ➤ Control Panel from the Classic Start menu) ➤ Network and Internet Connections. Next, click Internet Options to open the Internet Properties dialog. This dialog has seven tabs: General, Security, Privacy, Content, Connections, Programs, and Advanced.

TIP You can also access the Internet Options dialog (which displays the same options as the Internet Properties dialog) by choosing Tools ➤ Internet Options in Internet Explorer.

General Tab

The General tab allows you to configure your Internet home page and specify how you want to handle temporary Internet files and files in the History folder.

The Home Page section allows you to choose the page that IE displays when you first open it or when you click the Home button in the IE toolbar. Navigate to a Web page and click the Use Current button to change your home page to a specific URL. Click the Use Default button to use the address www.msn.com. Click the Use Blank button to display a blank page as your home page. You can also manually enter a URL in the Address text box.

Some Web sites use *cookies* to save information about the preferences you use when you visit the site; Internet Explorer stores these on your hard disk. IE also stores the content of visited Web pages in a *cache* on your hard drive. The next time you visit a page, IE uses the cached content and only downloads any new content that appears on the page, accessing the entire page more quickly. The options in the Temporary Internet Files section allow you to manage how all these temporary files are stored.

The Delete Cookies button allows you to delete Web page cookies that are stored on your hard drive. (For more on cookies, see the following section "Security Settings Dialog.") To delete the files in your cache, click the Delete Files button. Check or uncheck the option in the Delete Files dialog to also delete your offline content, then click OK.

The Settings button allows you to configure how IE handles new versions of files, and to specify the size of your Internet cache. Click the Settings button to open the Settings dialog, where you can check how often you would like IE to check the Web page against the version that is stored in your cache (Every Visit to the Page, Every Time You Start Internet Explorer, Automatically, or Never). Move the Amount of Disk Space to Use slider to adjust the maximum amount of disk space that your Internet cache consumes. Click Move Folder to specify a new location for your Internet cache. Click View Files to view a list of pages and images that reside in your cache, or View Objects to view ActiveX or Java controls that reside in your cache.

The History section stores links to the pages that you have viewed within a specified period of time (20 days by default). To adjust the number of days, enter a new value in the Days to Keep Pages in History field, or use the up and down arrows next to this field to increase or decrease the value. To remove all links from the History folder, click Clear History.

Colors button   Allows you to configure the colors for Web page text, backgrounds, and links. The default selection is Use Windows Colors.

TIP   To change the Windows colors, right-click the Desktop and choose Properties, then select the Appearance tab and make your changes.

Fonts button   Allows you to configure the language script and fonts for Web content that does not specify that a certain font be used.

Languages button   Allows you to configure the languages that IE uses for multilingual Web pages. In order to view multilingual content, you must use Regional and Language Options to add the appropriate language character set to your computer.

Accessibility button Allows you to configure accessibility options for Web pages you view. You can ignore the colors, font styles, and font sizes that appear on the pages and display them as configured in your options. You can also create and specify a style sheet that defines the default settings for font color, style, and size, as well as heading and text background.

NOTE The style sheets that you specify in the Accessibility dialog must be written using Cascading Style Sheet rules and saved with a CSS extension.

Security Tab

Use the options in the Security tab to assign Web sites and pages to one of four Internet content zones: Internet, Local Intranet, Trusted Sites, and Restricted Sites. To add or remove sites in a particular zone other than Internet, click a zone's icon, then click the Sites button to open the zone's dialog.

Internet IE places all Web sites into this zone unless you specify another zone for the site. The default security level is Medium.

Local Intranet Use this zone for pages and files on your company intranet. The default security level is Medium-Low.

Trusted Sites Use this zone for Web sites and pages that you know to be safe and that will not upload harmful content to your computer. The default security level for trusted sites is Low.

Restricted Sites Use this zone for Web sites and pages that you access but do not completely trust because you suspect that the sites may send potentially harmful content to your computer. The default security level is High.

Security Settings Dialog

Use the Security Settings dialog to customize the security level for any Internet content zone. To open the Security Settings dialog, open the Security tab in the Internet Properties dialog. Select the zone that you want to customize (Internet, Local Intranet, Trusted Sites, or Restricted Sites). Then click the Custom Level button to display the Security Settings dialog.

TIP Click the Default Level button in the Security tab to return the selected security zone to its default security settings.

 TIP Some sites use cookies to save information in relation to the preferences you use when you visit the site. For example, an online bookstore might keep track of the books that you order so that it can provide additional recommendations for you; or you might frequent message boards on an online community, and a cookie keeps track of the date that you last visited so that you only see new messages when you return. Cookies are used in many ways, and IE stores these cookies on your hard disk unless you disable or delete them.

IE provides several security level settings, each of which offers a different set of options for handling dynamic content such as Java applets, ActiveX controls, and cookies. You can select from the following security levels:

High   The most secure setting. Some features may be disabled; cookies are disabled. This setting reduces functionality of Web pages that depend on these features to work properly.

Medium   Displays a warning before you download ActiveX controls or Java applets, and does not download ActiveX controls that are not signed.

Medium-Low   Does not display a warning before you download ActiveX controls or Java applets. Does not download ActiveX controls that are not signed.

Low   Provides the least amount of security. Downloads most dynamic content without prompting. May display a few warning prompts. Do not use this setting unless you trust the Web site.

Choose one of the above security settings for the zone that you want to configure. If you want to customize the settings, select a radio button to select new security levels for ActiveX controls and plug-ins, cookies, downloads, Java, miscellaneous files, scripting, and user authentication. Click the Reset button to return to the default security level settings.

Privacy Tab

The Privacy tab allows you to set the privacy level for the selected Internet content zone. Move the Privacy slider up to increase your privacy or down to decrease it. As you move the slider, a description of the privacy level appears at the right of the slider. To override cookie handling for individual Web sites, click the Edit button. The Per Site Privacy Actions dialog allows you to allow or block cookies from specific Web page addresses. After you specify the addresses click OK to return to the Internet Properties dialog.

Content Tab

The Content tab allows you to restrict access to certain sites, manage certificates, and manage and configure personal information. Three different areas are available on the Content tab: Content Advisor, Certificates, and Personal Information.

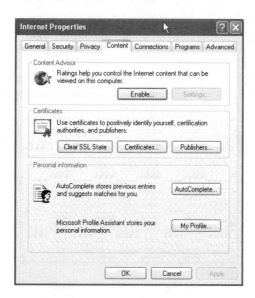

Content Advisor Section

The Content Advisor allows you to control the content that you view on your computer. To turn the Content Advisor on, click Enable to open the Content Advisor dialog. You use four tabs to configure the settings for the content advisor: Ratings, Approved Sites, General, and Advanced.

TIP The Content Advisor is very useful for restricting Internet access for children.

Ratings tab Allows you to select a rating level defined by the Internet Content Rating Association (ICRA, formerly known as RSACi). This rating system identifies Web sites based on the language, nudity, sex, or violence they contain. The default level for all categories is Level 0 (Inoffensive Slang) and prevents the download of anything with a higher rating, providing that the owner of the Web site has labeled the site with an ICRA rating. Increase the level to allow IE to download stronger content.

 NOTE To obtain more information on this rating system, or to learn how to apply ratings to your own Web site, click the More Info button to navigate to the ICRA Web page (http://rsac.org/ratingsv01.html).

Approved Sites tab Allows you to specify Web addresses that users can always or never view, regardless of their rating.

General tab Allows you to specify whether users can see sites that are not rated by RSACi/ICRA. By default, users must enter a password, set by the computer administrator, in order to view content that is not rated. To assign or change the password, click the Create Password button. Enter the old password for verification (leave this field blank when you assign the password for the first time), then enter the new password twice (the second entry confirms the first entry). Enter a password hint, then click Apply to set the password permanently.

NOTE Once you set the password, the Content Advisor is enabled, and you need to enter the password to make any other changes in the Content Advisor. After you enable the Content Advisor, the Content tab displays a Disable button in the Content Advisor section. Click Disable and enter your password to disable this feature.

Use the Rating Systems section to add and remove additional ratings systems for your Web pages. When you click Find Rating Systems, Internet Explorer browses to the Internet, where you can select additional rating systems for your Web pages.

Advanced tab   Allows you to choose a ratings bureau that sends Internet ratings to your rating systems, and allows you to view, import, or remove PICSRules files that determine whether a specific site should be viewed by the user.

Accessing a Restricted Page   When the Content Advisor is enabled, a dialog appears when you try to access pages that are configured for restricted access, including pages that are not rated. The dialog informs you that you are not allowed to see the site. If you know the password for the Content Advisor, you can check the appropriate radio button to choose how you want to handle the site, and enter the Content Advisor password to make the change.

Certificates Section

The Content tab of the Internet Properties dialog also contains a Certificates section that allows you to manage digital certificates used by applications and certain security services. Certificates enable secure communication, authentication, and data integrity over the Internet or other insecure networks.

Click Clear SSL State to clear the Secure Sockets Layer cache.

Click Certificates to open the Certificate Manager, where you can import, export, remove, and configure your own (personal) certificates, certificates for other people, certificates for immediate certification authorities, and certificates for trusted root certification authorities.

Click Publishers to view or configure software publishers and credential issuers you've specified as trusted. You can remove publishers and issuers from the list, configure certificate purposes and export format, and display certificates by purpose.

TIP   You must have administrative privileges to manage certificates.

Personal Information Section

Click the AutoComplete button (on the Internet Properties dialog Content tab) to open the AutoComplete Settings dialog, where you can specify in what situations Windows XP should try to match items you've previously typed so that you don't have to type the same information over and over.

If you specify AutoComplete for usernames and passwords, you can also choose to be prompted to save passwords. You can also choose to remove some Auto-Complete entries by clicking Clear Forms and Clear Passwords. To remove Web address AutoComplete entries, you'll have to clear the History folder on the General tab of Internet Properties.

WARNING Saving passwords poses a potential security risk if you leave your computer unattended without logging out of Windows XP. Anyone could walk up to your computer and access password-protected sites for which you saved the password.

Click the My Profile button on the Content tab to set up a profile that you can send to Web sites that request personal information. Clicking My Profile opens the Address Book—Choose Profile dialog, where you can either choose an existing profile from your Address Book or create a new entry in the Main Identity Properties dialog, which adds your profile to your Address Book.

Connections Tab

Use this tab of the Internet Properties dialog to configure Internet dial-up and LAN connections. You can create new dial-up connections, edit and remove existing ones, and configure LAN connection settings.

Connecting to the Internet

You can start the New Connection Wizard to configure a connection by clicking Setup. This wizard is explained in detail under its own main topic.

Configuring Dial-up Connections

You can configure your existing dial-up and VPN connections by selecting a connection in the Dial-up and Virtual Private Network Settings list and clicking Settings. You can also add a new connection by clicking Add and following the prompts in the New Connection Wizard (see the main topic "New Connection Wizard"), or you can remove a connection by selecting it in the list and clicking Remove.

You can also specify what action Internet Explorer should take if you are trying to access Internet resources and a connection to the Internet is not yet established. The default selection is to never dial a connection. Alternatively, you can choose to dial your default dial-up connection, either always or only when a network connection is not available. If you choose to dial a connection, you can change your default connection setting by selecting a different connection in the Dial-up and Virtual Private Network Settings list and clicking Set Default.

Configuring LAN Connection Settings

If you are connecting to the Internet over a LAN, you can click LAN Settings and choose to automatically detect your proxy server settings, specify an address for an automatic configuration script, or specify a physical address and port for your company's proxy server. If you do this, you can also specify to bypass the proxy server if you are accessing local addresses. Click Advanced to specify addresses for individual proxy servers (such as HTTP, FTP, and Gopher).

Programs Tab

Use this tab of the Internet Properties dialog to identify which programs you want to use for various Internet services. The types of programs from which you can choose depend on the service; examples are Outlook Express for e-mail and Microsoft NetMeeting for Internet calls. You can specify an application for each of the services shown.

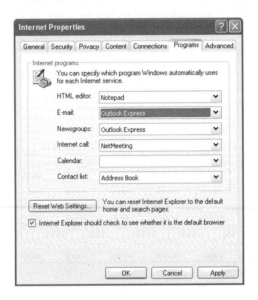

If you've installed another browser and your default settings for home and search pages have been changed, you can click Reset Web Settings to make Internet Explorer settings the default settings again.

If you have multiple browsers installed on your computer but want to retain IE as your default browser, select the "Internet Explorer should check to see whether it is the default" check box. IE then checks every time it starts up; if it determines that another browser has been set as the default, a prompt will ask whether you want to make IE the default browser again.

Advanced Tab

The Internet Properties dialog Advanced tab allows you to configure advanced Internet settings, in categories such as accessibility, browsing, HTTP 1.1,

Microsoft Virtual Machine, multimedia, printing, searching, and security. If you have made changes on the Advanced tab and want to return to the Windows XP defaults, simply click Restore Defaults.

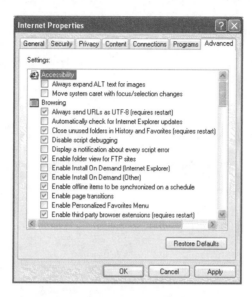

See also   Accessibility, Internet Explorer, New Connection Wizard, Regional and Language Options

IP Security Monitor

Optional MMC snap-in for Windows XP that allows a computer administrator to monitor Internet Protocol Security (IPSec) policies and authentication methods used in generic filters, specific filters, IKE policies, and security associations.

See also   Microsoft Management Console (Creating a New MMC Console)

IP Security Policy Management

Optional MMC snap-in for Windows XP that allows a computer administrator to manage Internet Protocol Security (IPSec) policies for secure communications with other computers in the current Active Directory or on another Active Directory.

See also   Microsoft Management Console (Creating a New MMC Console)

Keyboard

Lets you configure your keyboard's settings, such as character repeat settings, cursor blink rate, and hardware-related settings. Choose Start ➤ Control Panel (or Start ➤ Settings ➤ Control Panel in the Classic Start menu) ➤ Printers and Other Hardware. Next, click the Keyboard control panel icon to open the Keyboard Properties dialog. This dialog contains two tabs: Speed and Hardware.

Speed Tab

Use this tab to configure character repeat and cursor blink rate options.

Repeat Delay   Controls the amount of time from the instant you press a key to the instant the character associated with that key starts to repeat. Move the slider toward Long to increase the delay or toward Short to decrease it.

Repeat Rate   Controls the amount of time between each repetition of a character when you press and hold a corresponding key. Move the slider toward Slow to increase the rate or toward Fast to decrease it.

Test Repeat Rate   To test your Repeat Delay and Repeat Rate settings, click in the test box under the Repeat Rate slider. Then press and hold down a key.

Cursor Blink Rate   Controls the speed at which the cursor blinks. Observe the blinking cursor at the left of the slider while you adjust the settings.

Move the slider toward None to blink the cursor at a slower rate or toward Fast to blink it faster.

The adjustments that you make in the Speed tab take effect immediately in the Keyboard Properties dialog while you test your new settings. To apply the changes permanently so that they will work in all your Windows applications, click Apply or OK.

Hardware Tab

Use this tab to view, configure, and troubleshoot the hardware settings of your keyboard. The keyboard that is installed on your system appears in the Devices list. The Device Properties area displays additional information about your keyboard, including manufacturer, location, and device status. The Device Status line should indicate that the device is working properly. If your keyboard is not working properly, the Device Status line displays a description of the problem, a problem code, and a suggested solution, if available.

Two buttons appear in the Hardware tab:

Troubleshoot   Starts the Keyboard Troubleshooter in the Help and Support Center window. Follow the prompts in the troubleshooter to resolve keyboard-related problems.

Properties   Displays the Properties dialog that is unique to the keyboard that you have installed. It has two tabs:

General tab   Displays some of the same information about the device that you saw in the Hardware tab in the Keyboard Properties dialog box.

Driver tab   Displays information regarding the keyboard driver, including the driver provider, driver date, driver version, and the digital signer. Click Driver Details to open the Driver File Details dialog, which displays information about the drivers installed for the keyboard. Click Update Driver to install a new keyboard driver using the Hardware Update Wizard. If the keyboard fails after you update the driver, click Roll Back Driver to revert back to the previously installed driver. Click Uninstall to uninstall your keyboard driver completely.

 TIP   You can also access your keyboard properties through Device Manager. Choose Start ➤ Control Panel ➤ Performance and Maintenance. Next, click the System icon to open the System Properties dialog. Click the Hardware tab, then click the Device Manager button. Expand the Keyboards list, and click your keyboard device to display its properties.

See also   Device Manager, Regional and Language Options, System   **167**

Local Security Policy

WINDOWS XP PROFESSIONAL Local Security Policy is a feature of Windows XP Professional only.

Local Security Policy
Shortcut
2 KB

Lets you view and configure account, local, public key, and IP security policies for the local computer. To access Local Security Policy, choose Start ➤ Control Panel (or Start ➤ Settings ➤ Control Panel in the Classic Start menu) ➤ Performance and Maintenance ➤ Administrative Tools, then double-click Local Security Policy.

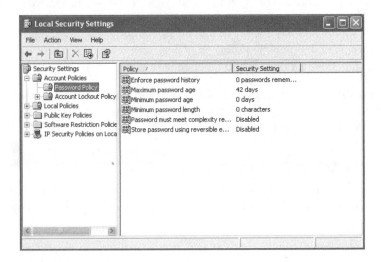

Configuring Security Policies

To configure a specific security policy, navigate the console tree on the left until individual policies appear in the Details pane on the right. The Details pane displays each policy's name, local setting, and effective setting. To configure the policy's local setting, right-click a policy and select Properties, or double-click a policy. If the computer is part of a domain and domain-level policy settings are configured, local policy settings are overridden by domain-level policy settings.

Account Policies Node

Lets you configure settings for password and account lockout policies. Examples of password policies include Maximum Password Age, Minimum Password Age, and Minimum Password Length. Account lockout policies include Reset Account Lockout Counter After and Account Lockout Duration.

Local Policies Node

Lets you configure settings for:

- Audit policies (such as "Audit account logon events")

- User rights assignments (such as "Add workstations to domain")

- Security options (such as "Allow system to be shut down without having to log on")

Public Key Policies Node

Allows you to add encrypted data recovery agents. Other policies will likely be added to this node later.

Software Restriction Policies Node

Allows you to configure security levels (disallowed or unrestricted), and to assign additional security rules. To assign a security rule, choose Action ➢ Create New Policy. Then right-click Additional Rules and choose a rule type. You can also configure settings for trusted publishers, designated file types, and enforcement.

IP Security Policies on Local Machine Node

Lets you configure Windows Internet Protocol Security (IPSec) to thwart network attacks (internal, private network, and Internet or extranet) by encrypting data that travels between computers in the network. Several policies are predefined for use on computers that are part of a domain. They include Server (Request Security), Secure Server (Require Security), and Client (Respond Only).

Each policy has certain rules that apply to any computer to which the policy is assigned. You can change these rules by double-clicking a policy and making changes, or by right-clicking the policy and selecting Properties from the short-cut menu.

To assign an IP security policy to a computer, right-click the policy and select Assign. To remove the assignment, right-click the policy and select Unassign.

You can create new IP security policies. To do so, right-click IP Security Policies on Local Machine and select Create IP Security Policy. Follow the steps in the IP Security Policy Wizard.

 TIP You can also click the Create an IP Security Policy button on the toolbar to create a new IP security policy.

You can create new IP filter lists and actions. To do so, right-click IP Security Policies on Local Machine and select Manage IP Filter Lists and Filter Actions. In the dialog that opens, select the Manage IP Filter Lists tab. Click Add to open a dialog, and click Add again to open the IP Filter Wizard. Follow the wizard's instructions to create a new IP filter list. Or select the Manage Filter Actions tab and click Add to open the Filter Action Wizard, and follow the wizard to create a new filter action. If you don't want to use the wizards, deselect the check box Use Add Wizard in the appropriate dialog.

TIP You can also click the Manage IP Filter Lists and Filter Actions button on the toolbar to perform these actions.

See also Group Policy, Microsoft Management Console, Network and Internet Connections

Local Users and Groups

WINDOWS XP PROFESSIONAL This snap-in is a feature of Windows XP Professional only.

Local Users and Groups MMC snap-in for Windows XP Professional that lets you create and configure user and group accounts on the local computer. Local user and group accounts let you assign rights and permissions as necessary to control access to resources on the local computer. Any user who has a local user account set up can log on to the computer using their username and password.

Groups allow you to assign access to resources to multiple people at the same time rather than to each individual user. All group members share the same rights and permissions. To do this, create a group and add users and groups to the group. Then, assign group rights and permissions to a resource.

To access Local Users and Groups, choose Start ➢ Control Panel (or Start ➢ Settings ➢ Control Panel in the Classic Start menu) ➢ Performance and Maintenance ➢ Administrative Tools, then double-click Computer Management. Locate the System Tools folder, which includes Local Users and Groups. Local Users and Groups contains two subfolders: Users and Groups.

Action Menu

While the Action menu for Local Users and Groups and its subcategories has many familiar options, it also has some unique options. Available options change depending on whether you select an item in the console tree or in the Details pane.

New User   Allows you to create a new user account. Available with Users selected in the console tree.

Set Password   Allows you to change the password for the user account that is selected in the Details pane.

Properties   Opens the Properties dialog for the user or group selected in the Details pane.

New Group   Allows you to create a new group. Available when you select Groups in the console tree.

Add to Group   Allows you to add users or groups to the group selected in the Details pane.

Users Node

Lets you view and configure existing user accounts and create new accounts. Details about each user account in the Details pane include name and description. An account icon for a disabled user account has a red circle with an *X* in it.

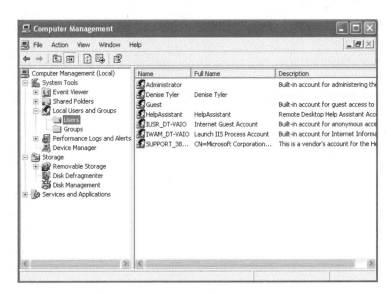

Built-in User Accounts

Built-in user accounts are created by the system during installation. Windows XP Professional has two built-in user accounts: Administrator and Guest.

NOTE When you install Internet Information Server on a Windows XP Professional computer, two additional built-in user accounts appear: IUSR_servername (for anonymous access to IIS) and IWAM_servername (for starting IIS out-of-process applications).

Administrator Provides access and all-encompassing rights and permissions to all areas of Windows XP computers. Administrator is a member of the Administrators group. You cannot delete or disable this account or remove it from the Administrators local group.

Guest Enables users to log on to a Windows XP computer without having an account set up on the computer. By default, the Guest account is disabled and does not have a password, although you can assign one later. By default, Guest is a member of the Guests group.

Creating a New User Account

To create a new user account, follow these steps:

1. Select Users in the console tree, then choose Action ➤ New User. The New User dialog appears.

2. Enter a username, full name, and description. Then enter a password and confirm the password.

3. Make any applicable choices relating to the user's password, such as User Must Change Password at Next Logon, User Cannot Change Password, Password Never Expires, and Account Is Disabled. Then click Create to create the account.

4. If you want to create another user account, repeat Steps 1 through 3. Click Close when you are finished.

Configuring a User Account

Use the Properties dialog to configure a user account. You can access this dialog from the Action menu or the shortcut menu. The Properties dialog box has three tabs: General, Member Of, and Profile.

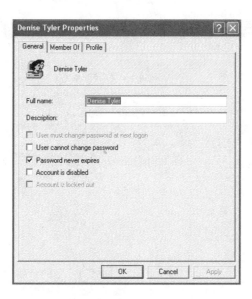

General   Allows you to specify the full name and description for the user account and to set password options. If a user has exceeded the number of unsuccessful logon attempts specified in the Password policy, Account Is Locked Out will be checked on this tab. Deselect it to unlock the account.

Member Of   Allows you to add a user to a group or groups. Click Add, select one or more groups, click Add, and then click OK to add the user to one or more groups. To remove a user from a group, select that user and click Remove.

Profile   Allows you to specify the path to the user's roaming profile (this enables roaming profiles to be used), to a logon script, and to a home folder located either on the local computer or on the network.

Groups Node

Lets you view and configure current groups, create new groups, and add users and groups to groups. Details about each group account in the Details pane include name and description.

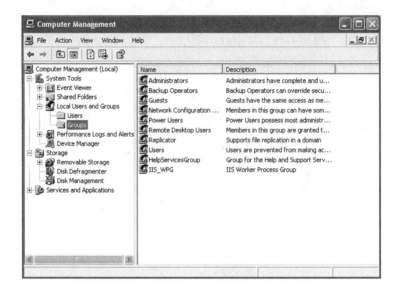

Built-in Groups

Windows XP creates built-in groups during the Windows XP installation. Several built-in groups exist. Some examples are Administrators, Backup Operators, Guests, Power Users, and Users. These groups have rights and permissions assigned by default to enable members of the groups to perform certain functions, such as performing administrative tasks, backing up files or folders, and installing programs.

Creating a New Group

To create a new group, follow these steps:

1. Select Groups in the console tree, then choose Action ➤ New Group. The New Group dialog appears.

2. Enter a name and description for the group.

3. Click Add and select one or more global groups or users from the list. Click OK. To see users and groups on other computers or in the Active Directory, make the appropriate choice from the Look In drop-down list. Click OK when you've finished adding users and groups.

4. Click Create. You can now create another group or click Close to return to Local Users and Groups.

Configuring Group Properties

To configure group properties, right-click a group in the Details pane and choose Properties from the shortcut menu. The Properties dialog displays the name of the group, a description of the group's rights, and the members of the group. To add a new member, click Add, then select a user or global group from the list, click Add, and click OK. To remove a user or group from the list, select the user or group, then click Remove.

See also   Microsoft Management Console

Log On/Log Off

Logs the current user on or off the computer. Each user in Windows XP has a user profile (either a local profile, or a roaming profile that is configured on a network) that contains such items as Desktop preferences, password, synchronization options, and accessibility options. When a user logs on, this profile is used to ensure that the environment is restored to the way the user previously configured it. Logging off enables you to stop working as the current user and then begin working as another user without having to shut down the computer.

When you start Windows XP, a logon screen displays icons for all accounts that are configured on the local computer. Click an icon to log on to a user account. Windows XP prompts you to enter a username and password if the user account is password protected. Click OK to log on.

  TIP   You may have to click Options to see all fields available in the Log On to Windows dialog box.

To log off the computer, choose Start ➤ Log Off to display the Log Off dialog. Then click Log Off again.

See also   System

Magnifier

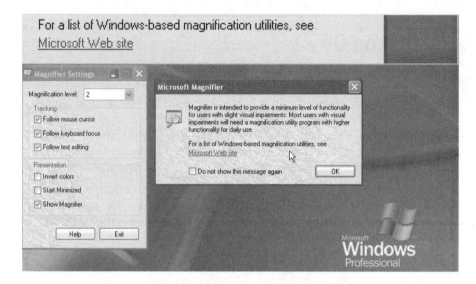

Magnifier Enlarges certain areas of the screen so that users with vision problems can read them more easily. Choose Start ➤ All Programs (or Start ➤ Programs in the Classic Start menu) ➤ Accessories ➤ Accessibility ➤ Magnifier. Read the message about the limitations of Magnifier, then select the Do Not Show This Message Again option to disable the message if desired. Click OK to access the Magnifier window (at the top of the screen by default) and the Magnifier dialog.

Move the mouse pointer to any area in the Desktop to display an enlarged view of the area in the Magnifier window. To change the size of the Magnifier window, drag its bottom edge downward. Drag the Magnifier window itself to turn it into a floating window.

The Magnifier dialog allows you to change how Magnifier is set up (changes to the Magnifier window take place immediately). The following options are available:

Magnification Level   Adjust the amount of magnification from 1 (no magnification) to 9.

Tracking   Select Follow Mouse Cursor to magnify the screen area beneath the mouse pointer. Select Follow Keyboard Focus to magnify areas while you navigate with keyboard keys, such as the Tab or arrow keys. Select Follow Text Editing to magnify text around the insertion point while you type.

Presentation   Select Invert Colors to reverse colors in the Magnifier window. Choose Start Minimized to minimize the Magnifier dialog when Magnifier starts. Choose Show Magnifier to display the Magnifier window when the Magnifier dialog is open.

To turn off Magnifier, click Exit in the Magnifier dialog or right-click Magnifier in the taskbar and select Close.

See also   Accessibility, Display

Make Available Offline

See   Offline Files

Map Network Drive

Map Network Drive...   If you're connected to a network, you can assign a drive letter to a share on the network (either on another workstation or a server). This is called *mapping* a drive. When you assign a drive letter, you can easily access specific shares from within Explorer windows or applications—for example, those shares that you need to access frequently.

To map a network drive, perform these steps:

1. Open an Explorer window (by opening Windows Explorer, My Computer, My Network Places, or My Computer).

2. Choose Tools ➤ Map Network Drive, or right-click My Computer or My Network Places and choose Map Network Drive. The Map Network Drive dialog appears.

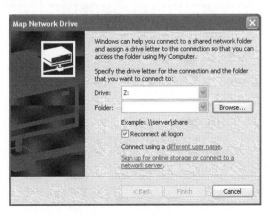

3. Use the Drive drop-down list to assign a drive letter. Enter the path to the folder in the Folder text box, or click Browse to locate the folder.

4. To permanently map the drive, select Reconnect at Logon. Leave this option unchecked to map the drive for this Windows XP session only. To connect as a different user, click "Connect using a different user name;" enter the username and password and click OK. To connect to a Web folder or FTP site, click "Sign up for online storage or connect to a network server." Follow the prompts in the Add Network Place Wizard.

5. Click Finish to map the drive. Windows XP adds the mapped drive to My Computer. You can also see it in any Explorer window or in the Open, Save, and Save As dialogs in any Windows XP application.

NOTE To disconnect a mapped drive, open Explorer. Choose Tools ➤ Disconnect Network Drive (or right-click My Computer or My Network Places and select Disconnect Network Drive). In the next dialog, select the drive you want to disconnect and click OK.

Maximize and Minimize

Allows you to change the display of a Windows XP application window. Click the Minimize button to hide the application window and place it on the taskbar. Click the taskbar icon to bring the application window back to its original size. Click the Maximize button to display the application window filling the full screen.

Microsoft Management Console (MMC)

Used to create, save, and open *MMC consoles,* which can contain administrative tools, containers, folders, Web pages, and other administrative items such as snap-ins, snap-in extensions, tasks, wizards, and documentation. You use MMC consoles to administer all aspects of your computer.

Many MMC console snap-ins are built into Windows XP. For example, you can access Component Services, Computer Management, Event Viewer, Performance, and Services through the Windows XP Control Panel. You can also use MMC to create new consoles to hold optional snap-ins that you frequently use.

To start MMC, choose Start ➤ Run, then enter **mmc** to open MMC. Here you can create new and open existing consoles. The MMC window consists of a menu bar, a toolbar, and a main area, called the workspace, in which you can display existing MMC consoles or create new ones.

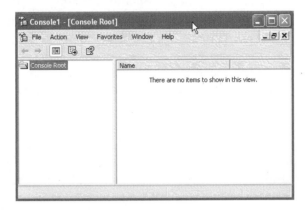

MMC Menus

MMC has six menus—File, Action, View, Favorites, Window, and Help—that you can use to work with MMC and consoles. The Action, View, Favorites, and Window menus only appear when a console window is opened.

Although all MMC consoles have some menus and toolbar buttons in common, individual menu options and additional buttons may be available depending on the item you've selected in the console tree.

File menu Allows you to create, open, and save consoles; add or remove a snap-in from the current console; change console options; select recent files; and exit MMC. Also lists the four most recently accessed consoles.

Action menu Contains equivalent menu options for actions you can perform by right-clicking in the right pane. The options here depend on the console snap-in or extension snap-in you select. Default options allow you to display the console in a new window, create a new taskpad view, rename the selected item, export the list of items from the workspace, and display help for MMC.

View menu Allows you to change the view in the workspace. You can add or remove columns in the display window, display the list of items in one of several ways, and show or hide various MMC and snap-in options (using the Customize command).

Favorites menu Functions the same as in Internet Explorer or Windows Explorer—allows you to add or organize console-tree items to your MMC favorites and then quickly access those items.

Window menu Provides commands to control MMC console windows. You can open another console in a new window, cascade or tile console windows, and arrange the icons for the windows. The bottom of the Window menu lists all the windows that are currently open, with a check mark next to the active window. Select another window from the list to bring it to the front.

Help menu Allows you to view MMC-related topics in the Help and Support Center or to display version number and licensing information for MMC.

MMC Toolbar

The buttons available on the MMC console standard toolbar depend on the item you have selected in the console tree. The following buttons are commonly available on the standard MMC console toolbar when you select an item in the console root:

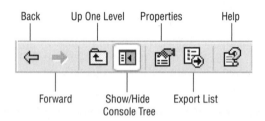

Back Goes back to the previously selected item in the console tree.

Forward Returns to the item in the console tree that was selected before you clicked the Back button.

Up One Level Moves up one level in the console tree hierarchy.

Show/Hide Console Tree Toggles the display of the tree on and off.

Properties Displays properties for the currently selected item.

Export List Exports the contents of the Details pane to a text file.

Help Opens the Windows XP Help and Support Center to the related topic.

MMC Consoles

MMC consoles host the tools that allow you to administer some aspect of your computer or network. MMC consoles have two panes: the console tree pane and the Details pane.

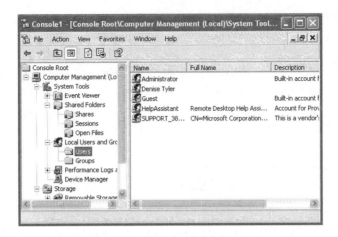

The console tree appears in the left pane and displays snap-ins, extension snap-ins, and other console items. Select an item from the tree to display its functions and information in the Details pane at the right.

The Details pane in an MMC console can also display *taskpad views*. A taskpad view contains the items that normally appear in the Details pane, along with icons for the tasks you add. Create taskpad views and add commonly used actions (tasks) to them (see the later subtopic "Creating Taskpad Views and Tasks"). This makes it easier to use the console, especially for users who are unfamiliar with MMC console functions and how to find actions.

MMC Console Modes

MMC consoles can be saved and then used in one of four modes:

- In Author Mode, users can add and remove snap-ins and extension snap-ins and create new windows, taskpad views, and tasks. Users can also see the entire console tree.

- In User Mode-Full Access, users can create new windows and see the entire console tree. They cannot add or remove snap-ins, taskpad views, and tasks or otherwise change the properties of the console.

- In User Mode-Limited Access, Multiple Window, users can see only the portion of the console tree that was saved by its author. They can open new windows but cannot close existing windows.

- In User Mode-Limited Access, Single Window, users can see only the portion of the console tree that was saved by its author. They cannot create new windows.

You must be a member of the Administrators group to open a console in Author mode that was saved in one of the User modes. Use one of the following methods:

- Choose Start ➤ Run, then enter **mmc *pathname* /a**, where *pathname* represents the complete path to the console file..

- From MMC, choose File ➤ Open. Right-click the console file in a Browse dialog and choose Author from the pop-up menu.

Creating a New MMC Console

To create a new MMC console, follow these steps:

1. Choose File ➤ New to open a new MMC console window in MMC.

2. Choose File ➤ Add/Remove Snap-in to open the Add/Remove Snap-in dialog.

3. On the Standalone tab, click Add. The Add Standalone Snap-In dialog appears. Select a snap-in from the list to include in the console and click Add. If a wizard starts, follow the prompts.

4. Repeat Step 3 for additional snap-ins. After you finish, click Close.

5. To remove a snap-in, select one from the list and click Remove.

6. To enable available snap-in extensions, select a snap-in from the list, then select the Extensions tab.

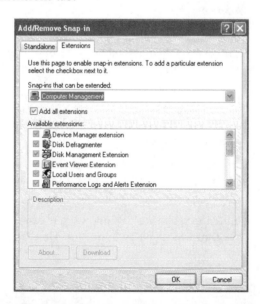

7. If extensions are available, uncheck Add All Extensions. Check or uncheck extensions to enable or disable them. Click OK to return to the console.

8. Choose File ➤ Options to open the Options dialog.

9. On the Console tab, enter a name for the console. Click the Change Icon button to change the console's icon, if desired.

10. In the Console Mode drop-down list, select the mode you want to use for this console.

11. If you selected one of the three User modes, specify whether you want to save changes that are made to the console, or allow the user to customize views. Click OK to save your changes.

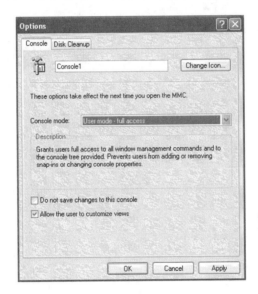

12. Choose File ➤ Save As. Enter a name for the console, browse to the folder where you want to save the console, and click Save. Windows XP saves console files with an .MSC extension into the logged-on user's Administrative Tools folder by default.

Creating Taskpad Views and Tasks

To make working with an MMC console easier for users, you can create taskpad views and add commonly used tasks to the view. To create a taskpad, perform these steps:

1. Open an MMC console in Author mode.

TIP See the previous subtopic "MMC Console Modes" for how to open a console in Author mode.

2. Select a snap-in or snap-in extension in the console tree.

3. Choose Action ➤ New Taskpad View. The New Taskpad View Wizard appears. Click Next.

4. Choose how you want the Details pane and task descriptions to appear. If you choose a list display, also specify the list size. Click Next.

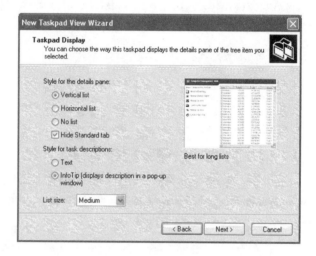

5. Specify whether you want the taskpad view to apply to the current console-tree item or to all console-tree items of this type. Click Next.

6. Enter a name and description for the taskpad view. Click Next.

7. Perform one of the following:

- To exit the New Taskpad View wizard, uncheck Start New Task Wizard. Click Finish. Windows returns you to the console where the new taskpad view appears. You do not need to complete the remaining steps.

- To add a new task to the taskpad view now, check Start New Task Wizard. Click Finish to display the New Task Wizard, then click Next.

8. Select the type of command you want to add to the taskpad view: Menu Command, Shell Command, or Navigation. Click Next.

9. The options you choose next depend on the command type chosen. Follow the screen and enter information as necessary, including a name, description, and icon for the task. Click Next to move from screen to screen.

10. If you want to add another task, select Run This Wizard Again, then click Finish. Otherwise, just click Finish. The new taskpad view and new task(s) appear in the Details pane.

See also   Explorer, Internet Explorer

Mouse

 Allows you to control the settings of your mouse, such as mouse button and pointer usage, pointer speed, and hardware configuration settings. Choose Start ➢ Control Panel (or Start ➢ Settings ➢ Control Panel in the Classic Start menu) ➢ Printers and Other Hardware, then click Mouse to open the Mouse Properties dialog. This dialog contains five tabs: Buttons, Pointers, Pointer Options, Wheel, and Hardware.

Buttons Tab

Controls how your mouse buttons function:

- Configure the mouse for left-handed or right-handed use. Select the Switch Primary and Secondary Buttons option to make the right mouse button the primary button (for left-handed use). Right-click to uncheck the option, which changes back to the left mouse button as the primary button.

185

- Set the speed at which a double-click is recognized. To test the setting, double-click the folder icon. The folder opens if you click at the correct speed. If the folder doesn't open, adjust the slider to a lower setting.

- Check the Turn On ClickLock option to enable a feature that allows you to highlight or drag without holding down the mouse button. Instead, you briefly press the mouse button to set the feature, and click the mouse button again to release the feature. Click the Settings button to adjust the click response time between short and long.

Pointers Tab

Use this tab to choose the pointer's appearance during various actions, such as when you select a help, text, or normal item; when the pointer is unavailable; and when you want to resize an item.

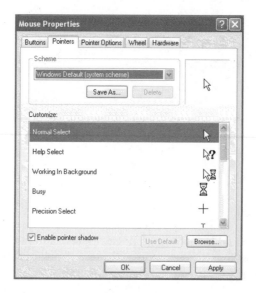

Windows XP comes with several predefined pointer schemes. Select a scheme from the drop-down list; the Customize list displays the default pointer icons for that scheme. The upper-right corner of the tab shows an example of the cursor. You can use the default options, or click OK or Apply to use the default options for the scheme.

To create a custom scheme, select an entry from the Scheme drop-down list. Click Browse to select a different pointer icon; cursor files use ANI and CUR extensions. When you return to the Pointers tab, click Save As to save your custom scheme.

To delete a scheme, select it from the drop-down list and click Delete. To return to the Windows XP default pointer settings, click the Use Default button.

Pointer Options Tab

Controls how your pointer moves.

- Set the speed of the pointer when you move it. Check or uncheck the option to enhance pointer precision.

- Check the Snap To option to automatically move the pointer over the default button in a dialog box when it opens.

- You can display pointer trails while you drag the mouse, hide the pointer while you type, and show the location of the pointer when you press the Ctrl key.

Wheel Tab

Allows you to adjust the amount of scrolling that occurs when you move forward or backward one notch on the wheel. You can specify a number of lines, or one screen at a time.

Hardware Tab

Use this tab to view and change the hardware configuration and properties of your mouse. The name and type of your mouse appears in the Devices list. Device properties appear below the list. Click Troubleshoot to start the Mouse Trouble-shooter in the Help and Support Center. Click Properties to configure the hardware properties of your mouse (including enabling or disabling it), view information about the device, and make changes to the driver.

See also   Device Manager, Help and Support Center, System

Moving Files and Folders

Windows XP allows you to move files and folders in a variety of ways. You can use the Edit menu in Windows Explorer windows, drag and drop, or use the shortcut menu that appears when you right-click a file or folder. When you move a file or folder, Windows removes it from the original location and places it in the new location.

To move files and folders in Explorer, select the items you want to move. Choose Edit ➤ Cut (or type Ctrl+X, or right-click the selection and choose Cut). Then select the destination folder and choose Edit ➤ Paste (or type Ctrl+V, or right-click the destination folder and choose Paste).

You can also drag and drop files between folders to move them:

1. Display both the source and destination folders in the Explorer Folders pane or on the Desktop.

2. Select the items you want to move from the source folder.

3. Perform one of the following:

   - Left-click and drag the selection to a destination folder on the same drive.

   - Right-click and drag the selection to a destination folder on a different drive. When you release the mouse button, choose Move from the pop-up menu.

See also   Copying Files and Folders, Explorer

MSN Explorer

MSN Explorer   Allows you to log in to your MSN user account, where you can browse and shop on the Internet, communicate with friends, manage finances, and listen to music in one integrated interface. To start MSN Explorer, choose Start ➤ All Programs (or Start ➤ Programs in the Classic Start menu) ➤ MSN Explorer.

NOTE A hotmail.com or msn.com e-mail address is required to use MSN Explorer.

The first time you start MSN Explorer, a dialog asks whether you would like to use it to get on the Internet and check e-mail. To disable this dialog, check Don't Show Me This Message Again. If you don't yet have an account set up on MSN, MSN Explorer guides you through simple setup options. After you complete the setup, you can log in to MSN Explorer.

NOTE After you configure your MSN account name and password, you must enter the password each time you open MSN Explorer.

My Computer

Allows you to view and navigate the contents of your computer, such as drives, folders, and files. To open My Computer, choose Start ➤ My Computer.

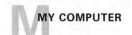

 NOTE You can also choose My Computer from the Folders pane in Explorer to display My Computer contents in the right pane of Explorer.

The right pane in My Computer displays the top-level contents of your computer. Large icons appear by default, but you can change views in this window the same way you can in any Explorer window. These contents include shared and personal documents on this computer, hard disk drives, and removable storage drives. Single-click a drive or folder to display details about the selected item in the left pane.

To view the contents of a drive or folder in My Computer, double-click the item. The right pane changes to display the contents of the item, and the left pane displays helpful information, related tasks, and links to other places. Click the Back, Forward, and Up One Level buttons in the toolbar to navigate to previous or higher-level locations.

The left pane of the My Computer window also displays links to system tasks and other places. System tasks allow you to view information in the System Properties dialog, add or remove programs, or change a setting in a selected Control Panel category. Links to other places include My Network Places, My Documents, Shared Documents, and Control Panel.

See also Control Panel, Explorer, My Documents, My Network Places, Shared Folders

My Documents

 Default folder where Windows XP stores documents created in such applications as WordPad and Paint. My Documents allows any user that is logged on to the computer to organize and quickly access his or her own personal documents.

To open the My Documents folder, choose Start ➤ My Documents, or navigate to it using the Folders pane or Address bar in any Explorer window.

TIP To change the location of the My Documents folder, right-click the My Documents shortcut on the Start menu and choose Properties. On the Target tab, enter a new path in the Target text box and click OK, or click Move and then browse to the new target folder.

By default, the My Documents folder contains folders such as My Music, My Pictures, My eBooks, My Received Files, and My Videos. Single-click any folder to display details in the left pane. Windows XP may create additional My Documents subfolders automatically as you work with applications; for example, the Fax Cover Page Editor creates a Fax subfolder. The left pane also allows you to create new folders, publish selected folders to the Web, and share folders over the network.

See also Desktop, Explorer, Fax Services, My Computer, My Music, My Network Places, My Pictures, Shared Folders

My Music

 Default folder (within the My Documents folder) that stores music files that you copy from a CD or download from the Internet.

The right pane in the My Music folder displays large icons for each music folder in your music library. If you have ripped songs from a CD, a small picture of the CD cover appears on the folder. The left pane displays a list of music tasks that change, depending on the selections you make in the main pane. When no folder is selected, click Play All to play all songs from the My Music folder in Windows Media Player.

When you select a folder from the main pane, details about it appear in the left pane. Additional options appear in the Music Tasks list, depending on the type of folder you select. Choose Play Selection to play all music in a selected folder. Choose Copy to Audio CD to burn the contents of a selected folder to CD.

My Network Places

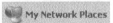 Allows you to view and navigate network resources, such as network shares and other computers. To open My Network Places, choose Start ➤ My Network Places. The My Network Places folder displays two panes. The right pane displays large icons for folders that are shared on your network. Select a folder to display details in the left pane, which also includes links to other locations on your computer and to network tasks that allow you to configure additional network options:

- Add a Network Place opens a wizard. Follow the instructions to configure online storage space, shortcuts to a Web site, an FTP site, or other network location.

- View Network Connections opens the Network Connections folder, where you can view and configure your connections.

- Set Up a Home or Small Office Network opens a wizard that sets up your computer for networking.

- View Workgroup Computers allows you to access other computers in your network workgroup.

You can also access My Network Places by selecting it from the Folders list or Address drop-down list of any Explorer window. When you display My Network Places in the Folders pane of Explorer, you can navigate all network resources using the Entire Network icon. Select Entire Network to display a hierarchical list of all computers on your network. You can access shared files on the network or print to network printers or faxes.

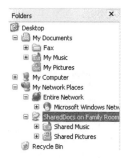

See also   Explorer, Network Connections

My Pictures

Default folder (in the My Documents folder) that allows you to store, view, and print image files that you create with image programs or obtain from a scanner or camera. To open the My Picture folder, choose Start ➤ My Pictures.

The main pane of the My Pictures folder displays large thumbnails of the files and folders that appear in My Pictures. Select a thumbnail to display file or folder properties in the left pane, which also contains a list of picture tasks. Click Get Pictures from Camera or Scanner to obtain photos from these devices. Click View as a Slide Show to display all pictures as a full-screen slide show; to end the slide show, press the Esc key. Click Order Prints Online to open the Online Print Ordering Wizard. Click Print Pictures to open the Photo Printing Wizard. Click Copy All Items to CD to add selected pictures to the files ready to be written to the CD.

See also   CD Writing Wizard, Explorer, My Documents, Online Print Ordering, Photo Printing Wizard

My Recent Documents

Start menu option that provides a list of shortcuts to the 15 most recently accessed documents so that you can quickly access them again when necessary. The list remains after you shut down and restart Windows XP. To use the My Recent Documents list, choose Start ➣ My Recent Documents, and click any item in the list to open the document in the appropriate application.

NOTE   The submenu also contains a shortcut to My Documents and My Pictures, which are default folders that Windows XP uses to save documents or images from many Windows XP applications.

Naming a Disk

You can add a label (name) to a floppy or hard disk. To name a disk, perform the following steps:

1. From Windows Explorer, right-click the disk that you want to name, and choose Properties. The Disk Properties dialog opens to the General tab.

2. Enter a name for the disk in the text box at the top of the dialog.

3. Click OK to save your changes.

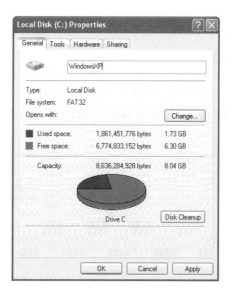

Narrator

Narrator   Aids users with vision impairments by "narrating" (reading aloud) on-screen text, menus, buttons, and dialogs. A sound card and speakers, or other audio output device, is required to use this feature.

To open Narrator, choose Start ➤ All Programs (or Start ➤ Programs in the Classic Start menu) ➤ Accessories ➤ Accessibility ➤ Narrator. Windows XP displays a message that explains the limited functionality of Narrator. Check Do Not Show This Message Again to disable this dialog, then click OK to display the Narrator dialog.

Four options appear in the Narrator dialog; place a check mark next to the ones you want to activate. The Voice button allows you to adjust the speed, volume, and pitch for the selected voice.

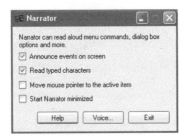

See also   Accessibility

.NET Passport Wizard

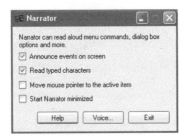 Set up my account to use a .NET Passport   Helps you set up your account to use a .NET Passport, which gives you personalized access to Passport-enabled services by using your e-mail address. You store your name and password in a single sign-in profile that encrypts your personal information. The information that you store is safe on public and shared computers.

For each of the following actions, first go to Start ➤ Control Panel (or Start ➤ Settings ➤ Control Panel in the Classic Start menu) ➤ User Accounts. Then:

- To start the .NET Passport Wizard on a domain computer, locate the .NET Passport section in the Advanced tab, then click .NET Passport Wizard.

- If you have a computer administrator account on a domain computer, click your account name, then choose Set Up My Account to Use a .NET Passport.

- If you have a limited account on a domain computer, click Set Up My Account to Use a .NET Passport.

NetMeeting

NetMeeting   Allows you to use voice and video to communicate with other people over the Internet. To run NetMeeting, your computer must have speakers or headphones, a microphone, and a video camera installed.

NetMeeting enables you to engage in real-time chats, work together in shared applications, send files, and create drawings together on a shared whiteboard. Voice, video, and images display on the screen while you participate in online conferences.

The first time you run NetMeeting, a wizard helps you configure NetMeeting and tune your audio settings. Subsequently, you will be brought directly to Microsoft NetMeeting.

NOTE To install NetMeeting in Windows XP, open the Help and Support Center topic "What's new in other areas of Windows XP Home" (or Professional). Expand the NetMeeting subtopic to select "Using NetMeeting." Finally, click the "Open NetMeeting" link to start the Microsoft NetMeeting Wizard.

When you complete the wizard, check the option to display a shortcut to NetMeeting on your desktop. Click this connection to start NetMeeting at any time.

The Microsoft NetMeeting Wizard helps you configure NetMeeting the first time you use it. At each screen, enter the requested information or choose settings, then click Next to move on. You'll be prompted to enter:

- Personal information about yourself that you want to use with NetMeeting

- The directory server you want to use, and whether to log on automatically

TIP The directory servers you log on to are called Internet Locator Servers, or ILS servers. Use your browser and favorite search engine to find available ILS servers.

- The speed/type of connection you use to connect to the Internet

- Sound settings (the wizard tests both the volume to use with your headphones or speakers and the recording level to use with your microphone)

When you have completed the wizard, click Finish to start Microsoft NetMeeting. If you are connected to the Internet, NetMeeting automatically tries to log on to the directory server you specified.

WARNING If you are not connected to the Internet, NetMeeting displays a warning that the directory server can't be found. Connect to the Internet, then choose Call ➤ Log On to *Directory Server Name* to log on to the directory server.

TIP To run the Audio Tuning Wizard again, choose Tools ➤ Audio Tuning Wizard in NetMeeting. Many of these settings can also be adjusted later in the Tools ➤ Options dialog.

NetMeeting Window

After you configure NetMeeting, click the NetMeeting shortcut on your desktop to use NetMeeting at any time. NetMeeting logs you on to the default directory server or the directory server you specify under Tools ➤ Options. After you log on, other NetMeeting users around the world can see the personal information you specified and place a call to you.

 TIP You must connect to the Internet before you log on to a directory server.

The Microsoft NetMeeting window includes menus, buttons, the video area (which displays video images of other users or of yourself), the data area (which displays the names of participants in a call or meeting), and the status bar.

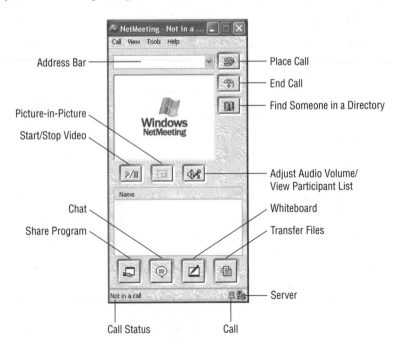

Most of the NetMeeting buttons perform functions equivalent to the commands on the NetMeeting menus. Find Someone allows you to search the current directory, other directories, the Speed Dial list, the history list, or Windows Address Book for a user's address. (See "Finding a User" later in this topic.) The Adjust Audio Volume/View Participant List button displays either the names of participants in the current call or meeting, or sliders that adjust the microphone and speaker volume.

The left side of the status bar tells you whether you are currently in a call. The right side of the status bar displays two icons: the first indicates whether you are in a call, and the second indicates the server to which you are connected. Hover the mouse over the server icon to see the name of the server that you are logged on to.

NetMeeting Menus

Four NetMeeting menus allow you to work with and configure NetMeeting: Call, View, Tools, and Help.

Call Menu

New Call   Opens the Place a Call dialog. Enter information about the user you want to call or select a previous contact from the To drop-down list. From the Using drop-down list, choose how you want to locate the user (Automatic, Network, or Directory). Optionally, check the Require Security for This Call (Data Only) option to establish a secure connection with your contact. Click the Call button to place the call.

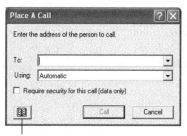

Find Someone in a Directory

 TIP   Alternatively, you can enter the user's address in the Address bar in the NetMeeting window and then click the New Call button.

After you place the call, the user receives a notification message that you are calling. The user can either accept or ignore the incoming call. To establish the call, the user must click Accept. After a call is established, the names of the participants appear in the data area of the NetMeeting window.

Host Meeting When you host a meeting, others can join. Before the meeting, contact the participants to inform them when the meeting will take place. At the specified time, choose Call ➤ Host Meeting to open a dialog where you establish a meeting password, enable or disable a secure meeting, and specify the users who can participate.

To remove a user from a meeting you are hosting, right-click the user's name in the data list of the main NetMeeting window, and choose Remove from Meeting.

Meeting Properties Displays the name of the meeting, whether you can place incoming and outgoing calls, and whether you can start Sharing, Whiteboard, Chat, and File Transfer.

Log On to *Directory Server Name* Logs on to the specified server. After you log on, this option changes to Log Off from *Directory Server Name*.

NOTE To change the directory server, choose Tools ➤ Options to open the Options dialog. In the General tab, enter the name of the directory server that you want to use.

Directory Opens the Find Someone dialog. Select a directory in which to search for a user. Enter a username in the Type Name text box or select a user from the list of users.

NOTE You must have an active MSN Messenger Service account to use the Directory. If Windows XP does not detect an active MSN Messenger Service account, it helps you create one automatically.

Do Not Disturb Check this option to prevent NetMeeting from notifying you when other calls come in. To resume incoming call notifications, choose Call ➤ Do Not Disturb again to clear the check mark.

TIP When you have Do Not Disturb active, callers have the option to send you e-mail when they try to call you.

Automatically Accept Calls Enable this option to automatically accept all incoming calls. To turn off this feature, select Automatically Accept Calls again to clear the check mark.

Create SpeedDial Opens a dialog where you can manually create a Speed Dial entry. Enter the user's address in the Address field. Use the Call Using drop-down to select how you want to place the call. Check or uncheck options to add the entry to your Speed Dial list or to save a shortcut on your Desktop.

Hang Up Ends the current call or meeting.

View Menu

Status Bar Shows or hides the status bar.

Dial Pad Displays a telephone-style dial pad in place of the video display in the NetMeeting window. Use the dial pad to place calls to an automated telephone system. To revert back to the video display, choose View ➤ Dial Pad to clear the check mark.

Picture-in-Picture Displays the video image you send to others in a small window within the video window.

My Video (New Window) Displays the video image you send to others in a separate window.

Compact Shows or hides the data area of the NetMeeting window; displays only the video area when the Compact option is checked.

Data Only Shows or hides the video area of the NetMeeting window; displays only the data area when the Data Only option is checked.

Always on Top Displays the NetMeeting window on top of other open windows.

Tools Menu

Video Allows you to send or receive video, and to specify the size of the video window (100, 200, 300, or 400 percent).

Audio Tuning Wizard Starts the Audio Tuning Wizard, which allows you to configure your audio settings, such as playback and recording volume.

TIP The Audio Tuning Wizard option is available only when you are not in a call.

Sharing Allows you to share an application with other people in the meeting.

Chat   Opens a window that allows you to send and receive messages during a call or meeting. The top area of the dialog displays the conversation (messages that you send and receive from other participants). Enter text in the Message text box. Select a recipient from the Send To drop-down list. Then click the Send button.

Whiteboard (1.0–2.x)   Displays the Whiteboard on the screen of each user who participates in the call or meeting. The Whiteboard functions similarly to a physical whiteboard; for example, users can jot down meeting notes or agendas, or sketch ideas. You can save the Whiteboard contents as a Whiteboard (.WHT) file.

TIP   The Whiteboard works similar to Paint. See the main topic "Paint" for more information.

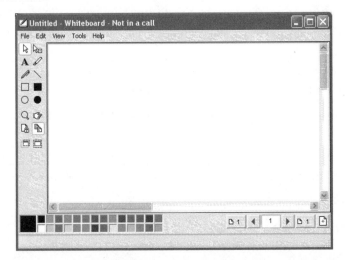

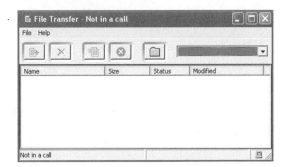

File Transfer   Allows you to send and receive files from other NetMeeting users during a call or meeting. Also allows you to open file folders, including the Received Files folder (which stores files you received from other users).

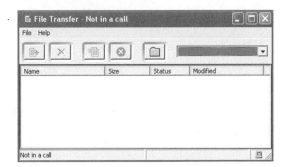

Remote Desktop Sharing   Allows you or another user to connect to your Desktop through another computer that is running NetMeeting. The remote computer can access files, run programs, and download files from your Desktop. The first time you choose this command, a wizard helps you configure your computer to listen for incoming Remote Desktop Sharing calls when NetMeeting is not running. After you configure settings with the wizard, this command opens the Remote Desktop Sharing Settings dialog.

TIP   You must have administrator privileges to access a computer using Remote Desktop Sharing.

Options   Allows you to configure directory options, general information, and security and video settings for NetMeeting.

NetMeeting Options

Use the NetMeeting Options dialog to configure NetMeeting to best serve your Internet conferencing needs. To open the Options dialog, choose Tools ➤ Options. The dialog has four tabs: General, Security, Audio, and Video.

General tab   Allows you to specify general, network bandwidth, and advanced calling settings, including the data you entered in the NetMeeting Wizard (personal information that other NetMeeting users can view, default directory, connection type and speed). Additional options allow you to run NetMeeting in the background when Windows starts, and to display the Net-Meeting icon on the taskbar. The Advanced Calling button opens a dialog where you can choose a gatekeeper to place calls, and a gateway to call telephones and videoconferencing systems.

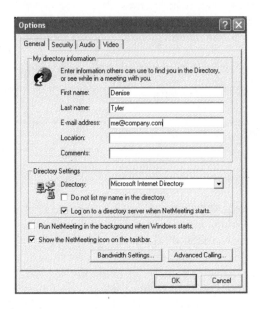

Security tab   Configure whether you want incoming and/or outgoing calls to be secure and whether to use a certificate.

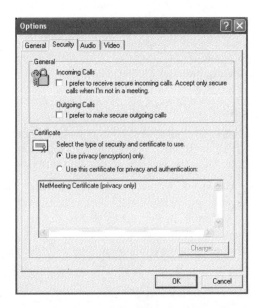

Audio tab   You can choose to enable full duplex audio and auto-gain control, automatically adjust the volume of your microphone while you are in a call, and enable DirectSound for better audio performance. Click the Tuning Wizard button to open the Audio Tuning Wizard; click the Advanced button to configure audio compression settings. Choose whether you want the silence detection sensitivity adjusted automatically or manually with a slider (this feature helps compensate for background noise in your room).

Video tab   Check or uncheck options to automatically send and/or receive video; choose an image size; and adjust the video quality. Use the Video Camera Properties drop-down list to select which video capture device you want to use. Click the Source button to configure video card settings (provided by the manufacturer). If the Source button is grayed out or missing, the Format button may be available, which serves the same function as the Source button.

TIP   The Source button may be available only if you're viewing an image in the Video window.

Finding a User

If you want to place a call but don't know the user's directory address, choose Call ➤ Directory, or click the Find Someone in a Directory button to open the Find Someone dialog.

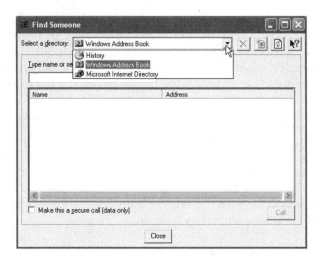

Choosing a Directory

Use the Select a Directory combo box to select or enter the name of a directory, or to select an entry from your Speed Dial or History view, or from the Windows address book. All entries from the selected source appear in the list box below. If you choose a directory other than the one you are currently logged on to, it displays the users that are logged on to that directory but does not log you on.

After you make a selection in the combo box, either select a user from the list, or enter a username in the Type Name or Select from List text box to select the closest match.

User Information

Information about each logged-on user appears in a list. An audio or video icon appears if the user has audio or video capabilities. The list also displays the user's last name, first name, e-mail address, location, and comments. A computer icon appears at the left of each person's e-mail address. If the user is in a call, the monitor in the icon is blue and a red star appears in the top-left corner of the icon. If the user is not in a call, the icon is grayed out.

Click a column header to sort the user list by that information; click the column again to sort the list in the reverse order. Drag a column header left or right to rearrange the order of the columns.

Available Actions

Right-click any user listed in the directory to choose from several actions, such as:

- Make a call to the user

• Access the user's properties

- Add the user to your Speed Dial list
- Add the user to the Address Book
- Refresh the directory list (or stop NetMeeting from refreshing the directory)

Sharing an Application

To share an application with other people in the call or meeting, choose Tools ➤ Sharing. The Sharing dialog allows you to select an application or document to share with the other participants from a list of items on your computer. Select the item you want to share, and click the Share button. When you share an item, meeting participants can see the information you enter in an application, but they cannot make any changes themselves.

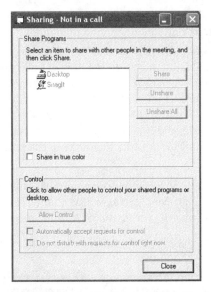

To stop sharing an item, select it in the list and click Unshare. Click Unshare All to stop all sharing. Place a check mark in the Share in True Color check box to share the application in true color (using up to 16 million colors).

WARNING Microsoft recommends that you don't check the Share in True Color option, as it makes application sharing very slow, especially over dial-up connections.

NOTE In order for others to view the item you share, they must have the associated application installed on their computer (for example, if you are sharing a Word document, they must have Word installed). The shared document must appear in an active window that appears on top of all other windows on their Desktop. **207**

> **TIP** Remote users can choose a command from the shared application's View menu to display the shared item in a full screen.

Enabling Control by Other Users

The Sharing dialog displays options that allow other users to make changes in your shared application. To enable these options, click the Allow Control button. When you enable user control, you can automatically accept requests for control or can temporarily disallow requests for control (the "Do not disturb me with requests for control right now" option).

After you enable user control, the Allow Control button toggles to a Prevent Control button. Click Prevent Control to prevent others from making changes to your application.

Requesting Control

To request control of a document, a user must choose Request Control from the Control menu of the shared application window. If you configured NetMeeting to automatically accept all requests, control of the document switches to the user that made the request. If you didn't select that option, NetMeeting informs you that a remote user would like to take control of the shared program. Click Accept to honor (or Reject to deny) the request. The user must then choose Control ➤ Release Control to turn control back over to the person who is sharing the application.

To grant control directly to a user without a request, right-click the user's name in the data area of the main NetMeeting window, and choose Grant Control. This option is available only if you've shared at least one application.

See also Address Book, Paint

Network and Internet Connections

Windows XP Control Panel group that provides access to utilities that configure (or create) your network connections and set Internet properties. Includes links to Network Connections, Internet Options, Phone and Modem Options, My Network Places, and Printers and Other Hardware. There are also links to troubleshooters for home networking, Internet Explorer, and network diagnostics. For further information on these topics, refer to individual topics listed below.

See also Internet Explorer, Internet Properties, My Network Places, Network Connections, Network Diagnostics, Network Setup Wizard, Phone and Modem Options, Printers and Other Hardware

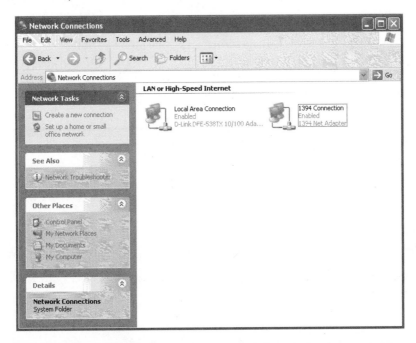

Network Connections

Folder where you can create, view, and configure network and dial-up connections on your computer. You use network connections to establish communications between two computers, between a computer and a local area network or wide area network, or between a computer and host on the Internet. Once you establish a connection, you can access and use resources on the computer, network, or Internet. For example, you can use files from the computer or network to which you are connected, or print to printers that are connected to the computer or network. If you connect to the Internet, you can view Web sites and download files.

Network connections can be either local or remote. Dial-up connections you create with the New Connection Wizard appear in this folder.

You can configure security for network and dial-up connections by using such features as callback, data encryption, authentication, and Windows XP login and domain security.

To open the Network Connections folder, choose Start ➢ All Programs (or Start ➢ Programs in the Classic Start menu) ➢ Accessories ➢ Communications ➢ Network Connections. (The folder is also available through shortcuts or links in Control Panel.)

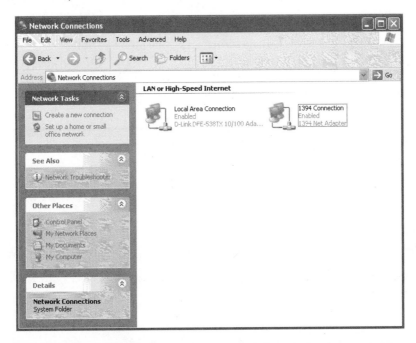

The folder includes an icon for each connection that is currently configured on the computer. When the connection is active, the screen areas of the two computers in the icon are blue. When the connection is inactive, the computers are grayed out. If your network card is disconnected, a red *X* appears over the network line. When you select a connection in the folder, the Details section in the left pane displays information such as connection type, status, adapter, IP address, and subnet mask for the connection. The Network Tasks area displays a list of file tasks that allow you to disable, repair, rename, view the status of, or change settings for the connection.

Network and Dial-up Connection Types

Windows XP supports six types of network and dial-up connections: Dial-up, Broadband, Local Area, Virtual Private Network (VPN), Direct, and Incoming. Each connection type has a different icon and default name associated with it that appears when you create a connection in the Network Connections folder.

 Dial-up Connection   A connection to the remote computer via standard telephone lines using a modem, via ISDN lines using an ISDN card, or via an X.25 network. Typically used for connections to the Internet or to connect remote users to a corporate network.

 Broadband Connection   A connection to the remote computer via a cable or DSL modem. Typically used for connections to the Internet or to connect remote users to a corporate network.

 Local Area Connection   A connection to another computer in a network, typically over Ethernet, Token Ring, cable modem, Fiber Distributed Data Interface (FDDI), DSL, T1, frame relay, and others. Typically used to connect computers in a corporate local area network (LAN).

 Virtual Private Connection   A dedicated, secure connection between two LANs over Point-to-Point Tunneling Protocol (PPTP) or Layer-2 Tunneling Protocol (L2TP). Allows you to establish a secure connection between a remote computer and a computer on a corporate network over the Internet.

 TIP   VPN connections over PPTP use MPPE (Microsoft Point-to-Point) encryption, and connections over L2TP use IPSec (IP Security Protocol) DES (Data Encryption Standard) encryption.

Direct Connection   A direct serial, parallel, or infrared connection between two computing devices. Typically allows you to connect Desktop computers with handheld computing devices.

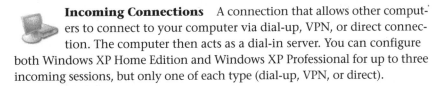 **TIP**   Use an RS-232C null modem cable to make a serial connection between two computers. The computers cannot be located more than 50 feet from each other.

Incoming Connections   A connection that allows other computers to connect to your computer via dial-up, VPN, or direct connection. The computer then acts as a dial-in server. You can configure both Windows XP Home Edition and Windows XP Professional for up to three incoming sessions, but only one of each type (dial-up, VPN, or direct).

Local Area Connection

 When you install Windows XP on a computer that has a network card installed, Windows XP automatically creates a local area connection for the card. The icon for this connection appears in the Network Connections folder. When you connect the computer to a network, this connection automatically activates without further action required by the user. If you install additional adapters, Windows XP creates a local area connection for each adapter and displays an icon for each connection in the Network Connections folder.

If the connection to the network is broken (for example, if you disconnect the patch cable from the hub or network card, or if a cable connecting the computer to the network is faulty), the icon displays a red *X* to indicate that this connection is no longer connected. When the connection to the network is reestablished (for example, you plug the patch cable back in), the local area connection automatically reconnects and the red *X* disappears.

As with all other connections, you can right-click the appropriate icon and choose Disable to manually disable a local area connection. If you do this, the local area connection no longer connects automatically. This feature is useful for laptop computers when you travel and cannot connect your adapter to your company's local area network. When you return to the office, right-click the connection icon and choose Enable (or double-click the icon) to reconnect the local area connection.

To configure local area connection properties, such as installed network clients and protocols, right-click the Local Area Connection icon and choose

Properties. The Properties dialog has three tabs: General, Authentication, and Advanced.

General tab   Displays the network adapter that you use for the connection; click Configure to open a Properties dialog for the adapter. Also displays a list of components (clients, services, and protocols) that the connection uses. Click Install or Uninstall to add or remove components; click the Properties button to configure a component. For example, selecting Internet Protocol (TCP/IP) and clicking Properties lets you set your IP address, subnet mask, default gateway address, and DNS server addresses, or choose to obtain your IP and DNS server addresses automatically from a DHCP server.

Authentication tab   Allows you to enable or disable authenticated network access for wired and wireless Ethernet networks. Check the Network Access Control Using IEEE 802 1X option to enable this feature. Choose the authentication method (MD-5 Challenge or Smart Card Or Other Certificate) from the EAP Type drop-down list. Click the Properties button to view or edit the properties for the EAP type that you select.

NOTE   In order to use smart cards to authenticate, you must have a smart card reader attached to your computer. You must enable the Use Extensible Authentication Protocol (EAP) option in the Advanced Security Settings of the connection's Security tab.

Advanced tab   Allows you to enable or disable Internet Connection Firewall, which prevents unauthorized access to your computer from the Internet. Also enables or disables Internet Connection Sharing (ICS), which allows other network users to connect through the computer's Internet connection. The tab provides direct links to help topics about the firewall, ICS, and the Network Setup Wizard, which automatically configures the firewall for you.

Create a New Connection

Create a new connection   Located in the Network Tasks section in the left pane; creates a new network or dial-up connection. Click the Create a New Connection link, or choose File ➤ New Connection, to start the New Connection Wizard. At the Welcome screen, click Next to display the Network Connection Type screen, which allows you to choose the type of connection you want to create. The following choices are available.

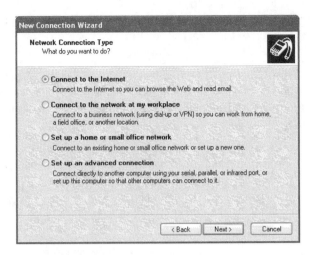

Connect to the Internet Allows you to create a dial-up connection or a broadband connection to an Internet service provider (ISP). You can choose from a list of ISPs, set up the connection manually, or use a CD that you received from an ISP. Choose the Dial-up Connection option to create a connection for a standard or ISDN modem. You must enter the phone number for your ISP, and the username and password that are required to connect to your account.

If you have a Broadband Connection, such as a cable or DSL modem, you can create a connection that requires a user name and password, or connect using a broadband connection that is always on and does not require you to sign in.

Connect to the Network at My Workplace Allows you to create a dial-up connection for a modem or ISDN, or a virtual private network (VPN) connection. A dial-up or broadband connection is required to use a VPN connection.

Choose the Dial-up Connection option to create a connection for a standard or ISDN modem. You must enter the phone number for your ISP, and the username and password that are required to connect to your account.

Choose the Virtual Private Network Connection option to create a secure, dedicated connection between your computer and a computer on a corporate network, over the Internet. You can automatically connect to the VPN connection using a dial-up or broadband connection that is configured on your computer. If you elect not to dial an Internet connection, you must manually establish a connection before you connect with the VPN connection. During setup of the VPN connection, you must provide the host name or IP address of the computer to which you want to connect.

Set Up a Home or Small Office Network   Starts the Network Setup Wizard, which helps you set up the computer to run on a network. You can share an Internet connection, set up Internet Connection Firewall, and share files, folders, and printers.

Advanced Connection   Choose this option to accept incoming connections from other computers, or to connect directly to another computer.

Choose the Accept Incoming Connections option to configure your Windows XP computer as a dial-in server that receives communications from other computers through a communications cable, modem, or direct parallel cable. You are prompted to select the type of connections in use (COM, modem, or LPT port). You can allow or disallow virtual private connections, specify users that are authorized to use this connection, and configure networking software to use with the connection.

Choose the Connect Directly to Another Computer option to create a connection between two computers using a serial, parallel, or direct connection cable. Specify whether the computer is the host (the computer that will be accessed) or the guest (the computer that will access the host computer), and choose the device you want to use for the connection.

If you're logged in without administrative privileges, Windows XP configures the computer to act as guest and creates it only for you. The only item you can specify is the device you want to use for the connection.

TIP   When you set up a direct connection with the machine acting as a host, you're effectively setting up the machine to accept incoming connections. If you have already configured the computer to accept incoming connections and later create a direct connection with the machine acting as host, you only change the parameters of the existing incoming connection.

Incoming Connections

To configure an eligible Windows XP computer to accept incoming connections and thus become a dial-in server, do the following:

1. Click the Create a New Connection task from the Network Tasks section in the left pane. The New Connection Wizard opens. Click Next.

2. Select Set Up an Advanced Connection. Click Next.

3. Select Accept Incoming Connections. Click Next.

4. Select the device or devices you want to use to accept incoming connections (such as a serial cable, modem, or parallel cable). To change the properties of a device, select it from the list and click the Properties button. When you're done, click OK to return to the wizard, then click Next to continue.

5. Select whether you want to allow VPN connections. Click Next.

NOTE You must have a valid Internet host name or IP address to allow VPN connections.

6. In the User Permissions screen, the Users Allowed to Connect list displays all users that currently have an account on the computer. Place a check mark next to any user you want to allow to use this incoming connection.

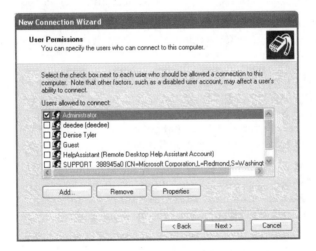

Add or remove users by clicking the appropriate buttons. To change the entry information for a user in the list, select the user and click the Properties button. In addition to basic properties such as name, you can enable the callback feature, which directs your computer to authenticate the user, then hang up and call them back. This reduces cost to the user, and it adds security by preventing incoming connections from unknown or authorized telephone numbers. (VPN connections do not support callback.)

WARNING If you delete a user from this dialog, Windows XP also deletes the user from the SAM database. Do not delete a user unless you are certain that this is what you want to do. To prevent a user from making an incoming connection to this computer, simply leave the check box next to their name empty.

After you configure the general and callback properties for the user, click OK to return to the wizard. Then click Next to continue.

7. In the Networking Software screen, select and configure the networking components (protocols, file and printer sharing services, and client services) that you want to use for incoming connections. The wizard lists all currently installed services; click the appropriate buttons to install or uninstall components. Place a check mark beside the components you want to enable, and clear the check mark to disable a component. If a check box for a service is grayed out, you cannot disable the service. To further configure protocols (such as TCP/IP, IPX/SPS, NetBEUI, and AppleTalk) for incoming connections, select the protocol and click Properties.

8. Click Finish to create the incoming connection. Windows returns you to the Network Connections folder and displays the Incoming Connections icon in the folder.

If you need to make changes to your Incoming Connections configuration, right-click the Incoming Connections icon and choose Properties. Use the General, Users, and Networking tabs to make configuration changes. These tabs display the same settings and options that appear when you create an incoming connection, along with some additional options.

For instance, on the General tab you can choose to display an icon in the taskbar notification area when users connect to the computer. On the Users tab, you can choose to require users to secure their passwords and data, and allow directly connected devices such as palmtop computers to connect without a password.

 NOTE If you require users to secure their passwords and data, users must enable two options in the Properties dialog that pertains to the connection they use to access this computer: on the Security tab, they must choose the Require Secured Password to validate their identity, and then check the Require Data Encryption (Disconnect If None) option.

Connection Properties

To further configure any network connection, right-click the connection you want to configure to open the Properties dialog.

- The Properties dialog for Incoming Connections is described in the preceding subsection.

- The Properties dialog for Local Area Connections is covered earlier in "Local Area Connection."

- The Properties dialog for all other connection types consists of five tabs: General, Options, Security, Networking, and Advanced.

General Tab

This is the only Properties dialog tab that differs significantly for each of the connection types. The bottom of the General tab usually offers an option to display an icon in the notification area of the taskbar when a user is connected.

Dial-up Connections The General tab for dial-up connections displays the device that you use to make the connection. Click the Configure button to configure connection speed and hardware features that are specific to your device. This tab is also where you change the phone number the device is dialing, and enable or disable dialing rules that utilize country and region codes. Click the Alternates button to add additional phone numbers to dial when the first number does not connect, and to specify the order in which Windows XP dials numbers. An option allows you to automatically place successful numbers at the top of the list.

Broadband The General tab for broadband connections only allows you to change the service name that is assigned to the connection.

Virtual Private Connections (VPN) The General tab for the Virtual Private Connection Properties dialog is where you specify the host name or IP address of the destination server to which you want to connect. You must establish a dial-up or broadband connection before you establish a VPN connection, and can configure the VPN connection to automatically dial a specified connection before you establish the VPN connection.

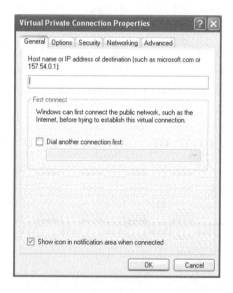

Direct Connections The General tab for direct connections only allows you to specify and configure the device (such as parallel or null modem) that Windows XP uses to make the connection.

Options Tab

Allows you to configure dialing and redialing options. You can specify the following:

- Show connection progress information while Windows XP establishes the connection.

- Prompt for authentication information, such as name, password, and certificate, before the connection is established.

- Include the Windows logon domain information.

- For dial-up connections, prompt for the phone number that is used for the connection.

- Redial the connection if the line is dropped.

NOTE The automatic redial feature only works when the Remote Access Auto Connection Manager service is running. To view the status of this service, choose Start ➤ Control Panel (or Start ➤ Settings ➤ Control Panel in the Classic Start menu) ➤ Performance and Maintenance ➤ Administrative Tools, and then double-click Component Services. Select Services from the console tree, then highlight Remote Access Auto Connection Manager to enable or disable this service.

The Options tab for Dial-up Connections includes one unique option: Click the X.25 button to specify X.25 logon settings.

Security Tab

Allows you to set up the level of security used when a connection is made. You can allow unsecured passwords, require secured passwords, or use a smart card. For secure passwords, you can automatically use the user's Windows logon name, password, and domain during authentication. You can enable or disable data encryption for secure passwords and smart card authentication. If you use data encryption and connect to a dial-in server that does not use this feature, the user is disconnected from the server.

TIP If you do not check the Require Data Encryption option, Windows XP still attempts to use data encryption when available. If the dial-in server doesn't use encryption, the connection is established without data encryption.

Select the Advanced (Custom Settings) option and click Settings to configure advanced encryption options. You can make encryption optional, not allow encryption, or require encryption. You can also specify the security protocols that the connection uses.

The Security tab for dial-up connections allows you to display a terminal window after you connect. The remote terminal server prompts you for logon information in the terminal window, and authenticates you after you provide the information. You can optionally specify a script that contains the necessary information to automate this process for the connection.

The Security tab for VPN connections contains a IPSec Settings button. Click this button to use a specified pre-shared key for authentication.

Networking Tab

Allows you to specify the connection method that is used.

Connection Type	Possible Connection Methods
Dial-up connections	PPP: Windows 95/98/NT4/2000, Internet (the most common)
	SLIP: UNIX Connection

Broadband connections	Point-to-Point Protocol over Ethernet (PPPoE)
Direct connections	Communications Cable between Two Computers (COM1)
	Direct Parallel (LPT1)
VPN connections	Automatic (Windows will attempt to connect via PPTP first, then via L2TP)
	PPTP VPN (Point-to-Point Tunneling Protocol)
	L2TP IPSec VPN (Layer-2 Tunneling Protocol)

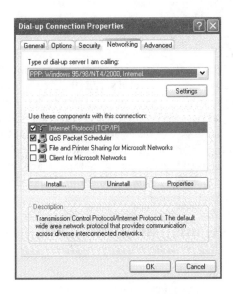

You can place a check mark beside the networking components that the connection uses, and install, uninstall, or view the properties of existing networking components.

Advanced Tab

The Advanced tab allows you to enable or disable the Internet Connection Firewall and Internet Connection Sharing. For further information on these topics, see their respective main headings elsewhere in this guide

Pop-up Menu Options

When you right-click a connection icon in the Network Connections folder, a pop-up or shortcut menu displays several choices. These vary, depending on the type of connection you select and whether the connection is active or enabled. Unique commands here include the following:

Connect/Disconnect   Not available for Incoming or LAN connections. To establish a connection, right-click the connection's icon and choose Connect, or select the connection and double-click the connection's icon. To disconnect a connection, either right-click the connection's icon and choose Disconnect or open the connection's Status dialog and click Disconnect on the General tab.

NOTE   If you choose to display a connection icon in the notification area of the taskbar, you can right-click the icon and choose Disconnect.

Status   Opens the Status dialog, which always has a General tab and may have a Support tab. The General tab displays the connection's status (for example, Connected), duration, and speed. It also displays activity information, such as the number of bytes sent and received, the compression ratio, and any errors that occurred during the connection. Click the Properties button to open the Properties dialog for the connection. Click Disconnect or Disable to disconnect or disable the connection. The Support tab, if available, displays items such as the IP address, subnet mask, and default gateway. Click the Details button to view more detailed connection information. Click the Repair button to fix the connection.

TIP   If you selected the option to display a connection icon in the notification area of the taskbar, you can right-click this icon and choose Status or single- or double-click the icon to open the Status dialog. Place the cursor over the icon to view the name of the connection, the connection's speed, and the number of bytes sent and received.

Set as Default Connection   Uses the selected connection as the default connection. Not available for Incoming or LAN connections.

Create Copy   Creates a copy of the connection, using the same properties as the original. Not available for Incoming or LAN connections.

Create Shortcut   Creates a shortcut to the connection and places it on your Desktop. Not available for Incoming connections.

Repair   Attempts to automatically repair problems with your connection. A dialog notifies you when the repairs are successful, or informs you of problems that may exist with the configuration.

Bridge Connections Creates a network bridge, which simplifies the setup and configuration of small networks that have mixed network connections. For detailed information about network bridges, see the "Network bridge overview" topic in Windows XP Help and Support Center.

Advanced Menu

Advanced The six options on the Network Connections folder Advanced menu open dialogs that allow you to adjust related settings and options, some of which are highlighted here:

Operator-Assisted Dialing Allows you to configure dial-up connections that allow you to manually dial a number through a telephone handset or have an operator dial the number for you.

Dial-up Preferences Allows you to configure Autodial and Callback options. Autodial learns which connections you used to access remote resources, and automatically dials a connection after you unsuccessfully attempt to access resources on a remote network. Callback changes the direction of the connection, connecting from the server to the user.

TIP Individual users that are granted the right to establish incoming connections can use the Callback tab of the Incoming Connections properties dialog to specify callback settings. These individual settings take precedence over Callback settings for outgoing connections.

Network Identification Opens the System Properties dialog to the Computer Name tab. Here you can change the computer's name, as well as the domain or workgroup the computer belongs to.

Bridge Connections Allows you to create a network bridge for a LAN connection. Network bridges simplify the setup and configuration of small networks that have mixed network connections.

Advanced Settings Allows you to configure applicable advanced network adapter options, such as connections and their bindings, NetBIOS network route LANA numbers, and the order in which the computer accesses network resources and information.

Optional Networking Components Starts a wizard that guides you through installing additional Windows networking components on the computer.

See also Administrative Tools, Device Manager, DHCP, New Connection Wizard, System, System Information

Network Diagnostics

Subset of Windows XP Help and Support Center. Network Diagnostics scans your system to gather information about your network hardware, software, and connections. Choose Start ➤ Help and Support to open the Help and Support Center window. From the Pick a Task area, click Tools, and then choose Network Diagnostics from the Tools section in the left pane.

See also Help and Support Center

Network Identification Wizard

See System (Network Identification tab)

Network Passwords

Allows you to maintain the list of passwords that are stored on your system to log in to Web sites. If you are logged on as a Limited user or Guest, choose Start ➤ Control Panel (or Start ➤ Settings ➤ Control Panel in the Classic Start menu) ➤ User Accounts to access the User Accounts window. Choose Change an Account, select the account you want to alter, then choose Manage My Network Passwords from the Related Tasks section.

Network Setup Wizard

Network Setup Wizard   Helps you connect multiple home computers. The screens in the wizard help you configure your Internet connection settings, bridge network adapters together to create a home network, and set up a firewall that prevents unauthorized users from gaining access to your files and folders.

NOTE Before you use the Network Setup Wizard, you must first install and configure your network communication devices (network cards, modems, cables, and device drivers). If you are going to use Internet Connection Sharing (ICS) to share a single Internet connection with more than one computer on your network, run the Network Setup Wizard on the ICS host computer first (the computer that connects directly to the Internet). Then, run the wizard on the other computers that will use the same Internet connection.

To use the Network Setup Wizard, choose Start ➤ All Programs ➤ Accessories ➤ Communications ➤ Network Setup Wizard. The introductory screen appears. Choose Next to continue through each step of the wizard, based on the responses you choose in each screen.

See also Internet Connection Firewall, Internet Connection Sharing

New Connection Wizard

 New Connection Wizard Guides you through the process of setting up either a dial-up or LAN connection to the Internet and setting up Internet e-mail. To start the wizard, use one of the following methods:

- Choose Start ➤ All Programs (or Start ➤ Programs in the Classic Start menu) ➤ Accessories ➤ Communications ➤ New Connection Wizard.

- Choose Start ➤ Control Panel (or Start ➤ Settings ➤ Control Panel from the Classic Start menu) ➤ Network and Internet Connections. Next, click the Internet Options control panel icon to open the Internet Properties dialog. Select the Connections tab, and click Setup.

When the New Connection Wizard starts, click Next to display the Network Connection Type screen. This screen gives you four options:

- Choose Connect to the Internet to set up an Internet connection. You can choose from a list of Internet service providers (ISPs), set up a connection manually, or use the CD that you received from an ISP.

- Choose Connect to the Network at My Workplace to use a dial-up or VPN connection to connect to your business network.

- Choose Set Up a Home or Small Office Network to open the Network Setup Wizard. This wizard helps you configure the computer to run on a network.

- Choose Set Up an Advanced Connection to connect directly to another computer using a serial, parallel, or infrared port, or to allow other computers to connect to your computer.

NOTE If you already have an account set up with an ISP and you use different computers frequently, it might be a good idea to store a record of this account and connection information. Then, you can use the New Connection Wizard and the information to quickly set up an Internet connection on a new computer.

Setting Up a Dial-up Internet Connection

The following steps describe how to use the New Connection Wizard to configure a new dial-up connection on your computer, using a modem that connects to an existing ISP. Follow these steps:

1. Choose Start ➤ All Programs (or Start ➤ Programs in the Classic Start menu) ➤ Accessories ➤ Communications ➤ New Connection Wizard.

2. Click Next to display the Network Connection Type screen.

3. Choose Connect to the Internet. Click Next to continue.

4. Choose Set up My Connection Manually. Click Next to continue.

5. Choose Connect using a Dial-Up Modem. Click Next to continue.

6. The Connection Name screen appears. Enter a name for your ISP connection. Click Next.

7. Enter the phone number of your ISP. Click Next.

8. The Internet Account Information screen appears. Enter your username and password, and confirm the password. Check or uncheck options to use this account name and password when anyone connects to the Internet, to make this the default Internet connection, and to turn on Internet Connection Firewall.

9. The wizard displays a summary of your choices and displays an option to add a shortcut to the connection on your desktop. Click Finish to exit the wizard. If you choose the option to display the shortcut on your desktop, click the connection to connect to your ISP.

Setting Up a LAN Internet Connection

You use a LAN Internet connection to configure your computer to connect to the Internet through your home or office network, or to connect to the Internet with a cable or DSL modem. To set up this type of connection, follow these steps:

1. Choose Start ➤ All Programs (or Start ➤ Programs in the Classic Start menu) ➤ Accessories ➤ Communications ➤ New Connection Wizard.

2. Click Next to display the Network Connection Type screen.

3. Choose Connect to the Internet. Click Next to continue.

4. Choose Set up My Connection Manually. Click Next to continue.

5. Choose Connect Using a Broadband Connection That is Always On. Click Next to continue through the remaining steps in the wizard.

Once you establish a LAN connection to the Internet, simply open a Web browser or e-mail application. You do not need to dial in to an ISP because your connection is made through the proxy server on the LAN, which is permanently connected to the Internet.

TIP   When you are using a LAN connection to connect your home computer or network to a DSL or cable modem, the use of a firewall is highly recommended. Enable the Internet Connection Firewall feature of Windows XP, or use a third-party firewall to protect your computers from unwanted intruders.

Setting Up an E-Mail Account

The following steps describe how you can use the Internet Connection Wizard to connect to an e-mail address that you already have. To set up an e-mail account with the wizard, follow these steps:

1. Open Outlook Express (for example, double-click the Outlook Express icon on your Desktop).

2. Choose Tools ➤ Accounts to open the Internet Accounts dialog.

3. Click the Add button, and choose Mail from the submenu. The wizard appears.

4. In the Your Name screen, enter the name that you want to use when you send an e-mail message or post a message to a newsgroup. Click Next.

5. In the Internet E-mail Address screen, enter your e-mail address. Click Next.

6. In the E-mail Server Names screen, choose the mail server type (POP3, IMAP, or HTTP) that your e-mail account uses. Then, enter the addresses

for your incoming mail (for example: mail.myisp.com) and outgoing mail (for example: smtp.myisp.com). Click Next to continue.

7. In the Internet Mail Logon screen, enter the account name and password that you use to log in to your email account.

8. If you want Outlook Express to automatically remember your password, check the Remember Password option. Uncheck this option if you want to enter your password each time you connect to your e-mail account.

9. If your ISP requires that you use Secure Password Authentication, check the Log On Using Secure Password Authentication check box.

10. Click Next to continue. The wizard informs you that your information is complete. Click Finish to complete your account setup.

TIP To modify your e-mail account settings at any time, open Outlook Express and choose the Tools ➤ Accounts command to open the Internet Accounts dialog. Click the Mail tab, select the account you want to change, and click the Properties button. For further information, see the main topic "Outlook Express."

Connecting to the Internet with a Modem

The Connect dialog appears when you choose to connect to the Internet for browsing, or when you choose to send or retrieve e-mail. If you have more than one dial-up connection set up, use the Connect To drop-down list to select the connection you want to dial.

Verify that the username and password are correct for the account you selected. Check the "Save this user name and password for the following users" option to store the password so that you do not have to enter it each time you connect to your account. You can save the information for yourself or for anyone who uses the computer. The Connect dialog also has the following buttons:

Dial Connects to your ISP. The modem dials your ISP, and the bottom of the dialog displays messages that tell you that you are connected to the remote computer and your password is being verified.

Properties Opens the Properties dialog to the General tab. For more information, refer to the main topic "Internet Properties."

TIP While you are connected, an icon with two overlapping (connected) computers appears in the notification area of the taskbar. Double-click this icon to obtain information about the connection, such as how long you've been connected, the speed of the connection, how many bytes have been sent and received, the server type used, and the client and server's IP addresses.

Closing a Modem Connection

After you connect to the Internet for browsing, you can disconnect in one of these ways:

- When you close Internet Explorer, the Auto Disconnect dialog appears. Choose Disconnect Now.

- Right-click or double-click the Connection icon in the notification area of the taskbar, and choose Disconnect.

See also Internet Explorer, Internet Properties, Network and Internet Connections, Outlook Express

Notepad

Notepad Program used to view, create, and edit small text files, such as configuration text files, readme files, or the contents of the Windows Clipboard.

Choose Start ➤ All Programs (or Start ➤ Programs in the Classic Start menu) ➤ Accessories ➤ Notepad to open Notepad. The Notepad window consists of a menu bar, text area, and status bar.

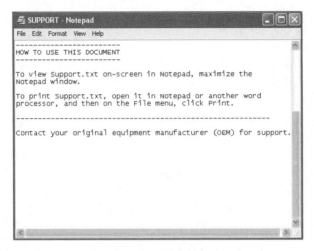

File menu   Contains common options such as New, Open, and Save. However, when you open a file in Notepad, existing formatting is stripped from the file and it is converted into ASCII format.

Edit menu   Contains options to find, select, or replace words and phrases in the document, go to a particular page number, or insert the time and date.

Format menu   Includes commands to toggle Word Wrap on and off (text automatically wraps around to the next line) and to choose a font.

View menu   The sole command shows or hides the status bar.

Working with Text

You can work with text in Notepad in one of the following ways:

- Create a new text file by typing in the text area and saving the file.

- Open an existing text file by choosing File ➤ Open.

- Place the contents of the Windows Clipboard into Notepad by choosing Edit ➤ Paste.

See also   WordPad

NTFS

File system for Windows XP computers. NTFS has many advantages over older file systems, such as FAT and FAT32. You can format a disk partition with the NTFS file system during the Windows XP operating system installation, or you

can convert an older file system (FAT or FAT32) to NTFS during or after the Windows XP operating system installation using convert.exe.

TIP For more information on how to convert a file system using convert.exe, choose Start ➤ All Programs (or Start ➤ Programs in the Classic Start menu) ➤ Accessories ➤ Command Prompt, then type **help convert** at the C:\> command prompt.

Features that are available only if you're using NTFS include, among others:

- Active Directory

- File encryption

- Permissions set on files

- Remote Storage

- Disk Quotas

See also Active Directory, Command Prompt, Permissions

Offer Remote Assistance

Subset of Windows XP Help and Support Center. Choose Start ➤ Help and Support to open the Help and Support Center window. From the Pick a Task area, click Tools and choose Offer Remote Assistance from the Tools section in the left pane.

See also Help and Support Center

Offline Files

✓ Make available offline Allows you to use network or shared files or folders when you're not connected to the network. From Windows Explorer, right-click a file or folder and choose Make Available Offline.

TIP To display this menu option in Windows Explorer, choose Tools ➤ Folder Options, and check Enable Offline Files on the Offline Files tab.

WARNING You cannot make files available offline when Fast User Switching is enabled. To disable this feature, see the main topic "Fast User Switching."

The *first* time you choose the Make Available Offline command, the Offline Files Wizard appears. Complete it as follows:

1. In the Welcome screen, click Next.

2. If you don't want files to synchronize automatically when you log on and off the computer, uncheck the Automatically Synchronize option. Click Next.

3. Check Enable Reminders to receive a periodic message that reminds you that you're working offline. It is also strongly recommended that you check the option "Create a shortcut to the Offline Files folder on my Desktop."

4. Click Finish. The wizard synchronizes the file or folder to the Offline Files folder and you return to Windows Explorer.

Thereafter, whenever you choose the Make Available Offline command, Windows Explorer automatically synchronizes the selected file or folder to the Offline Files folder. Two opposite-facing arrows appear in the bottom-left portion of the icon for an offline file or folder.

TIP To remove a file from the Offline Files folder, right-click the file and select Make Available Offline. This removes the check mark on the menu item.

When you are offline, you can access your offline files or folders as though you are connected to the network. Click the computer icon in the notification area of the taskbar to see your current offline file status. If you have reminders set up, a pop-up message periodically tells you that you're working offline. Choose Folder Options from Control Panel to further configure reminders.

Offline Files Folder

Offline files are also accessible through the Offline Files folder. Double-click the shortcut on your Desktop (if you created one) to open the Offline Files folder. This folder displays the names of all offline files, the synchronization status, availability, and the access rights you have to each file. If you delete a file from the Offline Files folder, the network version of the file remains.

TIP You can also browse to offline files or folders with Windows Explorer or My Network Places. The left side of Explorer displays a message that tells you when a folder is offline.

To work on a file offline, select it from the Offline Files folder. Open it and make any changes you need. Synchronization occurs automatically when you connect to the network (unless you change default settings in Synchronization or in the Offline Files Wizard).

To synchronize manually, open the Offline Files folder. Choose View ➣ Details if necessary. The Synchronization column indicates local files that have been modified. To synchronize files, close any offline files that are opened. To synchronize all files, choose Tools ➣ Synchronize, then click Synchronize. To synchronize an individual file, select the file and choose File ➣ Synchronize, or right-click the file and choose Synchronize.

See   Folder Options, Synchronize

Online Print Ordering

Allows you to order prints of your photos from the Internet. Depending on the vendor you select, you can also print your photos on gift items such as poster-size prints, mugs, mouse pads, sweatshirts, and T-shirts. You must have an Internet connection to use this feature.

To use the Online Print Ordering Wizard, follow these steps:

1. Choose Start ➣ My Pictures. Windows XP opens your My Pictures folder.

2. Select the picture or pictures that you want to order.

3. From the Picture Tasks section in the left pane, choose Order Prints Online. The Online Print Ordering Wizard appears. Click Next to continue.

4. The first screen displays your picture selections. Check pictures to order prints, or clear the check box to remove the picture from your order. You can also use the Select All or Clear All buttons to add or remove all pictures. Click Next to continue.

5. Select the Internet printing company that you would like to print your photos. Highlight a selection in the list, and click Next.

6. The wizard downloads a catalog of product and ordering options from the company you select. The options you see in this screen may vary from vendor to vendor. You can optionally set up a user account and password that allows you to track your orders.

7. Select items that you want to add to your shopping cart, and enter quantities for each item.

8. When you are ready to process your order, click the Check Out button in the company product catalog. You will be prompted to enter payment and shipping information.

9. Continue with the prompts in the wizard until your order is complete.

See also My Pictures, Scanners and Cameras

On-Screen Keyboard

 On-Screen Keyboard Designed for users who have difficulty using a standard keyboard. Users can control On-Screen Keyboard with the mouse or with a switch input device. To display On-Screen Keyboard, choose Start ➤ All Programs ➤ Accessories ➤ Accessibility ➤ On-Screen Keyboard.

Alternatively, you can use the Windows Logo Key + U shortcut to open the Utility Manager. Select the On-Screen Keyboard from the list of utilities and click Start. The Utility Manager also allows you to start the utility automatically when you log on, when you lock your desktop, or when the Utility Manager starts.

NOTE The program in which you want to enter text must be active when you're using On-Screen Keyboard.

The Keyboard menu allows you to choose the type of keyboard you want to display. Your choices are Enhanced Keyboard (with a numeric keypad) or Standard Keyboard, Regular or Block Layout, and 101 (U.S. Standard), 102 (Universal), or 106 (additional Japanese characters) keys.

The Settings menu allows you to configure the behavior of On-Screen Keyboard. Choose Always on Top to always display the keyboard on top of other windows. Choose Use Click Sound to play a clicking sound when you press a key on the On-Screen Keyboard. Choose Typing Mode to configure options for typing with a mouse or joystick.

The Typing Mode dialog lets you set up different typing modes; for example, you can specify that either clicking a key or hovering over a key selects that key. Alternatively, you can choose Joystick or Key to Select and then set up a scan interval to activate scanning of the keyboard. During the scan, each key on On-Screen Keyboard is highlighted and you can select keys by using a dedicated key on the physical keyboard or an external switching device. To specify a key or device, click Advanced and select "Serial, Parallel, or Game Port;" or select Keyboard Key and choose the key you want to use from the drop-down list.

Back on the Settings menu, you can also change the font used for the keys on the keyboard, perhaps making it larger so it's easier to read.

See also Utility Manager

Other Control Panel Options

Section of Windows XP Control Panel that stores additional Control Panel options that are installed by other Windows software. Items that you may find in this section include additional Desktop themes and user interface selectors, digital camera settings, live updates for software, and links to additional media players. To view other Control Panel options, choose Start ➤ Control Panel. Select Other Control Panel Options from the See Also section in the left pane.

See also Control Panel

Outlook Express

Application that allows you to send and receive Internet e-mail and to read and post newsgroup messages. To start Outlook Express, choose Start ➤ E-mail or Start ➤ All Programs ➤ Outlook Express. To open Outlook Express from within Internet Explorer, choose any option from Tools ➤ Mail and News, or select any option that appears when you click the Mail button in the Internet Explorer toolbar.

In order to send and receive e-mail with Outlook Express, you need to set up at least one e-mail account, either with an Internet service provider (ISP) or through your corporate intranet. When you launch Outlook Express, the Internet

Connection Wizard opens automatically if you have not yet configured your e-mail account for Outlook Express. You can also use this wizard to configure additional e-mail accounts at any time. To do so from Outlook Express, choose Tools ➢ Accounts ➢ Add ➢ Mail. Follow the steps in the wizard to create your e-mail account.

Outlook Express Window

The Outlook Express window in Windows XP consists of the menu bar and toolbar at the top of the window. The Folders and Contacts panes appear in the left portion of the window, and the main Outlook Express pane appears at the right. The main pane changes, depending on the folder you select in the Folders pane.

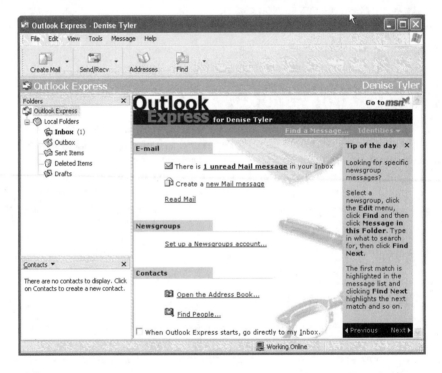

Menus

Outlook Express menus contain many familiar Windows XP menu options, many of which are accessible via toolbar buttons. The commands you see in the menus depend on where you are and what you have selected. Menu options allow you to configure Outlook Express; import and export Address Book entries, messages, and account settings; mark messages as read; move messages; change views; synchronize Outlook Express; create rules for messages; and set up and configure accounts.

File menu   Create new messages, folders, or contacts, or save messages, attachments, and stationery to your hard drive. You can also import messages and contacts from other mail software, print messages, switch identities, view properties of messages and folders, and choose to work offline.

Edit menu   Perform simple operations such as selecting and copying text from a message, finding specific messages or people, moving or copying messages to another folder, deleting messages from folders and emptying the Deleted Items folder, and marking messages as read or unread.

View menu   Select the messages you want to view in each folder (view all messages, hide read messages, or hide read and ignored messages). You can group messages by conversation, or display and sort them in various categories. The View menu also allows you to customize the layout of your Outlook Express window and navigate to or expand and collapse folder lists and message groups.

Tools menu   Send and receive e-mail messages, synchronize newsgroup messages, manage Address Book, and configure message rules that automatically organize messages as you receive them. You can also configure or modify new and existing mail accounts and set additional Outlook Express options.

Message menu   Send new messages with or without stationery, reply to or forward messages, create message rules based on a selected message, block messages received by certain senders, or flag messages and watch conversations.

Toolbar

When you first open Outlook Express, or when you have the Outlook Express Local Folders level selected in the Folders pane, the toolbar contains the following icons: New Mail, Send/Recv, Addresses, and Find. When you choose any folder that appears beneath the Local Folders level (such as Inbox, Outbox, or Sent Items), the Reply, Reply All, Forward, Print, and Delete buttons become available.

Create Mail   Opens a dialog where you can create a new e-mail message. To choose from a list of stationery options for the message, click the down arrow that appears to the right of the Create Mail button. To preview the stationery options, choose Select Stationery from the menu that appears. Choose No Stationery if you don't want to use stationery. Choose Web Page to create an e-mail using a saved HTML file.

Reply   Begins a reply to the original author of the selected message. The text from the original message appears in your reply. Outlook Express places the cursor above the original text so that you can write your reply. Attachments to the original message are not sent with the reply.

Reply All   Begins a reply to all individuals who received the original message, as listed in the To and Cc fields. Outlook Express places the cursor above the original text so that you can write your reply. Attachments to the original message are not sent with the reply.

TIP   When you reply to a message, Outlook Express automatically adds the recipient(s) to your contact list and Address Book. To disable this feature, choose Tools ➤ Options and click the Send tab. Uncheck the "Automatically put people I reply to in my Address Book" option.

Forward   Begins a message with a copy of the original message and its attachments, to send to a different recipient. You can add new text above the original message.

Send/Recv   Sends all messages in your Outbox and receives all messages waiting on your mail server (or servers, if you have more than one set up). For other send and receive options, click the down arrow that appears to the right of the Send/Recv icon. Here, choose to only receive all messages or to only send all messages. If you have more than one mail server configured, select the mail server you want to query from the bottom of the menu.

Addresses   Opens Address Book.

Find   Opens a dialog that helps you find messages in any of Outlook Express's folders. Click the arrow to the right of the Find button to look for messages in a specific folder or to find the next message that contains your search criteria. Other choices let you find text contained in a specific message or find people.

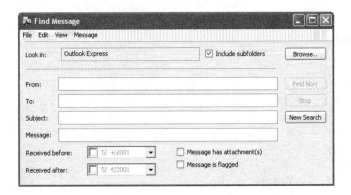

To customize the Outlook Express toolbar, right-click the toolbar and choose Customize to open a dialog that allows you to add, remove, or change the order of toolbar buttons. You can also display, hide, and format text labels and change icon sizes. Click Reset to revert back to toolbar defaults.

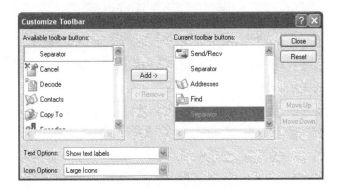

Folders Pane

The Folders pane appears at the right side of the Outlook Express window and allows you to navigate through, create, and organize folders that hold the messages you receive and send.

Outlook Express automatically places messages into several default folders:

Inbox   Holds messages when you first receive them.

NOTE To help with organizing your Inbox messages, you can create additional subfolders such as the Family, Friends, and Work subfolders shown here. All incoming messages first appear in the Inbox folder, unless you create message rules that direct them to other folders as they come in. You can also drag and drop message between folders.

Outbox   Holds messages that you have not yet sent.

Sent Items   After you send messages, they automatically appear in the Sent Items folder.

Deleted Items   Stores messages that have been deleted from other folders.

TIP To remove all items from the Deleted Items folder, right-click it and choose Empty Deleted Items Folder.

Drafts   Stores messages that you are still working on.

NOTE When a folder contains unread messages, the folder name appears in bold text, and the number of unread messages appears in parentheses next to the folder.

Contacts Pane

The Contacts pane displays Address Book contacts for the current identity. For further information about how multiple identities (or users) can use Outlook Express, see the subsection "Working with Identities" later in this topic.

To send a message to one or more contacts, select them from the contact list (using the Shift or Ctrl keys to select multiple contacts). Right-click the selection and choose Send E-Mail. The contact names automatically appear in the To list. To display or edit the Address Book information for a contact, right-click a contact and choose Properties.

Creating and Sending a Message

To create a new message, click Create Mail on the toolbar, or choose File ➤ New ➤ Mail Message. The New Message dialog appears.

Type the recipient's e-mail address in the To field. Separate multiple addresses with semicolons or commas. If you have entered contacts in your Address Book, you can click the To icon and select addresses from the list. If you want to send copies to other recipients, type their addresses in the Cc field, or click the Cc icon to select addresses from the Address Book. Type a subject for the message in the Subject field.

Type the message in the New Message body area in the lower part of the window. You can format the message by selecting a font, font size, and other attributes for the text.

When you send messages to several recipients, each person who receives the message can view the names and e-mail addresses of all other recipients. This is often undesirable and can lead to spamming and unwanted e-mail messages if the recipient list accidentally gets in the wrong hands. As an alternative, consider using the blind copies feature, which instead displays the list of recipients as "Undisclosed recipients." To send blind copies, click the Cc icon in the New Message dialog and, when the Select Recipients dialog appears, add the recipients' names to the Bcc area there.

Use the Insert menu in the New Message dialog to add other items such as attachments, text files, images, and business cards to the message. Options in the Format menu allow you to further format your message. The Tools menu offers spell-checking, message encrypting, and receipt options. Choose Message ➢ Set Priority to assign a priority level to your message.

Sending a Message

After you create your message, you're ready to send it. To immediately send the message, click the Send button on the toolbar, or choose File ➢ Send Message. To store the message for later delivery, choose File ➢ Send Later.

All outgoing messages appear in the Outbox until Outlook Express sends them to your mail server. If you're not connected to the Internet, the message stays in the Outbox until the next time you connect. Even if you are connected to the Internet, messages that you choose to Send Later will not be sent until you click the Send/Recv toolbar button or choose Tools ➢ Send and Receive ➢ Send and Receive All (or Send All).

Attaching a File to a Mail Message

Outlook Express also lets you send files you have created in other programs to your e-mail contacts. To attach a file to a mail message, simply choose Insert ➢ File Attachment, or click the Attach button on the toolbar. (If the button is not visible, you may need to resize the New Message dialog). Browse for and select one or more files, then click Attach. A new Attach field displays the name and size of the attached file.

TIP Many ISPs limit the amount of data that your mailbox will hold or send to others, and some ISPs won't allow you to send individual attachments larger than a particular limit. Other services may only allow you to attach one file to a message. Before you attach a very large file to your e-mail message, verify your ISP's limit.

Reading Mail

To read new mail, click the Inbox folder in the Folders pane. Next, select a message header from the Preview pane that appears in the upper portion of the main pane. The lower portion of the main pane displays the contents of the message. You can read messages in any other folder in the same fashion.

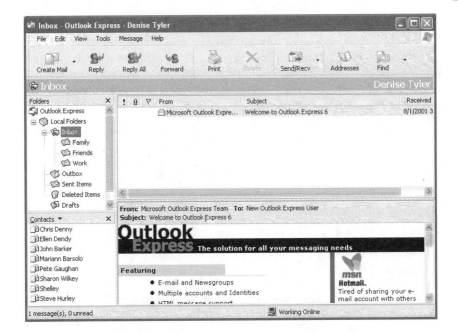

Right-click any message header to display an options menu. You can open or print the message, reply to the sender or all recipients, or forward the message either as a mail message or as an attachment. You can also mark the message as read or unread, move or copy it to a different folder, or delete it. Finally, you can add the sender to your Address Book and access message properties.

Reading News

Outlook Express also serves well as a newsreader for Internet-based newsgroups. To configure your news account, choose Tools ➤ Accounts ➤ Add ➤ News; the Internet Connection Wizard provides instructions to complete the account setup. After you create your news account, you can download a list of newsgroups to which your ISP has access. To search for groups of interest, select the news server name from the Folders pane. Then click the Newsgroups button that appears in the Preview pane to open the Newsgroups Subscription dialog. After you select a newsgroup, you can read articles others have posted and post your own articles to newsgroups using procedures that are similar to Outlook Express's e-mail functions.

Working with Identities

Outlook Express allows you to configure multiple identities, so that several users can receive and send e-mail and read news. Each identity sees its own mail messages, uses its own contacts, and so forth. If multiple identities are configured, the name of the current identity appears in the far-right corner of the Outlook Express bar (right below the toolbar).

When you first open Outlook Express, the default identity, Main Identity, is used.

NOTE You can also use identities when in Address Book.

Creating a New Identity

To create a new identity in Outlook Express, follow these steps:

1. Choose File ➤ Identities ➤ Add New Identity. The New Identity dialog appears.

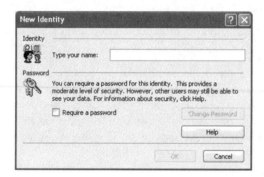

2. Enter a name for the new identity in the text box.

3. Check Require a Password if you want to password protect your identity. Enter the password in the Enter Password dialog and click OK to return to the New Identity dialog.

4. Click OK.

5. Click Yes to switch to the new identity now, or click No to continue using the current identity.

Switching to Another Identity

To switch to another identity, choose File ➤ Switch Identity and select the identity you want from the list box. Enter the password if necessary, and click OK.

If you're connected to the Internet, you're prompted to choose whether you want to keep the current connection for the next identity. Choose Yes to stay connected or No to break the connection.

Logging Off of an Identity

To log off the current identity, follow these steps:

1. Choose File ➤ Switch Identity.

2. Click Log Off Identity.

3. Click Yes to confirm.

4. If you're connected to the Internet, click Yes to keep the current connection for the next identity, or No to break the connection. Outlook Express then closes. If you're connected to the Internet while Auto Disconnect is enabled, you'll have to specify whether you want to stay connected or disconnect from the Internet.

After you log off an identity, the Identity Login dialog appears the next time you start Outlook Express. Use one of the available identities to log in.

Configuring Outlook Express Options

The Options dialog (Tools ➤ Options) allows you to further configure Outlook Express.

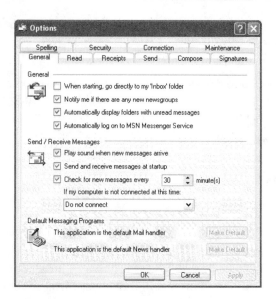

General tab   Contains options for configuring Outlook Express startup and for sending and receiving messages. Also lets you set Outlook Express as the default mail and news program.

Read tab   Configures the appearance of mail and news messages, and selects fonts and international settings for reading messages.

Receipts tab   Allows you to request receipts that notify you when a recipient has read your message, and to send receipts when you read a message delivered to you. You can also configure secure receipts for messages that are digitally signed.

Send tab   Configures how messages are sent and allows you to send mail and news messages in HTML or plain text format.

 TIP   Though HTML messages and stationery are attractive and easier to read than plain text, mail and news readers that do not support these features will display your nicely formatted HTML messages and pretty backgrounds as raw HTML code. This makes your messages difficult to read for those users. To remedy this situation, choose Plain Text format to send mail and news messages.

Compose tab   Lets you specify the fonts you use to create messages, the stationery for HTML messages, and whether Outlook Express should include your business card with new messages. Click the Edit button to create or edit your business card.

Signatures tab   Allows you to create and configure a signature that signs each outgoing message.

Spelling tab   Allows you to specify settings for spell-checking your messages and to specify language and custom dictionaries used.

Security tab   Lets you configure virus protection and security zone settings for Internet Explorer and messaging. Also allows you to obtain and manage digital IDs, and to specify whether you want to encrypt and digitally sign outgoing messages.

Connection tab   Contains options for configuring dial-up and Internet connection settings.

Maintenance tab   Configures how you want Outlook Express to handle message cleanup. The Cleaning Up Messages section includes such options as "Empty messages from the Deleted Items folder on exit" and "Compact messages in the background." There is also an option to create error log files for troubleshooting purposes. If you select this option, the error log appears in your message store folder and is named pop3.txt.

Creating Mail Message Rules

To keep incoming messages organized, you can create message rules. For example, you can create rules that automatically:

- Move certain messages to certain folders

- Highlight messages from specific senders

- Automatically forward messages from certain senders to other people

To create a rule that will be applied automatically to all incoming messages, follow these steps:

1. Choose Tools ➤ Message Rules ➤ Mail. If no other message rules exist, the New Mail Rule dialog appears.

NOTE   If at least one other rule already exists, the Message Rules dialog appears. Select New to display the New Mail Rule dialog.

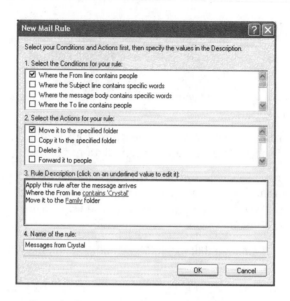

2. In list box number 1, check one or more conditions for the rule you want to create. For example, you can choose Where The From Line Contains People and Where The Message Is Marked As Priority. When you check a condition, a description for the rule appears automatically in list box number 3.

3. In list box number 2, check one or more the actions to perform if the conditions you selected in the preceding step are met. For example, you can move the message or messages to a specific folder, delete the message, or forward the message to another recipient.

4. In list box number 3, click each hyperlink to configure more specific details about the conditions and actions. For example, you may need to specify the names of the senders that apply to the rule, or the folder to which you want to move the messages.

TIP If you have multiple conditions, click the And link to open the And/Or dialog, where you can specify whether a message must match *all* of the criteria (AND) or *any one* of the criteria (OR).

WARNING You must specify details for each condition and action; otherwise, you won't be able to save the rule.

5. In text box number 4, type a name for the rule.

6. Click OK. The Message Rules dialog displays the name and rule description for the rule you just created. Here you can create another rule; modify, copy, or remove existing rules; and change the order of rules.

7. If you want to apply your new rule to messages that already exist in your Outlook Express folders, click Apply Now (otherwise, click OK to exit the Message Rules dialog). In the Apply Mail Rules dialog, select the rule(s) you want to apply. Browse to the folder where you want to apply them and, again, click Apply Now. Click OK, and then click Close.

Blocking Senders

Outlook Express also lets you choose *not* to receive messages from specific e-mail addresses, or newsgroup messages posted by specific individuals by blocking senders. For example, you can block e-mail addresses that are known for "spamming" (sending junk e-mail to an endless number of recipients). When you receive a message from a blocked sender, Outlook Express automatically moves the message to the Deleted Items folder, keeping your Inbox uncluttered.

To block a sender, perform these steps:

1. Choose Tools ➤ Message Rules ➤ Blocked Senders List. The Message Rules dialog opens to the Blocked Senders tab.

2. Click Add. The Add Sender dialog opens.

3. Type the e-mail address or domain name you want to block in the Address text box.

4. Check the appropriate radio button to block mail, news, or both.

5. Click OK to return to the Blocked Senders tab. The new blocked e-mail address appears in the list of blocked senders. Verify that the information is correct and click OK.

TIP An alternative method for blocking senders is to select a message in any folder and choose Message ➤ Block Sender. The message sender's e-mail address is then automatically added to the Blocked Senders list.

Watching and Grouping Conversations

Outlook Express lets you keep track of conversations (the original message and replies) by either "watching" or grouping conversations.

 When you choose to watch a conversation, Outlook Express marks all new messages pertaining to that conversation with a Watch icon (a pair of eyeglasses). This visual indicator helps you easily identify the messages and threads that you feel are important to monitor.

To watch a conversation, perform these steps:

1. Choose View ➤ Columns.

2. Select Watch/Ignore to turn on the Watch/Ignore column and click OK.

TIP You have to turn this column on separately for each folder in which you want to watch conversations.

3. Select a message.

4. Choose Message ➤ Watch Conversation. The Watch icon appears next to all messages pertaining to that thread.

TIP Outlook Express highlights messages in watched conversations with red text by default. To change the color, choose Tools ➤ Options and select the Read tab. Choose your highlight color from the Highlight Watched Messages drop-down list.

It is easier for you to track conversations when you group all messages in a conversation together. To group messages, choose View ➤ Current View ➤ Group Messages by Conversations. After you group your messages, a plus sign appears to the left of the original message in the conversation. To see the replies, click the plus sign to expand the grouped conversation. To collapse the conversation, click the minus sign.

See also Address Book, Internet Explorer, Network and Internet Connections, New Connection Wizard

Paint

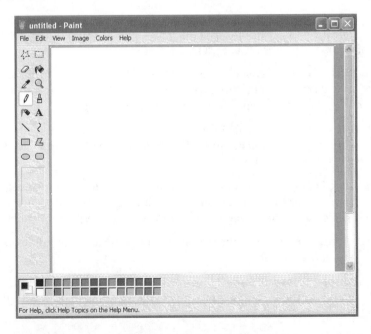 Paint   Allows you to create black-and-white, grayscale, or color drawings, which you can paste into other documents, print, or use as Windows XP backgrounds. Paint allows you to open BMP, JPG, GIF, EMF, WMF, TIF, PNG, and ICO images, and save BMP, DIB, JPG, GIF, TIF, and PNG images.

To open Paint, choose Start ➤ All Programs (or Start ➤ Programs in the Classic Start menu) ➤ Accessories ➤ Paint.

The Paint window consists of a menu bar at the top of the window, a toolbox at the left side of the window, and a main drawing area. It also contains a color palette and status bar at the bottom of the window.

Toolbox

The Paint toolbox consists of many buttons that activate drawing tools, such as a pencil, brush, and magnifier. When you click a toolbox button to activate a drawing tool, additional selections may appear in the field beneath the toolbox. For example, when you activate the Brush tool, Paint displays a variety of brush-strokes from which you can choose.

Click a toolbox button to activate the tool. Select additional options, such as stroke width or shape, from the options area. Select foreground and background colors from the color palette at the bottom of the interface, or choose Colors ➢ Edit Colors to create custom colors. Then drag the mouse in the drawing area to create strokes, lines, and shapes in your image window.

TIP When drawing, "left-drag" indicates you should press and hold the left mouse button, then drag the mouse to form a line or shape. "Right-drag" is the same action with the right mouse button.

You can use the tools in the Paint toolbox to perform the following functions:

Free-Form Select Select an irregularly shaped portion of the drawing, using an opaque or transparent background. You can cut or copy the selection to the Clipboard or move it to another area in the drawing.

Select Select a rectangular portion of the drawing, using an opaque or transparent background. You can cut or copy the selection to the Clipboard or move it to another area in the drawing.

Eraser/Color Eraser Erase a portion of the drawing, using one of several eraser shapes. When you erase, the Eraser removes existing colors and replaces them with the current background color.

Fill with Color Fill portions of the drawing. Left-click to fill an area with the current foreground color; right-click to fill an area with the current background color.

Pick Color Pick a color from the drawing and use it for subsequent line or shape drawing. Useful for matching colors within drawings. Left-click to pick up a foreground color; right-click to pick up a background color.

Magnifier Change the magnification of the drawing, using one of several magnification strengths.

Pencil Draw a free-form line with a width of one pixel. Left-drag to draw with the current foreground color; right-drag to draw with the current background color.

Brush   Draw a brush stroke using one of several brush shapes and sizes. Left-drag to draw with the current foreground color; right-drag to draw with the current background color.

Airbrush   Draw with an airbrush using one of several airbrush sizes. Left-drag to draw with the current foreground color; right-drag to draw with the current background color.

Text   Add text to the drawing, using an opaque or transparent background. Your current foreground color determines the color of the text, and the current background color determines the color of the text box. To create a text box, click inside the drawing area. Drag the mouse pointer to determine the width of the text box. Release the mouse button to choose the font, font size, and font style from the Text toolbar. Then enter your text in the text box.

NOTE   The text box remains active until you choose another tool from the toolbox.

Line   Draw a straight line, using one of several line widths. Left-drag to use the current foreground color; right-drag to use the current background color.

Curve   Draw a curved line, using one of several line widths. Left-drag to use the current foreground color; right-drag to use the current background color. To draw a curved line, draw a straight line with the Curve tool. Then click anywhere on the line and drag the mouse to create the curve. You can select another point on the line and drag again to change the shape of the curve.

Rectangle   Draw a rectangle, using one of several fill styles. The outline of the rectangle uses the current foreground color; the rectangle is filled with the current background color.

Polygon   Draw a polygon, using one of several fill styles. The outline of the polygon uses the current foreground color; the polygon's fill uses the current background color. To create a polygon, draw a straight line, then click where you want the next line to end. Continue in this manner until you nearly complete the shape. When you double-click to complete your polygon, Paint automatically connects the end of the current line to the start of the first line.

Ellipse   Draw an ellipse, using one of several fill styles. The outline of the ellipse uses the current foreground color; its fill uses the current background color.

Rounded Rectangle   Draw a rectangle with rounded edges, using one of several fill styles. The outline of the rounded rectangle uses the current foreground color, and its fill uses the current background color.

Line Width   Select one of five different line widths to draw your objects.

Color Palette

Two overlapping squares appear at the left of the color palette. The front square represents your foreground color (black by default), and the back square represents your background color (white by default).

To choose new colors for strokes, lines and shapes, click the foreground or background color square. Then select a color from the color palette. You can select colors before or after you choose a drawing tool.

TIP   To select colors without first selecting the foreground or background color square, left-click the color palette to choose the fill color, and right-click to choose the outline color.

Menus

The Paint menus contain many standard Windows options as well as some that are unique to Paint; the unique ones are described here.

File Menu

From Scanner or Camera   Opens the Scanner and Camera Wizard, which allows you to obtain images from your scanner or camera.

Set as Background (Tiled)   Allows you to use the current drawing as a tiled background for your Desktop.

Set as Background (Centered)   Allows you to use the current drawing as a centered background for your Desktop.

View Menu

The main options on the View menu show or hide the named element (the toolbox, color palette, status bar, and Text toolbar).

Zoom   Allows you to choose various zoom options from a submenu. Options include Normal Size, Large Size, and Custom. The Show Grid command displays a "graph-paper" grid over the selected drawing area, and the Show Thumbnail command displays a selected portion of the drawing as a thumbnail.

NOTE   The Grid and Show Thumbnail options are active only if the drawing is zoomed to a size other than normal.

View Bitmap   Displays a full-screen preview of your current image. Press any key or click anywhere in the bitmap to return to the Paint window.

Image Menu

Flip/Rotate   Opens a dialog where you can flip the selection or image horizontally or vertically, or rotate the selection or image clockwise by a 90, 180, or 270 degrees.

Stretch/Skew   Opens a dialog where you can stretch or skew a selection or image horizontally, vertically, or by a percentage you specify.

Invert Colors   Changes the colors of a selection or image to their complementary colors.

Attributes   Opens a dialog where you can adjust the width and height of the drawing; specify its measurements in inches, centimeters, or pixels; and specify whether to use black and white or colors. You can also choose a color to represent transparency. Click Default to return to the default settings.

Clear Image   Replaces all colors in an image or selection with the current background color. You can restore it by choosing Edit ➢ Undo.

Draw Opaque   Toggles opaque or transparent drawing. Opaque drawing covers the existing image; transparent drawing allows the underlying image to show through.

Colors Menu

Edit Colors   Opens a dialog where you can create custom colors.

See also   Image Preview

Password Reset Wizard

See   Forgotten Password Wizard

Performance

MMC snap-ins that display system performance data as graphs and lets you configure alerts and data logs. To open Performance, choose Start ➤ Control Panel (or Start ➤ Settings ➤ Control Panel in the Classic Start menu) ➤ Performance and Maintenance ➤ Administrative Tools, and then double-click Performance.

Performance contains two MMC console snap-ins: System Monitor and Performance Logs and Alerts.

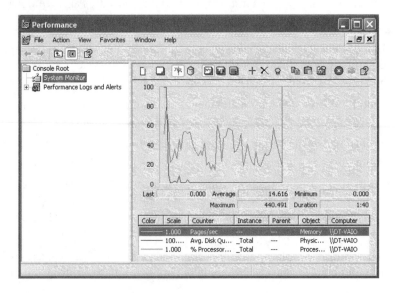

TIP   You can also access Performance Logs and Alerts through Computer Management in Administrative Tools. You'll find it under System Tools in the console tree.

System Monitor

The System Monitor snap-in displays system performance in one of three views: graph, histogram, or report. It displays performance counters that track several different performance objects, including such items as Browser, Cache, Indexing Service, Memory, Network Interface, and Processor, to name but a few. The counters that appear depend on the performance objects you select.

Adding and Viewing Performance Counters

In order to view performance information, you need to add one or more counters that track a performance object. To make your choices, select System Monitor in the console tree, and then follow these steps:

1. Right-click anywhere in the Details pane and choose Add Counters, or click the Add button (+) on the toolbar. The Add Counters dialog appears.

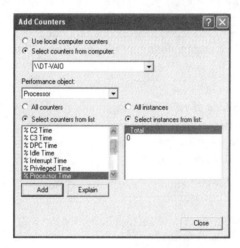

2. Check Select Counters from Computer, and choose the computer from the drop-down list.

3. Use the Performance Object drop-down list to select the object you want to monitor.

4. Check the All Counters radio button to display all available counters for the performance object, or check the Select Counters from List radio button and choose the counter or counters you want to display.

TIP If you're not sure which counter to add, select a counter and click Explain for a description.

5. Click the Add button. System Monitor adds the specified counters to the Details pane.

6. To add additional counters, select counters from the list and click the Add button. Continue in this fashion until you add all the counters you want to view.

7. Choose the All Instances radio button to display all instances, or choose the Select Instances from List to choose specific instances from the list.

8. Click Close.

The System Monitor assigns a different color to each counter so that you can distinguish it in the graph. The list of counters and their color assignments appear in a legend below the graph. The legend also displays the counter scale, counter name, instance, parent, object, and computer. When you select a counter from the legend, the value bar beneath the graph displays last, average, minimum, maximum, and duration values for the selected counter.

Managing Counters and Displays

Highlighting counters When you include many counters in the System Monitor, it might be difficult to view a specific counter. Click the Highlight button to display the selected counter with a bold black line.

Deleting counters Clicking the Delete button removes the selected counter from the legend.

Resetting counters To remove all counters and start over, click the New Counter Set button.

Viewing a histogram To change the view to histogram, click the View Histogram button.

Viewing a report To change the view to report, click the View Report button.

Clearing the display To clear the display for the current counters, click the Clear Display button.

Stopping and starting the display To stop the counters temporarily, click the Freeze Display button. To continue the counters, click this button again.

Refreshing the display After you stop the counters, the Update Data button allows you to display the most current data. Click this button to refresh the display to the most current data.

Viewing data from a log file To display data from a log file instead of the current activity, click the View Log Data button and open the desired log.

Changing System Monitor Properties

To customize the System Monitor, right-click System Monitor in the Details pane and choose View ➤ Customize from the shortcut menu. The Customize View dialog allows you to show or hide the console tree, Action and View menus, standard toolbar, status bar, description bar, taskpad navigation tabs, and Menu and Toolbars snap-ins.

Performance Logs and Alerts

The Performance Logs and Alerts MMC snap-in allows you to configure performance-related logs and alerts. Two log types exist: counter logs and trace logs.

To start logging, right-click a log or alert and choose Start, or choose Action ➤ Start. A green icon indicates a log or alert that is started.

To stop logging, right-click a log or alert and choose Stop, or choose Action ➤ Stop. A red icon indicates a log that is stopped.

To delete a log or alert, select it from the Details pane, and click the Delete button on the toolbar.

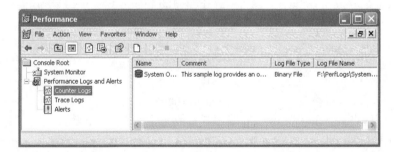

Counter Logs

Counter logs allow you to obtain information from System Monitor counters and record the information in a log. Counter logs record all activity that takes place during a specified period, or when you manually run the counter log. To create a counter log, follow these steps:

1. Select Counter Logs in the console tree.

2. Right-click anywhere in the Details pane and choose New Log Settings.

3. In the New Log Settings dialog, enter a name for the log and click OK. A new dialog appears for the log.

4. On the General tab, click Add Counters to open the Add Counters dialog. Use the steps discussed earlier in the "Adding and Viewing Performance Counters" subsection to add counters for your new log.

5. Use the Log Files tab to specify a log file type and path, configure auto-naming options, add comments, or enable/disable overwriting of previous log files.

6. Use the Schedule tab to schedule run times for the new log, or to disable scheduling and run the log whenever you choose.

7. Click OK to exit the new log dialog. If you are prompted to create a new folder, click OK. The new log appears in the Details pane. To view the data in the log, use System Monitor's View Log Data button.

Trace Logs

Trace logs record data only when activity occurs, such as a process creation/deletion, disk I/O operation, or page fault. To create a new trace log, follow these steps:

1. Select Trace Logs in the console tree.

2. Right-click anywhere in the Details pane and choose New Log Settings.

3. In the New Log Settings dialog, enter a name for the log and click OK. A new dialog appears.

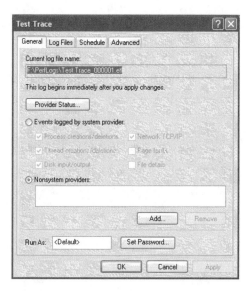

4. Use the General tab to specify events that are logged by the system provider, or add non-system providers to the list. Click the Provider Status button to select a provider, which might include the Windows Kernel Trace Provider (system provider), Active Directory: Kerberos, Active Directory: NetLogon, Active Directory: SAM, Local Security Authority (LSA), and others.

TIP You can use each system or nonsystem provider in only one trace log at a time.

5. Use the Log Files tab to specify a log file type and path, configure auto-naming options, add comments, or enable/disable overwriting of previous log files.

6. Use the Schedule tab to schedule run times for the new log, or to disable scheduling and run the log whenever you choose.

7. Use the Advanced tab to specify buffer sizes and the minimum and maximum number of buffers to use. You can also specify the number of settings at which data is transferred from the buffers to the log file.

8. Click OK to create the log. Use System Monitor's View Log Data button to view the data in the log file.

PERFORMANCE

Alerts

Alerts allow you to send messages, run programs, or start a log when a counter value equals, exceeds, or is less than the value specified in the alert setting.

To create a new alert, follow these steps:

1. Select Alerts in the console tree.

2. Right-click anywhere in the Details pane and choose New Alert Settings.

3. In the New Alert Settings dialog, enter a name for the alert and click OK. A new dialog appears.

4. In the General tab, add a comment for the alert. Click Add Counters to open the Add Counters dialog. Use steps discussed earlier in the "Adding and Viewing Performance Counters" subsection to add counters for your new log. Then specify when you want System Monitor to trigger the alert and how frequently it should sample the data.

5. Use the Action tab to select the action that occurs when an alert is triggered, such as logging an entry in the application event log, sending a message to a user you specify, starting a performance log, or running a program.

6. Use the Schedule tab to schedule run times for the new log, or to disable scheduling and run the log whenever you choose. You can also start a new scan automatically after the previous scan is completed.

7. Click OK to create the log. Use System Monitor's View Log Data button to view the data in the log file.

Creating New Logs and Alerts from Saved Files

You can save logs and alerts as HTML files and then use them to create other logs and alerts. Right-click the log or alert, choose Save Settings As. Enter a name for the HTML file, then click Save. To use the saved file to create a new log or alert, right-click anywhere in a blank area of the Details pane and choose New Log Settings From or New Alert Settings From. Then select the applicable HTML file and click Open.

See also   Computer Management, Microsoft Management Console

Performance and Maintenance

Control Panel category that provides access to administrative tools, scheduled tasks, system configurations, and power options. Also displays tasks that allow you to free up space on your hard drive, rearrange your hard disk so that programs start more quickly, change performance settings, and restore your system.

See also   Administrative Tools, Disk Cleanup, Disk Defragmenter, Performance, Power Options, Scheduled Tasks, System, System Restore

Permissions

WINDOWS XP PROFESSIONAL   Setting permissions is a feature of Windows XP Professional only.

Windows XP Professional feature that allows you to grant access permissions to users or groups when they access objects or object properties. The permissions you can assign depend on the object type, and can include the following:

- Change Owner
- Delete
- Full Control
- Modify
- Read
- Read and Execute
- Write
- Special Permissions

NOTE For detailed information on available permissions, see the "Permissions and user rights" topic in Windows XP Professional Help and Support Center. This entry also provides more detailed information on other permissions-related information.

Explicit and Inherited Permissions

You can assign permissions directly to an object (an explicit permission) or inherit permissions from a parent object (inherited permission). Windows XP Professional assigns explicit permissions when you first create an object. An administrator can manually assign explicit permissions.

By default, Windows XP Professional assigns inherited permissions to any objects that you create in a container object. For example, if you create a folder called Data and later create subfolders and files in the Data folder, the subfolders and files inherit the permissions of the original Data folder (unless you change them individually). The Data folder uses explicit permissions, and the subfolders and files in the Data folder use inherited permissions.

See also Help and Support Center

Personalized Menus

Windows XP feature that displays Start Menu programs and documents that you most frequently and most recently accessed. You can disable this feature to display all menu items, or change the number of items that appear in the menus.

TIP To access programs that do not appear in personalized menus, choose Start ➤ All Programs, and click the down arrow at the bottom of the menu to display additional programs.

To change personalized start menu options, follow these steps:

1. Right-click the Start button and choose Properties. The Taskbar and Start Menu Properties dialog opens to the Start Menu tab.

2. Click the Customize button to open the Customize Start Menu dialog.

3. Use the General tab to specify the number of frequently used programs that appear in the start menu. You can enter any number between and including 0 through 9. Click the Clear List button to remove existing programs from the list.

4. Use the Advanced tab to enable or disable the Show Most Recently Used Documents feature. Click the Clear List button to remove existing documents from the list.

See also   Taskbar and Start Menu

Phone and Modem Options

Allows you to configure modem properties and telephone dialing rules. Modem properties determine the configuration of the modem, while dialing rules specify how Windows dials the phone numbers for the locations you identify.

To configure phone and modem options, choose Start ➤ Control Panel (or Start ➤ Settings ➤ Control Panel in the Classic Start menu) ➤ Network and Internet Connections. From the See Also list in the left pane, click the Phone and Modem Options link to open a dialog with three tabs: Dialing Rules, Modems, and Advanced.

Dialing Rules Tab

Used to add, edit, or delete dialing locations (the areas from which you are dialing). You can also specify dialing rules for each location that appears in the Locations list box.

When you add or edit a location, you configure the dialing rules in a dialog that consists of three tabs: General, Area Code Rules, and Calling Card.

General tab Allows you to specify the name of the location, the country/region from which you are calling, and the area code for the location. In the Dialing Rules section, enter the numbers that you dial to reach an outside line for local or long-distance calls, or the carrier code that you use to place long-distance or international calls. To disable call waiting, check the To Disable Call Waiting option and enter the number that you dial to disable this feature with your phone service.

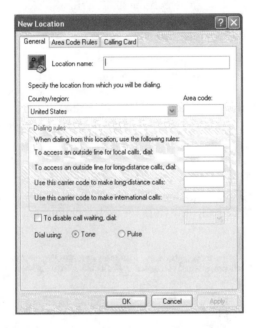

Area Code Rules tab Lists rules for the area codes that you use (including your own area code). Click New to open the dialog where you specify an area code, specific prefixes if needed, any numbers that you dial before you dial the area code (such as 1 for a long-distance call), and whether you include the area code when you dial the phone numbers. Click OK to finish. Your new rule appears in the Area Code Rules list box.

Calling Card tab   Allows you to specify the calling cards you use. Select a calling card type from the list of predefined card types, or click New to open the dialog where you create a new entry for the list. To use a predefined card type, specify your account number and PIN number.

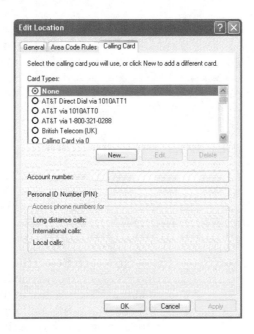

Modems Tab

Used to view the modems on your computer or to view and change their properties. You can also add or remove modems.

Select a modem and click Properties to open the Modem Properties dialog. This dialog contains seven tabs: General, Modem, Diagnostics, Advanced, Driver, Resources, and Power Management.

General tab   Displays modem information such as device type, manufacturer, location, and current status. Click the Troubleshoot button to diagnose problems that appear in the status area. Use the Device Usage drop-down list to enable or disable the modem.

Modem tab   Allows you to adjust the volume of your modem speaker, select the maximum port speed, and enable or disable the dial tone before you dial.

Diagnostics tab   Allows you to run diagnostics on the modem to see if it is functioning properly. Click Query Modem to send standard AT commands to the modem. The responses from the modem appear in the lower list box. Check the Append to Log option to append new log information to an existing log file, or uncheck the option (default) to overwrite the existing log file. Click the View Log button to view the log file.

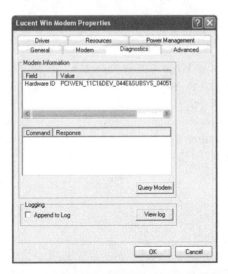

Advanced tab   Allows you to specify additional modem initialization commands. These commands are sent after the commands you previously configured, and override the other settings. Enter the extra commands in the Extra Settings field.

Click the Change Default Preferences to change the default preferences for your modem, such as disconnecting calls if the computer is idle after a specified period or stopping the call if your modem cannot connect within a specified period. Additional options depend on your hardware but typically include data connection preferences (port speed, data protocol, compression, flow control) and hardware settings (data bits, parity, stop bits, modulation).

The Advanced tab may also display an Advanced Port Settings button for some modems. Click this button to configure these settings, which vary depending on your hardware.

Power Management tab   Allows you to enable or disable the "wake up" feature of your modem. When enabled, your computer wakes up from standby mode when your modem receives an incoming call. When disabled, your computer remains in standby mode and the modem does not respond to the call.

NOTE   The Driver and Resources tabs in the Modem Properties dialog contain the same information that you find in most other device properties dialogs. For a description of the features and options you see in these two dialogs, and to learn how to view device properties from within the device manager, refer to the main topic "Device Manager."

Advanced Tab

Used to view telephony drivers installed on the computer, configure any installed driver, and add and remove drivers.

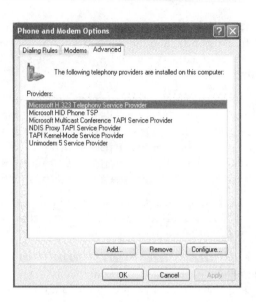

See also   Device Manager, System

Photo Printing Wizard

Allows you to print photos and images from your My Pictures folder. To open the Photo Printing Wizard, choose Start ➢ My Pictures. Open the folder that contains the pictures you want to print. Then, choose Print Pictures from the Printer Tasks pane on the left side of the screen.

The Photo Printing Wizard prompts you to select a printer and paper size. Next, you select the type of pictures that you want to print. Most standard photo sizes are available, ranging from 8×10 to contact sheets, and you can also print a full-size image. After you complete the steps in the wizard, your printer prints the photo or image.

Portable Device

See   Windows Media Player

Power Options

Provides settings that reduce the amount of power that your computer consumes. Conserving energy is becoming ever more important, both from an environmental and a cost-savings perspective. Power Options help you conserve valuable resources, such as the electricity you use to run your desktop computer or the batteries on your laptop computer. In the latter case, Power Options can extend the amount of time you use your laptop while you run it on battery power. The options you configure depend on your hardware and system configuration.

To open the Power Options Properties dialog, choose Start ➤ Control Panel (or Start ➤ Settings ➤ Control Panel in the Classic Start menu) ➤ Performance and Maintenance ➤ Power Options. The tabs you see depend on the power management features that your hardware supports. Common tabs include Power Schemes, Advanced, Hibernate, and UPS. If your computer supports advanced power management (which helps reduce battery power consumption and provides battery status information), the Power Options Properties dialog also displays an APM tab.

Power Schemes Tab

Power schemes are preset collections of power-usage settings. Windows XP includes several default power schemes and allows you to create your own custom power schemes. The options you see depend on your hardware and system configuration.

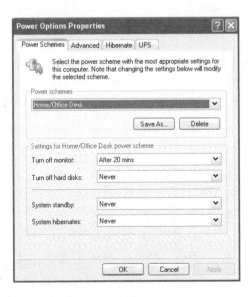

You can specify the amount of idle time that elapses (from never to after five hours) before Windows XP applies power-saving features to your computer hardware. Possible power scheme settings include:

- Placing the system on standby (where it uses less power)

- Placing the system into hibernation

- Turning off the monitor or hard disks (controlled separately)

- Settings for AC and battery power on laptops

WARNING When a computer enters standby mode, Windows XP does not save your open files to disk. If you lose power while you are in standby mode, you may lose unsaved data. Be sure to save your data before you leave your computer idle for an extended period.

TIP If your hardware supports standby, you can also choose Start ➤ Turn Off Computer and then select Standby to manually place the computer on standby.

To apply a power scheme, select a scheme from the Power Schemes drop-down list, and click either the Apply or OK button. To create a new power scheme, select an existing scheme from the Power Schemes list. Modify the settings for the scheme and click the Save As button. To delete a power scheme, select an existing power scheme and click the Delete button.

Advanced Tab

This tab contains advanced power options that depend on your hardware and system configuration. Examples of the options you see are:

- Display or remove a power icon on the taskbar.

- Display a laptop battery usage power meter on the taskbar

- Prompt for a password when the computer comes out of standby mode

You may also be able to configure Windows XP to place your computer on standby when you press the power button on a desktop computer or close the lid on a laptop computer.

Hibernate Tab

This tab is available when your hardware supports hibernation. When your computer enters hibernation mode, Windows XP stores all data from memory onto your hard disk and shuts down the computer. When you bring the computer out of hibernation, Windows XP retrieves the data from the hard disk, opens the necessary programs automatically, and restores your environment to its pre-hibernation state.

Options in the Hibernation tab allow you to enable or disable the hibernation feature. Select the Enable Hibernate Support check box and click the OK or Apply button. Then, choose Start ➤ Turn Off Computer to display the Turn Off Computer dialog. Choose Hibernate to place the computer into hibernation.

The Hibernate tab also displays the amount of disk space required to enter hibernation and the amount of free disk space on your hard disk.

UPS Tab

This tab lets you configure settings for an uninterruptible power supply (UPS). The Status area displays your UPS power source, estimated run-time and capacity, and battery condition. The Details section displays the manufacturer and model of the UPS.

To select your UPS, click the Select button and choose the manufacturer and model of your UPS and the port to which the UPS is connected. Click Finish to add the information to the UPS tab.

To configure UPS settings (such as notifications and alarms), click the Configure button. You can also specify the actions you want Windows to take in case of power failure (such as shutdown), and turn off the UPS after the computer completes the actions.

Printers and Faxes

 Used to manage all aspects of printing. Allows you to add, remove, and share printers; assign permissions; set the default printer; change printer properties; set; view and manage job queues; and pause or cancel printing. You can also set print server properties.

 TIP   See the main topic "Fax Services" elsewhere in this book for information about faxing.

To open the Printers and Faxes folder, choose Start ➤ Control Panel ➤ Printers and Other Hardware ➤ Printers and Faxes. From the Classic Start menu, choose Start ➤ Settings ➤ Printers and Faxes. Alternatively, you can access the Printers folder through My Computer, Windows Explorer, or Control Panel.

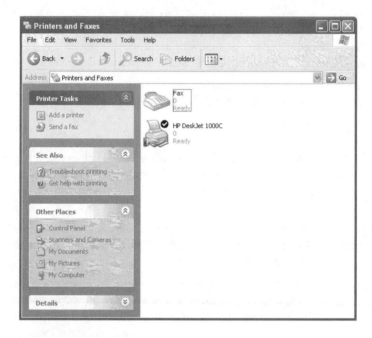

You configure the majority of your printer options through printer properties. You can also use File menu commands or right-click any printer icon to perform some printing-related actions or access configuration pages. For example, you can:

- Set a printer to be the default printer

- Access the printing preferences pages

- Pause printing

- Cancel printing of all documents

- Share a printer

- Use a printer offline

- Create a shortcut to the printer

- Delete or rename the printer

- Access the printer property sheet

- Access the print server property sheet (available only on the File menu)

Adding a New Local Printer

To add a new local printer, follow these steps:

1. From the Printer Tasks area in the left pane, click Add a Printer. The Add Printer Wizard appears. Click Next to continue.

2. Choose the Local Printer radio button, and check or uncheck the option to specify whether you want Windows to automatically detect a Plug and Play printer. If you check the option, click Next and proceed with Step 3. If you do not check the option, click Next and proceed to Step 4.

3. If you selected "Automatically detect and install my Plug and Play printer," Windows XP tries to find the printer.

   - If Windows finds the printer, it adds the printer automatically and returns you to the Printers folder. You can now customize printer settings.

   - If Windows cannot find your printer, it prompts you to click Next to install the printer manually. Click Next to continue.

4. Select the printer port to which your printer connects, or create a new port. Click Next.

5. Select your printer manufacturer and model, then click Next.

NOTE If your printer does not appear in the list, click Have Disk to install the Windows XP–compatible drivers that came with your printer, or click Windows Update to find a list of drivers that are available online.

6. Enter a name for the printer, and check or uncheck the option to use the printer as your default printer for Windows applications. Click Next.

NOTE When you assign a name to your printer, or to a print server that shares printers, limit the name to 31 characters or less. This ensures compatibility with clients and software applications that cannot recognize longer printer names.

7. Specify whether you want to share the printer. If you share the printer, enter a shared printer name, using eight characters or less, followed by a period and three-letter extension if you need to provide Windows 3.*x* or MS-DOS client compatibility. Click Next. If you chose not to share the printer, skip to Step 9.

8. If you share the printer, enter a location for the printer (such as the name of a building or office). You can also add a comment that further identifies the printer (such as Creative Dept. or Executives' Printer). Click Next.

9. Specify whether you want to print a test page. Click Next.

10. Review your choices and settings and click Finish to close the Add Printer Wizard. Windows XP adds the printer to the Printers folder.

TIP In the Printers folder, a check mark appears at the top of the default printer's icon.

Connecting to a Network Printer on Another Computer

To connect to a printer on another computer on your network, follow these steps:

1. From the Printer Tasks area in the left pane, click Add a Printer to start the Add Printer Wizard. Click Next.

2. Click the "A network printer, or a printer attached to another computer" radio button. Click Next.

3. You can find the printer in one of three ways: browse for the printer in your network folder, enter the qualified name of the printer (such as \\server-1\hp_laserjet), or enter the URL for a printer that is located on the Internet or your company or home network. Enter any necessary information, and click Next. If you specified the printer's name or URL, skip to step 5.

4. If you chose to browse for the printer, the Browse for Printers screen appears. Select the printer you want to use from the list of shared printers, or enter the printer name in the text box. As you select the printer, information in the lower portion of the window displays the comments for the printer, the printer status, and the number of documents that are waiting to be printed. After you select the printer, click Next.

5. Specify whether you want this printer to be the default printer for Windows programs. Click Next.

6. Review your choices, then click Finish to close the Add Printer Wizard.

NOTE When you use the Add Printer Wizard, some steps might be different if settings for certain group policies are different from their defaults.

Printer Properties

Right-click the appropriate printer icon and choose Properties. The Properties dialog has seven tabs for configuring different aspects of the printer: General, Sharing, Ports, Advanced, Color Management, Device Settings, and Services. Because each printer has different features and functionality, the options available and features you see on some of these tabs differ from printer to printer.

General tab   Allows you to specify the printer name and location. You can also add comments, such as who typically uses the printer and who to contact if there's a problem. The General tab also displays the printer features, which differ for each printer type and model.

Click the Printing Preferences button to configure settings for page layout and paper source and quality. Click Advanced to configure other advanced printing features. Click the Print Test Page button to verify that the printer is connected and functioning properly. If the test page doesn't print, click the Troubleshoot button, to open the Windows XP Help and Support Center Printing Troubleshooter.

Sharing tab   Allows you to configure the printer as a local computer (not shared) or to share the printer with other users in the network. You can also specify additional printer drivers for those who use a different hardware and/or operating system platforms. The correct drivers download automatically when a computer connects to the printer.

WARNING You can share a printer only if you log on as a member of the Administrators group or if you have Manage Printers permissions.

Ports tab   Allows you to specify, delete, and configure the port to which the printer is attached. You can also enable bidirectional support and printer pooling.

Advanced tab   Allows you to configure advanced options, such as printer availability, logical printer priority, printer drivers, spooling options, printing defaults, print processor options, and separator pages.

Color Management tab   Allows you to automatically or manually select a color profile to use when you print images. You can add or remove color profiles from the list, and select a default color profile.

Device Settings tab   The options available on this tab depend on the capabilities and functions of your printer. Use this tab to view and manage printer-specific settings. Some examples include:

- Assigning forms to specific paper trays
- Substituting unavailable fonts with available fonts
- Setting printer-specific installation options, such as the amount of installed memory

Refer to your printer documentation for specific settings and their values.

Services tab   The availability of this tab depends on the printer you have installed. This tab can include service options such as aligning or cleaning print cartridges on inkjet printers.

NOTE To change printer properties, you must be the creator of the printer, or log on as a computer administrator or member of the Administrators or Power Users group, or have Manage Printers permissions.

Sharing a Printer

You must share a computer in order for the printer to be accessible to other users on your network. To share a printer, right-click it in the Printer and Faxes window and choose Properties. Then select the Sharing tab in the Printer Properties dialog.

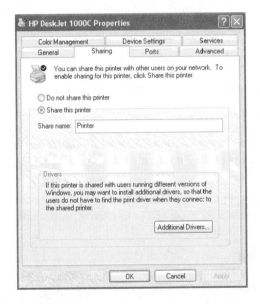

To share the printer, check the Share This Printer radio button and enter a name for the shared printer in the Share Name field (this can be different from the printer name). The name should consist of no more than eight characters, followed by a period and three-letter extension if you need to provide Windows 3.*x* or MS-DOS client compatibility. The name you enter appears when other users browse the network in My Network Places and Windows Explorer.

If you need to provide support for older versions of Windows (such as Windows NT 3.5 or 4, Windows 95 or 98) or for different hardware platforms, click the Additional Drivers button. Select the appropriate hardware and OS version, and click OK to install the drivers. When users connect to the printer, their workstation downloads the correct drivers.

> **TIP** Windows 95 and 98 workstations download the driver only when the workstation connects to the printer the first time. You need to manually install newer drivers on these platforms when you update your printer driver. Windows 3.x, NT 4, and 2000 clients automatically download driver updates.

Printing Documents

There are several ways to print documents with Windows XP. To send a print job to your default printer, use one of the following methods:

- Open the document in any Windows application and click the Print icon.

- In Windows Explorer, My Documents, My Computer, or My Network Places, select a file or files. Right-click the selection and choose Print, or choose File ➤ Print.

- Drag and drop one or more selected files to a printer in the Printers folder, or to a printer shortcut on the Desktop.

To print a document to a printer that is not your default printer, open the document in the applicable Windows application (for example, open Microsoft Word to open a Word document). Choose File ➤ Print in the application to open the Print dialog. Select the printer that you want to print to, and click the Print button to print.

Once you click the Print button to print your document, Windows XP sends it to a print queue on your local computer or on the print server. The document stays in the queue until it is printed.

The Print Dialog

The tabs in the Print dialog vary depending on your printer's capabilities (specified through the printer driver). What follows are examples of tabs and settings you commonly see in the Print dialog. Other printer-specific tabs and settings may be available for your printer. Click Apply to save any changes you make on these tabs without closing the dialog.

Choose the printer you want to print to and whether you want to print to a file (the default is printing to a printer). You can search for printers and view the status of the currently selected printer. You can print the entire document, the selected portion of a document, the current page, or a specific range of pages. You can also specify the number of copies you want to print and whether the printer should collate the copies.

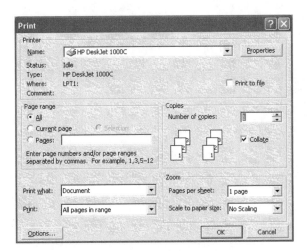

Click the Properties button in the Print dialog to configure layout and paper options for your document. The Properties dialog displays two tabs: Layout and Paper/Quality. In either tab, click the Advanced button to open the Advanced Options dialog; the settings you find in this dialog are printer-specific.

Layout tab   Used to make document layout choices. Examples are orientation, print order, and pages per sheet.

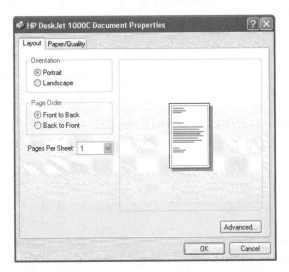

Paper/Quality tab   Allows you to select the paper source and media type. Options vary depending on the capabilities of your printer. Refer to your printer documentation for more information about specific settings.   **281**

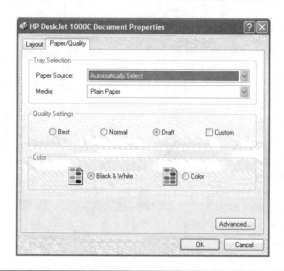

 TIP You can also access printing preference tabs using one of these other methods: right-click any printer icon and choose Printing Preferences; or click the Printing Preferences button on the General tab of the Printer Properties dialog.

Print Queue

The Print Queue stores print jobs from the time a user sends a document to the printer until after they have printed. You can use the print queue to manage and view the status of print jobs. Double-click a printer icon in the Printers folder to access the print queue for the selected printer.

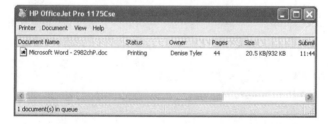

The print queue dialog displays the following information for every print job in the queue:

Document Name The name of the document that is currently printing or waiting to be printed.

Status The status of the document (printing, spooling, paused, or error).

Owner The user name of the person who sent the print job.

Pages   The total number of pages in the document (for print jobs that are waiting in the queue), or the number of pages printed and total number of pages for jobs that are currently printing.

Size   Total and printed document size in kilobytes.

Submitted   The time and date when the document was sent to the printer.

Port   The port the printer uses.

The status bar at the bottom of the print queue dialog displays the number of print jobs in the queue.

Use the Printer menu to connect to the printer, set the printer as the default printer, set up printing preferences, pause printing, cancel all documents, configure printer sharing options, use the printer offline, access printer properties, and perform other functions. Most of these functions are also available on the File menu of the Printers folder when you select a printer.

TIP   If you choose to use a printer offline, the printer icon is gray (disabled) in the Printers folder.

Use the Document menu to perform such functions as pausing, resuming, restarting, and canceling the print job and to access document properties.

TIP   You can pause, resume, restart, cancel, and access properties for more than one print job at a time by selecting multiple print jobs and then making your choice from the Document menu.

NOTE   By default, only the creator of a job can manage his or her own print jobs. A user needs Manage Documents permission or administrative privileges in order to manage other people's print jobs.

Document Properties

Contains settings related to the document to be printed. Select a print job in the queue and choose Document ➤ Properties.

The General tab displays the name of the document, its size, number of pages, data type, processor, owner, and the date and time the job was submitted. By default, Windows notifies the owner of the document when the print job is complete, but you can specify that Windows notify a different user by typing the name in the Notify text box. You can move a slider left or right to change the priority of the print job in relation to other print jobs in the queue. Finally, you can specify a time range in which to print the job.

You can also access other printing preference tabs, such as the Layout and Paper/Quality tabs, from the Document Properties dialog.

Print Server

You can designate a Windows XP Home or Professional computer to be a print server, and then add and share printers from it. Print servers do not have to be dedicated as print servers; they can also serve other functions as well.

Users connect to these shared printers as necessary. When a user sends a print job to a shared printer on a print server, it goes into the print queue on the print server. Users can double-click the printer in the Printers folder to view the print queue and determine when their print job is likely to print in relation to the other print jobs in the queue. When errors occur, messages appear on all computers that connect to the printer, allowing problems to be reported and resolved quickly. Finally, the print server receives the print jobs and spools them to the printer, freeing some of the processing from the local computer.

In the Printers folder, choose File ➤ Server Properties to access the Print Server Properties dialog, which has four tabs you can use to configure the print server: Forms, Ports, Drivers, and Advanced.

Forms tab   Lists the printer forms available on the print server and tells you the measurements of each form in either metric or English format. Also allows you to create new forms.

Ports tab   Enables you to view, add, delete, and configure print server ports.

Drivers tab   Enables you to view, add, remove, and update printer drivers and view and configure printer driver properties.

Advanced tab   Enables you to specify the location of the print server's spool folder, as well as log spooler events, such as error, warning, and information events. Allows you to specify whether you want Windows to sound an audible alarm when a remote document encounters an error. Also lets you specify whether you want Windows to send out a notification when a remote document is printed, and whether you want that notification sent to the user or to the computer.

See also   Fax Services

Printers and Other Hardware

Control Panel category that provides access to information and configuration dialogs for printers, faxes, scanners, cameras, game controllers, mice, and keyboards. To open the Printers and Other Hardware category, choose Start ➤ Control Panel (or Start ➤ Settings ➤ Control Panel in the Classic Start menu) and click the Printers and Other Hardware icon.

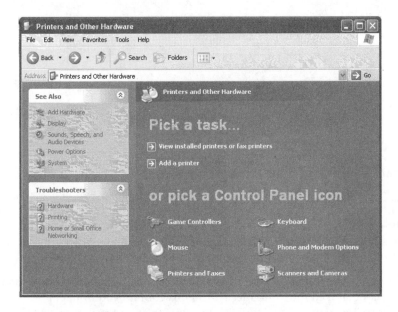

See also   Game Controllers, Keyboard, Mouse, Printers and Faxes, Scanners and Cameras

Private Character Editor

Allows you to create and add new characters to the Unicode character set. You can link characters to a specific font or all fonts. To start Private Character Editor, choose Start ➢ Run, then type **eudcedit** and click OK.

> **NOTE** This feature is recommended for advanced users.

When you first open the Private Character Editor, select a square in the Select Code dialog to assign a Unicode code for the new character. Your choice appears in the Code area below the grid. Click OK to open the Private Character Editor window.

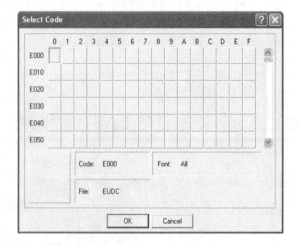

Private Character Editor Window

The Private Character Editor window consists of a toolbar, a guidebar, an Edit window, and menu options. The toolbar has several drawing tools, including Pencil, Brush, Straight Line, Hollow Rectangle, Filled Rectangle, Hollow Ellipse, Filled Ellipse, Rectangular Selection, Freeform Selection, and Eraser. Click a toolbar button to select a tool, then create a new (private) character in the Edit window.

The guidebar, located beneath the menu bar, displays such items as the character set, code, linked font, and file. The menus contain additional options you can use to create new characters. Descriptions follow of the menu options that are specific to Private Character Editor.

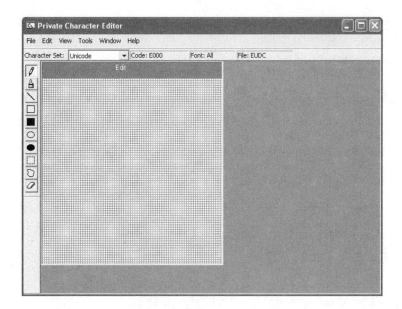

File ➤ Font Links Allows you to link the newly created character with all available fonts or with fonts you select.

Edit ➤ Copy Character Allows you to copy characters from any available font into the Edit window of Private Character Editor. You can then modify the character in the Edit window.

Edit ➤ Select Code Allows you to select a Unicode code for the character you want to create.

Edit ➤ Save Character Saves the current character using the currently selected Unicode code.

Edit ➤ Save Character As Allows you to save the current character using a different Unicode code.

View ➤ Guidebar Shows or hides the guidebar.

View ➤ Toolbar Shows or hides the toolbar.

View ➤ Grid Shows or hides the grid in the Edit window.

View ➤ Next Code Displays the next code in the Edit window.

View ➤ Prev Code Displays the previous code in the Edit window.

View ➤ Show/Hide Outline Displays or removes an outline around the line components of the new character in the Edit window.

287

Tools ➤ Item   Displays a submenu that contains all of the items available in the toolbar, such as Pencil, Brush, and Eraser.

Tools ➤ Flip/Rotate   Allows you to flip the character horizontally or vertically, or rotate the character by 90, 180, or 270 degrees.

Window ➤ Reference   Allows you to select another character from any available font and display the character in a separate Reference window, next to the Edit window. Use the Reference window to compare your newly created character to an already existing character. It helps you make decisions about the size of the character, the thickness of lines, and so forth.

See also   Character Map

Program Compatibility Wizard

Program Compatibility Wizard   Helps you select and test compatibility settings to fix programs that worked correctly on an earlier version of Windows but do not run correctly on Windows XP.

To start the Program Compatibility Wizard, choose Start ➤ All Programs (or Start ➤ Programs in the Classic Start menu) ➤ Accessories ➤ Program Compatibility Wizard. The wizard opens in the Help and Support Center. Click Next to step through the wizard.

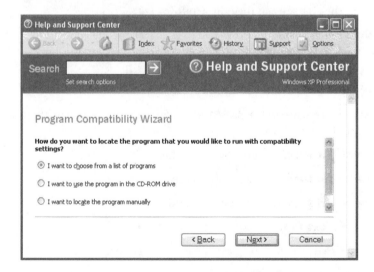

The wizard helps you test programs that are installed on your system or on a CD. During the process, you select items such as the operating system that the program was designed for and the display settings for the software. After you make your selections, the wizard tests the application and asks you whether it started correctly. If so, you can set the program to always use the compatibility settings that you selected in the wizard; otherwise, you can try different compatibility settings or exit the wizard.

Recovery Console

Command-line utility that allows you to perform basic file and disk management commands in the event that you are unable to log in to Windows XP. For example, through the Recovery Console, you can format disks, copy and delete files, create directories, and perform other basic file and folder operations.

You can start the Recovery Console in one of two ways: by booting your computer with the Windows XP CD inserted, or through a Startup menu that appears when you boot up your computer. However, in order to use the second method, you must install the Recovery Console onto your hard disk while Windows XP is running.

Starting the Recovery Console from the CD-ROM

If you are unable to start your computer, you can start the Recovery Console from the Windows CD. The steps are as follows:

1. Insert the Windows XP CD into your CD-ROM drive and turn on or reboot your computer.

2. After your computer reboots, you will be prompted to press any key to boot from the CD. Press any key immediately after this prompt appears. The Windows XP Setup screen appears.

3. At the Setup Notification screen, press Enter.

4. At the Welcome to Setup screen, press **R** to repair a Windows XP installation using Recovery Console.

5. The Windows XP Recovery Console screen appears and lists the paths to the Windows XP installations that are installed on your computer. If you have only one Windows XP installation, enter **1** to repair or recover that

installation. If you have a dual-boot or multiple-boot system, enter the number that corresponds with the installation you want to repair.

6. Enter the Administrator password to log on to the Recovery Console.

Installing the Recovery Console as a Startup Option

You can install the Recovery Console on your computer so that it appears as a startup option in the list of available operating systems when you are unable to start Windows XP during startup. To install the Recovery Console as a startup option, log in to Windows XP as a Computer Administrator or as a member of an Administrator Group. Then complete the following steps:

1. With Windows XP running, insert the Windows XP CD into your CD-ROM drive. When the menu screen appears, click Exit to return to the Windows XP Desktop.

2. Choose Start ➤ All Programs (or Start ➤ Programs in the Classic Start menu) ➤ Accessories ➤ Command Prompt.

3. At the command prompt, type the letter of your CD-ROM followed by a colon (for example, **D:**) to switch to your CD-ROM drive. Enter one of the following commands:

   - To install the Recovery Console for 32-bit computers, enter **\i386\ winnt32.exe /cmdcons**

   - To install the Recovery Console for 64-bit computers, enter **\ia64\ winnt32.exe /cmdcons**

4. The Windows Setup screen asks if you want to install the Recovery Console. Click Yes to continue. After the files are installed, choose OK to complete the setup.

5. Type **exit** at the command prompt to close the Command Prompt window.

NOTE After you reinstall the Recovery Console as a startup option, a Startup menu appears each time you reboot your computer. You are prompted to select your Windows installation or the Recovery Console. If you do not make a selection within 30 seconds, your default Windows XP installation starts automatically.

Using Recovery Console

The Recovery Console provides commands that you can use to perform simple operations. The Recovery Console supports the following commands (which are not case sensitive):

attrib	delete	fixmbr	more
batch	dir	format	net
cd	disable	help	rd
chdir	diskpart	listsvc	ren
chkdsk	enable	logon	rename
cls	exit	map	rmdir
copy	expand	md	systemroot
del	fixboot	mkdir	type

To obtain help for these commands, type **help** followed by the command name (for example, **help diskpart**) at the Recovery Console command prompt.

To exit the Recovery Console, type **exit**.

NOTE A user can run the Recovery Console without logging on. To implement this feature, enable the Automatic Administrative Logon When Using Recovery Console option in the Group Policy snap-in. You can find this attribute in the console tree under Local Computer Policy ➤ Computer Configuration ➤ Windows Settings ➤ Security Settings ➤ Local Policies ➤ Security Options.

Deleting the Recovery Console Startup Option

If you installed the Recovery Console as a Startup option, there are several steps required to remove it from your computer. You will need to remove some hidden system files and folders, and you will also need to edit the BOOT.INI file that appears in your root directory.

WARNING This procedure is not recommended unless you are an advanced Windows XP user. Improper editing of the BOOT.INI file will cause your computer to not boot at all.

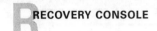

To delete the Recovery Console, follow these steps:

1. Choose Start ➤ My Computer.

2. Double-click the drive onto which you installed the Recovery Console (usually your boot drive).

3. Choose Tools ➤ Folder Options. The Folder Options dialog appears.

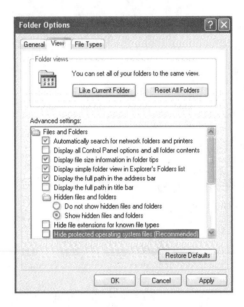

4. Click the View tab. In the Advanced Settings area, locate the Hidden Files and Folders option. Select the Show Hidden Files and Folders radio button.

5. Unselect the Hide Protected Operating System Files check box. Click Yes to respond to the warning that appears.

6. Click OK to exit the Folder Options dialog. You return to the drive folder.

7. Delete *only* the following items in your root directory:

- The cmdcons folder
- The cmldr system file

8. Right-click the BOOT.INI file and choose Properties from the shortcut menu.

9. Unselect the Read-Only check box, and then click OK.

10. Right-click the BOOT.INI file again, and choose Open. The file opens in Notepad.

11. Remove the entry for the Recovery Console. It looks similar to this:

```
c:\cmdcons\bootsect.dat="Microsoft Windows Recovery Console" /cmdcons
```

WARNING When you edit the BOOT.INI file, be sure to *only* delete the entry for the Recovery Console.

12. Save the BOOT.INI file and close Notepad.

13. Right-click the BOOT.INI file, choose Properties from the menu, and select the Read-Only check box. Click OK to exit the Properties dialog.

14. To hide your system files and folders again, repeat Steps 3 through 7, except revert the settings back to their original state.

Recycle Bin

Folder that stores files and folders you deleted from your hard disk until you permanently remove them. It allows you to quickly restore files that you may have deleted in error.

WARNING The Recycle Bin does not store files that are deleted from floppy disks, removable disks (such as a Zip or Jaz disks), or from network drives. Use caution when you delete files from these types of drives, as they are permanently deleted.

NOTE The Recycle Bin is not a substitute for a tape backup system. It is limited in size and only holds the files you most recently deleted.

To open the Recycle Bin, double-click the wastebasket icon on the Desktop. When there are no files in the Recycle Bin, the icon appears as an empty wastebasket. When you delete files from your hard disk (using the Delete key, or through pop-up menus, or by dragging and dropping files to the Recycle Bin), the Recycle Bin icon appears as a full wastebasket to show that it contains files.

NOTE You can also use My Computer or Windows Explorer to browse to and open the Recycle Bin folder.

The Recycle Bin folder displays a list of all the files that you deleted. If you view the Recycle Bin folder in Details view (choose View ➤ Details, or click the Views button on the toolbar and choose Details), you can also see the original location of each file, the date it was deleted, and the type and size of the file.

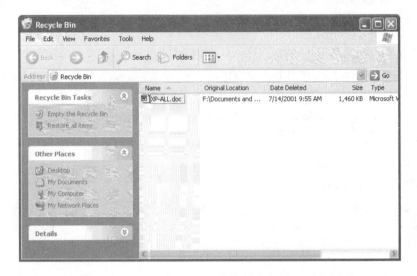

The left pane of the Recycle Bin folder displays two tasks. The first task allows you to empty the recycle bin. The second task allows you restore one or more files to their original location.

Emptying the Recycle Bin

Files that are in the Recycle Bin still take up space on your hard disk. To reclaim that space, you have to delete some files from the Recycle Bin or completely empty the Recycle Bin. As a general rule, you should empty the Recycle Bin once a week. Various methods are available:

- To remove all files when the Recycle Bin window is open, choose the Empty the Recycle Bin icon from the left pane. Alternatively, you can choose File ➤ Empty Recycle Bin from the Recycle Bin menu.

- To delete one or more selected files when the Recycle Bin window is open, select the file or files you want to delete. Choose File ➤ Delete, or right-click the selection and choose Delete.

TIP You can also empty the Recycle Bin from your Desktop. Right-click the Recycle Bin icon and choose Empty Recycle Bin from the shortcut menu.

Restoring a File

When you restore a file, you remove it from the Recycle Bin and move it back to its original location on your hard drive. To restore one or more files, select them in the Recycle Bin. Choose File ➤ Restore, or right-click the selection and choose Restore from the shortcut menu.

TIP You can also restore files using the Restore command in the left pane of the Recycle Bin. This command changes, depending on how many files you select from the Recycle Bin window. With no files selected, click Restore All Items. With one file selected, click Restore This Item. With multiple or all files selected, click Restore the Selected Items.

Changing the Size of the Recycle Bin

Each fixed drive or partition on your computer has its own Recycle Bin. By default, each Recycle Bin is allocated 10 percent of the total space available on its respective hard disk or partition. If you are logged on as a Computer Administrator, you can change the default settings. From your Desktop, right-click the Recycle Bin icon and choose Properties. The Recycle Bin Properties dialog opens to the Global tab. This tab offers two different methods of managing the Recycle Bin:

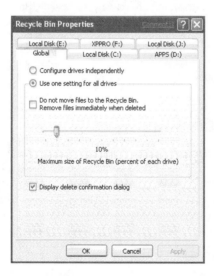

- If you have one or more drives on your system and want to use the same settings on each drive, select the Use One Setting for All Drives radio button. (This is the default option.) Move the Maximum Size of Recycle Bin slider

295

toward the left to decrease the percentage or toward the right to increase the percentage. If you do not want to use the Recycle Bin at all, select the Do Not Move Files to the Recycle Bin check box.

WARNING When you choose the Do Not Move Files to the Recycle Bin option, any files you delete are removed from your system immediately. You don't have a second chance to retrieve them. Use this option with care.

- If your drives or partitions are sized differently, you can configure the space allocated for the Recycle Bin for each drive separately. To apply different settings to each drive on your system, select the Configure Drives Independently radio button. Click the tab that is associated with the drive you want to configure. Adjust the Maximum Size of Recycle Bin slider accordingly, or check the Do Not Move Files to the Recycle Bin box for the selected drive or partition. Repeat these steps for each drive or partition on your system.

If you want to display a confirmation dialog before files are removed from the Recycle Bin, select the Display Delete Confirmation Dialog check box. This option is checked by default.

WARNING Be careful not to make your Recycle Bin too small. If you delete a file that is larger than the Recycle Bin's storage capacity, the file is permanently deleted.

See also Disk Cleanup

Regional and Language Options

Enables you to customize the display of fractional or large numbers, currencies, dates, and times as used in your geographical location. Windows XP also supports the use of multiple languages. You can view or change the languages and methods available to enter text, and allow non-Unicode programs to display menus and dialogs in your native language.

To display the Regional and Language Options dialog, choose Start ➤ Control Panel (or Start ➤ Settings ➤ Control Panel in the Classic Start menu) ➤ Date, Time, Language, and Regional Options. Next, select the Regional and Language Options control panel icon. The Regional and Language Options dialog opens, containing three tabs: Regional Options, Languages, and Advanced.

Regional Options Tab

Select your geographical region here and choose how to format numbers, currencies, times, and short or long dates. You can also select a region for local information such as news and weather.

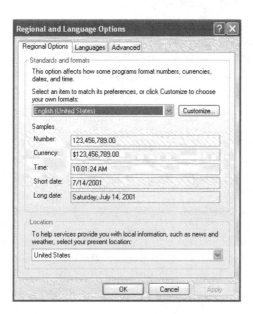

In the Standards and Formats area is a drop-down list where you choose the geographical region that you want to use. By default, this field displays the language option that you selected during Windows XP installation. When you choose another option from the drop-down list, the Samples fields display noneditable examples to show how numbers, currency, time, short date, and long date are formatted in that region. The Location drop-down, at the bottom of the tab, allows you to select a region for local information such as news and weather.

Customizing Regional Options

To customize your regional options, click the Customize button in the Regional Options tab. This opens the Customize Regional Options dialog, which features four tabs: Numbers, Currency, Time, and Date.

Numbers tab Adjust the display of decimal symbols, the number of decimal digits, the digit grouping symbol, digit grouping, the negative sign symbol, negative number format, display of leading zeros, list separators, and the measurement system. As you enter or select new values for each field, the Sample area displays examples for positive and negative numbers.

Currency tab   Adjust the display of the currency symbol, the positive and negative currency formats, the decimal symbol, the number of digits after the decimal, and the digit grouping and digit grouping symbol options. As you enter or select new values for each field, the Sample area displays examples for positive and negative currency values.

Time tab   Adjust the display of times on the clock that appears in the notification area of your taskbar and in related dialog boxes. These times appear in hours (*h, hh, H,* or *HH*), minutes (*mm*), and seconds (*ss*). Use *h* or *hh* to display time in 12-hour format, and *tt* to display A.M. or P.M. Use *H* or *HH* to display time in 24-hour format. This dialog also allows you to enter or select symbols for the time separator, as well as for the A.M. and P.M. symbols. As you enter or select new values for each field, the Sample area displays an example of your customized time values.

Date tab   Adjust the display of dates in dialog boxes and in documents that you create with applications such as Microsoft Word. When you enter a two-digit number for a year (such as 02 for 2002) in any dialog or application that recognizes dates, Windows XP automatically interprets any value starting at 1930 and ending with the value you specify in the ending year field of the Calendar area. In the Short Date area, you can customize the format and separator used to display short dates; the Short Date Sample box displays an example of your customized short date format. In the Long Date area, you can specify how long dates are displayed and see a sample of your customized format.

Languages Tab

Allows you to view or change the languages and methods you use to enter text. The Supplemental Language Support section contains two options:

- Select the Install Files for Complex Script and Right-to-Left languages check box if you want to install Arabic, Armenian, Georgian, Hebrew, Indic, Thai, and Vietnamese language files on your computer. These additional files use approximately 10 MB of disk space.

- Select the Install Files for East Asian languages check box to install additional files for Chinese, Japanese, and Korean language files. These files use approximately 230 MB of disk space.

To configure language services, click the Details button to open the Text Services and Input Languages dialog.

Text Services and Input Languages Dialog

The drop-down list in the Default Input Language area allows you to specify the default language that you use to enter text. This language is used when you start up or log on to your computer.

The Installed Services area displays all language and text services that are installed and loaded into memory when you start your computer. The text services you can select for each language installed on your computer include keyboard layouts, input method editors, and handwriting and speech recognition options. Use this area to add, remove, or check properties for additional language services.

To install additional language services, follow these steps:

1. From the Text Services and Input Languages dialog, click Add. The Add Input Language dialog appears.

2. Use the Input Language drop-down box to select the input language that you want to add.

3. The Keyboard Layout/IME field displays a keyboard layout to correspond with the selection you made in Step 2. You can choose another keyboard layout if you desire.

4. Click OK to return to the Text Services dialog. The new service appears in the Installed Services list.

299

NOTE Language services require computer memory and can affect performance.

NOTE When you install a new language service, Windows XP may prompt you to insert your Windows XP CD to install additional files, and to reboot your computer in order for settings to take effect.

To remove an installed language service, highlight the service you want to remove, and click Remove.

The Preferences area at the bottom of the Text Services and Input Languages dialog allows you to specify options for the language bar. If you have speech recognition, handwriting recognition, or an input method editor installed as a text service, a Language Bar button is available; it opens a dialog that allows you to change the look and behavior of the language bar.

Click the Key Settings button to open the Advanced Key Settings dialog. This dialog allows you to configure the hot key settings that you use to switch between your installed language services and to turn off the Caps Lock function. The default hot key to switch languages is Left Alt+Shift.

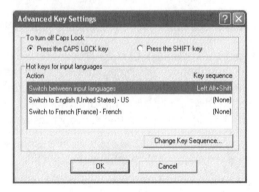

Creating a Document Using Multiple Languages

When you have more than one language service installed on your system, you can create documents that use multiple languages. The following example demonstrates how you can create a multilanguage document in WordPad:

1. Choose Start ➤ All Programs (or Start ➤ Programs in the Classic Start menu) ➤ Accessories ➤ WordPad to open WordPad.

2. Enter text to begin your document in your default language.

3. To switch to another language service, press Left Alt+Shift.

4. Enter the text that you want to display in the alternate language.

5. To return to your original language, or to switch to another language, press Left Alt+Shift again. Select the language you want to use, and enter more text.

NOTE If you distribute your multilanguage document to others, those who read your document must have the same language services installed in order to read it properly.

Advanced Tab

Unicode is a standard encoding scheme that allows computers to display text-based data in almost all of the written languages of the world. The Advanced tab in the Regional and Language Options dialog allows you to display menus and dialogs in their native language within programs that do not support the Unicode standard.

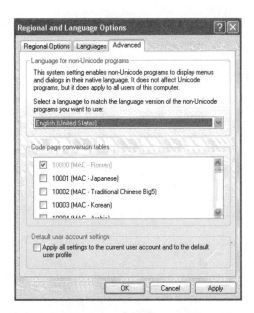

Language for Non-Unicode Programs Use the drop-down menu in this area to select the language of the non-Unicode applications that you want display in their native language. If a language option differs from region to region, you can also specify a localized version of a language. For example, if you are using an older program that was written for French Canadian users, click French (Canada).

Code Page Conversion Tables   These tables allow Windows XP to interpret letters and other characters that a program uses and to display them correctly on your screen. The list displays the available tables, with check marks to the left of tables that are installed. Computer Administrators can install or uninstall code page tables. Click to place a check mark next to additional tables that you want to install, or clear a check mark to remove an installed table.

Default User Account Settings   Select the check box in this area to apply the settings in the Regional and Language Options dialog to your own user account and to all new user accounts that are created on this computer.

See also   Keyboard

Registry

Database that holds all information about your system, such as defaults and properties for folders, files, users, preferences, applications, protocols, devices, and any other resources. Information about program installation and changes are saved in the Registry when you install new applications or hardware, or when you make any changes to your system using Control Panel.

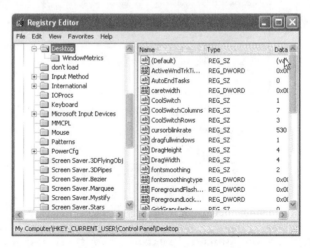

Advanced users can use the Registry Editor to manually edit the Registry. To open the Registry Editor, choose Start ➤ Run, then type **regedit** and click OK.

WARNING You can cause serious problems with your Windows XP installation, such as the system not functioning properly or not functioning at all, if the Registry changes you make are not correct. Do not make any manual changes to the Registry unless you are *very* familiar with how the Registry database works.

Remote Assistance

Subset of Windows XP Help and Support Center. Remote Assistance allows you to connect over the Internet with another Windows XP user that you trust to remotely view and control your computer with your permission.

Choose Start ➢ Help and Support (or press F1 from the Desktop) to open the Help and Support Center window. From the Pick a Task area, click Tools, and then choose Remote Assistance to display the Remote Assistance options in the main pane of the Help and Support Center window.

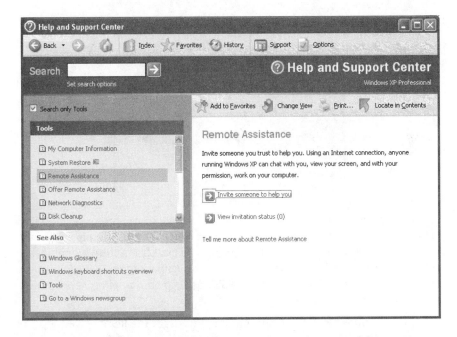

To send an invitation to a trusted Windows XP user, click Invite Someone to Help You. You can send the invitation as an e-mail message, through Windows Messenger, or as a file. Follow additional prompts to complete your invitation.

To view the status of your invitation, click View Invitation Status. This screen displays the status of all invitations that you have sent and allows you to expire, resend, or delete invitations from the list.

See also Help and Support Center, Windows Messenger

Remote Desktop Connection

 Remote Desktop Connection — Allows you to connect to a computer's Desktop from a remote location and to run applications as if you were sitting at its console. Both computers must be running Windows XP, and you must have network access and permissions to connect to the other computer.

TIP To enable a computer to accept remote connections, open the System Properties dialog, click the Remote tab, and select the "Allow remote assistance invitations to be sent from this computer" check box.

To establish a Remote Desktop connection, choose Start ➤ All Programs (or Start ➤ Programs in the Classic Start menu) ➤ Accessories ➤ Communications ➤ Remote Desktop Connection.

Use the Computer field to enter or choose a remote computer for connection, or choose Browse for More from the Computer drop-down list to select from a list of available computers. Then click Connect to establish a connection to the remote computer. Click Cancel to abort the connection and close the Remote Desktop Connection dialog. Click Help to display help on how to use remote Desktop connections.

Click the Options button to display more options for the Remote Desktop Connection dialog. You now see five tabs in the dialog: General, Display, Local Resources, Programs, and Experience.

General Tab

Includes the same Computer drop-down list that appears in the smaller Remote Desktop Connection dialog. In addition, the following options appear:

User Name   Enter your user name to log on to the remote computer.

Password   Enter your logon password in this field if you want to automatically log on to a selected computer.

Domain   Enter the domain name for the remote computer, if applicable.

Save My Password   Check this box if you want Windows XP to automatically log you on with your password.

Save As   Allows you to save the settings for the selected computer. The connection information is saved to the Remote Desktops folder with an RDP extension.

Open   Allows you to open remote Desktop connections that you previously saved to your Remote Desktops folder.

Display Tab

Allows you to configure the Desktop appearance when you log on to a remote computer. You can specify the remote Desktop size and number of colors. (The settings on the remote computer may override this Colors setting and display fewer colors than you select.) The check box at the bottom of the tab allows you to display the connection bar, which lets you manipulate the window and perform functions such as disconnecting when your display is set to full screen.

Local Resources Tab

Allows you to determine how sounds, keyboard combinations, and devices react to your remote connection. The Remote Computer Sound drop-down list allows you to choose how sounds from the remote computer play on your local Desktop. Choose Bring to This Computer, Do Not Play, or Leave at Remote Computer.

The Keyboard list allows you to configure how Windows key combinations (shortcut keys) are handled when you are connected to a remote Desktop. Options are On the Local Computer, On the Remote Computer, and In Full Screen Mode Only.

The check boxes in the Local Devices area allow you to select the devices from your local computer that automatically connect when you are logged on to a remote computer. You can use the check boxes to select disk drives, printers, or serial ports.

Programs Tab

Allows you to start a program when you log on to a remote computer. Select the Start the Following Program on Connection check box to run a specified program when you connect to a remote computer. Use the Program Path and File Name field to enter the path and filename of the program you want to run. Use the Start In the Following Folder field to enter the path to the working directory of the program.

Experience Tab

Choose your connection speed and select additional performance options. You can allow or disallow Desktop background, display the contents of windows while you drag them, use menu and window animation, use themes, and enable or disable bitmap caching.

See also NetMeeting, Windows Messenger

Removable Storage Management

MMC snap-in that lets you manage hardware libraries. Hardware libraries consist both of hardware devices (such as jukeboxes and changers) that can read removable media (for example, tapes and optical discs), and the removable media itself.

Use Removable Storage Management to track, label, and catalog your removable media and to control hardware libraries' physical aspects, such as door, slots, and drives. You can also use Removable Storage Management to clean hardware library drives.

Removable Storage Management complements your backup software, which you would use to manage the physical data contained on your removable media. For further information on removable storage, consult the topic "Removable Storage" in the Windows XP Help and Support Center.

See also   Computer Management, Microsoft Management Console

Restore Down

 Button that appears at the top-right corner of opened windows. Click the Restore Down button to return a window to its original size after you maximize it with the Maximize button.

See also   Close, Maximize and Minimize

Roaming User Profile

WINDOWS XP PROFESSIONAL   Roaming User Profiles is a feature of Windows XP Professional only.

The first time you log on to any computer on your network, Windows XP automatically creates a local user profile and stores it on the computer's local hard disk. The local user profile stores your user preferences on that computer only. When you customize your Desktop environment, display settings, network and printer connections, and other settings, the changes are stored in your local user profile and are specific to the computer on which you made the changes.

Later, if you log on to another computer on the network, Windows XP creates a local user profile that is specific only to that computer. In order to use the same preferences that you configured for the first computer, you must also configure them on the second computer to store them in the local user profile on that computer.

Roaming user profiles allow you to use the same settings on any computer in the network, without having to reenter them into every computer that you use.

Your system or network administrator creates roaming user profiles on the main server, where all roaming user profiles are stored.

When you use your network logon information to log on to any computer in the network, you can choose your local user profile (which you typically use on the computer in your own office) or a roaming user profile (which you typically use when you log on to any other computer in the network). When you choose the latter, the server sends your roaming user profile information to that computer.

When you make changes to a roaming user profile, the changes are updated on the server and are available when you log on to any computer as a roaming user.

To switch between a local user profile and a roaming user profile, follow these steps:

1. Choose Start ➤ Control Panel (or Start ➤ Settings ➤ Control Panel in the Classic Start menu) ➤ Performance and Maintenance, then click System to open the System Properties dialog.

2. On the Advanced tab, in the User Profiles section, click Settings.

3. Under Profiles Stored on This Computer, click the user profile you want to change.

4. Click Change Type. The Change Type dialog appears.

5. Click Local Profile or Roaming Profile.

NOTE If Roaming Profile is not available, this indicates that the only profile is a local user profile.

NOTE When you use a roaming profile on more than one computer simultaneously, the settings used on the last computer that logs off are preserved on the server.

Run

Used to open programs, folders, documents, and Internet resources. Most frequently used to run installation programs. To use this function, follow these steps:

1. Choose Start ➤ Run. The Run dialog appears.

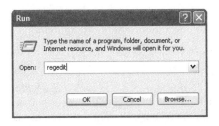

2. In the Open text box, enter the full path and name of the resource you want to open, or use the Browse button to locate the resource on your hard drive. You can also use the drop-down list to select a resource that you previously opened.

3. Click OK to open the resource.

Run As

Used to run a program or MMC tool as a user other than the one currently logged on (for example, as an administrative user). Follow these steps to access the Run As dialog box:

1. In Windows Explorer, select a program you want to run as another user.

2. Hold down the Shift key and right-click.

3. From the shortcut menu, select Run As.

4. In the Run As dialog, select the The Following User radio button.

5. Enter the username and password for the user that you want to run the program as.

6. Click OK.

> **NOTE** By default, the Run As dialog runs the selected program as the current user and displays the name of the user that is currently logged on to the computer. When you run a program as the Current User, you can choose to run the program with or without virus protection. If virus protection causes a program to function improperly, uncheck the "Protect my computer and data from unauthorized program activity" option.

Safely Remove Hardware

Option that appears in the notification area of the Windows XP taskbar if you have installed removable storage media such as Zip disks, Jaz disks, FireWire drives, compact flash card readers, or SmartCard readers. The Safely Remove Hardware feature allows you to safely dismount your storage device before you unplug the drive.

To safely remove a drive, click the Safely Remove Hardware button in the notification area of the taskbar. A list of removable drives that are installed on your computer appears. Select the device you want to remove. A notification box then tells you that you can safely unplug the device.

To view properties of a removable storage device, right-click the Safely Remove Hardware button in the notification area of the taskbar; or, right-click the Safely Remove Hardware button to display the dialog shown here. Click the Properties button to view the properties of the selected device, or to troubleshoot the device and update its drivers.

Safe Mode

Startup option that allows you to troubleshoot system problems when you cannot properly start Windows XP. Safe mode starts Windows XP with a minimal set of drivers so that you can correct installation problems or check driver versions. To access the Safe Mode startup options on the Windows XP Advanced Options menu, follow these steps:

1. If you are currently in Windows, choose Start ➤ Turn Off Computer. Select Restart from the dialog.

NOTE If you are unable to start Windows, restart your computer using the Ctrl+Alt+Del keys on your keyboard.

2. Press F8 when your system reboots, and before the Windows XP startup screen appears. The Windows Advanced Options menu appears and displays the options listed below.

3. Use the Up and Down arrow keys to highlight your choice, and press Enter to select it. NumLock must be off in order for the arrow keys to work.

The menu options that appear in the Windows Advanced Options menu are as follows:

Safe Mode   Starts Windows XP but bypasses the startup files (such as the Registry) and loads only basic device drivers (standard VGA, keyboard, mouse, and other basic drivers required to start Windows).

TIP If you can't start Windows XP in Safe mode, you might need to repair your Windows XP system using Automated System Recovery. See the main topic "Backup" for more information.

Safe Mode with Networking   Starts Windows XP but bypasses the startup files. Loads network (NIC card) drivers in addition to basic device drivers.

Safe Mode with Command Prompt   Bypasses the startup files and, after logging on, displays the DOS command prompt.

Enable Boot Logging   Starts Windows XP and creates a log file of all of the services and drivers that load during startup. The file, called ntbtlog.txt, is saved in your Windows installation folder.

Enable VGA Mode   Starts Windows XP with the standard VGA driver. You can use this mode to troubleshoot problems you might be having after installing a different video driver.

Last Known Good Configuration   Starts Windows XP using the Registry information that was saved the last time you successfully shut down Windows XP.

Directory Services Restore Mode (Windows Domain Controllers Only)   Restores the Active Directory and the SYSVOL folder on a Windows XP domain controller.

Debugging Mode   Starts Windows XP and sends debugging data to another computer via a serial connection.

Start Windows Normally   Lets you proceed with a normal boot.

Reboot   Exits the Windows Advanced Options menu and reboots your computer.

Return to OS Choices Menu   On a computer where multiple operating systems are installed, returns to the Please Select Operating System to Start screen and allows you to start the selected operating system in the mode you selected.

See also   Backup

Scanners and Cameras

 Lets you configure scanners and cameras that are installed on the Windows XP computer.

Choose Start ➤ Control Panel (or Start ➤ Settings ➤ Control Panel in the Classic Start menu) ➤ Printers and Other Hardware. Next, click the Scanners and Cameras control panel icon to display the Scanners and Cameras folder. This folder contains icons for the scanners and cameras that are installed on your system. The Add an Imaging Device task, in the left pane, allows you to install cameras and scanners that Windows XP does not automatically detect.

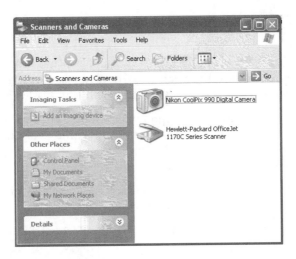

When you right-click a scanner or camera, a pop-up menu displays several options for the device. These allow you to delete or rename the device, or to get pictures using the Scanner and Camera Wizard. To view or modify the properties of a scanner or camera, select it in the list and click Properties. The properties you see vary depending on your hardware but may include such items as port settings used for the device and color management. The Properties dialog also includes options to test and troubleshoot problems with your scanner or camera and to configure color management profiles.

Scanner and Camera Installation Wizard

In most cases, Windows XP automatically detects your imaging device when you connect it to your computer and prompts you to install the drivers and any third-party software that came with your device. In the event that Windows XP does not detect your hardware, you can use the Scanner and Camera Installation Wizard to install your hardware.

To use the Scanner and Camera Installation Wizard, follow these steps:

1. Choose Start ➣ Control Panel (or Start ➣ Settings ➣ Control Panel in the Classic Start menu) ➣ Printers and Other Hardware. Next, click the Scanners and Cameras control panel icon to display the Scanners and Cameras folder.

2. From the Imaging Tasks section in the left pane, choose Add an Imaging Device. The Scanner and Camera Installation Wizard appears.

3. Click Next. A dialog prompts you to select the device driver to install for your hardware.

4. Select the manufacturer of your device from the Manufacturers list in the left portion of the dialog.

5. The Models list (on the right) displays a list of available products. Select your device from the list. If your device does not appear in the list, click Have Disk to install the drivers that came with your hardware device.

6. Click Next to continue. You are prompted to connect your device to the computer, and to select the port to which it is connected. Choose Automatic Port Detection to detect the port automatically, or manually select the port from the list of available ports.

7. Click Next to continue. The wizard prompts you to choose automatic port detection or to select from a list of ports.

8. Click Next to continue. Enter a name for your device. Edit the name if desired.

9. Click Next to display the final wizard screen. To complete the installation, click Finish.

Scanner and Camera Wizard

 Scanner and Camera Wizard Once you install a scanner, you use the Scanner and Camera Wizard to scan or retrieve your images and photos. To open the Scanner and Camera Wizard, choose Start ➤ All Programs (or Start ➤ Programs in the Classic Start menu) ➤ Accessories ➤ Scanner and Camera Wizard.

NOTE If you have both a camera and scanner installed, the Select Device dialog prompts you to select the device you want to use before you continue with the Scanner and Camera Wizard. Select your scanner and choose OK to continue.

Scanning a Document

To scan a document, follow these steps:

1. When the first screen in the Scanner and Camera Wizard appears, click Next.

2. A screen prompts you to choose your scanning preferences. The options that are available here depend on the features of your scanner. For example, you may be prompted to select a picture type (color, grayscale, black and white, or custom). If you choose custom, click the Custom Settings button to configure such properties as brightness, contrast, or DPI (dots per inch).

3. Click the Preview button to scan a preview of the image or document you want to scan.

4. After the preview image appears in the right portion of the wizard, adjust the rectangular selection to surround the area you want to scan. Click Next to continue.

5. The wizard prompts you to enter a name for your scanned document and to choose a file format and folder in which to save your scanned image. After you make your selections, click Next to continue.

6. The Scanner and Camera Wizard scans your document. After the scan is complete, the Other Options screen displays additional choices. You can publish the pictures to a Web site, order prints from a photo printing Web site, or complete the wizard. After you make your selection, click Next.

The options you see next depend on the choice you made in Step 6. Follow the remaining prompts to complete the wizard.

Obtaining Photos from Your Digital Camera

The Scanner and Camera Wizard also allows you to retrieve photos from your digital camera. To use the Scanner and Camera Wizard for digital cameras, follow these steps:

1. Connect your camera to the correct port before starting the wizard.

2. Choose Start ➤ All Programs (or Start ➤ Programs in the Classic Start menu) ➤ Accessories ➤ Scanner and Camera Wizard, or double-click the camera icon in the Scanners and Cameras folder. The wizard scans for pictures on your camera.

3. At the Welcome screen, click Next to continue.

4. On the Choose Pictures to Copy screen, check the pictures that you want to copy and uncheck those that you do not. Click Next.

5. Enter a name for this group of pictures, and select the folder in which to save them. You can also check an option to delete the pictures from your camera after the wizard copies them. Click Next.

6. The wizard copies the pictures into the designated folder. Click Cancel to stop the copying process at any time. When the copies are finished, click Next.

7. The Scanner and Camera Wizard displays the Other Options screen, which allows you to publish the pictures to a Web site, order prints from a photo printing Web site, or complete the wizard. After you make your selection, click Next.

The options you see next depend on the choice you made in Step 7. Follow the remaining prompts to complete the wizard.

Scheduled Tasks

 Windows XP allows you to schedule tasks, so that you can run programs and scripts or use documents at a certain time, date, or interval. Scheduled Tasks allows you to create, view, and configure tasks as needed.

To open the Scheduled Tasks folder, choose Start ➢ Control Panel (or Start ➢ Settings ➢ Control Panel in the Classic Start menu) and click the Performance and Maintenance control panel icon. Then click the Scheduled Tasks icon. You can also choose Start ➢ All Programs (or Start ➢ Programs in the Classic Start menu) ➢ Accessories ➢ System Tools ➢ Scheduled Tasks.

 TIP Make sure your system time settings are accurate if you want to set up scheduled tasks.

Scheduled Tasks Folder

The Scheduled Tasks folder displays the tasks that you schedule with several details, including task schedule, next and last run times, status, last result, and creator of the task. The Add Scheduled Task icon allows you to manually add additional tasks with the Scheduled Task Wizard.

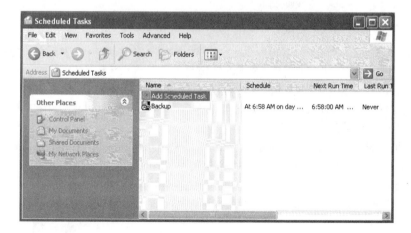

Run and End Task

Right-click any task to display a submenu of options. Two of these options are specific to scheduled tasks. To run the scheduled task immediately, choose Run.

To stop a task that is currently running (as shown in the Status column), choose End Task.

TIP End Task is handy when you want to use the computer and a scheduled task is currently running. End the task and then restart it later, using Run Task. It may take several minutes for the task to actually stop.

Properties

To view or edit properties for a task, double-click a task in the list. You can also right-click any task and choose Properties from the menu that appears. The Properties dialog has three tabs: Task, Schedule, and Settings.

Task Tab Use this tab to specify information about the task. The Run field displays the location of the file currently associated with the task. To change the path, simply enter a new path or use the Browse button to locate another application, folder, or file. Use the Start In field to specify the directory that contains the file, or the location of any other files that are required to run the task (which may be located in the same folder, or in a different location). Use the Comments field to enter any comment about the task, such as a description of what the task does.

TIP To specify command-line parameters for a program, enter them in the Run field after you enter the path to the task's associated file.

If spaces appear in any portion of the path to the task's associated file, enclose the path inside double quotation marks.

By default, the creator of the task runs a scheduled task. You can also run a task as a different user: Use the Run As field to specify the user you would like to run the task. The syntax is *computername_or_domainname\username*. Next, click the Set Password button to specify the user's password.

Use the Enabled option (at the bottom of the Task tab) to enable or disable the scheduled task.

Schedule Tab The Schedule tab allows you to change the task's schedule—for example, you can change the task to run daily instead of weekly, or change the times the task runs. Choose an option from the Schedule Task drop-down list. With the exception of the At System Startup or At Logon options, the area below the list changes to display scheduling options for the type of schedule you selected (such as days of the month for a Monthly task). As you make your choices, the top section of the tab updates the scheduling information.

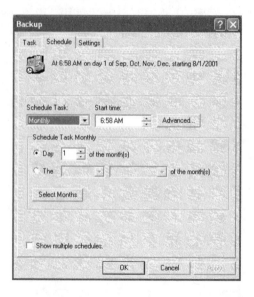

Check the Show Multiple Schedules box to configure more than one schedule for the same task. The top area of the tab now displays a drop-down list of all the schedules you configured for the task. Click New to create additional schedules for the task.

NOTE Once you create multiple schedules, they always appear; you cannot disable the display of multiple schedules unless there is only one schedule.

To configure advanced scheduling options (such as start and end dates and additional repeat options), click the Advanced button in the Schedule tab to open the Advanced Schedule Options dialog. Select a start date for the task. To specify an end date, check the End Date box and choose a date from the drop-down calendar. Use the Until section to specify when you want the Repeat functions to end or how long you want them to last. Click OK to save your advanced settings.

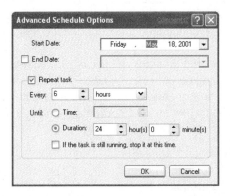

Settings Tab   Use the Settings tab to configure special circumstances for the task. Use the Scheduled Task Completed section to specify how to handle the task after it runs. You can delete the task if it is not scheduled to run again, or stop the task if it runs over a certain amount of time.

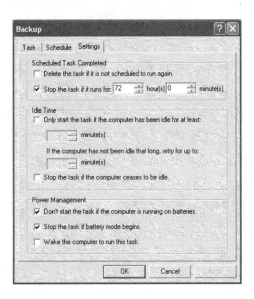

Use the Idle Time section to specify how to handle the task if your computer is in idle mode. You can start the task if the computer has been idle for at least a specified amount of time, and specify a time limit within which Windows retries to start the task. You can also end the task when your computer ceases to be idle.

NOTE Idle-time configuration can come in handy if you want tasks to run but you still want to be able to use your computer without the task tying up your computer's resources.

Use the Power Management section to specify how to handle the task while your computer is running on batteries, or when your computer wakes up from power management. You can choose not to run the task if your computer is in battery mode, stop the task when your computer goes into battery mode, or wake the computer up to run the task.

Advanced Menu

The Advanced menu is unique to the Scheduled Tasks folder. This menu contains the following five options (the first four are only available for users with administrative privileges):

Stop/Start Using Task Scheduler   Stops or starts the task scheduler service (choose this option to toggle between using the task scheduler and not using it). When you stop the service, any tasks that are scheduled to run won't run until the next time they are scheduled to run, providing the task scheduler has been restarted. Choose Start Using Task Scheduler to start the scheduler again after it has been stopped. When you stop the task scheduler, the Pause/Continue Task Scheduler and AT Service Account menu options are disabled.

Pause/Continue Task Scheduler   Available only if the task scheduler is running. Pause Task Scheduler temporarily pauses the task scheduler service; any tasks that are scheduled to run won't run until the next time they are scheduled to run, providing the task scheduler has been continued. Choose Continue Task Scheduler to resume the operation of the task scheduler after you pause it.

Notify Me of Missed Tasks Choose this option to receive notification from Windows XP if a task did not run. Click this option to place a check mark next to the option, indicating that it's active. Click the option again to turn off notification.

AT Service Account Lets you specify which account can run or list scheduled tasks using the command-line AT command.

TIP For more detailed information about the AT command, search the Help system's index for the words **AT COMMAND**.

View Log View a log of messages relating to scheduled events and the status of the task scheduler. The log file includes success as well as error messages, and messages regarding starting, stopping, pausing, and continuing the task scheduler service.

Add Scheduled Task

Add Scheduled Task Starts the Scheduled Task Wizard, which guides you through the process of creating scheduled tasks. To create a scheduled task, follow these steps:

1. In the Scheduled Tasks folder, double-click Add Scheduled Task. The Scheduled Task Wizard appears.

2. Click Next. The wizard displays a list of applications. Select an application from the list, or click the Browse button to locate another application on your local or network computer.

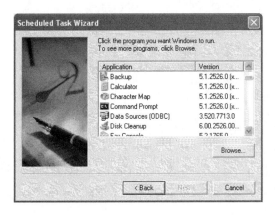

3. Click Next. Enter a name for your task, and then click the radio button that corresponds with how often you want the task to run. Your choices are daily, weekly, monthly, one time only, when your computer starts, or when you log on. Skip to Step 5 if you choose either of the last two options.

TIP A scheduled task icon has a visual indicator to denote that it is a scheduled task. You may find it easier to distinguish scheduled tasks from actual programs if you use a name that is different than the program you are scheduling—for example, name a scheduled disk cleanup something like My Scheduled Disk Cleanup.

4. Click Next. The options that appear in the next dialog depend on your choice in Step 3. In this screen, you can specify such items as the time to run the task, or on which days (or weeks, or months) you want to run the task.

5. Click Next to enter your username and password.

6. Click Next. The wizard informs you that your task is scheduled and confirms when it will run. Click Finish to complete the steps in the wizard.

NOTE The screen in Step 6 provides an option to open an advanced properties dialog after you click the Finish button. You can also double-click any task in the list to open the properties dialog, where you can view or modify the settings and schedules of your task. You can also limit the amount of time that a task runs, set idle times, and configure power management options.

See also Help and Support Center

Screen Saver

See Display (Screen Saver Tab)

Search

Use this Windows XP feature to search for files, folders, Internet resources, printers, and people. Choose Start ➤ Search to open the Search Results window.

NOTE Search options in the Classic Start menu include four subcommands: For Files or Folders, On the Internet, For Internet Audio/Video, or For People.

The left pane of the Search Results window initially displays a menu that allows you to choose whether or not you want to search with an animated screen character. This is a one-time option. After you make your selection, the menu in the left pane displays different categories for your searches. These categories are described in the following sections.

NOTE If you later decide to change your choice for the animated screen character, choose Change Preferences from the Search Companion pane and change your configuration in the menu that appears.

TIP You can also browse My Computer or My Network Places through Windows Explorer to search for files on your local or network hard drive.

Several search categories display the following buttons or options:

Use Advanced Search Options Click this button to displays additional search criteria that allow you to perform more specific searches for files or folders. The options you see here depend upon the type of search you are performing.

Back   Click to display the previous screen in the left pane of the Search Results window.

Search   Click to perform your search.

Pictures, Music, or Video

Searches your computer for multimedia files. Click Pictures, Music, or Video to display the following options:

Pictures and Photos   Check this option to search your computer for still images.

Music   Check this option to search your computer for music files.

Video   Check this option to search your computer for video files.

All or Part of the File Name   Allows you to search for files with a specific name. You can also use * and ? wildcard characters to broaden your search.

Documents

Allows you to search for documents (such as those created in word processing, spreadsheet, or similar programs) based on the date they were last modified or by name. Click Documents to display the following options:

Don't Remember   Check this option if you do not remember the date on which you created or modified the file. It returns all files that contain all or part of the document name that you specify.

Within the Last Week   Check this option to search for a document that you worked on in the last seven days.

Past Month   Check this option to search for a document that you worked on during the last month.

Within the Past Year   Check this option to search for a document that you worked on during the past year.

All or Part of the Document Name   Allows you to search for documents with a specific name. You can also use * and ? wildcard characters to broaden your search.

All File and Folders

Use this option to search for files and folders based on part or all of a filename, or by a word or phrase in the file. You can also search a specific drive, by date modified, or by file size. Click All File Types to display the following options:

All or Part of the File Name Enter all or part of a filename in this box to search for a specific file, or for any filename that contains the text you enter.

A Word or Phrase in the File Enter a word or phrase that you are certain appears in the file you are seeking. Note, however, that searches of this type can take a long time if this is the only search criterion that you enter. It helps to add additional criteria in the other fields.

Look In Use this drop-down list to select the drive or folder in which you want to perform the search.

When Was It Modified? Click this option to choose how long ago the file was created or last modified.

What Size Is It? Click this option to specify a size for the file you are searching for.

More Advanced Options Click this option to search for system folders or hidden files and folders. You can also search subfolders, add case sensitivity, and search tape backups.

Computers or People

This option allows you to search for a computer on a network, or for people in your Address Book. An additional option also allows you to search the Internet. Click Computers or People to display the following options:

A Computer on the Network This option allows you to search another computer on your network for the same types of files that you can find on your local computer. Click this option to enter the name of the computer you want to search. To locate specific files on that computer, click Search This Computer for Files. A list of search categories (arranged like your own search window) appears for that computer.

Click Search the Internet to search for documents on the Internet. Enter a sentence for search criteria and click the Search button to display a list of web pages in the main pane.

People in Your Address Book This option allows you to search for people in your contacts list, or allows you to find a person on the Internet by using one of several Internet search directories. Click this link to display the Find People dialog.

Use the Look In drop-down list to select your contacts list. You can search by any combination of name, e-mail address, postal address, phone, or other criteria. Click Find Now to complete the search.

Search the Internet   Choose Search the Internet to search for Web pages or e-mail addresses on the Internet, as described shortly.

Information in Help and Support Center

 Choose this option to search through Windows XP Help and Support Center for additional help on Windows XP (see the main topic "Help and Support Center").

Search the Internet

Choose this option to search the Internet for Web pages, people's addresses, businesses, maps, encyclopedia entries, and newsgroups. The Search Companion prompts you to enter your search in the form of a question. Click Search the Internet to display the following options:

TIP   You can also click Search on the Windows Explorer toolbar to perform a search on the Internet.

What Are You Looking For?   This field allows you to enter a sentence, word, or phrase for your search terms. For example, enter **buy a book online** to search for online bookstores. After you enter your search term, click Search. The Search Companion displays a list of links in the right pane. Select a link to navigate to the Web page.

Search This Computer for Files   Displays the default Search Companion menu.

Change Preferences

Click Change Preferences to configure options for the Search Companion. This menu offers the following options:

With/Without an Animated Screen Character   The option that appears in this area depends on whether you are using an animated screen character. Choose this option to switch your current decision.

With a Different Character   This option appears only if you are using an animated screen character to assist in your searches. Click this option to display a list of optional characters that you can select from. Check the character that you want to use, and click OK to assign your new choice.

With/Without Indexing Service (for Faster Local Searches)   To enable indexing services enabled, choose With Indexing Service. The top of the pane reports that Indexing Service is currently disabled, and then displays options to enable or disable the indexing service. Select Yes, Enable Indexing Service, then click OK. Windows XP indexes the files on your hard drive so that you can search through them more quickly.

To disable indexing, choose Without Indexing Service. The top of the pane reports that Indexing Service is currently enabled. Choose No, Do Not Enable Indexing Service, then click OK.

To set advanced properties for the Indexing Service, click Change Indexing Service Settings (Advanced). This opens the Indexing Service dialog (see the main topic "Indexing Service"). To obtain more help about Indexing Service, click Learn More About Indexing Service.

Change Files and Folder Search Behavior   Allows you to search in Standard mode (using step-by-step instructions) or Advanced mode (where you manually enter search crireria).

Change Internet Search Behavior   Refreshes the display of the options menu.

Don't Show/Show Balloon Tips   Toggles balloon tips on and off.

Turn AutoComplete Off/On   Toggles AutoComplete on and off.

See also   Help and Support Center, Indexing Service

Security Configuration and Analysis

 WINDOWS XP PROFESSIONAL Security Configuration and Analysis is a feature of Windows XP Professional only.

MMC snap-in for Windows XP Professional that allows a computer or network administrator to create and open databases that are used to analyze and configure security options. Items in the Action menu allow the computer administrator to open a database, analyze the local computer, configure the computer, import and export security templates, and view log files. For a complete overview and description of how to configure security and analysis, refer to the Windows XP Help and Support topic titled "Security configuration management tools."

See also   Microsoft Management Console (Creating a New MMC Console)

Security Templates

WINDOWS XP PROFESSIONAL   Security Templates is a feature of Windows XP Professional only.

MMC snap-in for Windows XP Professional that allows a computer or network administrator to use predefined or custom security templates to secure a computer on a network. Several security templates are installed by default, and custom templates can be saved. For complete information on security templates, refer to the Windows XP Help and Support topic titled "Security templates overview."

See also   Microsoft Management Console (Creating a New MMC Console)

Send To

Send To   ▸   Lets you send a file or folder directly to a compressed folder, your Desktop (as a shortcut), a mail recipient, a floppy, Zip, or CD disk, your My Documents folder, or to publish to the Internet.

To send an item to a destination using Send To, perform these steps:

1. In any Explorer window, right-click a file or folder and choose Send To from the menu that appears.

2. Select the destination:

- Choose Compressed (Zipped) Folder to create a ZIP file that contains the item(s) you selected.

- Choose Desktop (Create Shortcut) to create a shortcut on your desktop that opens the selected item.

- Choose Mail Recipient to send the file to a contact from your Address Book, or to the e-mail address you enter.

- Choose 3-1/2 Floppy to copy the selection to a floppy disk.

- Choose My Documents to send the document to your My Documents folder.

- Choose CD-Drive to write the selected file(s) to CD.

See also   Address Book, Compressing Drives, Folders, and Files, Desktop, Explorer, My Documents, Web Publishing Wizard

Services

 Services Shortcut 2 KB   MMC snap-in that lets you start and stop services that are installed or running on your Windows XP computer. Some examples of services are Fax Service, Indexing Service, Event Log, Plug and Play, and Utility Manager.

To access Services, choose Start ➤ Control Panel (or Start ➤ Settings ➤ Control Panel in the Classic Start menu), Performance and Maintenance. Click Administrative Tools, and then double-click Services (or double-click Computer Management and expand the Services and Applications category to select Services in the console tree).

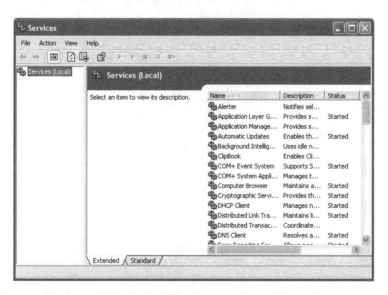

The Details pane displays information about all services installed on your computer, including name, description, status, startup type, and the account the service uses to log on.

Working with Services

Services lets you start, stop, pause, resume, and restart services installed on your Windows XP computer. To do so, right-click a service name and choose the appropriate action (Start, Stop, Pause, Resume, or Restart) from the pop-up menu; or, select a service and choose Start, Stop, Pause, Resume, or Restart from the Action menu.

TIP The Services toolbar displays Start Service, Stop Service, Pause Service, and Resume Service buttons.

Service Properties

To view and configure properties for any service installed on your computer, right-click a service name and choose Properties from the pop-up menu. The Service Properties dialog has four tabs: General, Log On, Recovery, and Dependencies. The General tab appears here.

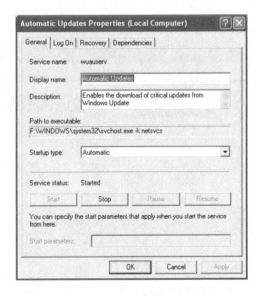

General tab Lets you view and configure general settings, such as the display name, description, startup type, status of the service (started, stopped, or paused), and start parameters. Click the appropriate button to start, stop, pause, or resume the service. Use the Start Parameters field to enter parameters to apply when you start the service.

Log On tab   Lets you log on to the Local System account or to an account you specify by name and password. Check the Allow Service to Interact with Desktop option to provide a user interface that anyone can use to interact with the service.

Recovery tab   Allows you to choose computer responses for cases when the service fails. You can choose different actions for the first, second, and subsequent failures. The default actions vary from service to service. Available options include Take No Action, Restart the Service, Run a File, and Reboot the Computer. If you select Run a File, specify the file you want Windows to run. If you select Restart the Service, specify the number of minutes that should elapse before the service restarts. If you select Reboot the Computer, click Restart Computer Options to specify the number of minutes that should elapse before the computer reboots. You can also send a custom message to network users before the reboot. On the Recovery tab, you can also specify the number of days that should pass before Windows resets the fail count.

Dependencies tab   Lets you view any services that depend on the currently selected service and any services on which the currently selected service depends. This information can help with troubleshooting service-related problems.

See also   Computer Management, Microsoft Management Console

Settings

 Settings   The Settings option on the Start menu is only available when you use the Classic Start menu. The Settings option gives you access to many Windows XP configuration tools, such as Control Panel, Network Connections, Printers and Faxes, and Taskbar and Start Menu. Choose Start ➤ Settings and make your choice from the submenu.

TIP   To choose the Classic-style Start menu, right-click the Start button and choose Properties. The Taskbar and Start Menu Properties dialog opens to the Start Menu tab. Select Classic Start Menu and choose OK.

See also   Control Panel, Network and Internet Connections, Printers and Other Hardware, Taskbar and Start Menu

Shared Folders

 Shared Folders   MMC snap-in that lets you view and manage shares on the computer you're using, remote connections to that computer, and files in use by remote users.

TIP   To use Shared Folders, you must be a member of the Administrators, Power Users, or Server Operators group, and your computer must be on a network.

To access Shared Folders, choose Start ➤ Control Panel (or Start ➤ Settings ➤ Control Panel in the Classic Start menu) ➤ Performance and Maintenance, click Administrative Tools, and double-click Computer Management. From the System Tools category in the console tree, select Shared Folders.

Shared Folders Nodes

Shared Folders contains three nodes: Shares, Sessions, and Open Files.

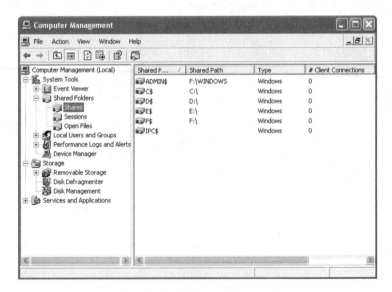

Shares   Lets you view, stop sharing, and configure properties (such as permissions and security) for existing shares. You can also create new shares. Some default shares for Windows XP are ADMIN$, C$, IPC$, print$, and SharedDocs. Detail columns for each share include the name and path of the share, its type, the number of client (user) connections, and any comments attached to the share.

Sessions   Lets you see which users are currently connected to the computer, disconnect a single session, or disconnect all sessions. Detail columns for each session include User, Computer, Type, Open Files, Connected Time (the time elapsed since the user connected), Idle Time (the time elapsed since the user performed an action), and Guest (whether the user is connected as Guest).

Open Files   Lets you see which files are currently open by remote users on shared folders. Here you can also close a single file or all files. Detail columns for each open file include Open File, Accessed By, Type, Number of Locks, and Open Mode (the permission granted when the file was opened).

Action Menu

Action   The Action menu in Shared Folders contains many familiar items and some unique ones. The items available depend on whether you're selecting a node in the console tree or an item in the Details pane, and also on the node or item you've selected.

All Tasks ➢ Send Console Message   Opens the Send Console Message dialog, where you can create and send a message to one or more individuals. Available with Shares selected in the console tree.

Disconnect All Sessions   Lets you disconnect all currently open sessions by remote users. Available with Sessions selected in the console tree.

Close Session   Closes the open session that is selected in the Details pane.

Disconnect All Open Files   Closes all files open in shared folders. Available with Open Files selected in the console tree.

Close Open File   Closes the open file that is selected in the Details pane.

New Window from Here   Displays the Share node and shared files in a new window.

Refresh   Allows you to refresh the display of items in the Details pane.

Export List   Opens the Export List dialog and allows you to save the items in the Details pane as a text file.

Properties   Opens the Properties dialog for the shared resource, which allows you to set user limits, caching, and share permissions.

See also   Microsoft Management Console, Sharing

Sharing

Sharing and Security... Lets you share folders, disks, printers, and other resources on your computer with other users on a network. When you share a folder or disk, you can specify which users have access to the resource and configure the permissions for them. Sharing settings are configured on the Sharing tab of the resource's property sheet. Users can see and access your shared resources through My Network Places.

Sharing a Folder or Disk

To share a folder or disk with users of the network, perform the following steps:

1. In any Explorer window, right-click the folder or disk you want to share and select Sharing and Security. The Properties dialog opens to the Sharing tab.

 TIP Alternatively, you can right-click the folder or disk, select Properties, and then select the Sharing tab.

2. Select Share This Folder on the Network and enter a name for the share.

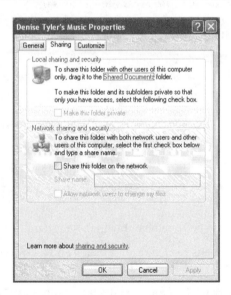

3. Check or uncheck the option to allow network users to change the files.

4. Click OK to apply your selections.

See also Explorer

Skin Chooser

See Windows Media Player

Snapshots

See Backup

Sound Recorder

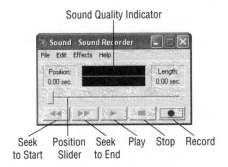

Sound Recorder Lets you record, edit, play, and mix audio files from audio input devices installed in your computer. Examples of audio input devices are a microphone (using a sound card) and a CD-ROM player.

Choose Start ➤ All Programs (or Start ➤ Programs in the Classic Start menu) ➤ Accessories ➤ Entertainment ➤ Sound Recorder to open the Sound Recorder dialog.

Sound Recorder Display

The Sound Recorder display provides information about the sound track you're recording or playing back. Several buttons allow you to control recording and playback of the sounds you record.

Sound Quality Indicator

Seek   Position   Seek   Play   Stop   Record
to Start   Slider   to End

Position Displays the current location on the sound track during play and recording.

Sound quality indicator Provides a visual display of the sound during playback or recording.

TIP If you do not see a green line in the sound quality indicator, this indicates that the sound file is compressed and can't be modified.

Length   Displays the total length of the currently opened audio file.

Position slider   Displays the relative position in the audio file while you record or play it. The slider moves toward the right to indicate the current position, relative to the entire length of the audio file. You can move the slider to change the position.

NOTE When you record a new track, the entire length of the new track is set to a default of 60 seconds, and the position of the slider is relative to that length while you record.

Seek to Start   Click to position the slider at the beginning of the audio file.

Seek to End   Click to position the slider at the end of the audio file.

Play   Click to play the audio file, beginning at the current position of the slider.

Stop   Click to stop playback or recording of the audio file.

Record   Click to start recording an audio file.

Menus

The commands in the File, Edit, and Effects menus of the Sound Recorder dialog allow you to create, edit, and add effects to your audio files.

File

Commands in the File menu allow you to open, save, and view properties of audio files. The options are as follows:

New   Creates or records a new audio file. The Sound Recorder prompts you to save changes to your current file before it creates a new one.

Open   Provides a dialog where you can choose an existing audio file to open.

Save   Saves the current audio file to your My Documents folder, or to the location from which the file was originally opened. The Save command overwrites any previous version of the file that is saved to your hard drive. To keep the original version of the file, use the Save As command to save a new version of the file to a different filename or folder.

Save As   Provides a dialog where you can save the current audio file to a new folder or using a different filename. If you want to change the format of the audio file, click the Change button to open the Sound Selection dialog (described later in this section).

Revert   Undoes all changes to the file since you last saved it. This reverts back to the file as you originally opened it. Click Yes to confirm the changes, or No to cancel.

Properties   Provides a dialog for the sound file that displays copyright information, file length, file size, and audio format. The Properties dialog also allows you to convert your audio file to a different file playback or recording format. Choose the format you want to display (All formats, Playback formats, or Recording formats) from the drop-down menu in the Format Conversion area. Then click the Convert Now button to open the Sound Selection dialog, described later in this section.

Edit

Commands in the Edit menu allow you to copy, paste, mix, and delete portions of the current audio file. You can also view the properties of the audio file.

Copy   Places a copy of the current audio file into your Clipboard.

TIP   To combine or mix two audio files using the Clipboard, open the first audio file in the Sound Recorder and copy it to your Clipboard. Then open the second file, and position the slider at the point at which you want to add the first file. Use the Paste Insert or Paste Mix command to paste the file from the Clipboard into the current file. Save the new file under a new name to keep the original file untouched.

Paste Insert   Inserts the contents of the clipboard at the current slider position. The size of the original file expands to make room for the clipboard contents.

Paste Mix   Mixes the contents of the current file with the contents that you have in your clipboard, starting at the current slider position. Files are mixed at equal volume.

Insert File   Provides a dialog where you can choose a file to insert at the current slider position. The size of the current file expands to make room for the file you insert.

Mix with File   Provides a dialog where you can choose a file to mix with the currently opened file, beginning at the current slider position. Files are mixed at equal volumes.

TIP To combine or mix two audio files that are saved to your hard disk, open the first file in the Sound Recorder. Then use the Insert File or Mix with File command to add or mix the second file. Save the combined version under a new filename to keep the two original files untouched.

Delete Before Current Position   Deletes the area between the beginning of the audio file and the current slider position.

Delete After Current Position   Deletes the area between the current slider position and the end of the audio file.

Audio Properties   Opens the Audio Properties dialog to the Audio Devices tab, where you specify the audio devices that Sound Recorder should use for playback and recording. This tab also lets you specify volume and advanced settings. More information about the Audio Devices tab is available under "Sounds and Audio Devices."

Effects

The Effects menu allows you to increase or decrease volume or speed of the audio file, or add additional effects such as echo or reverse. Options include Increase Volume (by 25%), Decrease Volume, Increase Speed (by 100%), Decrease Speed, Add Echo, and Reverse. When you increase or decrease volume or speed or add an echo, Sound Recorder applies the change to the entire audio file. The Reverse command physically reverses the file so that it plays backward from end to beginning.

See also   Sounds and Audio Devices, Volume Control

Sound Selection Dialog

The Sound Selection dialog allows you to change the format of your current audio file. To open the Sound Selection dialog from the Sound Recorder, choose File ➤ Save As and click the Change button.

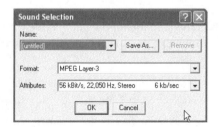

After you choose an audio format in the Sound Selection dialog, click OK to return to the Save As dialog and save your file in the new audio format.

The following options in the Sound Selection dialog allow you to create custom presets that you can use to convert your audio files:

Name   Allows you to select a *preset* audio format from a drop-down list. When you select a preset, the Format and Attributes drop-down lists display the settings that apply to each preset. Three presets appear by default: CD Quality (PCM, 44.100 kHz, 16 Bit, Stereo, 172 kb/sec), Radio Quality (PCM, 22.050 kHz, 8 Bit, Mono, 21 kb/sec), and Telephone Quality (PCM, 11.025 kHz, 8 Bit, Mono, 10 kb/sec). These default formats are not compressed.

Format   Allows you to select a custom audio format for a preset. The PCM option creates an audio file that is not compressed; all other options create a compressed audio file. Common choices for compressed audio include MPEG Layer 3 (which creates MP3 audio files), Windows Media Audio V1, and Windows Media Audio V2.

Attributes   Allows you to select a custom target download rate for your audio file. Choose the speed, quality (frequency in Hz), and number of channels (mono or stereo) that is appropriate for your target audience and mode of delivery.

TIP   You can immediately cut the size of an audio file in half by choosing mono instead of stereo. When you compress sound files, they become smaller in size, making them easier to download from the Internet. However, this also reduces the quality of the sound file when compared to its original uncompressed version. Higher "kBit/s" or "Hz" choices sound better but take much longer to download. You will need to experiment with the settings for each sound file to achieve the right balance between file size and sound quality.

Save As   Allows you to save your custom settings as a preset. To create a custom preset, follow these steps:

1. Select an audio format from the Format drop-down list.

2. Select the desired target rate for download speed (kBit/s), quality (Hz), and number of channels (stereo or mono) from the Attributes list.

3. Click the Save As button, and assign a name to your custom preset.

Remove   To remove a preset from the Name list, highlight the preset you want to delete and click Remove.

Sounds and Audio Devices

Sounds and Audio Devices Lets you assign specific sounds to Windows XP system events, such as receiving e-mail or exiting Windows, and for sound and multimedia device configuration.

Choose Start ➤ Control Panel (or Start ➤ Settings ➤ Control Panel in the Classic Start menu) ➤ Sounds, Speech and Audio Devices, then click Sounds and Audio Devices to open the Sounds and Audio Device Properties dialog. This dialog contains five tabs: Volume, Sounds, Audio, Voice, and Hardware.

Volume Tab

The top of the Volume tab displays the name of your WAVE audio device. Move the Device Volume slider to adjust speaker volume. Check the Mute box to turn off the sound completely while remembering the previous volume setting. You can also check an option to display a volume icon in your taskbar's notification area. Click the Advanced button to open the Volume Control dialog (see the main topic "Volume Control").

Click the Speaker Volume button to open a dialog where you can individually adjust the balance and volume for stereo or surround-sound speakers. To move all sliders at the same time, check Move All Slide Indicators at the Same Time. Click the Restore Defaults button to revert to the original default settings.

To choose advanced speaker settings, click the Advanced button in the Volume tab. This opens the Advanced Audio Properties dialog, which consists of two tabs: Speakers and Performance. In the Speakers tab, select your speaker setup from the setup types in the Speaker Setup drop-down list. The settings in the Performance tab allow you to control how Windows XP handles audio acceleration and sample rate conversions. If you are experiencing problems with audio playback, adjust the Hardware Acceleration and Sample Rate Conversion Quality sliders as necessary to improve performance.

TIP When you move the sliders for hardware acceleration and sample rate conversion quality, the description underneath each slider displays information about the current setting and under which circumstances you should use it.

NOTE The Advanced buttons in the Audio tab and Voice tab (discussed in following sections) also open the Advanced Audio Properties dialog.

Sounds Tab

Use the Sounds tab of the Sounds and Audio Device Properties dialog to assign individual sounds to Windows XP events, such as when Windows XP starts or when you receive an incoming fax. Choose a sound scheme from the Sound Scheme drop-down list. You will be prompted to save any changes you made to your previous scheme if you have not already done so.

NOTE Sound schemes do not assign a sound to every possible event. After you select a scheme, you may still need to assign specific sounds to additional events.

Use the Program Events list to customize your sound scheme, or to add sounds for events that have no assignment. Highlight the event to which you want to assign a sound, then choose a sound from the Sounds drop-down list at the bottom of the tab. Optionally, use the Browse button to select or preview a sound from your Media folder or another folder on your computer.

Audio Tab

Use the Audio tab to choose the default devices that Windows XP uses to play or record sound or to play MIDI music. Each audio device has a Volume button that opens the Volume Control dialog, which allows you to adjust volume and speaker balance for each device, or to control bass and treble settings, if available; see the main topic "Volume Control" for additional information. The Advanced buttons open the Advanced Audio Properties dialog, discussed under "Volume Tab" earlier in this main topic.

Voice Tab

Use the Voice tab to select and configure the device that you use to play back and record voice. Choose your default devices from the Voice Playback and Voice Recording drop-down lists. Use the Volume buttons to open the Volume Control dialog, which allows you to adjust playback and recording volumes for each device. See the main topic "Volume Control" for additional information. The Advanced buttons open the Advanced Audio Properties dialog, discussed under "Volume Tab" earlier in this main topic.

Click the Test Hardware button to open the Sound Hardware Test Wizard, which tests your sound hardware to ensure that you can play sounds and capture your voice properly. Follow the instructions in the wizard to test your sound hardware. You will be prompted to speak into a microphone to test and adjust recording settings and to adjust volumes for playback.

Hardware Tab

Use the Hardware tab of the Sounds and Audio Device Properties dialog to configure hardware settings for your sound and multimedia devices and drivers (including CD-ROM drives).

To troubleshoot problems with a device, select an item from the Devices list. Then click the Troubleshoot button to open the Help and Support Center troubleshooter. Follow the prompts in the troubleshooter to resolve the problem.

To view or adjust settings for a device, select an item from the Devices list. Then click the Properties button to open a properties dialog for the device. This dialog displays several tabs, depending on the device you select. Typical information in these tabs includes device type, manufacturer, device status, and driver information.

 TIP You can also view and edit device properties through the Device Manager. Choose Start ➣ Control Panel (or Start ➣ Settings ➣ Control Panel in the Classic Start menu), and click Performance and Maintenance. Click the System control panel icon to open the System Properties dialog. Select the Hardware tab, and click the Device Manager button to open the Windows XP Device Manager. Expand the appropriate device heading to right-click a device, and choose Properties.

See also Accessibility, Sound Recorder, System, Volume Control

Start Menu

The Start menu provides access to programs, documents, Control Panel, network connections, help and support, searches, and program execution functions. To access the Start menu, click the Start button. By default, the Start button appears in the bottom-left corner of the taskbar.

start Right-click the Start button to display a shortcut menu of additional options:

- Choose Open to display the Start Menu folder for the current user.

- Choose Explore to open Windows Explorer.

- Choose Search to search for files, folders, computers, printers, and people.

- Choose Properties to configure display options for the Start menu and taskbar, or to switch between Windows XP and Classic Start menu.

If you are logged on as a computer administrator, two additional options appear in the Start shortcut menu. Choose Open All Users or Explore All Users to open the C:\Documents and Settings\All Users\Start Menu folder in Windows Explorer with the Folders view in the Explorer bar either not displayed (Open All Users) or displayed (Explore All Users).

In Windows XP, you have the option to use one of two layouts for the Start menu: the default Windows XP style, or the traditional "classic" Windows style. The options in each are described in the following subsections.

TIP If you place the mouse pointer over submenu items (and also items in Windows Explorer), in many cases, a brief explanation of the item or additional information about it is shown as a ScreenTip.

Windows XP Start Menu

To use or switch to the Windows XP–style Start menu, right-click the Start button and choose Properties to open the Taskbar and Start Menu Properties dialog. From the Start Menu tab, click the Start Menu option, and choose OK.

Internet Connects to your Internet connection, and opens Internet Explorer (or your default browser) for browsing.

E-mail Connects to your Internet connection and opens Outlook Express (or your default e-mail program) so that you can retrieve, send, and read e-mail and news messages.

Recent Files Area Displays your most recently used files.

All Programs Opens a submenu that provides access to program groups and programs located on your computer.

My Documents   Opens the My Documents folder for the user that is currently logged on.

My Recent Documents   Stores a list of the 15 most recent documents that you have worked on.

My Pictures   Opens the My Pictures folder for the user that is currently logged on.

My Music   Opens the My Music folder for the user that is currently logged on.

My Computer   Opens the My Computer folder, which displays links to shared documents, hard disks, and removable storage devices. Options let you search for files or folders, view system information, add or remove programs, and change settings.

My Network Places   Opens the My Network Places folder, where you can connect to other computers on the network.

Control Panel   Opens the Control Panel window, which allows you to customize and configure desktop appearance, hardware and software configurations, network connections, user accounts, and accessibility options.

Connect To   Allows you to connect to the Internet through your ISP or other connections that you have configured.

Printers and Faxes   Opens the Printers and Faxes folder, where you can add, remove, print to, or troubleshoot printers and faxes.

Help and Support   Opens the Windows XP Help and Support Center, for answers to your Windows XP–related questions. You can browse the help contents, query the help index, search by keyword, or add help topics to a favorites list. You can also obtain additional help from other Windows XP users through your network or on the Internet.

Search   Opens the Search Companion window, which allows you to search for files, folders, people, and other resources on your local or network computer or on the Internet.

Run   Opens the Run dialog, which allows you to enter or browse for a command or path to run programs, open folders or documents, or browse to Internet resources.

Log Off   Opens the Log Off dialog, which prompts the current user to log off the computer. After the current user logs off, the Windows XP logon screen appears and allows any user to log on or turn off the computer.

Turn Off Computer Opens the Turn Off Computer dialog, which allows you to place the computer in Standby mode, turn the computer off, or restart (reboot) the computer.

Classic Start Menu

To use or switch to the classic Windows–style Start menu, right-click the Start button and choose Properties to open the Taskbar and Start Menu Properties dialog. From the Start Menu tab, click the Classic Start Menu option, and choose OK.

The following options are part of the "Classic" Start menu:

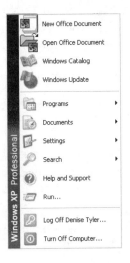

Windows Catalog Connects you to the Windows Catalog on Microsoft's Web site, where you will find products made for Windows.

Windows Update Connects you to the Windows Update section of Microsoft's Web site, so that you can automatically update your Windows XP installation with new features, device drivers, and so forth.

Programs Opens a submenu that gives you access to program groups and programs located on your computer.

TIP Click the double arrow at the bottom of the program list to display programs that you have not used recently. You can disable this auto-hide feature in the Taskbar and Start Menu Properties dialog.

Documents   Opens a submenu of options to open the My Documents or My Pictures folders. Also displays shortcuts to your most recently used files. Click a filename to open it.

Settings   Opens a submenu with options to open Control Panel, to view and configure network connections, to add or configure printers and faxes, and to set options for the taskbar and Start menu.

Search   Opens a submenu with options to search for files or folders, on the Internet, or for people. Each option you select opens the Search Companion to the appropriate screen.

Help and Support   Opens the Windows XP Help and Support Center, which helps you find answers to your Windows XP–related questions. You can browse the help contents, query the help index, search by keyword, or add help topics to a favorites list. You can also obtain additional help through other Windows XP users through your network or from the Internet.

Run   Opens the Run dialog, which allows you to enter or browse for a command or path to run programs, open folders or documents, or browse to Internet resources.

Log Off (username)   Opens the Log Off dialog, which prompts the current user to log off the computer. After the current user logs off, the Windows XP logon screen appears and allows any user to log on or turn off the computer.

Turn Off Computer   Opens the Turn Off Computer dialog, which allows you to place the computer in Standby mode, turn the computer off, or restart (reboot) the computer.

See also   Taskbar, Taskbar and Start Menu

Synchronize

Synchronize   Allows you to update the content of Web pages that you have selected to view offline. The Synchronize feature compares versions on your hard disk to versions on the Internet, and updates your local version accordingly.

Choose Start ➤ All Programs (or Start ➤ Programs in the Classic Start menu) ➤ Accessories ➤ Synchronize to open the Items to Synchronize dialog. This dialog displays any files or Web pages that are available for offline viewing. Check the items that you want to synchronize, and uncheck those that you do not. The Items to Synchronize dialog contains four buttons:

Properties   Opens the Properties dialog for the selected item. The Schedule tab in the Properties dialog allows you to synchronize the item automatically, or based on a schedule that you configure. The Download tab allows you to specify what content to download when you synchronize the item, or to notify you by e-mail when the online item changes.

Synchronize   Synchronizes the selected items.

Setup   Opens the Synchronization Settings dialog. Use the Logon/Logoff tab to specify the items you want to synchronize automatically when you log on or off the computer. Use the On Idle tab to specify the items you want to synchronize when the computer is idle. Use the Scheduled tab to configure a schedule for synchronizing items (using the Scheduled Synchronization Wizard).

Close   Closes the dialog.

See also   Offline Files

System

 Controls system properties, including network identification configuration, hardware device configuration (including hardware profile configuration), user profile configuration, and advanced properties, including performance, environment variable, and system startup and recovery configuration.

Choose Start ➤ Control Panel (or Start ➤ Settings ➤ Control Panel in the Classic Start menu), then choose Performance and Maintenance. Then, click the System control panel icon to open the System Properties dialog. This dialog contains seven tabs: General, Computer Name, Hardware, Advanced, System Restore, Automatic Updates, and Remote; these are described in the following subsections.

 TIP   Alternatively, you can right-click My Computer and choose Properties to access the System Properties dialog.

General Tab

The General tab provides information about your system, such as the version of the operating system you are running, to whom the operating system is registered, and information about the physical computer.

Computer Name Tab

Use this tab to view and configure the full name of your computer and the workgroup or domain to which it belongs. Each computer in a network must have a unique name by which you and other users can identify it. If the computer is a member of a domain and you've specified a DNS domain name for the computer, then the DNS domain name becomes part of the full name.

Click the Network ID button to open the Network Identification Wizard, which helps you join a domain and create a local user account.

To assign a new name for your computer, click the Change button to open the Computer Name Changes dialog. Enter a new name for your computer and click OK to apply it.

Hardware Tab

Use this tab to configure the hardware on your computer. This tab gives you access to the Add Hardware Wizard, driver signing options, Device Manager, and hardware profiles.

Add Hardware Wizard

Click the Add Hardware Wizard button to start the Add Hardware Wizard. This wizard allows you to add new hardware to a Windows XP computer after you have installed it on your machine. It also prepares removable hardware so that you can safely remove or unplug it from your computer, and allows you to troubleshoot devices that are not operating correctly.

The wizard automatically makes required changes to your Registry and configuration files. It also installs, loads, removes, or unloads drivers as necessary. For further information about the wizard, see the main topic "Add New Hardware."

Driver Signing

Driver Signing   Click the Driver Signing button to open the Driver Signing Options dialog, where you can configure how you want to handle file signatures that ensure the integrity of a file. This allows you to prevent the installation of files that may adversely affect the operation of your system.

Choose the verification level that you want to use from the File Signature Verification section. You can ignore the file signatures completely, receive a warning when a file is not signed, or block unsigned files so that they are not installed on your computer. If you are logged on as an administrator, you can also check Make This Action the System Default to use this setting for each user that logs in to the computer.

Device Manager

Device Manager   Click the Device Manager button to open the Windows XP Device Manager, which lists all hardware installed in the computer. Device Manager also enables you to configure the properties of hardware devices, check the status of installed devices, view and update device drivers, and disable and uninstall devices. Device Manager is explained in detail under "Device Manager."

Hardware Profiles

Hardware Profiles   Hardware profiles allow you to select the drivers that Windows XP loads at system startup in the event that you frequently change your hardware configurations. For example, you may use a modem to connect to the office and to the Internet while you are on the road with a laptop computer. Then, when you return to the office, you may attach your laptop to a docking station that connects to the network and the Internet through a network adapter. To handle these different hardware configuration needs, Windows XP allows you to set up multiple hardware profiles. At system startup, you can then choose which profile to use.

NOTE If the computer is a laptop, the default profile will be called either Docked Profile or Undocked Profile.

To configure a hardware profile, click the Hardware Profiles button to open the Hardware Profiles dialog. By default, this dialog displays your original hardware profile as Original Configuration. Where there are multiple profiles, use the up and down arrows to move the highlighted selection to a new location in the list. The hardware profile that is currently being used appears at the top of the list, with (Current) appended to the hardware profile name.

NOTE By default, when you add new hardware, the settings are saved in the Original Configuration hardware profile.

Click Copy to create a duplicate of the current profile under a new name. Click Rename to assign a new name to the selected profile. Click Delete to remove the selected profile from the list.

NOTE You must be logged on as a computer administrator to copy hardware profiles.

Click the Properties button to open the Properties dialog for the selected hardware profile. Use this dialog to view and configure the properties of the selected profile; it displays information such as the manufacturer's dock ID and serial number of a docking station. To specify settings for portable computers, check the This Is a Portable Computer option, then select the radio button that applies to your docking station (docked, undocked, or unknown docking state). Check the Always Include This Profile as an Option When Windows Starts option to make the hardware profile available when your computer starts.

Advanced Tab

Use the Advanced tab to configure advanced system settings that relate to the performance of your computer, user profiles on the computer, or startup and recovery options. This tab presents three Settings buttons (one each for Performance, User Profiles, and Startup and Recovery) plus buttons for Environment Variables and Error Reporting.

Performance Settings

To control how your computer uses resources for visual effects, processor scheduling, memory usage, and virtual memory, click the Settings button in the Performance section. This opens the Performance Options dialog, which consists of two tabs: Visual Effects and Advanced.

Visual Effects Tab   Use the Visual Effects tab in the Performance Options dialog to configure how your computer handles various graphical elements. You can let Windows choose the settings that are best for your computer, or select from additional options. Choose Adjust for Best Appearance to select all of the features in the features list (such as animated windows, gradients in dialog boxes, menus that fade in and out, and other graphic options). Choose Adjust for Best Performance to disable all of the options. Choose Custom to check or uncheck options manually.

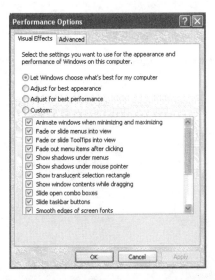

Advanced Tab   Use the Advanced tab in the Performance Options dialog to choose how you want your computer to utilize its processor, physical memory, and virtual memory.

Processor Scheduling   This choice controls how your computer optimizes processor usage for the applications you run. Choose the Programs radio button to optimize processor usage for applications that are running in the foreground. Choose the Background Services radio button to optimize your processor usage so that all applications receive equal amounts of processor resources.

Memory Usage   This choice controls how your computer optimizes memory usage for the applications you run. Choose the Programs radio button to use all physical memory for applications before using the system cache. Choose System Cache to balance memory usage between physical memory and system cache.

Virtual Memory   The Virtual Memory section displays the current size of the virtual memory paging files on your hard drives. To change the size of the paging file, click the Change button to open the Virtual Memory dialog. Select a drive from the Drive list, and perform one of the following operations:

- To customize settings for the paging file on the selected drive, click the Custom Size radio button. Enter new values (in MB) for the Initial Size and Maximum Size boxes. Size recommendations appear at the bottom of the dialog, along with the minimum allowed and the amount that is currently allocated.

- To have Windows XP manage the size of your paging files, check the System Managed Size radio button. Initial Size and Maximum Size fields are disabled when you choose this option.

- To eliminate the use of paging files, check the No Paging File radio button.

After you choose one of the above options, click the Set button to apply the new settings.

TIP   The Initial Size is the size of the paging file when Windows XP starts. The Maximum Size is the maximum size that you want to allow for the paging file. As a general rule, the Initial Size should be 1.5 times the amount of RAM that is installed in your computer.

NOTE When you reduce the size of the Initial or Maximum paging files, Windows XP prompts you to restart your computer. You do not have to restart the computer when you increase the size of the paging files.

User Profiles Settings

To view or edit user profiles that are stored on the computer, click the Settings button in the User Profiles section of the Advanced tab in the System Properties dialog. This opens the User Profiles dialog, which displays a list of user profiles that are set up on the computer. If you are logged on as a computer administrator, use the buttons to edit the items in the list.

- To change the user account type, highlight the user account that you want to change, and click the Change Type button. In the Change Profile Type dialog, choose Roaming Profile or Local Profile. Then click OK to apply the change.

- To delete a user account from the computer, highlight the user account that you want to delete, and click the Delete button.

- To create a copy of a user account, highlight the account you want to copy, and click the Copy To button. The Copy To dialog allows you to choose a directory in which to copy the file, and to configure which users or groups are permitted to use the profile.

Startup and Recovery Settings

To view or edit startup and recovery settings, click the Settings button in the Startup and Recovery section of the Advanced Tab in the System Properties dialog. This opens the Startup and Recovery dialog, which consists of two sections: System Startup and System Failure.

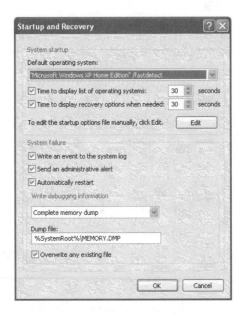

If you have more than one operating system installed on the computer, a list of operating systems appears when you first start your computer. Settings in the System Startup section of the dialog allow you to configure options for this list. Use the Default Operating System drop-down list to select which operating system you want your computer to start automatically if no alternate selection is made. You can also specify how long to display the list of operating systems and recovery options before starting the default operating system if no selection is made. Click the Edit button to open the Boot.ini file in Notepad.

 WARNING Do not make any changes to the Boot.ini file if you are unfamiliar with how it works. Improper editing can result in your computer not booting at all.

Use options in the System Failure section to specify actions to perform if the computer suddenly stops. Items include writing an event to the system log, sending an administrative alert, or automatically rebooting the computer.

You can also specify whether to write debugging information to a file (this process is called a *dump*) and how much information you want to record. Under Write Debugging Information, you can select from None (Do Not Write Debugging Information), Small Memory Dump (64 KB), or Kernel Memory Dump. You can specify a path for the dump file and choose whether to overwrite the file if it already exists.

Environment Variables

Environment Variables · Windows XP and its programs use environment variables to behave in a certain way under certain conditions. An *environment variable* is a symbolic name that is associated with a value (string). Environment variables might include items such as paths for saving certain file types (such as temp files), paths to certain files (such as files needed by an application to run), the number of processors, and the processor architecture.

Click the Environment Variables button to open the Environment Variables dialog. The upper portion of the dialog displays variables that are defined for the current user. Use the New, Edit, and Delete buttons in this section to create new user variables.

The lower portion of the dialog displays system variables. Variables in this list are created by the computer administrator, by users of the computer, or by Windows applications. You must be logged on as a Computer Administrator to make changes to these variables. Use the buttons in the lower section of the dialog to make changes to system variables.

> **TIP** You can also use the SET command at the command prompt to create environment variables.

Error Reporting

Error Reporting Click the Error Reporting button in the System Properties dialog to specify how you want to report Windows errors to Microsoft. This button opens the Error Reporting dialog, which is described under the main topic "Error Reporting."

System Restore Tab

The System Restore tab in the System Properties dialog allows you to track and reverse changes that are made to your computer. To disable the System Restore features, check the Turn Off System Restore on All Drives option that appears in the upper portion of the dialog.

Click the Settings button in the Drive Settings section to change the amount of disk space used on each drive for System Restore files. This displays the Drive Settings dialog. Move the Disk Space Usage slider toward the left (Min) to reduce the amount of space or toward the right (Max) to increase the amount of space. Click OK to apply your settings.

Automatic Updates Tab

Use the Automatic Updates tab in the System Properties dialog to configure how you want to handle automatic updates for your software. Three options appear in the Notification Settings area. They allow you to download updates automatically, receive notification before you download and install files, or turn off automatic updating completely.

Use the Previous Updates section to display update notifications that you previously declined. Click the Restore Hidden Items button to redisplay them.

Remote Tab

Use the Remote tab to choose how remote users (such as those on your network or on the Internet) can connect to your computer. Check the "Allow remote assistance invitations to be sent from this computer" option to allow others to connect to your computer. Uncheck this option to turn this feature off.

Click the Advanced button to open the Remote Assistance Settings dialog. You can enable or disable remote control of the computer and set the maximum amount of times that invitations remain open.

The Remote Desktop section of the Remote tab allows you to enable or disable remote desktop connections to this computer. Click the Select Remote Users button to add or remove user names that can connect to the computer.

See also Add New Hardware, Device Manager, Error Reporting, Safely Remove Hardware, User Accounts

System Configuration Utility

Allows you to view and make changes to your system configuration files. To run the System Configuration Utility, choose Start ➤ Run, and enter **msconfig** in the Run dialog.

The System Configuration Utility displays six tabs: General, SYSTEM.INI, WIN.INI, BOOT.INI, Services, and Startup.

General Tab

The General tab allows you to choose which files Windows XP processes when your system starts up. Choose Normal Startup to load all device drivers and services. Choose Diagnostic Startup to load basic device drivers and services so that you can diagnose and troubleshoot system-related problems. To customize your startup files, choose Selective Startup. Then check or uncheck the startup options you want to perform.

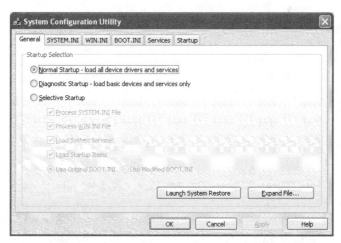

Click the Launch System Restore button to open the System Restore window (which is described in the main topic "System Restore"). Click the Expand File button to open the Expand One File from Installation Source dialog. This dialog

allows you to extract compressed files from Windows XP installation disks and copy them to a specified folder on your hard drive.

SYSTEM.INI and WIN.INI Tabs

The SYSTEM.INI and WIN.INI tabs display lists of items that these files load upon startup. Check or uncheck any item in the list to enable or disable these resources, or click the Enable All or Disable All buttons. Use the buttons in the right side of the dialog to move items up or down in the list or to enable or disable individual items. Click the Find button to locate a specific item. Click the New button to create a new item at the current cursor location. Click the Edit button to change an existing item.

BOOT.INI Tab

The BOOT.INI tab displays your BOOT.INI file in the upper section of the dialog.

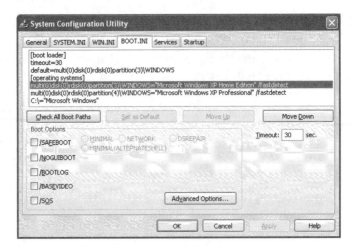

Check or uncheck options in the Boot Options section of the dialog to configure the boot-up options when your computer starts.

Click the Check All Boot Paths button to verify that the entries in your BOOT.INI file are valid.

When you have multiple operating systems on your computer, you can change the order in which they appear in the list. Highlight the line that starts one of the operating systems, and use the Move Up or Move Down buttons to move it up or down in the list.

Use the Set as Default button to select the operating system that you want the BOOT.INI file to use for the default operating system.

Services Tab

The Services tab in the System Configuration Utility dialog displays a list of services that start when your system starts. It also displays whether or not the service is essential to operation, the manufacturer of the service, and the status of the service. Check the Hide All Microsoft Services button to hide all services that were written by Microsoft. Check or uncheck items that you want to include or exclude from your startup options, or click the Enable All or Disable All buttons to include or exclude all items.

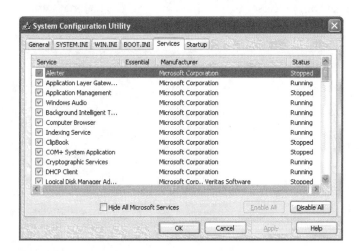

Startup Tab

The Startup tab in the System Configuration Utility dialog displays applications that Windows XP runs when your system starts. Check or uncheck items that you want to include or exclude, or click the Enable All or Disable All buttons to enable or disable all items in the list.

See also Help and Support Center

System Information

System Information MMC snap-in that collects and displays information about your Windows XP computer. To access System Information, choose Start ➢ All Programs (or Start ➢ Programs in the Classic Start menu) ➢ Accessories ➢ System Tools ➢ System Information.

System Information includes a system summary, along with many different items that are grouped into four categories: hardware resources, components, software environment, and Internet Explorer. You can see details about your configuration or provide the information collected by System Information to service technicians who are troubleshooting your computer.

System Summary

Displays a summary of essential system information, such as operating system name and version, processor type, Windows directory, regional settings, and memory information, just to name a few.

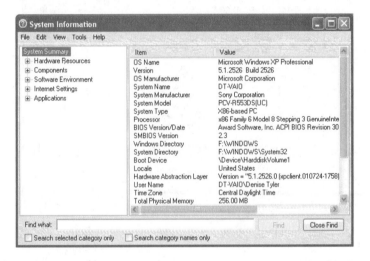

Hardware Resources

Displays information about your hardware resources in several subfolders, including Conflicts/Sharing, DMA, Forced Hardware, I/O, IRQs, and Memory. Select each subfolder from the console tree to display detailed information in the Details pane. The type of information you see depends on the type of resource you selected. To see whether any hardware items share resources or whether resource conflicts exist, select the Conflicts/Sharing folder.

Components

Displays detailed information about the components of your Windows XP computer in several subfolders that may also contain other subfolders. Examples include Multimedia, Display, Infrared, Input, Modem, Network, Ports, Storage,

Printing, Problem Devices, and USB. Select a subfolder from the console tree to display detailed information about a component. Information displayed in the Details pane includes the item (such as Resolution and Bits/Pixel for display) and the item's value (such as 640×480×60 hertz and 32).

Software Environment

Displays detailed information about the software that is currently loaded in memory. This information appears in several subfolders that may also contain other subfolders. Examples include System Drivers, Environment Variables, Print Jobs, and Windows Error Reporting. Select a subfolder to display detailed information in the Details pane. The type of information that appears in the Details pane depends on your selection in the console tree.

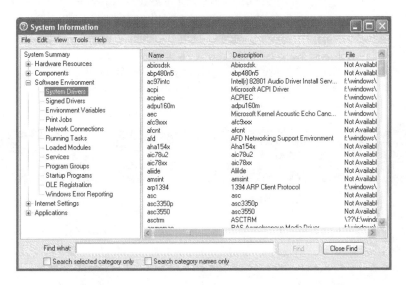

Internet Settings

Displays detailed information about Internet Explorer in several subfolders that can contain other subfolders. Examples include Summary, File Versions, Connectivity, Cache, Content, and Security. The type of information that appears in the Details pane depends on your selection in the console tree.

See also   Add New Hardware, Backup, Device Manager, DirectX, Disk Cleanup, Dr. Watson, File Signature Verification Utility, Microsoft Management Console, Network and Internet Connections

System Monitor

Allows you to monitor the performance of your system. To open the System
Monitor, choose Start ➤ Control Panel (or Start ➤ Settings ➤ Control Panel in
the Classic Start menu), and select Performance and Maintenance. Click Administrative Tools, and double-click Performance to open the System Monitor in the
console root. For further information, see the main topic "Performance."

System Restore

Subset of Windows XP Help and Support Systems that allows you to restore your
system to a configuration that you used on a previous date. System Restore allows
you to resolve problems that might occur as a result of installing improper driver
versions or software that is incompatible with existing hardware and software on
your system.

To open the System Restore window, choose Start ➤ All Programs (or Start ➤
Programs from the Classic Start menu) ➤ Accessories ➤ System Tools ➤ System
Restore.

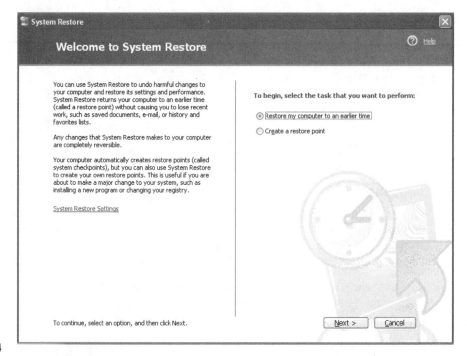

The left side of the System Restore window displays a link called System Restore Settings. Click this link to open the System Properties dialog to the System Restore tab, which is explained in the section "System Restore Tab" under the main topic "System."

The right portion of the System Restore window displays three tasks:

Restore My Computer to an Earlier Time   Choose this option to restore your computer to a configuration that you saved previously. To continue the system restore, follow these steps:

1. Click the Next button to select any bold date from a calendar, or from a list of restore points.

2. Click Next to receive a confirmation of the restore point that you selected. Windows XP prompts you to save your changes and close any programs that are currently open.

3. Click Next to restore your computer to the selected date and time. Windows XP shuts down, and restarts using the settings from the date and time that you specified.

4. After your system restarts, a Restoration Complete screen appears if your computer has been successfully restored. Click OK to exit the System Restore window. If the restoration does not correct the problem, you can choose another restore point or undo the restoration you just completed.

Create a Restore Point   Windows XP creates restore points for you automatically, but you can also choose to create your own restore points. To create a restore point, choose the Create a Restore Point option, and then complete the following steps:

1. Click the Next button to enter a description for your restore point. You can enter a word or phrase (such as "Before Installing Program XYZ") or enter a date and time. You cannot change the name of the restore point after you create it.

2. Click the Create button. The System Restore window notifies you that the restore point has been created.

3. Click Home to perform another system restore task, or Close to close the System Restore window.

Undo My Last Restoration   This option appears after you restore your computer to an earlier time. Choose this option to undo the last restoration that you performed.

See also   Help and Support Center

System Tools

 System Tools Predefined Windows XP program group that contains several utilities you can use to perform system maintenance and configure your system. Choose Start ➢ All Programs (or Start ➢ Programs in the Classic Start menu) ➢ Accessories ➢ System Tools to choose from the following system tools: Activate Windows, Backup (Windows XP Professional only), Character Map, Disk Cleanup, Disk Defragmenter, File and Settings Transfer Wizard, Scheduled Tasks, System Information, and System Restore.

See also Backup, Character Map, Disk Cleanup, Disk Defragmenter, File and Settings Transfer Wizard, Scheduled Tasks, System Information, System Restore

Taskbar

Interface panel that appears at the bottom of your screen by default.

TIP To move the taskbar to the top, left, or right side of the screen, click an empty area of the taskbar and drag it to a new location.

The taskbar allows you to quickly launch and switch between applications. It contains three primary areas:

Start button On the left end of the taskbar. Click the Start button to display shortcuts that launch your Windows XP operating system and additional software.

Taskbar button area The main area of the taskbar. When a program is running, a button for that program appears in the main area of the taskbar. To switch to another opened application, simply click its button.

Notification area At the right end of the taskbar. This area contains your system clock. It may also contain additional icons that allow you to adjust sound or Desktop properties, monitor anti-virus software, or enable and disable hardware and software control panels. Icons also appear here when you are printing a document or when you have received e-mail. Finally, some applications flash or display icons and message balloons in the notification area to alert you to problems or other actions that you need to perform.

TIP Hover the cursor over the system clock to display the current date. Double-click the system clock to adjust the date and time.

Toolbars

You can also display or hide additional toolbars in the taskbar. To add a new toolbar, right-click an empty area of the taskbar. Choose Toolbars from the shortcut menu, then drag your mouse to select a menu option.

NOTE The Toolbars option will not be available if the taskbar is locked.

The five additional toolbars that you can display in the taskbar are:

Address Allows you to enter a URL and click Go to automatically open Internet Explorer and navigate to the URL.

Links Provides you with quick links to Hotmail and to the Microsoft Windows and Windows Media home pages. It also allows you to add your own custom links.

Desktop Places shortcuts for the items found on your Desktop (such as My Computer and My Network Places) in the taskbar.

Quick Launch Lets you quickly launch applications, such as Internet Explorer and Outlook Express, by clicking the corresponding button. Also contains the Show Desktop button, which you can use to bring the Desktop to the front.

TIP To create a Taskbar shortcut that points to an application, simply drag an application from My Computer or Windows Explorer to the Quick Launch toolbar. To remove the shortcut, right-click it and choose Delete.

New Toolbar Allows you to create a shortcut to a folder or a URL.

To remove a toolbar from the taskbar, right-click the toolbar and click Close Toolbar. If the Confirm Toolbar Close dialog appears (you can optionally disable it), choose OK to close the toolbar.

NOTE You may need to resize toolbars that are already in the taskbar to create enough space for your new toolbars. To resize or move toolbars, move the cursor over the vertical bar at the left of the toolbar. Then click and drag the toolbar left or right. You can also drag and drop the toolbar to the Desktop to create a floating toolbar.

Switching between Applications

Windows XP allows you to multitask your applications, so you can run more than one application at the same time. There are two ways to switch between open applications: You can use the taskbar or a keystroke shortcut.

Using the Taskbar

When you open an application, the taskbar displays a button with the icon and name of the application. To switch to any other open application, click the appropriate button on the taskbar. A taskbar button may at first show the entire name of the application and any open documents or folders.

Windows XP also groups similar buttons into a single button. For example, if you have multiple documents open in Word, or if you have several Explorer windows open, the taskbar displays a common button that displays the number of open documents. Click the application button to display a submenu of open documents, and select the document you want to bring to the front.

TIP Drag the top of the taskbar upward, and you'll have two bars available on which to place buttons. However, keep in mind that this reduces the size available to the Desktop.

Using the Alt+Tab Key Combination

As you open more applications, the taskbar buttons become smaller and the names truncate to fit all the buttons into the taskbar. When several applications are open at the same time, it can become difficult to determine which buttons are associated with which applications. In these cases, you can use the Alt+Tab key combination to switch between applications. To do so, follow these steps:

1. Hold down the Alt key and keep it held down while you complete the next steps.

2. Press and release the Tab key. A dialog displays a selection border around the icon for the application you last used. The name of the selected icon appears in the bottom of the dialog. Additional icons appear for each window that is open.

3. Press and release the Tab key to move through the list one icon at a time until the border surrounds the application you want to open.

4. Release the Alt key to bring the selected application to the foreground.

See also   Start Menu, Taskbar and Start Menu

Taskbar and Start Menu

 Customizes the taskbar and Start menu. To open the Taskbar and Start Menu Properties dialog, choose Start ➤ Control Panel (or Start ➤ Settings ➤ Control Panel in the Classic Start menu) ➤ Appearance and Themes, and then click the Taskbar and Start Menu control panel icon. Alternatively, you can right-click an empty area of the taskbar and choose Properties. The Taskbar and Start Menu Properties dialog has two tabs: Taskbar and Start Menu.

Taskbar Tab

Use this tab to customize the look and placement of the taskbar.

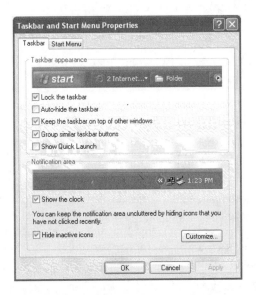

Lock the Taskbar   Locks the taskbar in its current position so that you cannot move it to another location. Uncheck this box to unlock the taskbar.

NOTE When you lock the taskbar, you will not be able to customize the toolbars that appear on the taskbar.

Auto-Hide the Taskbar   Displays the taskbar as a thin line until you move the pointer over it to reveal the taskbar.

TIP If you want the taskbar to still display as a thin line even if a full-screen window is displayed, select both Keep the Taskbar on Top of Other Windows and Auto-Hide.

TIP A different way to hide the taskbar is to drag its top edge down (or to the side if you've moved the taskbar to the side). Drag the line up (left or right) to display it again.

Keep the Taskbar on Top of Other Windows   Displays the taskbar on top of other opened windows so that you can always see it.

Group Similar Taskbar Buttons   Displays all files opened with the same application in the same area of the taskbar. If the button width shrinks below a certain width, the opened files collapse into a single button. Click the button to select the window you want, or right-click the button to close the application you want.

Show Quick Launch   Displays or hides the Quick Launch buttons at the right of the Start menu.

Show the Clock   Displays the clock on the right side of the taskbar. Enabled by default.

Hide Inactive Icons   Keeps the notification area uncluttered by hiding icons for applications you have not used for a while.

Customize   Allows you to customize the icons that appear in the notification area. Click to open a dialog that displays a list of icons that Windows XP and third-party software normally placed in the notification area. Use dropdowns in the Behavior column to select Hide When Inactive, Always Hide, or Always Show for each icon you want to customize. Click Restore Defaults to revert to installed defaults.

Start Menu Tab

Use this tab to customize the appearance and style of the Start menu. You can customize the appearance of the Windows XP Start menu, or change to and customize to the Classic Start menu style used in previous versions of Windows.

Start Menu

When you choose this option, Windows XP displays a Start menu that provides easy access to the Internet, e-mail, and your favorite programs. To customize this Start menu, click the Customize button that appears to the right of the Start Menu radio button. This opens the Customize Start Menu dialog, which features two tabs: General and Advanced.

The General tab allows you to configure the following options:

- To select an icon size for programs, choose the Large Icons (default) or Small Icons radio button.

- To specify the number of program shortcuts that appear on the Start menu, enter a new value in the Programs area. The list displays the applications you have used most recently. To clear the program list, click Clear List.

- Internet Explorer and Outlook Express appear as the default Internet and e-mail programs on the Start menu. To change these defaults, select another browser from the Internet drop-down list and select another mail reader from the E-mail drop-down list, or uncheck one or both boxes to disable any such program from appearing on the Start menu automatically.

The Advanced tab lets you specify Start menu settings, select other items that appear on the Start menu, and get quick access to documents you've used most recently. The Advanced tab has three sections:

Start Menu Settings   Allows you to open submenus when you hover the mouse over the parent menu, and to highlight newly installed programs.

Start Menu Items   Displays a list of items that you can include or remove from the Start menu. Select radio buttons to include the named items as a link or as a menu, or to never display them.

Recent Documents   To display your most recent documents on the Start menu, select the check box. Click Clear List to reset the list of documents.

Classic Start Menu

When you select this radio button in the Taskbar and Start Menu Properties dialog, Windows XP formats the Start menu using the classic style of previous releases of Windows. A preview appears in the upper portion of the Taskbar and Start Menu Properties dialog. To customize the Classic Start menu, click the Customize button that appears to the right of the Classic Start Menu radio button. This opens the Customize Classic Start Menu dialog.

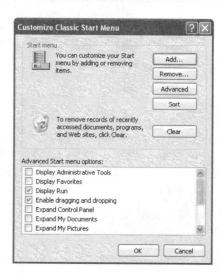

To add items to the Start menu, click Add; the Create Shortcut Wizard appears. Enter the path to the program you want to add, or use the Browse button to locate it. Click Next to select (or New Folder to create) the Start Menu folder in which to store the new item. Finally, click Next to assign a name to the new shortcut, and click Finish.

To remove shortcuts and folders from the Start menu, click Remove; the Remove Shortcuts/Folders dialog appears. When you remove a folder, you also remove all shortcuts contained in that folder. Locate the folder or shortcut you want to remove, and then click Remove. Click Close to exit the dialog.

Choose Advanced to open an advanced explorer view of your Start Menu folder. In this view, you can add submenus to the Start menu or to the Programs folder. First, highlight the item to which you want to add a submenu. Then, choose File ➤ New ➤ Folder and assign a name to the folder. After you add the subfolder, you can drag and drop shortcuts from other folders into your new folder. You can also use the Add button in the Customize Classic Start Menu dialog to add shortcuts.

Click the Sort button to rearrange items on the Programs menu so that they display in the default order.

Click the Clear button to remove records of recently accessed documents, programs, and Web sites from the Documents menu.

Choose Advanced Start Menu options from the scrolling list at the bottom of the dialog. Options here allow you to expand folders, scroll programs list, show small icons in the Start menu, and to display other program options. Select or unselect the check boxes for the options that you want to include or omit.

TIP You can also add items to the Start menu or any Programs submenu by dragging an item to it from My Computer or Windows Explorer. Note that when you start dragging, the Start menu won't be displayed. To display it, drag the item over the Start Menu button. Then continue to drag the item to the desired location.

See also Start Menu, Taskbar

Task Manager

Lets you view the status of and control programs and processes that are running on the Windows XP computer. You can also view performance indicators for processes. Using Task Manager, you can see which programs (tasks) are running, end them if they're no longer responding, see which processes are running, and view system resource information about these processes as well as overall system usage information.

To access Task Manager, press Ctrl+Alt+Delete. The Windows Task Manager dialog opens, with menus at the top of the window. Four tabs also appear in the main Task Manager dialog: Applications, Processes, Performance, and Networking. A status bar appears at the bottom of the dialog.

The status bar at the bottom of the Task Manager window displays information about the number of processes that are currently running, the current CPU usage, and the current memory usage.

Menus

Task Manager has several menus: File, Options, View, Windows, Shut Down, and Help. The options available on the View menu change depending on the Task Manager tab you have selected.

File Menu

New Task (Run...)   Opens the Create New Task dialog. Enter the path to a new task and click OK to run it.

Exit Task Manager   Ends Task Manager.

Options Menu

Always on Top   Check this option to run Task Manager on top of other programs.

Minimize on Use   Check this option to minimize Task Manager when you switch to another running program.

Hide When Minimized   Check this option to hide Task Manager when you minimize it. It does not appear in the taskbar.

Show 16-Bit Tasks   Appears only when you select the Processes tab. Check this option to include 16-bit Windows tasks in Task Manager.

Tab Always Active   Appears only when you select the Networking tab. Check this option to show the Networking tab when you open the Task Manager.

Other options, such as Show Accumulative Data, Auto Scale, Reset, and Show Scale, are only available when you are on a network and select the Networking tab.

View Menu

Refresh Now   Refreshes the Task Manager screen immediately.

Update Speed   Configures how often the Task Manager screen refreshes automatically. From the submenu, choose High (twice per second), Normal (every two seconds), Low (every four seconds), or Paused (no automatic refresh).

Large Icons, Small Icons, Details   Appear only when you select the Applications tab. Display tasks as large or small icons, or as a list of tasks and their status (the default setting).

Select Columns   Appears when you select the Processes, or Networking tab. Choose this option to open the Select Columns dialog, which allows you to configure columns that appear for each view.

CPU History   Appears only when you select the Performance tab. Displays one graph per CPU if your computer has more than one processor.

Show Kernel Times   Appears only when you select the Performance tab. Displays kernel time in the CPU and Memory Usage and Usage History graphs.

Network Adapter History   Appears only when you select the Networking tab. Displays kernel time in the CPU and Memory Usage and Usage History graphs.

Shut Down Menu

Stand By, Hibernate   Places your computer in the appropriate mode.

Turn Off, Restart   Turns your computer off, or shuts down and restarts it.

Log Off (Username)   Logs the current user off.

Lock Computer   Appears only when one user is configured on the computer. Click to lock the computer. You will need to enter your password to unlock the computer.

Tabs

Task Manager contains the Application, Processes, Performance, Networking, and Users tabs, which you can use to view and control tasks and processes as well as view performance information.

Applications   Displays all applications (tasks) that are currently running. To terminate a task, select it and click End Task. To switch to another task, select that task and click Switch To. To create a new task, click New Task.

Processes   Displays a list of processes that are currently running. Default columns display details about the image name of the application that is running, the user name, and the CPU and memory being used by the task. To add additional columns, choose View ➤ Select Columns. To terminate a process, select one from the list and click End Process.

You can also assign priorities to processes. Right-click a process and choose Set Priority. Choices in the submenu include Realtime, High, AboveNormal, Normal (default), BelowNormal, and Low.

Performance Graphically displays system performance information such as usage and history for CPU and memory.

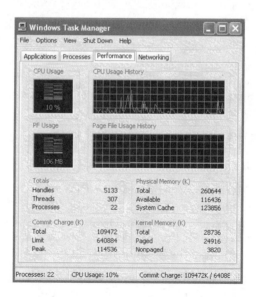

Networking Displays a graph of network connection usage for each network adapter installed on your computer.

Turn Off Computer

To turn off your computer, click the Start button to display the Start menu. Then click Turn off Computer, located in the bottom-right corner. The Turn Off Computer dialog appears.

Stand By   Click Stand By to put your computer a low-power state. In Stand By mode, you can quickly resume your Windows session when you press and release the on/off button on your computer.

Shift-click Stand By to put your computer in hibernation. This mode saves your Desktop state to your hard drive so that you can resume Windows where you left off. Then it shuts your computer down.

Turn Off   Powers down your computer. Windows XP prompts you to save any unsaved changes in programs that are currently opened before your computer shuts down.

Restart   Reboots your computer. Windows XP prompts you to save any unsaved changes in programs that are currently opened before it reboots your computer.

Updates

See   Windows Update

User Accounts

Windows XP makes it easy for several different users to use the same computer while retaining their own settings for Desktop, e-mail, and Internet settings. To open the User Accounts window, choose Start ➤ Control Panel ➤ User Accounts. The User Accounts home page differs, depending on whether you are logged in as a Computer Administrator, Limited user, or Guest.

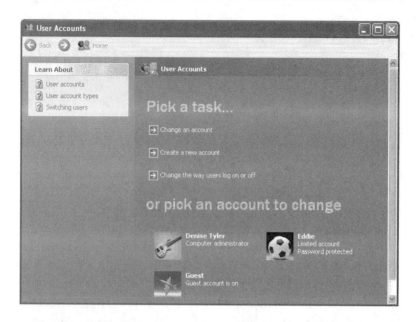

The main differences between the three types of user accounts are as follows:

Computer Administrator   Allows an individual to make system-wide changes to the computer. This includes installation of programs and hardware, accessing and reading all non-private files, creating and deleting user accounts, and changing the names, pictures, passwords, and account types of other users.

Limited   Prevents the user from changing most computer settings and deleting important files. Users that are assigned Limited accounts cannot install software or hardware, but can access programs that have already been installed on the system. Limited users can change their account name and picture. They will be unable to create, change, or delete their account password.

Guest   For users who do not have a user account on the computer. There is no password for this account, so all users that log in as guests will share common Internet and e-mail settings. Guest users cannot install hardware or software, but can access applications that are already installed on the computer. They will be unable to change the account type, but can change the Guest account picture.

The User Accounts toolbar appears in the top of the User Accounts window when you are logged in as any type of user. Click the Back and Forward buttons to navigate back and forth to topics that you have already viewed. Click Home to return to the main User Accounts window at any time.

Options Pane

The left side of the User Accounts window offers options and topics related to user accounts and their management. These depend on the account currently logged in and the task or option chosen. Possible categories and options include Related Tasks (such as Manage My Network Passwords or Prevent a Forgotten Password) and the Learn About section, which contains quick overviews about key User Accounts features, such as deleting your own account, switching users, or using a .NET Passport. Each option provides additional links to related topics in the Windows XP Help and Support Center.

Pick a Task

The Pick a Task section of the User Accounts window provides quick access to the main tasks that users typically need to perform. The options in this section vary, depending on whether you are logged on as a Computer Administrator, Limited user, or Guest. The steps to perform each task are described in the following sections.

Change an Account

This option appears for Computer Administrators only. Click Change an Account, then choose the account you want to change from the following screen. After you select the account, the following choices appear, depending upon whether you select your account or the account of another user on the machine:

Change My/the Name   Prompts you to enter a new name for the account on a separate screen. The name you enter appears in the Welcome screen and Start menu. After you enter the new name, click Change Name to apply the new settings.

Change My/the Password   This option appears if a password has been created for the account. See "Change My/the Password," later in this topic, for the procedure.

Remove My/the Password   This option appears if a password has been created for the account. See "Remove My/the Password," later in this topic, for the procedure.

Change My/the Picture This option appears when a Computer Administrator elects to change any type of account. See "Change My/the Picture," later in this topic, for the procedure.

Change My/the Account Type This option appears when a Computer Administrator elects to change a non-Guest account. The Computer Administrator can change another Computer Administrator to a Limited user or vice versa. After you select the new option, click Change Account Type to apply the change.

> **NOTE** A Computer Administrator cannot change their own account type to Limited unless there is at least one other Computer Administrator account present on the system.

Create a Password This option appears if the selected Computer Administrator or Limited account is not yet protected by a password. To create a password for the selected account, click Create a Password to open a dialog. Enter a password on the first line, and retype the same password (case-sensitive) to confirm it on the second line. Enter a word or phrase to use as a password hint on the third line. Then, click Create Password.

Set up my account to use a .NET Passport This option appears when a Computer Administrator elects to change their own account. Choose this option to open the .NET Passport Wizard, which allows you to configure personal access to MSN Web sites and other passport-enabled sites using your e-mail address.

Delete the Account This option appears when a Computer Administrator elects to change another user's Computer Administrator or Limited account. After you select the user, click Delete the Account. The next screen asks if you want to keep the files associated with the account:

- Click Keep Files to save the files. A new folder, using the same name as the account you are deleting, appears on your Desktop. The folder contains the user's Desktop and My Document files. E-mail messages, Internet favorites, and other settings are discarded.

- Click Delete Files to remove all files associated with the account.

Turn Off the Guest Account A Computer Administrator can remove the Guest account from the computer, providing that the Guest has logged off the computer. To remove the Guest account, choose Start ➤ Control Panel ➤ User Accounts. From the Accounts to Change section, click the Guest account. Then, click Turn Off the Guest Account.

TIP   To turn the Guest account back on, repeat the steps mentioned here. After you click the Guest account to change it, click Turn On the Guest Account to complete the task.

Create a New Account

This option appears for Computer Administrators only, and allows the administrator to create another Computer Administrator or Limited user account on the computer. To create a new account, follow these steps:

1. Choose Create a New Account. The Name the New Account screen appears.

2. Enter a name for the new account. This account name appears on the Welcome screen during the log-in procedure. Click Next to choose the account type.

3. Choose Computer Administrator to allow this user to make system-wide changes and account changes. Choose Limited if you only want to allow the user to run applications that are already on the computer, and to access their password-protected e-mail, Internet, and documents.

4. Click Create Account.

NOTE   New accounts are not password-protected when you first create them. The Computer Administrator or the account user can set up a password for the account after it is created.

Change the Way Users Log On or Off

This option appears for Computer Administrators only. It allows you to select whether or not users will be able to log on with the Welcome screen, by using Fast User Switching, or both. After you make your choices, click Apply Options to apply the settings.

NOTE   Windows XP prompts you to disable Offline Files before you enable Fast User Switching.

Set Up My Account to Use a .NET Passport

In the event that you forget your User Account password, you can use a password reset disk to gain access to your account. The Forgotten Password Wizard helps you create a password reset disk on a floppy drive or on a removable disk drive such as a Zip disk.

Change My/the Picture

To change your picture, use one of the following methods:

- If you are logged on as a Computer Administrator, choose Start ➤ Control Panel ➤ User Accounts. From the Pick a Task section, click Change an Account and select an account to change. Then click Change My/The Picture. Alternatively, click one of the accounts that appear in the Pick an Account to Change section of the User Accounts window. Then click Change My/The Picture. Select a new picture, then click Change Picture.

- If you are logged on as a Limited user or Guest, choose Start ➤ Control Panel ➤ User Accounts. From the Pick a Task section, click Change My Picture. Click to select one of the pictures on the page, then click Change Picture.

TIP You can also use any BMP, GIF, JPEG, PNG, or TIFF image that resides on your computer. Click Browse for More Pictures. Select the image you want to use and click Open. To use a picture from a scanner or camera, choose Get a Picture from a Camera or Scanner.

Change My/the Password

A Computer Administrator can change the password for any other user on the computer. A Limited user can only change his or her own password. To change your account password, follow these steps:

1. Open the Change My Password window using one of the following methods:

    - If you are logged on as a Computer Administrator, choose Start ➤ Control Panel ➤ User Accounts. From the Pick a Task section, click Change an Account and select an account to change. Then click Change My Password (or Change the Password). Alternatively, click one of the accounts that appear in the Pick an Account to Change section of the User Accounts window. Then click Change My Password or Change the Password.

    - If you are logged on as a Limited user, choose Start ➤ Control Panel ➤ User Accounts. From the Pick a Task section, click Change My Password.

2. Enter the current password in the first line. If you don't remember the password, click Show Password Hint for a reminder.

3. Enter a new password on the second line.

4. Retype the new password on the third line, using the same capitalization (passwords are case-sensitive).

5. Enter a word or phrase on the fourth line to use as a Password Hint. You can use this password hint at any time to help remember your password.

6. Click Change Password. The new password is now ready to use.

WARNING Remember that your password hint will be visible to anyone who tries to use your account to log on to the computer. Anyone who knows you really well might be able to guess your password based on the hint you enter. So make sure you enter a hint (and resulting password) that only you will recognize!

Remove My/the Password

Computer Administrators can remove passwords for any user on the computer. A Limited user can only remove his or her own password. This option will not be available unless the user account has a password assigned to it.

- If you are logged on as a Computer Administrator, choose Start ➤ Control Panel ➤ User Accounts. From the Pick a Task section, click Change an Account and select an account to change. Then click Remove My Password (or Remove the Password). Alternatively, click one of the accounts that appear in the Pick an Account to Change section of the User Accounts window. Enter your current password to confirm your identity. Then click Remove My Password or Remove the Password.

- If you are logged on as a Limited user, choose Start ➤ Control Panel ➤ User Accounts. From the Pick a Task section, click Remove My Password. Enter your current password to confirm your identity. Then click Remove Password.

Or Pick an Account to Change

This section appears at the bottom of the User Accounts window when you are logged in as a Computer Administrator. It displays icons for all user accounts that are configured on the computer. To change an account, simply click to select it. The options that appear are similar to those discussed previously in this topic.

See also   Fast User Switching, Forgotten Password Wizard, Help and Support Center, .NET Passport Wizard, Network Passwords

Utility Manager

 Utility Manager   Program used by Computer Administrators to manage the Windows XP Magnifier, Narrator, and On-Screen Keyboard Accessibility options.

The preferred way to start Utility Manager is to press the Windows Logo Key + U at the Windows XP Welcome screen. Starting Utility Manager using this method enables you to manage your programs when you lock or unlock your computer.

Alternatively, choose Start ➤ All Programs ➤ Accessories ➤ Accessibility ➤ Utility Manager. When you use this method, Utility Manager cannot manage your programs when you lock or unlock your computer, and some options will be disabled.

TIP You must have administrative privileges to run Utility Manager and to configure utility options.

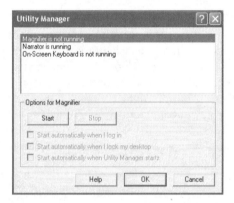

The Utility Manager displays the Accessibility utilities currently installed in Utility Manager: Magnifier, Narrator, and On-Screen Keyboard are installed automatically during Windows XP setup. The status of each device appears as Running, Not Running, or Not Responding. The Narrator utility runs automatically when you open Utility Manager.

To start or stop a utility, select it from the list and click Start or Stop.

Three additional options appear in the lower portion of the Utility Manager. These options are disabled if you start Utility Manager through the Start menu. They allow you to start the selected utility automatically when you log in, when you lock your Desktop, or when Utility Manager starts. Check or uncheck each of these options as desired for each utility.

See also Accessibility, Magnifier, Narrator, On-Screen Keyboard

Virtual Memory

See System

Volume Control

 Lets you control the volume, balance, and other audio settings for speakers and other audio devices used for sound recording and playback. To open the Volume Control dialog, choose Start ➤ All Programs ➤ Accessories ➤ Entertainment ➤ Volume Control.

TIP There are other ways to open the Volume Control dialog. One way is to double-click the Sound icon in the notification area of the taskbar. Or, in Sound Recorder's Audio Properties dialog, click Volume under any device on the Audio Devices tab. Or, from Sounds and Audio Devices (in Control Panel), click Volume for any audio device that appears in the Audio tab.

By default, the Volume Control dialog displays controls used for audio playback. The Volume Control portion of the dialog displays a master set of Balance and Volume sliders and a Mute All check box. These controls affect all of the audio devices that are shown in the Volume Control dialog. In addition, each audio device has its own controls that you can set independently.

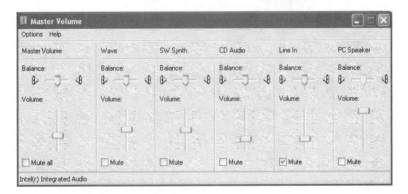

The Volume Control Options menu has three choices: Properties, Advanced Controls, and Exit.

Properties

Click Options ➤ Properties to open the Properties dialog. If you have more than one mixer device installed on your computer, use the Mixer Device drop-down to choose between them. The Adjust Volume For section allows you to choose devices that are displayed during Playback, Recording, or Other (depending on the capabilities of your mixer device). By default, the Volume Control dialog displays settings for Playback mode. (To configure recording settings, click the Recording radio button and your dialog and menu options will change accordingly.) The bottom of the Properties dialog contains a list of the audio devices that are installed on your computer. Check or uncheck any device to add or remove them from the Volume Control or Recording Control dialog, then choose OK to return to that dialog.

Advanced Controls

When you choose Advanced Controls from the Options menu, an Advanced button appears for each device that supports additional settings. Click it to open the Advanced Controls for *Device Name* dialog. Use the Bass and Treble sliders in the Tone Controls section to adjust between Low and High settings. Other control options may appear in the dialog, depending on your audio hardware. Consult your hardware documentation for further information on using these settings.

See also Sound Recorder, Sounds and Audio Devices

Web Publishing Wizard

Publish this file to the Web Allows you to publish your files to MSN or XDrive (each of which requires a user account). You can also publish your files to shared folders or shared webs on your network, or to an FTP site.

To open the Web Publishing Wizard, use one of the following methods:

- Choose Start ➤ My Documents. Select one or more files or folders. From the File and Folder Tasks section in the left pane of the My Documents window, click Publish This File (or Folder) to the Web.

- Choose Start ➤ My Computer. Double-click a drive on your computer. Select the files or folders you want to publish. From the File and Folder Tasks section in the left pane, click Publish This File (or Folder) to the Web.

After the Web Publishing Wizard screen opens, click Next to continue. Follow the prompts in the wizard to publish your selected files and folders to the location you specify in the wizard.

Welcome Screen

Screen that initially appears when Windows first starts. The Welcome screen allows you to log on to any user account that is set up on the computer. To log on, click the icon that applies to the user account you want to use. If the account is password-protected, Windows XP prompts you to enter the account password. Press Enter after you complete these steps to open Windows XP.

You can configure Windows XP so that the Welcome screen does not appear when you first start the computer. Instead, your computer will display the Windows Desktop when you first open Windows.

To disable the Welcome screen, follow these steps:

1. Log on to Windows XP as a Computer Administrator.

2. Choose Start ➤ Control Panel (or Start ➤ Settings ➤ Control Panel in the Classic Start menu) and click User Accounts to open the User Accounts window.

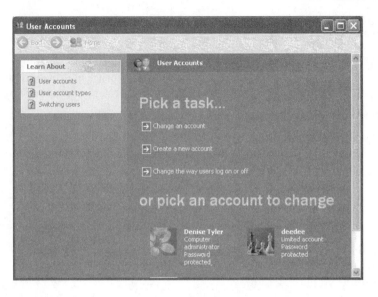

3. In the Pick a Task section, select Change The Way Users Log On Or Off. The Select Logon And Logoff Options window appears.

4. Deselect the Use the Welcome Screen option.

5. Choose Apply Options to apply the new settings.

NOTE When you disable the Use the Welcome Screen option, the Welcome screen no longer appears when you start the computer. Instead, the standard Log On to Windows dialog appears. Enter your user name, and password if you use one, in the dialog to log on to the computer.

To re-enable the Welcome screen, repeat these steps and, at Step 4, check the Use The Welcome Screen option.

What's This

Dialog feature that allows you to access context-sensitive help. To access What's This, right-click an item in a dialog. If available, the What's This selection pops up. Click it to read help information about the item.

Some dialogs display a question mark icon in the top-right corner. Click the icon to attach a What's This question mark to the cursor. Then place the cursor over the item in the dialog for which you want help. Click the item to read help information.

See also Help and Support Center

Windows Components

Windows XP Home and Professional install many Windows components on your computer, and also provide many other components to suit your specific needs. The default options installed with Home and Professional are not identical.

Examples of Windows components installed by default include WordPad, Calculator, HyperTerminal, Phone Dialer, Media Player, and Volume Control. Additional Windows components include Component Services, Data Sources, Event Viewer, Remote Storage, and so on.

To add additional components that Windows XP does not install by default, choose Start ➤ Control Panel (or Start ➤ Settings ➤ Control Panel in the Classic Start menu) ➤ Add or Remove Programs. Select Add/Remove Windows Components from the left pane. For information about each of the available components, look under the specific main topic elsewhere in this book or use Windows XP Help and Support Center.

See also Add or Remove Programs, Control Panel, Help and Support Center

Windows Explorer

See Explorer

Windows Media Player

Windows Media Player Allows you to play audio, video, and mixed-media files in a variety of different formats. For example, you can view video clips of a movie, listen to radio broadcasts (over the Internet), or enjoy a music video.

Windows Media Player supports both streaming and non-streaming media files. When you play a streaming media file, playback begins before the entire file is downloaded. Streaming files use a continuous process of downloading portions of the file, storing those portions in memory, and then playing them back while more of the file is downloaded and stored. This allows users to receive live media content, such as newscasts or live concerts.

TIP For a full list of supported file types, see the "Options" section later in this topic.

To access Windows Media Player, choose Start ➤ All Programs (or Start ➤ Programs in the Classic Start menu) ➤ Accessories ➤ Entertainment ➤ Windows Media Player.

The Windows Media Player window consists of several components, which will vary depending on the view you have selected and the type of file you are playing. Components can include the following:

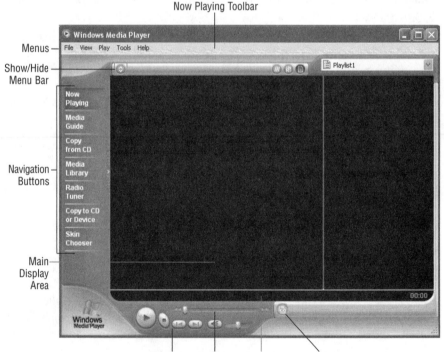

Menus   Let you use and configure Windows Media Player. To display or hide the menu bar, click the Show Menu Bar control in the left side of the Now Playing toolbar.

Now Playing toolbar   Appears immediately above the main display area of the media player. It contains buttons that allow you to display or hide the menu bar, turn shuffling on and off, show or hide equalizer controls, and display or hide the playlist. A drop-down list allows you to select any item in your Media Library so that you can play the media.

Navigation buttons   The buttons in the left portion of the Windows Media Player allow you to choose one of several windows to display in the main display area. Click a button to display one of the following windows: Now Playing, Media Guide, CD Audio, Media Library, Radio Tuner, Portable Device, or Skin Chooser.

TIP   These buttons are discussed individually in later subtopics.

Main display area   Depending on the window you choose to display in the Windows Media Player, the main area can display one of several different items: visualizations when you play audio files; video files; Internet Web pages with links to online media; items in your Media Library; track lists on a CD; a list of online radio stations; a list of items to burn to a portable device; and a skin chooser that allows you to customize the appearance of Windows Media Player when you view it in compact mode.

Status bar   Displays information about the media that you are currently playing, such as total length of the media file, bit rate, number of items in a list, total length and size of a selected group of files, and media player status (Ready, Playing, and so on).

Seek bar   Slider that displays the progress of a playing media file. You can move the slider to skip to a different place in the media file.

Controls   Allow you to use VCR-type controls to play, pause, stop, skip forward, skip backward, rewind, fast forward, and preview your media files, and mute or adjust the volume.

Switch to Skin Mode   Button to the right of the controls that allows you to display a Windows Media Player skin while you view the player in compact mode.

Menus

Windows Media Player's menus contain options that enable you to use and configure the application. Some are common to all Windows applications (Open, Exit, Help); the commands that are unique to Windows Media Player are described in the next few pages.

File Menu

File Menu commands allow you to perform the following operations (among others):

- Open files or URLs to play.

- Add the current track, file, or URL to your media library.

- Copy tracks from and to audio CDs and to portable playing devices.

- Import and export playlists.

- Listen to content while offline.

- Display the properties of the current media file.

View Menu

The View menu contains commands that control the appearance of the media player. You can choose from these options (among others):

- Display the media player in full mode or skin mode.

- Show or hide the menu bar or various taskbars.

- Show or hide the playlist, title, visualizations, equalizer, and settings, or resize bars.

- Choose the visualizations that you want to display.

- Display or hide file markers and file statistics.

Play Menu

The Play menu contains options that let you control the playback of media files, with traditional controls such as Play, Pause, Rewind, Fast Forward, and Stop. You can also perform the following:

- Play CD audio files on a selected CD or DVD drive.

- Shuffle or repeat playback of files in the playlist.

- Increase, decrease, or mute the volume.

- Eject the media from your media device.

Tools Menu

Commands in the Tools menu allow you to:

- Download visualizations from the Microsoft Web site.

- Search your computer for media files.

- Backup and restore license files for your media.

- Open the Options dialog (described in the following section).

Options

Choose Tools ➢ Options to display the Options dialog, which consists of eight tabs: Media Library, Visualizations, File Types, Network, Player, Copy Music, Devices, and Performance.

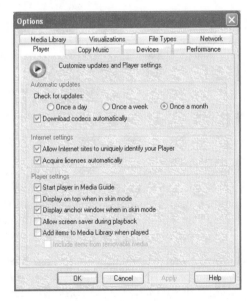

Media Library tab Configure the access rights of other applications and of Internet sites (No access, Read-only access, or Full access). Check or uncheck the option to automatically add purchased music to your Media Library.

Visualizations tab Add and configure the visualizations that you can display in Windows Media Player. To view or configure full-screen size and buffer settings for the selected visualization, click the Properties button.

File Types tab   Select the media formats that will automatically open Windows Media Player when you select them. Check or uncheck to automatically open the following file types:

File Type	Extension(s)
Windows Media	ASF, ASX, WM, WMX, WMP
Windows Media audio	WMA, WAX
Windows Media audio/video	WMV, WVX
CD audio tracks	CDA
Video	AVI
Audio	WAV
Movie	MPEG, MPG, MPE, M1V, MP2, MPV2, MP2V, MPA
MPEG3 format sound	MP3, M3U
MIDI sound	MID, MIDI, RMI
Indeo video	IVF
AIFF format sound	AIF, AIFC, AIFF
AU format sound	AU, SND

Network tab   Configure network protocols and proxy settings. Check the protocols you use to receive streaming media. To specify UDP ports, check the Use Ports option and enter the port address you want to use. The Proxy Settings list displays a list of protocols for your computer. Click the Configure button to configure proxy settings for the selected protocol.

Player tab   Customize updates and other settings for the Windows Media Player. You can automatically check for updates and download codecs. Check or uncheck options that allow Internet sites to uniquely identify your player, or to acquire licenses automatically. Check options in the Player Settings section to control display of Windows Media Player and the Media Guide.

Copy Music tab   Specify the location of your My Music folder. Use the File Format drop-down to select the file format you use by default when you copy files from CD.

Devices tab   Configure playback and copy settings for audio CDs, and copy settings for portable devices. Select a device from the list, then choose Properties to view or configure properties for the device.

Performance tab   Configure network or player performance. You can choose to automatically detect connection speed and use default buffering or to set these manually. You can also adjust hardware acceleration rate, apply a full screen mode switch, and adjust digital video acceleration settings.

Screens

Now Playing

Displays your current media in the left portion of the screen. If you are playing an audio file (such as a CD track, music file, or radio station), the right pane displays a computer-generated visualization that changes in time with the music. When you select a video or animation file, it also appears in the left pane.

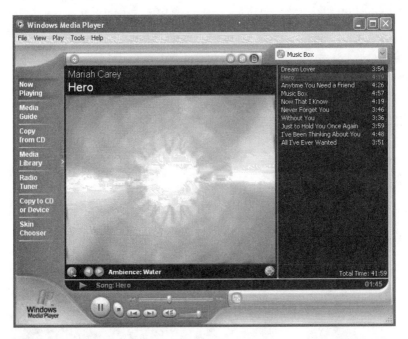

The right pane in the Now Playing screen displays the name of the media file that is currently playing. The lower section of the right pane displays the total length of the media file. Beneath the visualization is a toolbar that allows you to choose its type and display mode.

Media Guide

Navigates to the WindowsMedia.com home page, which streams the latest video and music files from the Internet. Media files are encoded for 56K modem connections and for broadband connections such as DSL and cable modems.

The left portion of the home page contains a Web Search that allows you to search WindowsMedia.com for media. Enter a search term and press the Go button to perform the media search. The navigation bar also contains links to other pages providing content related to music, radio, movies, entertainment, lifestyles, business, news, sports, and webcams.

Copy from CD

Allows you to listen to or save copies of songs from CD to your media library. The screen displays the CD title and a list of its tracks, and information such as track number, name, length, copy status (if copied to your media library), artist, composer, genre, style, data provider, and modified by. Buttons at the top allow you to copy selected files from the CD to your hard drive, search an online database for CD information, and display detailed information about the CD.

Media Library

Media Library Displays a list of all media files that you have added to your library and allows you to manage those files. The left pane arranges your media into several categories: Audio, Video, My Playlists, Radio Tuner Presets, and Deleted Items. Click the plus (+) sign to expand a category and select any item from the list. Click the minus (-) sign to minimize a category list.

The right pane of the Media Library window changes, depending on the type of item that you select from the right pane. Use the right pane to view and select your media files in a number of ways. For example:

- Select the Album category in the left pane to display a list of albums in the right pane.

- Expand an album subcategory (All Audio, Album, Artist, or Genre) to arrange your audio files based on the subcategory you select.

- Select the Video subcategory from the left pane to display a list of all video clips, or to select one by author name.

- Select a My Playlists subcategory from the left pane to display custom playlists in the right pane.

399

- Select Radio Tuner Presets from the left pane to display a list of Internet Radio stations in the right pane.

- Select Deleted Items from the left pane to view a list of media files that have been deleted from your media library. To remove the deleted items, right-click the Deleted Items header and choose Empty Deleted Items. To restore a deleted item into your media library, right-click the item you want to restore, and choose Restore (to restore all deleted items) or Restore Selected (to restore selected items only).

The Media Player toolbar lets you create and manage playlists, search for files in your media library, and get information on the current CD.

Radio Tuner

Radio Tuner Allows you to tune in to online radio stations and listen to radio broadcasts from all over the world as they are streamed over the Internet. The left pane contains a list of featured stations that allow you to quickly choose a radio broadcast. Expand the selection to add it to your stations list, visit the Web site, or play the broadcast. The left pane also includes the My Stations list and a list of recently played stations.

Copy to CD or Device

Copy to CD or Device Allows you to copy media files from your Media Library to a portable device, such as an MP3 players, handheld or pocket PC, CompactFlash card, SmartCard, Zip disk, or CD-R drive. Click the Portable Device button, and Windows Media Player scans your system for available devices.

Use the Music to Copy drop-down list to select the media that you want to copy to your portable device. Select a device from the Music on Device drop-down list. The Status column then reports whether there is enough room to copy the selected files. Insert media (CD-R, Zip disk, etc.) as necessary and click the Copy Music button at the top right.

The buttons above the Music on Device list allow you to configure properties and recording settings, create a new playlist, or delete selected items from your Media Library or portable device.

Skin Chooser

Skin Chooser Allows you to select one of a vast assortment of skins that change the appearance of the Windows Media Player whenever you place it in compact mode. Skins vary from traditional appearance (such as the default Windows Media Player Skin or the Classic skin) to more artistic and creative skins like Headspace (shown here) or Toothy.

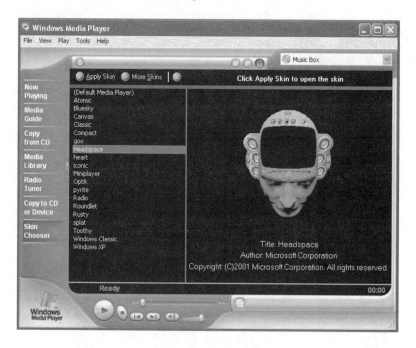

Select a skin from the left pane of the Skin Chooser to display a preview of the skin in the right pane. The appearance and functionality of the options on each skin vary, according to the skin design. Most skins have buttons that allow you to play, pause, stop, rewind, or advance the media file and to adjust its volume. Other skins may display a visualization while the media file plays. Three buttons appear above the skins list:

Apply Skin   Applies the selected skin to the Windows Media Player and places the Windows Media Player in compact mode. The skin appears over the items on your Desktop. A dialog in the lower-right corner of your Desktop displays a button that allows you to return to full mode, select a new skin, open a file, open a URL, or exit the Windows Media Player.

 More Skins   Navigates to the Microsoft Web site, where you can download more skins for the Windows Media Player.

Delete   Deletes the selected skin from the your skin library.

Windows Messenger

Windows Messenger   A communications utility that allows you to communicate in real time with other Windows Messenger users. To start Windows Messenger, choose Start ➤ All Programs ➤ Windows Messenger.

When you first open the Windows Messenger, you are prompted to sign in. Use the Click Here to Sign In link in the middle of the window (or choose File ➤ Sign In) to sign in to Windows Messenger. If you have not yet established a .NET Passport account, a wizard steps you through the process of configuring a new account; see ".NET Passport Wizard" elsewhere in this book for further information.

After you establish and connect through your .NET Passport account, the Windows Messenger dialog appears. This dialog displays the names of your contacts and shows whether they are online.

The main window displays three icons:

- Click the Add button to open the Add a Contact Wizard. This wizard helps you add contacts to your Windows Messenger contact list. Follow the steps in the wizard to search by email address or by contact name.

- Click the Send button to send a message to the selected contact.

- Click the Call button to call the selected contact.

Windows Messenger Menus

The Windows Messenger contains four menus: File, View, Tools, and Help. Menu commands are briefly described in the following sections.

File Menu

Commands in the File menu allow you to perform the following:

- Sign into or out from the Windows Messenger.

- Display your status as online, busy, be right back, away, on the phone, out to lunch, or appear offline.

- Add, delete, or display properties of a contact.

- Send a file to someone, or open received files.

- Close Windows Messenger.

View Menu

Commands in the View menu allow you to display or hide the toolbar or the status bar, and to always display the Windows Messenger window on top of other windows.

Tools Menu

Commands in the Tools menu allow you to establish contact with your online contacts in several ways:

- Send an instant message to a selected contact.

- Call a contact to participate in an audio or video conference.

- Send an invitation to a contact.

- Ask for remote assistance, using shared applications, remote assistance, or the whiteboard.

- Send e-mail or display your e-mail inbox.

- Open the Audio/Video Tuning Wizard to configure audio and video settings.

- Display the Options dialog, which allows you to configure Personal, Phone, Preferences, Privacy, and Connection information settings.

Windows Messenger Options

Choose Tools ➤ Options to display the Options dialog, which consists of five tabs: Personal, Phone, Preferences, Privacy, and Connection.

Personal tab   Use to enter your display name as you would like others to see it. You can also enable or disable the password prompt, and change the font that you use in instant messages. Check or uncheck the option to show graphics (emoticons) in your messages.

Phone tab   Use to choose a country/region code, and to enter your home, work, and mobile phone numbers. If you do not want others to view this information, leave these fields blank.

Preferences tab   Use to configure Windows Messenger preferences. You can run Windows Messenger whenever Windows starts, run it in the background, and automatically show you as "away" when the computer is inactive for longer than a specified time. You can also configure visual or audio alerts when contacts come online, when you receive an instant message, or when contacts sign in or send messages to you. Use the File Transfer dropdown to enter or choose a folder in which to store files that you receive from other contacts.

Privacy tab   Use to select users that are allowed to see your online status and who can send you messages. You can also add contacts to a block list, to prevent users from seeing your online status or sending you messages. Use the Allow or Block buttons to switch users from one list to the other.

To view the names of users that have added you to their contact list, click the View button. Check or uncheck the option to receive an alert when others add you to their contact list.

Connection tab   Windows Messenger automatically detects your Internet connection for you. If you have trouble with the Internet connection, you can use the Connection tab to configure a proxy server. Check the option to use a proxy server, then choose the proxy server type. Enter the server name and port and your user ID and password.

Windows Movie Maker

Windows Movie Maker   Allows you to capture, edit, and distribute your own home videos. You can capture video from a VCR, or from a digital camera. To start Windows Movie Maker, choose Start ➣ All Programs (or Start ➣ Programs in the Classic Start menu) ➣ Accessories ➣ Windows Movie Maker.

Windows Movie Maker consists of six menus: File, Edit, View, Clip, Play, and Help. The commands in each menu are described in the following sections.

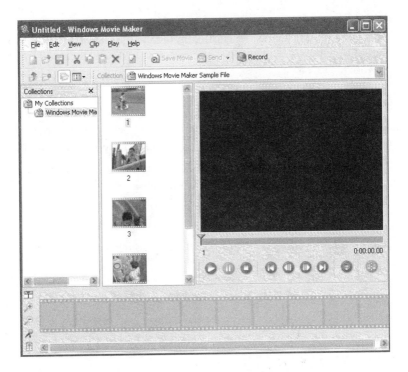

Beyond the typical menu bar and toolbars, the Windows Movie Maker inter-face includes the following areas:

Collection drop-down   Select a collection of movie clips that you have previously recorded.

Collections pane   Displays a list of video collections. When you high-light a collection in the list, thumbnails of each clip in the collection appear in the main display.

Thumbnails pane   Click a thumbnail to preview the clip in the video display, or drag and drop a clip into the storyboard or timeline.

Video display area   Allows you to preview the selected clip. Buttons beneath the preview window allow you to play, pause, stop, rewind, advance, or go to the start or end of the clip. You can also play the clip full-screen or split the clip at the current insertion point.

Storyboard/timeline The bottom section of the interface displays either the storyboard or timeline, depending on the view you select. Use the storyboard or timeline to add clips to your project, to add narration, and to edit your movie project.

File Menu

The File menu includes commands that allow you to create and open files, import content, and save or export your movies in a variety of ways, including these unique options.

Import Allows you to import content into your movie project. The types of media and extensions that you can import are video files (ASF, AVI and WMV) and movie files (MPEG, MPG, M1V, MP2, MPA, and MPE).

Record Choose this command to record Video and Audio, Video only, or Audio only from a VCR or digital camera.

Record Narration Enabled when the Timeline is displayed in the lower pane of the interface. Allows you to record a narration track for your movie.

Send Movie To Allows you to send your movie to an e-mail contact or publish it to your Web site.

My Videos Opens the My Videos folder in Explorer.

Recording Your Source Material

You can include pre-recorded video from a VCR or digital camera. You can also set your digital camera to record live video while you capture the video with Windows Movie Maker.

You will not hear audio while you capture your content. To record, follow these steps:

1. Choose File ➤ Record. The Record dialog appears.

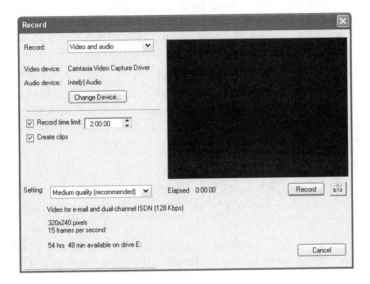

 NOTE When you use an IEEE 1394 card to record digital video, Windows Movie Maker may display a message that indicates your system may not provide acceptable performance while capturing full-screen video. To continue the recording process, press Yes.

2. From the Record drop-down, select the type of media that you want to record (Video and Audio, Video Only, or Audio Only).

3. The Record dialog displays your default video and audio devices. If desired, click the Change Device button to change the devices that you use to record your source material. Click Configure to configure the selected device.

4. By default, Windows Movie Maker automatically stops recording after two hours. To change the limit, enter a new value (in Hours, Minutes, and Seconds) in the Record Time Limit field. Uncheck this option if you do not want to set recording limits.

5. Check the Create Clips option to allow Windows Movie Maker to automatically generate smaller clips of your recorded material after you record it. A new clip begins when Windows Movie Maker detects a change in the scene. Uncheck this option to use the entire length of the recorded material as one clip.

6. Choose a quality setting from the Setting drop-down list. Optionally, select Other to choose from a variety of sources that optimize your video for 28K, 56K, ISDN, or broadband NTSC modem connections. As you choose quality settings, the dialog displays the resolution and frames per second that your choice produces.

7. Use the controls on your VCR or camera to locate the source material that you want to record. Start the VCR camera just before the segment that you want to record, or advance to the beginning of the segment and press the Pause button on your VCR or camera.

8. To record your material, choose one of the following in the Record dialog:

   • To record motion video, click the Record button to record full motion video and audio, video only, or audio only. Unpause your VCR or camera (if necessary) to begin playback.

   • To record still pictures from your video, unpause your VCR or camera (if necessary) to begin playback. Click the Take Photo button when the Record dialog displays a portion of the movie that you want to save as a still image.

9. Recording stops automatically when the recording exceeds the time limit you entered in Step 4. To stop recording manually, click the Stop button.

10. Enter a path and file name in the File Name field, and click Save to save your recording. Windows Movie Maker displays your clips as a collection.

11. Stop playback of your VCR or camera.

Edit Menu

The Edit menu includes commands that help you edit your movie content. You can cut or copy clips, then paste them into another location in your movie project. You can also delete and rename clips and adjust audio levels.

Cut, Copy, Paste Move the selected clip between the workspace and the Clipboard.

TIP You can also drag and drop a movie clip to move it from one location in the timeline to another. The position bar indicates the position at which the clip appears when you release the mouse button. Surrounding clips move to create space for the clip.

To quickly *copy* a clip to a new location, hold down the Ctrl key while you drag a movie clip from one location to another.

Delete Allows you to delete the selected media clip from the workspace.

Select All Selects all clips in a collection.

Select Storyboard/Timeline Selects all items in the storyboard or timeline.

Rename Allows you to rename a clip.

Audio Levels Allows you to adjust the balance between the sound in the video track and the sound in the audio (or narration) track.

View Menu

The View menu contains commands that allow you to customize the items you see in the Windows Movie Maker interface. You can show or hide the toolbars, status bar, and Collections pane; review clip or collection properties; and display your items in thumbnails, list, or details views. It also includes commands that allow you to view the movie storyboard or timeline and zoom in or out from them.

Changing Windows Movie Maker Options

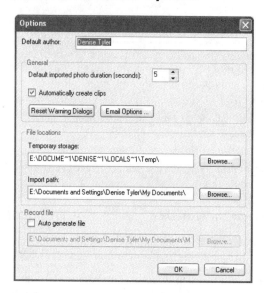

Choose View ➤ Options to open the Options dialog. The following options appear:

Default Author   Enter the name of the author that appears by default when you create a movie clip. Windows Movie Maker saves the author name with the movie and displays the author name when you play the clip in Windows Media Player.

Default Imported Photo Duration (Seconds)   When you import and add a photograph into your movie project, this value determines the length at which the photograph appears in your movie. Enter a new value, or use the dial to increase or decrease the default number of seconds.

Automatically Create Clips   Check this option to automatically divide your source material into smaller, more manageable sections that you can combine in the video editing window. Windows Movie Maker automatically creates a new clip when it detects an entirely new scene. Uncheck this option to use the entire length of a video as a single clip when you place it into your project.

Reset Warning Dialogs   Click this button to specify the warning boxes that you want to display in the Windows Movie Maker.

Email Options Click this button to select the e-mail program to use when you send your movies in an e-mail message. If your e-mail program does not appear in the list, select the option As an Attachment in Another E-mail Program.

Temporary Storage Use this field to enter the location that temporarily stores the movies you record, send by e-mail, or send to a Web server. Windows Movie Maker removes the temporary movie from the storage area after your task is complete. Click the Browse button to choose a folder on your local or network computer.

Import Path Use this field to enter the location that stores movies when you import them into your project. Click the Browse button to choose a folder on your local or network computer.

Auto Generate File Check this option to automatically generate movie files that do not exceed the Record Time Limit setting that you specify in the Record dialog. Windows Movie Maker assigns a generic file name, such as Tape1.wmv. When your recording time exceeds the Record Time Limit value, Windows Movie Maker automatically creates additional sequentially numbered files (such as Tape2.wmv, Tape3.wmv, and son on) until your recording is complete. Click the Browse button to choose a location in which to store the movie files.

Clip Menu

The Clip menu contains commands that allow you to edit the clips you use in your movie. You can add clips to your storyboard or timeline, set or clear the start and end trim points, split a clip, or combine two clips together as one.

Add to Storyboard/Timeline From the Collections pane, select the collection that contains the clip you want to add to your project. Then drag the clip to the workspace, or click Add to Storyboard/Timeline.

Set Start/End Trim Point   Position the cursor at the position where you want the clip to start or End, then choose the appropriate command.

Clear Trim Points   Select a trimmed clip from the workspace, and choose Clear Trim Points to remove the start and end trim points.

Split   Allows you to split a clip from the Collections pane into two smaller segments. Choose Play ➤ Play/Pause or position the playback indicator at the point you want to create the split. Then choose Clip ➤ Split to split the clip.

Combine   Combines two adjacent clips into a single clip, using the name and properties of the first clip in the sequence.

Play Menu

The Play menu contains commands that allow you to play and navigate through the frames in your movie. Besides the traditional Play, Pause, Stop, Back, and Forward commands, this menu also includes these:

Play Entire Storyboard/Timeline   Allows you to play all clips that appear in your storyboard or timeline, from start to finish.

Previous Frame, Next Frame   Moves to the previous or next frame in the storyboard or timeline.

TIP   You can use keyboard shortcuts to move forward or backward one frame at a time more quickly. Use the Alt+Left arrow key to move to the previous frame, or the Alt+Right arrow key to advance to the next frame.

Full Screen   Plays your movie file in a full screen window. Press the Esc key to return to Windows Movie Maker.

Windows Report Tool

See System Monitor

Windows Update

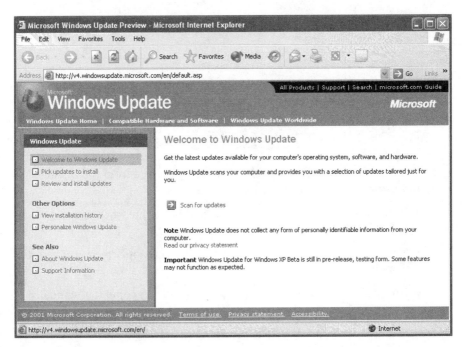

Windows Update   Choose Start ➤ All Programs (or Start ➤ Programs in the Classic Start menu) ➤ Windows Update to connect to the Microsoft Windows Update home page. Windows Update scans your computer and provides you with a list of the latest updates that help keep your Windows XP operating system, hardware, and software running at peak performance. Windows Update also tracks the updates you have already installed so that you do not have to download them again. Click the appropriate links to find the information you're looking for, such as critical updates, recommended updates, top picks, device drivers, additional Windows features, and help on using the site.

You can also configure Windows XP to automatically notify you when updates are available. To configure update notification, follow these steps:

1. Choose Start ➤ Control Panel (or Start ➤ Settings ➤ Control Panel in the Classic Start menu) ➤ Performance and Maintenance.

2. Click the System control panel icon to open the System Properties dialog.

3. Select the Automatic Updates tab.

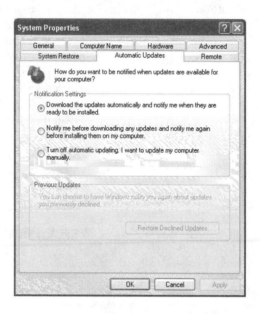

4. Choose one of the following self-explanatory options from the Notification Settings section of the dialog:

- Download the updates automatically and notify me when they are ready to be installed.

- Notify me before downloading any updates and notify me again before installing them on my computer.

- Turn off automatic updating. I want to update my computer manually.

5. By default, Windows Update hides update notification items that you previously declined. To make these updates available again, click the Restore Declined Updates button.

6. Choose OK to apply your settings and exit the System Properties dialog.

WMI Control

WMI Control MMC console snap-in for Windows XP Home and Professional that allows you to manage settings and configuration for Windows Management Instrumentation (WMI), which is designed to let you manage your enterprise over the Internet or an intranet.

To access WMI Control, choose Start ➤ Control Panel (or Start ➤ Settings ➤ Control Panel in the Classic Start menu) ➤ Performance and Maintenance. Next, click Administrative Tools, then double-click Computer Management. Expand the Services and Applications category in the console tree to view the WMI Control snap-in.

To work with WMI Control properties, select WMI Control in the console tree and choose Action ➤ Properties. This opens the WMI Control Properties dialog, which contains five tabs: General, Logging, Backup/Restore, Security, and Advanced.

General Allows you to view general information about the computer to which you are currently connected (such as processor, operating system, operating system version, WMI version, and WMI location). To connect to the WMI Control service as a different user, click Change, deselect Log On as Current User, specify the username and password of a different user, and click OK.

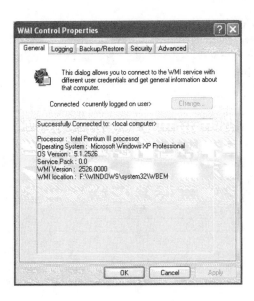

Logging   Allows you to specify the logging level (Disabled, Errors Only, or Verbose with extra information for Microsoft troubleshooting), and the maximum size and location of log files.

Backup/Restore   Allows you to back up the WMI repository to a file, if a change to the repository has occurred since the last time you performed a backup. Also allows you to restore from a backup and specify the automatic backup interval. To manually backup or restore the WMI repository, click the Back Up Now or Restore Now buttons, respectively, and follow the prompts.

Security   Allows you to configure permissions for any name space (directory) in the WMI directory structure.

Advanced   Allows you to specify advanced settings, such as the name space WMI Scripting should use by default.

TIP   For more information about WMI services, see the WMI software development kit (SDK), which is available on the Microsoft Developer Network (MSDN).

See also   Computer Management, Microsoft Management Console

WordPad

WordPad   Basic word processing program included with Windows XP. Allows you to create, edit, and view files using several different formats, including Word for Windows 6.0, Rich Text Format (RTF), text documents (ASCII), and Unicode text documents.

Choose Start ➤ All Programs (or Start ➤ Programs in the Classic Start menu) ➤ Accessories ➤ WordPad to open WordPad. The WordPad window consists of a menu bar, toolbar, Format bar, ruler, text area, and status bar.

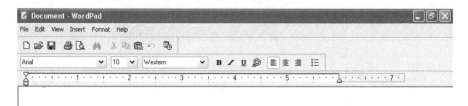

WordPad Menus

The WordPad menus contain many options you use to work with documents. You'll find many of these options are used with most other Windows programs.

File Menu

New   Creates a new document.

Open   Opens an existing document.

Save   Saves the currently active document.

Save As   Saves the currently active document using a different name, or to another folder on your hard drive.

Print   Opens the Print dialog, which allows you to print the currently active document. Here, you can specify the printer to use, the pages to print, the number of copies to print, whether you want to collate the print job, and whether you want to print to a file.

Print Preview   Displays a preview of how the currently active document will look when you print it at the current print settings.

Page Setup   Opens the Page Setup dialog, where you can choose settings for items such as paper size and source, orientation, and margins. You can also choose the printer to use and configure printer settings.

Send   Sends the currently active document by e-mail.

Exit   Closes WordPad and asks you to save unsaved documents.

Edit Menu

Undo   Reverses the last action.

Cut   Cuts a selected portion from the current document and places it into the Windows XP Clipboard.

Copy   Copies a selected portion from the current document to the Windows XP Clipboard.

Paste   Pastes the contents of the Windows XP Clipboard into the document at the insertion point.

Paste Special   Displays paste options before you paste Clipboard contents, allowing you to paste the Clipboard contents using different formats.

Clear   Erases the currently selected text.

Select All   Selects the entire document.

Find   Allows you to find a specific word or phrase in the document.

Find Next   Allows you to find the next occurrence of the search term you entered in the Find dialog.

Replace   Replaces text you find with different text.

Links   Allows you to edit linked objects. You can update the object from the original source, open or change the source, or break the link.

Object Properties   Opens the properties dialog for the currently selected object.

Object   Activates a linked or embedded object.

TIP   The title of the Object option may change to better reflect the type of object depending on the type of object you have selected. For example, if the selected object is a bitmap, this option reads Bitmap Image Object.

View Menu

Toolbar, Format Bar, Ruler, Status Bar   Shows or hides the named element.

Options   Opens the Options dialog, where you can configure the units of measurements that your document uses (inches, points, centimeters, or picas). You can also specify word wrap and toolbar options for each document format that WordPad supports (Text, Rich Text, Word, Write, and Embedded). Word wrap options include No Wrap, Wrap to Window, and Wrap to Ruler. Toolbars you can display include Toolbar, Format Bar, Ruler, and Status Bar.

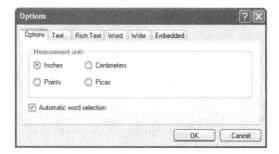

Insert Menu

Date and Time   Inserts the current date and time in one of several available formats.

Object   Creates and inserts objects (including images, media clips, wave sounds, and other object types) into the currently active document.

Format Menu

Font   Allows you to choose a font, font style, size, effect, and script for your entire document or selected portions of the document.

Bullet Style   Creates bulleted lists in your document.

Paragraph   Allows you to specify settings for the current paragraph, such as indentation and alignment.

Tabs   Allows you to specify tab stop positions.

WordPad Toolbars

WordPad has two toolbars: the Standard toolbar and the Format bar.

Standard Toolbar

The Standard toolbar contains these buttons:

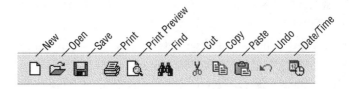

New   Creates a new document.

Open   Opens an existing document.

Save   Saves the currently active document.

Print   Prints the currently active document.

Print Preview   Allows you to preview the currently active document before you print it.

Find   Allows you to search the active document for specific text.

Cut   Cuts the selected portion of the document and places it into the Clipboard.

Copy   Copies the selected portion of the document and places it into the Clipboard.

Paste   Pastes the contents of the Clipboard into the currently active document at the insertion point.

Undo   Reverses the last action.

Date/Time   Inserts the current date and time into the currently active document. You can choose from several date/time formats.

Format Bar

The Format bar contains these buttons:

Font   Displays the font used for the selected text. If there is more than one font in a selection, the Font drop-down appears blank. You can also use the Font drop-down list to change the font for the entire document or for a selected portion of the document.

Font Size   Displays the size of the selected text. If there is more than one font size in the selection, the Font Size drop-down appears blank. You can also use the Font Size drop-down to change the font size in all or part of your document.

Font Script   Allows you to select the font script for the entire document or a selected portion of the document.

Bold   Toggles bold type on or off the selection.

Italic   Toggles italic type on or off the selection.

Underline   Toggles underlining on or off the selection.

Color   Allows you to select a color from a drop-down list and apply the color to selected text.

Align Left   Left-justifies the paragraph.

Center   Centers the paragraph.

Align Right   Right-justifies the paragraph.

Bullets   Allows you to create bulleted lists. Automatically adds bullets and tabs at the beginning of each bullet item.

Ruler

The ruler allows you to track your position on the current line. By default, the ruler displays units in inches. Choose the View ➤ Options command and select the Options tab to change the units to points, centimeters, or picas. To set tab stops for your document, click the desired position on the ruler.

To adjust right indentation, drag the right ruler marker left or right. The left ruler marker consists of three sliders. The top triangular slider sets the position for the first line in a paragraph. The bottom triangular slider sets the position for the remaining lines in a paragraph. The bottom square slider adjusts both markers at the same time.

Creating a Document in WordPad

You can create documents in WordPad in several ways. The most common is to place the insertion point in the document window and type your text. Use the menus, Standard toolbar, and Format bar buttons to format your text and adjust settings. Then choose File ➤ Save to name and save your document.

You can also cut or copy text from another document into the Windows Clipboard, and then paste the contents into your WordPad document. Follow these steps:

1. Open a document in WordPad or in another application.

2. Select text or other document contents.

3. Choose Edit ➤ Cut or click the Cut icon on the toolbar.

4. Create or open a second document in WordPad.

5. In the document window, place the cursor where you want to insert the contents of the Clipboard.

6. Click the Paste icon on the toolbar or choose Edit ➤ Paste.

7. Add other text and format your document as desired.

8. Choose File ➤ Save or click the Save button on the toolbar to save your document.

To insert objects into your document, perform the following steps:

1. Place the cursor where you want to insert the object.

2. Choose Insert ➤ Object.

3. Select Create New and choose an object type; or select Create from File and browse to the file's location.

4. Click OK.

5. Add any other text and format your document as desired.

6. Choose File ➤ Save or click the Save button on the toolbar to save your document.

See also Notepad

Index

Note to the reader: Throughout this index **boldfaced** page numbers indicate primary discussions of a topic. *Italicized* page numbers indicate illustrations.

A

abstracts, from Indexing Service, 140
Accessibility, **2–6**
  Internet Explorer options, 157
  Magnifier, **176–177**
  Narrator, **195–196**
  On-Screen Keyboard, *234*, **234–235**
  Options window, *2*, 2–3
  Utility Manager, **385–386**, *386*
Accessibility Options dialog, Keyboard
  tab, *3*, 3–4
Accessories, **6**
  Calculator, **37–38**
  Command Prompt, *46*, **46–47**
  Communications, 47
  Entertainment program group, 92
  Program Compatibility Wizard, *288*,
    288–289
  System Tools, **366**. *See also* Backup
  Character Map, 40
  Disk Cleanup, **69–71**, *71*
  Disk Defragmenter, **71–75**
  File and Settings Transfer
    Wizard, 112
  Scheduled Tasks, *316*, **316–322**
  System Information, **361–363**
  System Restore, *364*, **364–365**
  Windows Explorer, *97*, **97–106**
  Windows Movie Maker,
    406–414, *407*
Action menu
  for Device Manager, 59–63

for Local Users and Groups, 171
  in Shared Folders, 333
Active Directory, **7–8**
  for adding programs, 12
ActiveX controls, security settings
  for, 158
Add Counters dialog, *257*, 257–258
Add Excluded Files dialog
  (Backup), 35
Add Hardware Wizard, **8–10**, 350–351
Add or Remove Programs, **10–13**
address bar
  in Explorer, 101–102, *102*
  in Internet Explorer, 149
Address Book, **13–25**
  contact template, 20
  creating contacts, 16–17
  folders, 22–23
  groups, 20–22
  identities for, 24–25
  menus, 15–16
  retrieving e-mail addresses from, 241
  searching for people in, 325–326
  toolbar, 14, *15*
  window, *14*
Address toolbar, 367
Administrative Tools, **25–26**. *See also*
    Microsoft Management Console
    (MMC) snap-ins
  Active Directory, **7–8**
  for adding programs, 12
  COM+ (Component Services), **45**
  Data Sources (ODBC), **51–55**

Event Viewer, 93, **93–96**, *94*

Local Security Policy, *168*, **168–170**, **168–170**

Administrator account, 172

administrator, for Group Policy, 124

Advanced Audio Properties dialog, 341

Advanced Backup mode, 30–33

Restore and Manage Media tab, 32–33, *33*

AIF files, 396

AIFC files, 396

AIFF files, 396

Airbrush tool (Paint), 253

alerts, 262

from saved files, 263

from Windows Messenger, 406

alignment in WordPad, 422

Alt key, StickyKeys to keep active, 4

Alt+Tab key to switch between applications, 368–369

animated menus, 86–87

animated screen character, for searches, 326–327

Appearance and Themes control panel, **26**

for fonts, 117

Application log, 93, 94

applications. *See* programs

Arabic language, 298

area code, in phone dialing, 266

Armenian language, 298

ascii command (FTP), 122

ASCII format, 418

ASF files, 396

associating programs with file extensions, 116

ASX files, 396

attachments to e-mail, 242

attrib command, 291

AU files, 396

audio. *See also* Sound Recorder

device for Windows Movie Maker recording, 409

Windows Media Player for, 391

Audio Tuning Wizard, 201

authenticated network access, 212

author of movie clip, 412

auto-hide taskbar, 370

AutoComplete Settings dialog, 162, *162*

autodial configuration, 223

Automated System Recovery Wizard, 36

automatic redial feature, 219

Automatic Reset of accessibility options, 4

automatic updates. *See* Windows Update

AutoPlay, **27**

AVI files, 396

B

background for Desktop, 82

Backup, **27–36**

Advanced mode, *30*, 30–33

Automated System Recovery Wizard, 36

options, 33–35

of WMI repository, 418

backup jobs, 27

Backup or Restore Wizard, 27–30

What to Backup screen, *28*

What to Restore screen, *29*

basic disks, 77

batch command, 291
binary command (FTP), 122
blind copies of e-mail, 242
blink rate of cursor, 4
blocking senders of e-mail, 249–250
BMP files, 251
bold type in WordPad, 422
BOOT.INI file, 360
BounceKeys, 5
bridge connections, 223
broadband connection, 210
    general properties, 218
    for Internet, 213
Browse feature, **36**
Brush tool (Paint), 253
bullets in WordPad, 421, 422
burning CDs, **39–40**

C

cache for Web pages, 156
Calculator, **37–38**
call waiting, disabling, 266
callback for incoming connec-
    tion, 215
Called Station Identifier (CSID), 108
calling card for phone dialing, 267
camera
    configuration, **312–315**
    photographs from, 194, 315
    recording from, 408
canceling print job, 283
Caps Lock key, and accessibility, 4
capturing images, **38**
catalogs in Indexing Service, **139–143**
    searching, 143, *143*
cd command, 291

CD Quality audio, 339
CD-R drive, copying media files
    to, 401
CD-ROM
    adding program from, 12
    autoplay following insertion, 27
    copying songs from, 398
    starting Recovery Console from,
        289–290
CD Writing Wizard, *39*, **39–40**
CDA files, 396
Character Map, *40*, **40–42**
chat in NetMeeting, 202
chdir command, 291
Check Disk dialog box, **42**
Chinese language, 298
chkdsk command, 291
ClickLock option, 186
Clip menu (Windows Movie Maker),
    413–414
Clipboard, **43–45**
    capturing screen images to, 38
    to copy from Character Map, 41
    placing audio file in, 337
ClipBook
    accessing another user's, 45
    saving Clipboard contents to, 44
ClipBook Viewer, **43–45**
clock, 56, *366*, 366
    displaying, 370
Close button, **45**
closing
    modem connection, 229
    user sessions, 333
.CLP file extension, 43
cls command, 291
code page conversion tables, 302
collections of movie clips, 407

color
for Desktop, 82
in Internet Explorer, 156
maximum number, 87–88
in Paint, 254
in WordPad, 422
Color Eraser tool (Paint), 252
color management
for monitor, 90
for printers, 278
color scheme
for dialog boxes, 85
of screen items, 5
Colors menu (Paint), 255
COM+ (Component Services), **45**
Command Prompt, *46*, **46–47**
communications, network connections for, 209–210
Communications program group, **47**. *See also* Network Connections
Fax Services, **106–112**
NetMeeting, **196–208**
Network Setup Wizard, **224–225**
New Connection Wizard, *213*, 213–214, **225–229**
Phone Dialer, 9999
Remote Desktop Connection, **304–306**
CompactFlash card, copying media files to, 401
compatibility of programs, wizard to test, *288*, **288–289**
compression
of audio, 339
of drives, folders and files, **47–48**
computer administrator user account, 380

Computer Management (MMC snap-in), **48**
Disk Management, *76*
computers. *See also* System Properties dialog
acceptance of remote connection, 304
information about components, 362–363
logon/logoff, **175**
name and workgroup for, 350
power management for, **271–273**
searching for, 325
transferring files between old and new, **112**
turning off, 379
connection pooling, for ODBC, 54
contacts. *See also* Address Book
sharing between identities, 25
in Windows Messenger, 406
Contacts folder, 22
Content Advisor, 159–161
context-sensitive help for dialog boxes, 134–135, **390–391**
Control Panel, **48–49**, *49*. *See also* Microsoft Management Console (MMC) snap-ins
Add New Hardware, **8–10**
Add or Remove Programs, **10–13**
Appearance and Themes, **26**
Display, **80–90**
Folder Options, **114–117**
Game controllers, **123**
Keyboard, **166–167**
Local Security Policy, **168–170**
Mouse, **185–188**
Network and Internet Connections, **208**
opening, 346

other options, **235**
Performance and Maintenance, **263**
Phone and Modem Options,
   265–269
Power Options, **271–273**
Printers and Faxes, **273–285**
Printers and Other Hardware, **285**
Regional and Language Options,
   296–302
Scanners and Cameras, **312–315**
Scheduled Tasks, **316–322**
Sounds and Audio Devices, **340–344**
System, **349–359**
Taskbar and Start Menu, **369–375**
conversations, tracking in Outlook
   Express, 250–251
cookies, 155
   deleting, 156
   security settings for, 158
copy and paste, in Address Book, 16
copy command, 291
copying
   disks, **49**
   files and folders, **50**
   floppy disks, **49**
   songs from CD, 398
   user accounts, 355
counters
   logs, 259–260
   performance, 257–258
cover page for faxes, 110
   editor, *111*, 111–112
CSID (Called Station Identifier), 108
Ctrl key, StickyKeys to keep active, 4
currency, customizing regional
   options, 298
cursor blink rate, 166
cursor for visually impaired, 4

Curve tool (Paint), 253
Customize Classic Start Menu dialog,
   374, 374
Customize Toolbar dialog, 101

D

Data Sources (ODBC), **51–55**
date
   customizing regional options, 298
   inserting in WordPad, 421
Date and Time Properties dialog, *56*,
   56–57
deaf, sound features for, 4
debugging, writing information to
   file, 357
default connection, 222
default language, 299
default Web browser, Internet Explorer
   as, 164
del command, 291
delete command, 291
deleting
   contacts in Address Book, 15
   cookies, 156
   icons from Desktop, 83
   Recycle Bin for, **293–296**, *294*
   Scheduled Tasks, 319
   themes, 82
   user accounts, 355, 382
Desktop, *57*, **57–58**
   remote connection, **304–306**
   remote sharing in NetMeeting, 203
Desktop Items dialog, 82–84
   General tab, *83*, 83
   Web tab, 83–84
Desktop toolbar, 367

device drivers
  for keyboard, 167
  for ODBC, 53
  for printers, 278
  for shared printer, 279–280
  uninstalling, 60
  updating, 12, 58
Device Manager (MMC snap-in),
  58–64, *59*, 351
  Action menu, 59–63
  View menu, 63–64
DHCP (Dynamic Host Configuration
  Protocol), **64–65**
Diagnostic Startup, 359
dial-in server, 214–216
dial-up connections, 209
  configuration, 163
  general properties, 217, *217*
  for Internet, 213
  operator-assisted dialing for, 223
dialog boxes
  appearance of, *85*, 85–87
  help for, 134–135
  What's This, **390–391**
DIB files, 251
digital camera
  installing, 313–314
  photographs from, 194, 315
  recording from, 408
digital certificates, 161–162
digital IDs, in Address Book, 20
digital signatures, verification,
  112–113
dir command, 291
direct connection, 211
  general properties, 218
directories. *See* folders

DirectX, **66–69**
  Diagnostic tool, *67*
disable command, 291
disabling
  local area connection, 211
  Welcome Screen, 389–390
Disk Cleanup, **69–71**, *71*
Disk Defragmenter (MMC snap-in),
  71–75
Disk Management (MMC snap-in),
  75–80, *76*
disk Properties dialog box, General
  tab, *195*
disk space, **80**
  Disk Cleanup to increase available,
    69–71, *71*
  emptying Recycle Bin to increase, 294
  for hibernation, 273
  program use of, 11
diskpart command, 291
disks
  copying, **49**
  names for, **195**
Display Properties dialog, 58, **80–90**
  Appearance tab, *85*, 85–87
  Desktop tab, 82–84
  Screen Saver tab, 84–85
  Settings tab, 87–90
  Themes tab, *81*, 81–82
documents
  clearing from Start menu, 374
  creating
    using multiple languages, 300–301
    in WordPad, 423–424
  printing, 280–282
  properties, 283–284
  searching for, 324
domains, in Active Directory, 7

double-click speed, 186

Dr. Watson, *91*, **91–92**

Drafts folder in Outlook Express, 240

drag-and-drop, **90**

    to move files and folders, 188

    to print documents, 280

drawings. *See* images; Paint

drive Properties dialog box, General
    tab, *142*

drivers. *See* device drivers

drives

    compression of, **47–48**

    indexing, 141–142

    mapping network, **177–178**

    viewing contents in My Com-
        puter, 190

dump, 357

dynamic disks, 78–80

Dynamic Host Configuration Protocol
    (DHCP), **64–65**

E

e-mail. *See also* Outlook Express

    account setup, 227–228

    for alerts based on counter
        values, 262

    connection from Start menu, 345

    default program on Start menu
        for, 372

    to send movie clip, 413

e-mail addresses

    in Address Book, 14, 17

    sending files to, 328

East Asian languages, 298

Edit menu

    in Address Book, 16

    in Advanced Backup mode, 31

    in Explorer, 98–99

    in Internet Explorer, 150

    in Sound Recorder, 337–338

    in Windows Movie Maker, 410–411

    in WordPad, 419–420

Effects dialog, *86*, 86–87

Effects menu (Sound Recorder), 338

Ellipse tool (Paint), 253

EMF files, 251

enable command, 291

encryption, network connections
    options, 220

energy-saving power features,
    271–273

Entertainment program group, **92**

environment variables, 357

Eraser tool (Paint), 252

error reporting, **92–93**, 358

errors, checking drives for, **42**

Event Viewer, **93–96**, *94*

exist command, 291

expand command, 291

explicit one-way trust, 8

explicit permissions, 264

Explorer, *97*, **97–106**. *See also* Internet
    Explorer; MSN Explorer

    bars, 102–104

    to check for disk errors, 42

    to copy files and folders, 50

    to copy floppy disks, 49

    to create folders, 50

    to create shortcuts, 50–51

    folder customization, 105

    to label disk, 195

    to map network drives, **177–178**

    menus, 98–100

    to move files and folders, 188

printing documents from, 280
Send To feature, **328–329**
to share folders or disks, **334**
status bar, 106
toolbars, 100–102
Explorer Bar, 99, 102–104
exporting from Address Book, 15

F

Fast User Switching, **106**
fault tolerance, RAID-5 disk for, 78–79
Favorites menu
  in Explorer, 100
  in Internet Explorer, 151
Favorites view for Explorer Bar, 103
Fax Services, **106–112**
  configuration wizard, 107–108
  Fax Console, 109–110
  Fax Cover Page Editor, *111*, 111–112
  Fax status monitor, 110–111
  installing, 106–107
  Send Fax wizard, 108
faxes. *See also* Printers and Faxes control panel
File and Settings Transfer Wizard, **112**
file extensions
  associating programs with, 116
  in Media Player, 396
File menu
  in Address Book, 15
  in Explorer, 98
  in Fax Console, 109–110
  in Internet Explorer, 150
  in Media Player, 394
  in Paint, 254
  in Sound Recorder, 336–337
  in Task Manager, 376
  in Windows Messenger, 404
  in Windows Movie Maker, 408
  in WordPad, 419
File Signature Verification utility, **112–114**, 351
File Transfer Protocol (FTP), **122**
file types. *See* file extensions
files. *See also* Explorer
  compression of, **47–48**
  copying, **50**
  disk space for, 80
  drag-and-drop to move or copy, 90
  finding
    with Browse, 36
    with Search, 322–327
  indexing, 142
  moving, **188**
  offline, **231–233**
  in Recycle Bin, **293–296**
  saving Clipboard contents to, 43–44
  Send To feature, **328–329**
  sharing, **334**
  transferring between old and new computer, **112**
  transferring within NetMeeting call, 203
  writing to CD, **39–40**
Fill with Color tool (Paint), 252
filtering log events, 95
FilterKeys, 4
finding. *See also* Search feature
  events, 96
  messages in Outlook Express, 238, *239*
firewall, 227
  for Internet Connection, **144–146**, 212

fixboot command, 291
fixmbr command, 291
floppy disks
  adding program from, 12
  checking for errors, **42**
  copying, **49**
  files deleted from, 293
  for forgotten password, **119–120**
  formatting, **120–121**
  naming, **195**
Folder Options dialog, **114–117**
  General tab, *115*
folders, **113–114**. *See also* Explorer
  in Address Book, 22–23
  compression of, **47–48**
  copying, **50**
  creating, **50**, 98
  customizing, 105
  finding
    with Browse, 36
    with Search, 322–327
  moving, **188**
  My Documents, **191**, *191*
  My Music, **192**
  Offline Files, 232
  in Recycle Bin, **293–296**
  removing from Start menu, 374
  Send To feature, **328–329**
  shared, **332–333**
  sharing, **334**
  specifying for indexing, 140–141
  viewing contents in My Com-
    puter, 190
  writing to CD, **39–40**
Folders view for Explorer Bar, 104
fonts
  for dialog boxes, 86

displaying character sets for, 41
  for icon text, 88
  installing, 119
  in Internet Explorer, 156
  for Private Character Editor, 286, 287
  smoothing, 87
  viewing examples, *118*, 118–119
  in WordPad, 421, 422
Fonts folder, **117–119**
forests in Active Directory, 7
Forgotten Password Wizard, **119–120**
Format bar in WordPad, 422, *422*
format command, 291
Format dialog, *79*, 79–80
Format feature, **120–121**
Format menu (WordPad), 421
forwarding e-mail, 238
fragmented files, 71–72
Free-Form Select tool (Paint), 252
FTP (File Transfer Protocol), **122**
  publishing files to site, 389
full screen window, for playing
    movie, 414
full-text searches, in Help and Support
    Center, 130

G

Game controllers control panel, **123**
Games program group, **123**
Georgian language, 298
get command (FTP), 122
GIF files, 251
graphics
  Image Preview for, *135*, **135–137**
  My Pictures folder to store,
    193–4, *194*

retrieving from Web pages, 154

searching for, 324

graphics adapter. *See also* video
adapters

displaying information about, 89

graphs of system performance data,
256, *256*

Group Policy (MMC snap-in),
124–125

groups

in Address Book, 15

built-in, 174

creating, 174

local, 170, 173–175

properties, 174–175

guest account, 172, 380

turning off and on, 382–383

H

handedness of mouse, 5, 185

handheld computing devices

copying media files to, 401

direct connection to, 211

hard disk drives

checking for errors, **42**

clean-up, **69–71**

defragmenting, **71–75**

formatting, 79–80, **120–121**

naming, **195**

hardware. *See also* computers

Add Hardware Wizard, **8–10**,
350–351

Device Manager to display list,
58, *59*

displaying information about
resources, 362

profiles, 351–353, *352*

Safely Remove Hardware
feature, **310**

scanners and cameras, 313–315

scanning for changes, 61

System Properties dialog to configure, 350–353

troubleshooter, **125–127**, *126*

hardware libraries, managing,
306–307

hearing impaired, sound features
for, 4

Hebrew language, 298

Help and Support Center, **127–135**,
128, 346

for applications and dialogs,
134–135

Ask for Assistance area, 132

Did You Know? area, 132

List and Contents panes, 132–134

Network diagnostics, 224

Offer Remote Assistance, 231

Pick a Help topic area, 131–132

Pick a Task area, 132

Remote Assistance, *303*, **303–304**

Search area, 129–30, *130*

System Restore, *364*, **364–365**

toolbars, 128–129

help command, 291

Help menu

in Explorer, 100

in Internet Explorer, 153

hibernation, 272–273

hiding taskbar, 370

High Contrast option, 4

hint for password, 385

histograms, for performance
counters, 258

history, managing in Internet
  Explorer, 156
History view for Explorer Bar, 103
home network
  Internet Connection Sharing, **146**
  setup, 214
home page, for Internet Explorer, 155
hosting meeting in NetMeeting, 200

I

ICO files, 251
icons
  in Explorer, 99
  font size for text, 88
  hiding inactive, 370
  removing from Desktop, 83
  selecting for folder, 105
  size of, 87
ICRA (Internet Content Rating Association), 160
identities
  in Address Book, 24–25
  in Outlook Express, 24–25, 244–245
  sharing contacts between, 25
idle time
  before activating power-saving fea-
    tures, 272
  and scheduled tasks, 320
IEEE 1394 card, 409
Image menu (Paint), 255
Image Preview, *135*, **135–137**
images
  My Pictures folder to store,
    193–4, *194*
  retrieving from Web pages, 154
  searching for, 324

imaging device. *See* Scanners and
  Cameras control panel
importing
  to Address Book, 15
  to Windows Movie Maker, 408
Inbox in Outlook Express, 240
incoming connections, 211, 214–216
Indexing Service (MMC snap-in),
    137–144
  Action menu, 138–139
  catalogs, **139–143**
  configuration, 140
  searching, 143, *143*
  for searches, 327
  specifying directories, 140–141
Indic language, 298
infrared connection, 211
inherited permissions, 264
initialization commands for
    modem, 269
Insert menu (WordPad), 421
installing
  Fax Services, 106–107
  fonts, 119
  scanners and cameras, 313–314
Internet
  default program on Start menu
    for, 372
  Online Print Ordering Wizard,
    233–234
  searching, 326
Internet connection, 213
  New Connection Wizard, **225–229**
  dial-up connections, 226
  from Start menu, 345
  for Windows Messenger, 406
Internet Connection Firewall,
    144–146, 212

Internet Connection Sharing, **146**

Internet Connection Wizard, for e-mail account setup, 227, 236

Internet Content Rating Association (ICRA), 160

Internet content zones, 157

Internet Explorer, **147–154**, *148*

  editing current page, 153–154

  menus, 150–153

  retrieving images, 154

  settings, 363

  toolbars, 148–149

  viewing documents, 148

Internet Information Services, Web catalog for, 140

Internet profile, in Address Book, 16

Internet Properties dialog, **154–165**

  Advanced tab, 164–165, *165*

  Connections tab, 163–164

  Content tab, **159–163**

  General tab, *155*, **155–7**

  Privacy tab, **159**

  Programs tab, **164**, *164*

  Security tab, **157–159**

Internet Protocol Security, 165

Internet Protocol (TCP/IP) Properties dialog, 65, *65*

Internet Time, synchronization with time server, 56

IP addresses, DHCP to manage, 64–65

IP Security Monitor (MMC snap-in), **165**

IP Security Policy Management (MMC snap-in), **165**

italic type in WordPad, 422

IUSR_servername user account, 172

IVF files, 396

IWAM_servername user account, 172

J

Japanese language, 298

Java applets, security settings for, 158

Job menu, in Advanced Backup mode, 31

JPG files, 251

K

Kernel Memory Dump, 357

keyboard

  accessibility options, 4

  Alt+Tab to switch applications, 368–369

  configuration for remote connection, 305

  Ctrl+Alt+Del to access Task Manager, 375

  for input language, 299

  On-Screen, *234*, **234–235**

Keyboard control panel, **166–167**

keyboard shortcuts

  for accessibility options, 3

  for Unicode characters, 41

Korean language, 298

L

L2TP (Layer-2 Tunneling Protocol), 210

labels for disks, **195**

LAN (local area network)

  for computer connection, 210

  for Internet Connection, 163–164, 227

languages
  customizing regional options, 298–301
  document creation using multiple, 300–301
  in Internet Explorer, 156
  removing service, 300
laptop computers
  battery power conservation, **271–273**
  battery usage power meter, 272
  disabling local area connection on, 211
Last Known Good Configuration, 312
Layer-2 Tunneling Protocol (L2TP), 210
left-handed mouse, 5, 185
limited user account, 380
  changing password, 385
Line tool (Paint), 253
Line Width tool (Paint), 253
Links toolbar, 367
lists in Explorer, 99
listsvc command, 291
local area network (LAN)
  for computer connection, 210
  for Internet Connection, 163–164, 227
Local Intranet content zone, 157
Local Security Policy control panel, *168*, **168–170**
local user profile, 307
Local Users and Groups (MMC snap-in), **170–175**, *171*
locations, dialing rules for, 265–266
locking taskbar, 370
Log On/Log Off, **175**, 346
logical drives, creating, 77

logon command, 291
logon/logoff
  options, 383
  for Outlook Express identity, 245
logs
  of counters, 259–260
  for programs, security and system events, 93
  viewing on remote computer, 96
  from saved files, 263
  trace, 260–261
  from WMI Control, 418

M

M1V files, 396
M3U files, 396
Magnifier, **176–177**
Magnifier tool (Paint), 252
maintenance in Outlook Express, 247
Manage Identities dialog box, 24, *24*
map command, 291
Map Network Drive feature, 98, *177*, **177–178**
Maximize button, **178**
md command, 291
measurement system
  customizing regional options, 297–298
  in WordPad, 420
Media Library, 395, 399, *399*
Media Player (Windows), **391–402**
Media view for Explorer Bar, 104
meetings. *See* NetMeeting
memory
  information about software in, 363
  optimizing use, 354

Messenger (Windows), **403–406**
microprocessor, optimizing use, 354
Microsoft, error reporting to, **92–93**
Microsoft Knowledge Base, searching, 130
Microsoft Management Console (MMC), **178–185**
  consoles, 180–183, *181*
  creating, 182–183
  menus, 179–180
  taskpad views and tasks, 183–185
  toolbars, 180
Microsoft Management Console (MMC) snap-ins
  Computer Management, **48**
  Device Manager, **58–64**
  Disk Defragmenter, **71–75**
  Disk Management, **75–80**
  Group Policy, **124–125**
  Indexing Service, **137–144**
  IP Security Monitor, **165**
  IP Security Policy Management, **165**
  Local Users and Groups, **170–175**
  Performance, **256–263**
  Removable Storage Management, **306–307**
  Security Configuration and Analysis, **327–328**
  Security Templates, **328**
  Services, **329–331**
  Shared Folders, **332–333**
  WMI Control, **417–418**
MID files, 396
MIDI files, 396
Minimize button, **178**
mirrored disk, 78
mixing audio files, 337
mkdir command, 291

MMC. *See* Microsoft Management Console (MMC)
modem
  for Internet Connection, 228–229
  properties, 265, 267–269, *268*
    advanced, 269, *270*
    speaker volume, 268
monitor and graphics adapter Properties dialog, 88–90
  General tab, 88, *89*
monitors
  color management, 90
  multiple, 87
more command, 291
mouse
  handedness of, 5
  numeric keypad control of, 4
Mouse control panel, **185–188**
  Buttons tab, 185–186
  Hardware tab, 187–188
  Pointer Options tab, 187, *187*
  Pointers tab, 186, *186*
  Wheel tab, 187
mouse pointer, schemes, 186
MouseKeys, 5
Movie Maker (Windows), **406–414**, *407*
  Clip menu, 413–414
  Edit menu, 410–411
  File menu, 408–410
  options, *412*, 412–413
  Play menu, 414
  View menu, 411–413
moving
  files and folders, **188**
  Taskbar toolbars, 368
MP2 files, 396
MP2V files, 396

MP3 files, 396

MP3 players, copying media files to, 401

MPA files, 396

MPEG files, 396

MPEG Layer 3, 339

MPG files, 396

MPV2 files, 396

MS-DOS commands, 46

msconfig command, 359

MSN Explorer, **188–189**, *189*

MSN, publishing files to, 389

multimaster replication model, 8

multimedia
DirectX components for, **66–69**
DirectX Diagnostic tool, *67*
searching for, 324

music, searching for, 324

My Computer, **189–190**, *190*, 346

My Documents, **191**, *191*, 346
publishing file to Web from window, 389

My Music, **192**, 346
folder location, 396

My Network Places, **192–193**, *193*, 346

My Pictures, **193–194**, *194*, 346
printing photos and images from, 270

My Recent Documents, **194**, 346

My Videos folder, 408

My Workplace, for network connection, 213–214

N

names
of Address Book folder, changing, 23
for disks, **195**

for printers, 276

for scheduled tasks, 322

for user account, 381

narration in Windows Movie Maker, 408
adjusting balance, 411

Narrator, **195–196**

navigation buttons in Media Player, 393

net commands, 46–47, 291

.NET Passport, user account setup to use, 382, 383

.NET Passport Wizard, **196**, 403

NetMeeting, **196–208**
finding user, 205–207
menus, 199–203
options, 203–204
settings in Address Book, 19–20
window, *198*, **198–9**

network
adding program from, 12
connecting to printer on, 276–277
mapping drives, **177–178**
My Network Places, **192–193**, *193*
passwords, **224**
publishing Web files to, 389
searching for computer on, 325
user access to resources, 7

Network and Internet Connections control panel, **208**

Network Connections, *209*, **209–223**
Advanced menu, 223
creating new connection, 212–214
firewall configuration, 145
local area connection, 211–212
pop-up menu options, 221–223

properties
  Advanced tab, 221
  General tab, 217–218
  Networking tab, 220–221, *221*
  Options tab, 218–219
  Security tab, 219–220, *220*
  protocols for Media Player, 396
  red X on icon, 211
  types, **210–211**
Network Diagnostics, **224**
Network Identification Wizard, 350
Network Setup Wizard, **224–225**
firewall configuration, 144
New Connection Wizard, *213*,
  213–214, **225–229**
New Identity dialog (Outlook
  Express), 244
New Mail Rule dialog, 247–249, *248*
New Message dialog (Outlook
  Express), *241*, 241–242
New Taskpad View Wizard, *184*,
  184–185
New Volume Wizard, 79
newsreader, Outlook Express as, 243
Normal Startup, 359
Notepad, **229–230**, *230*
notification of Windows XP
  updates, 416
Now Playing toolbar (Media
  Player), 393
ntbtlog.txt file, 311
NTFS, **230–231**
  compression of files, **47–48**
null modem cable, RS-232C, 211
Num Lock key, and accessibility, 4
numbers, customizing display,
  297–298

O

objects
  in Active Directory, 7
  inserting in WordPad, 421, 423–424
ODBC Data Source Administrator
  dialog, 51
  About tab, *55*, 55
  Connection Pooling tab,
    54–55, *55*
  Drivers tab, 53, *53*
  File DSN tab, 53
  System DSN tab, 52
  Tracing tab, 54
  User DSN tab, 52, *52*
Offer Remote Assistance, **231**
offline files, 116–117, **231–233**
  folder for, 232
  from Web, 151–152
  synchronization, **348–349**
On-Screen Keyboard, *234*, **234–235**
one-way trust, explicit, 8
Online Print Ordering Wizard, 194,
  233–234
open command (FTP), 122
Open Type fonts, 117
operating system
  configuration of options during
    startup, 356
  version of, 349
operator-assisted dialing, for dial-up
  connection, 223
Options dialog (Backup), 33–35
  Exclude Files tab, *35*
  General tab, *34*
Options dialog (Media Player), Player
  tab, *395*, 396

Options dialog (Outlook Express), 246–247

General tab, *246*

Options menu (Task Manager), 376

organizational unit in Active Directory, 7

Organize Favorites dialog, *152*, 152–153

orientation of printing, 281

Outbox in Outlook Express, 240

Outlook Express, **235–251**

blocking senders, 249–250

configuration, 245–247

creating and sending message, 241–242

e-mail account setup, 227–228

identities in, 24–25, 244–245

mail message rules, 247–249

opening Address Book from, 13

reading mail, 242–243, *243*

reading news, 243

tracking conversations, 250–251

window, *236*, **236–241**

Contacts folder, 240–241, *241*

Folders pane, *239*, 239–240

menus, 236–237

toolbars, 237–239

P

page setup in WordPad, 419

paging files, size of, 354–355

Paint, **251–255**

color palette, 254

menus, 254–255

toolbox, 252–254

window, *251*

paragraph settings in WordPad, 421

parallel connection, 211

partitions, creating, 77

Passport. *See* .NET Passport

passwords

AutoComplete for, 162–163

for Content Advisor, 160

to end standby mode, 272

for identities, 24

for network, 219, **224**

in Outlook Express, 228, 244

policies, 168–169

for remote connection, 305

for screen saver, 85

for user account, 171, 381, 382

changing, 384–385

removing, 385

wizard for forgotten, **119–120**

pausing print job, 283

pausing services, 330

Pencil tool (Paint), 252

performance

System Monitor for, 364

Task Manager information about, *378*, 378

Performance (MMC snap-in), **256–263**

Performance and Maintenance control panel, **263**

Performance Logs and Alerts, **259–263**

Permission feature, **263–264**

Personalized menus feature, **264–265**

Phone and Modem Options control panel, **265–269**

phone dialing rules, 265–267

phone numbers in Windows Messenger, 406

Photo Printing Wizard, **270**
photographs
  default duration for Movie Maker
      import, 412
  from digital camera, 315
  ordering prints from Internet,
      233–234
physical disabilities. *See* Accessibility
Pick Color tool (Paint), 252
pictures. *See* images
Play menu
  in Media Player, 394
  in Windows Movie Maker, 414
Plug and Play device
  disabling, 59–60
  installing drivers, 60
PNG files, 251
pocket PC, copying media files to, 401
Point-to-Point Tunneling Protocol
    (PPTP), 210
Polygon tool (Paint), 253
port
  for printers, 278
  for scanners and cameras, 314
portable device, copying media files
    to, 401
power management
  for computer, **271–273**
  for modem, 269
Power Options control panel,
    271–273
Power Options Properties dialog, 85
power schemes, 271–272
PPTP (Point-to-Point Tunneling Proto-
    col), 210
Print dialog, 280–282, *281*
print queue, 282–283
print server, 284–285

Printers and Faxes control panel,
    273–285, *274*
  adding new local printer, 275–276
  connecting to network printer on
      another computer, 276–277
  printer properties, 277–279
    General tab, *277*, 278
  sharing printer, 276, 278, 279–280
Printers and Other Hardware control
    panel, **285**, *285*
printing
  from Address Book, 15
  documents, 280–282
  font examples, 118
  help topic, 133
  photos and images from My Pictures
      folder, 270
  to send fax, 108
  system summary, 61
  in WordPad, 419
privacy in Windows Messenger, 406
Private Character Editor, 41, *286*,
    286–288, *287*
processes, Task Manager list of run-
    ning, 377, *378*
processor, optimizing use, 354
Program Compatibility Wizard, *288*,
    288–289
programs
  adding or removing, **10–13**
  associating file extensions with, 116
  automatic updates, 358
  closing, 45
  help for, 134–135
  Run to open, **308–309**
  sharing in NetMeeting, 207–208
  starting on remote computer, 306
  switching between, 368–369

properties
of broadband connection, 218
of dial-up connections, 217, *217*
of direct connection, 218
of files and folders, 98
of groups, 174–175
of Volume Control, 388
Properties dialog (Address Book), 23
Business tab, 18
Digital IDs tab, 20
Home tab, 18, *18*
Name tab, 17, *17*
NetMeeting tab, 19–20
Other tab, 19
Personal tab, 18–19, *19*
Properties dialog for groups (Address Book), *21*, 21–22
Properties dialog (hardware), 61
Driver tab, 62
General tab, 61, *62*
Resources tab, 62–63, *63*
put command (FTP), 122

Q

quality of sound, indicator, 335
quick format, 121
Quick Launch toolbar, 367, 370
quit command (FTP), 122

R

Radio Quality audio, 339
radio stations, online, 400
RAID-5 disk, 78–79
RAM, optimizing use, 354

raster fonts, 117
rd command, 291
reading mail in Outlook Express, 242–243, *243*
reading news in Outlook Express, 243
recording with Windows Movie Maker, *409*, 409–410
recovery after service failure, 331
Recovery Console, **289–293**
deleting startup option, 291–293
installing as startup option, 290
starting from CD-ROM, 289–290
recovery disk, creating, 36
Rectangle tool (Paint), 253
Recycle Bin, **293–296**, *294*
emptying, 294
restoring file from, 295
size of, 295–296
red X on network connection icon, 211
redial feature, automatic, 219
refresh rate for monitor, 89
Regional and Language Options control panel, **296–302**
Advanced tab, *301*, 301–302
Languages tab, 298–301
Regional Options tab, *297*, 297–8
Registered File Types list, 116
Registry, **302–303**
Registry Editor, *302*
Remote Access Auto Connection Manager, 219
Remote Assistance, *303*, **303–304**
remote computer
allowing connection by, 358–359
viewing logs on, 96
Remote Desktop Connection, **304–306**

removable disks
  files deleted from, 293
  Safely Remove Hardware
    feature, 310
Removable Storage Management
  (MMC snap-in), 306–307
removing. *See* deleting
ren command, 291
rename command, 291
repair of network connection, 222
repeat delay for keyboard, 166
repeat rate
  FilterKeys and, 4
  for keyboard, 166
replies to e-mail, 238
reports from Disk Defragmenter,
  74–75, *75*
resources, and performance,
  353–354
Restore Down button, 307
restoring backups, 29–30
restoring computer to previous
  configuration, *364*, 364–365
restricted sites, 157
resuming services, 330
reversing audio file, 338
Rich Text Format (RTF), 418
rmdir command, 291
RMI files, 396
Roaming User profile, 307–309
Rounded Rectangle tool (Paint), 253
RS-232C null modem cable, 211
RSACi, 160
RTF (Rich Text Format), 418
ruler in WordPad, 422, *422*
Run As dialog box, 309–310

S

Safe Mode, 311–312
Safely Remove Hardware feature, 310
saving Clipboard contents to file,
  43–44
scan for disk errors, 42
scanner, getting pictures from, 194
Scanners and Cameras control panel,
  312–315, *313*
scanning hardware for changes, 61
Scheduled Task Wizard,
  321, 321–322
Scheduled Tasks control panel, *316*,
  316–322
  Advanced menu, 320–321
  properties, 317–320
scheduling backup jobs, 28, 32
schemes
  for event sounds, 341
  for mouse pointer, 186
scientific calculations, 37
screen images, capturing to Clipboard, 38
screen resolution, 87
screen saver, 84–85
ScreenTips, 87
Scroll Lock key, and accessibility, 4
Search feature, 322–327, *323*
  animated screen character for,
    326–327
  in Help and Support Center,
    129–30, *130*
  indexing for, 138
  queries of catalog, 143
Search view for Explorer Bar, *102*,
  102–103

security
for Internet connection, **157–159**
Local Security Policy, *168*, **168–170**
for NetMeeting, 204
for network connection, 219–220
for WMI Directory structure, 418
Security Configuration and Analysis
(MMC snap-in), **327–328**
Security log, 93, 94
Security Templates (MMC snap-in), **328**
Seek bar in Media Player, 393
Select tool (Paint), 252
Send To feature, 98, **328–329**
Sent Items folder in Outlook
Express, 240
SerialKey Devices, 4
Services (MMC snap-in), *329*,
329–331
services, displaying startup list, 361
sessions, 333
Settings, **331**
shadows for icons, 87
Shared Contacts folder, 22
Shared Folders (MMC snap-in),
332–333
sharing, **334**
ClipBook page, 44–45
printers, 276, 278, 279–280
programs in NetMeeting, 207–208
Shift key, StickyKeys to keep active, 4
shortcuts
creating, 50–51
removing from Start menu, 374
ShowSounds, 4
Shut Down menu in Task Manager, 377
signature
for e-mail messages, 247
for files, 351

simple disk, 78
sites in Active Directory, 7
size of screen items, adjusting, 5
sizing Taskbar toolbars, 368
skin for Media Player, 401–403
skin mode, 393
slide show from My Pictures, 194
Small Memory Dump, 357
small office network, setup, 214
SmartCard, copying media files
to, 401
SND files, 396
software. *See* programs
sorting Address Book, 14, 16
sound
assigning to system event,
340–344
from modem, 268
from remote connection, 305
Sound Hardware Test Wizard, 343
Sound Recorder, *335*, **335–339**
file format, 338–339
menus, 336–338
Sound Selection dialog, 338–339
sound scheme, 341
Sounds and Audio Devices control
panel, **340–344**
Audio tab, 342, *342*
Hardware tab, 343–344
Sounds tab, 341, *342*
Voice tab, 343, *343*
Volume tab, *340*, 340–341
SoundSentry, 4
spam, blocking senders, 249–250
spanned disk, 78
speed dial in NetMeeting, 201
spell check for e-mail messages, 247
SQL.LOG file, 54

Standard toolbar in WordPad, *421*, 421–422

standby mode, 272, 379

Start button, *366*, 366

Start menu, **344–348**

➤ All Programs, 264

classic version, *347*, 347–348

customizing, 373–374

customizing, 369, **371–375**

➤ My Recent Documents, **194**

personalized menus for programs and documents, **264–265**

➤ Settings, **331**

sorting programs, 374

Windows XP version, *345*

starting services, 330

startup

deleting Recovery Console as option, 291–293

files processed at, 359

installing Recovery Console as option at, 290

in Safe mode, **311–312**

Startup and Recovery dialog, *356*, 356–357

statistical calculations, 38

status bar

in Explorer, 106

hiding or displaying, 99

in Media Player, 393

of print queue, 283

status of network connection, 222

StickyKeys, 4, 5

still images from video, 410

stopping services, 330

storyboard in Windows Movie Maker, 408

adding clip to, 413

streaming media file, 391–392

striped disk, 78

support. *See* Help and Support Center

switching between programs, 368–369

synchronization

of Desktop Web page, 84

of offline files, 233

of time with Internet server, 56

Synchronize feature, **348–349**

system cache, 354

system catalog, 139

system clock, 56, 366, *366*

displaying, 370

System Configuration utility, **359–363**

BOOT.INI tab, 360, *360*

General tab, *359*, 359–360

Services tab, 361, *361*

Startup tab, 361

SYSTEM.INI tab, 360

WIN.INI tab, 360

system events, assigning sounds to, **340–344**

System log, 93, 94

System Monitor, **256–259**, **364**

System Properties dialog, **349–359**

Advanced tab, 353–358

environment variables, 357

error reporting, 358

performance, 353–354

Startup and Recovery, 356

user profiles, 355

Automatic Updates tab, 358, *416*, 416

Computer Name tab, 350, *350*

General tab, 349

Hardware tab, 350–353

Remote tab, 358–359

System Restore tab, 358

System Restore, *364*, **364–365**
system summary, 362
  printing, 61
system tasks in My Computer, 190
System Tools, **366**. *See also* Backup
  Character Map, 40
  Disk Cleanup, **69–71**, *71*
  Disk Defragmenter, **71–75**
  File and Settings Transfer
    Wizard, 112
  Scheduled Tasks, *316*, **316–322**
  System Information, **361–363**
  System Restore, *364*, **364–365**
system variables, 357
SYSTEM.INI file, 360
systemroot command, 291

T

Task Manager, **375–378**
  Applications tab, *375*, 377
  menus, 376–377
  Networking tab, 378
  Performance tab, 378, *378*
  Processes tab, 377, *378*
Taskbar, *366*, **366–369**
  customizing, 369–370
  to switch between applications, 368
  toolbars, 367
Taskbar and Start Menu Properties dia-
  log, **369–375**
  Start Menu tab, 264, *371*, 371–375
  Taskbar tab, *369*, 369–370
taskpad views, 183–185
tasks, scheduling, **316–322**
telephone. *See* phone dialing rules
Telephone Quality audio, 339

templates, folder type as, 105
temporary files
  clean-up, **69–71**
  managing in Internet Explorer, 156
temporary storage for movies, 413
terminal window for dial-up connection, 220
text files, Notepad for,
    229–230, *230*
Text tool (Paint), 253
Thai language, 298
themes, 26, 81–82
thumbnails
  in Explorer, 99
  of movie clips, 407
  in My Pictures, 194
TIF files, 251
time
  customizing regional options, 298
  inserting in WordPad, 421
  system clock setting, 56–57
time limits for Movie Maker recording, 409
timeline in Windows Movie
    Maker, 408
  adding clip to, 413
ToggleKeys, 4, 5
toolbars
  in Explorer, 100–102
    hiding or displaying, 99
  in Fax Console, 109
  in Help and Support Center,
    128–129
  in Image Preview, 136–137
Tools menu
  in Address Book, 16
  in Advanced Backup mode, 31
  in Explorer, 100

for Fax Console, 110
in Internet Explorer, 153
in Media Player, 395
in Windows Messenger, 405
trace logs, 260–261
tracking conversations in Outlook Express, 250–251
transitive trust, two-way, 7
Transmitting Station Identifier (TSID), 108
trees in Active Directory, 7
troubleshooting
Diagnostic Startup for, 359
Dr. Watson for, *91*, **91–92**
hardware, 61, **125–126**, *126*
keyboard, 167
modem, 268
sound and multimedia devices, 343–344
starting Windows XP in VGA mode for, 312
System Restore, *364*, **364–365**
video acceleration, 90
video display, 88
writing debugging information to file, 357
TrueType fonts, 117
trust relationships between domains, 7
trusted sites, 157
TSID (Transmitting Station Identifier), 108
Turn Off Computer, **379**, *379*
two-way transitive trust, 7
Type 1 fonts, 117
type command, 291
Typing Mode dialog, for On-Screen Keyboard, 235

U

underline in WordPad, 422
Unicode character set, 301
Private Character Editor to add characters, **286–288**
text files, 418
value for character, 41
uninstalling device drivers, 60
uninterruptible power supply (UPS), 273
updates. *See* Windows Update
updates to programs, automatic, 358
UPS (uninterruptible power supply), 273
user accounts, **379–385**
applying Regional and Language settings to, 302
built-in, 172
changing My/the Password, 384–385
changing My/the Picture, 384
changing type, 382
creating, 383
fast switching, **106**
local, **170–173**
logon/logoff, 389–390
window, *380*
Options pane, 381
Pick a Task area, 381–385
user permissions for incoming connection, 215
user profiles, 355
roaming, **307–309**
user Properties dialog box, *173*
usernames, AutoComplete for, 162
users
access to network resources, 7
current connections, 333

finding for NetMeeting, 205–207
information on faxes, 107
logon/logoff, **175**
with physical disabilities. *See*
    Accessibility
Utility Manager, **385–386**, *386*
to open On-Screen Keyboard, 234

V

VCR, recording from, 408
vector fonts, 117
version of operating system, 349
VGA mode, starting Windows XP
    in, 312
video
    on Internet, NetMeeting for,
        196–208
    searching for, 324
    Windows Media Player for, 391
    Windows Movie Maker for,
        406–414, *407*
video adapters
    displaying information about, 89
    multiple, 87
Video Display Troubleshooter, 88
Vietnamese language, 298
View menu
    in Address Book, 16
    in Advanced Backup mode, 31
    in Explorer, 99–100
    in Fax Console, 110
    in Internet Explorer, 150–151
    in Media Player, 394
    in Paint, 255
    in Task Manager, 376–377
    in Windows Messenger, 405

in Windows Movie Maker, *411,*
    411–413
in WordPad, 420
virtual memory, 354
virtual private connection, 210,
    213–214
    general properties, 218, *218*
virtual private networking, and fire-
    wall, 146
visual effects, performance vs. appear-
    ance, 353
Visual Studio Analyzer, 54
visualizations in Media Player, 395
visually impaired
    display options for, 4
    Magnifier to aid, **176–177**
    Narrator to aid, **195–196**
voice
    device configuration for record-
        ing, 343
    on Internet, NetMeeting for,
        196–208
Volume Control, *387,* **387–388**
volume (disk)
    defragmenting, 74
        analysis for, 73
    formatting, 79–80
volume (sound level)
    for audio device speaker, 340–341
    of audio file, 338
    of modem speaker, 268

W

wake up feature of modem, 269
wallpaper for Desktop, 82
WAV files, 396

WAX files, 396
Web browsers
    default, 164
    Internet Explorer, **147–154**, *148*
Web pages
    accessing restricted, 161
    displaying on Desktop, 83–84
    finding with Search, 322–327
    synchronization, **348–349**
Web Publishing Wizard, **389**
Web sharing of folders, 114
Welcome Screen, **389–390**
What's This, 135, **390–391**
whiteboard in NetMeeting, 197,
    202, *202*
window buttons
    Close button, **45**
    Maximize and Minimize but-
        tons, **178**
    Restore Down button, **307**
windows
    capturing image, 38
    closing, 45
Windows Components, **391**
    Fax Services, **106–112**
Windows Components Wizard, *12*,
    12–13
Windows Explorer. *See* Explorer
Windows logo key, StickyKeys to keep
    active, 4
Windows Management Instrumenta-
    tion (WMI)
    settings, **417–418**
        General tab, 417, *417*
Windows Media Audio, 339
Windows Media Player, **391–402**
    menus, 394–395
    options, 395–397

screens, 397–403
    Copy from CD, 398, *398*
    Copy to CD or Device, 401, *401*
    Media Guide, 398
    Media Library, 399, *399*
    Now Playing screen, *397*, 397
    Radio Tuner, 400, *400*
    Skin chooser, 401–403
    window, *392*, 393
Windows Messenger, **403–406**, *404*
    menus, 404–405
    options, *405*, 405–406
Windows Movie Maker, **406–414**, *407*
    Clip menu, 413–414
    Edit menu, 410–411
    File menu, 408–410
    options, *412*, 412–413
    Play menu, 414
    View menu, 411–413
Windows Update, 347, *415*, **415–416**
    to add system updates, 12
Windows XP, adding or removing
    components, 12–13
WIN.INI file, 360
wizards
    Add Hardware Wizard, **8–10**,
        350–351
    Automated System Recovery
        Wizard, 36
    Backup or Restore Wizard, 27–30
    CD Writing Wizard, **39–40**
    Fax configuration wizard, 107–108
    File and Settings Transfer Wizard, **112**
    Forgotten Password Wizard,
        119–120
    .NET Passport Wizard, **196**
    Network Identification Wizard, 350
    Network Setup Wizard, **224–225**

New Connection Wizard, **225–229**

New Taskpad View Wizard, *184*, 184–185

New Volume Wizard, 79

Online Print Ordering Wizard, 194, **233–234**

Photo Printing Wizard, **270**

Program Compatibility Wizard, **288–289**

Send Fax wizard, 108

Sound Hardware Test Wizard, 343

Web Publishing Wizard, **389**

WM files, 396

WMA files, 396

WMF files, 251

WMI Control (MMC snap-in), **417–418**

WMP files, 396

WMV files, 396

WMX files, 396

Word file format, 418

word processing with Notepad, **229–230**

word wrap, 420

WordPad, *418*, **418–424**
creating document, 423–424
menus, 419–421
ruler, 423
toolbars, 421–422

WVX files, 396

X

XDrive, publishing files to, 389

Z

Zip disk, copying media files to, 401

SYBEX BOOKS ON THE WEB

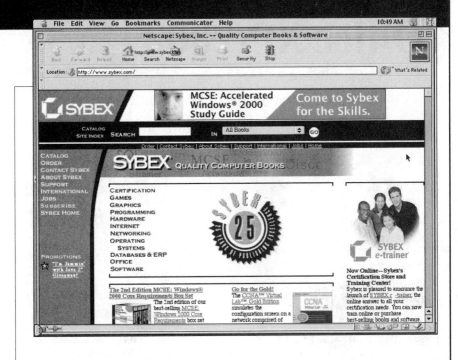

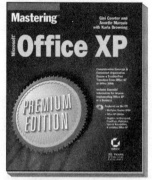

MAP SYMBOLS

≈≈≈	Expressway	◖	Highlight	✗	Airfield	⚓	Golf Course
∷∷∷	Primary Road	○	City/Town	✈	Airport	🅿	Parking Area
∷∷∷	Secondary Road	◉	State Capital	▲	Mountain	◬	Archaeological Site
─ ─ ─	Unpaved Road	⊛	National Capital	✛	Unique Natural Feature	⛪	Church
- - - -	Trail	★	Point of Interest			⛽	Gas Station
⋯⋯	Ferry	•	Accommodation	🦪	Waterfall	◌	Glacier
◆-◆-◆	Railroad	▼	Restaurant/Bar	▲	Park	🐊	Mangrove
▨▨▨	Pedestrian Walkway	■	Other Location	🚩	Trailhead	▨	Reef
⊞⊞⊞	Stairs	Λ	Campground	🎿	Skiing Area	▨	Swamp

CONVERSION TABLES

$°C = (°F - 32) / 1.8$
$°F = (°C \times 1.8) + 32$
1 inch = 2.54 centimeters (cm)
1 foot = 0.304 meters (m)
1 yard = 0.914 meters
1 mile = 1.6093 kilometers (km)
1 km = 0.6214 miles
1 fathom = 1.8288 m
1 chain = 20.1168 m
1 furlong = 201.168 m
1 acre = 0.4047 hectares
1 sq km = 100 hectares
1 sq mile = 2.59 square km
1 ounce = 28.35 grams
1 pound = 0.4536 kilograms
1 short ton = 0.90718 metric ton
1 short ton = 2,000 pounds
1 long ton = 1.016 metric tons
1 long ton = 2,240 pounds
1 metric ton = 1,000 kilograms
1 quart = 0.94635 liters
1 US gallon = 3.7854 liters
1 Imperial gallon = 4.5459 liters
1 nautical mile = 1.852 km

°FAHRENHEIT / °CELSIUS

°FAHRENHEIT	°CELSIUS	
230	110	
220		
210	100	WATER BOILS
200	90	
190		
180	80	
170		
160	70	
150		
140	60	
130		
120	50	
110		
100	40	
90		
80	30	
70	20	
60		
50	10	
40		
30	0	WATER FREEZES
20		
10	-10	
0		
-10	-20	
-20	-30	
-30		
-40	-40	

INCH 0 1 2 3 4

CM 0 1 2 3 4 5 6 7 8 9 10

MOON PORTLAND

Avalon Travel
a member of the Perseus Books Group
1700 Fourth Street
Berkeley, CA 94710, USA
www.moon.com

Editor: Leah Gordon
Series Manager: Erin Raber
Copy Editor: Deana Shields
Graphics Coordinator: Darren Alessi
Production Coordinator Darren Alessi
Cover Designer: Darren Alessi
Map Editor: Albert Angulo
Cartographer: Kaitlin Jaffe, Heather Sparks,
  and Kat Bennett

ISBN: 978-1-61238-507-5
ISSN: 2153-3741

Printing History
1st Edition – 2010
2nd Edition – July 2013
5 4 3 2

Front cover photo: Portland's St. Johns Bridge
  © Zeb Andrews
Title page: © Hollyanna McCollom

Interior color photos: page 18 © (inset) Courtesy
  of Travel Portland © Janis Miglavs, (bottom left)
  © Torsten Kjellstrand, (bottom right) Courtesy of
  Travel Portland © Janis Miglavs; page 19 Courtesy
  of Travel Portland © Michael Durham; page 21
  Courtesy of Travel Portland © Polara Studios;
  page 22 Courtesy of Travel Portland © Rob Finch;
  page 23 Courtesy of Travel Portland; page 24
  Courtesy of Travel Portland.

Printed in Canada by Friesens

KEEPING CURRENT

If you have a favorite gem you'd like to see included in the next edition, or see anything
that needs updating, clarification, or correction, please drop us a line. Send your comments via email to feedback@moon.com, or use the address above.